SAP BW Data Retrieval

 **PRESS**

SAP PRESS is issued by
Bernhard Hochlehnert, SAP AG

SAP PRESS is a joint initiative of SAP and Galileo Press. The know-how offered by SAP specialists combined with the expertise of the publishing house Galileo Press offers the reader expert books in the field. SAP PRESS features first-hand information and expert advice, and provides useful skills for professional decision-making.

SAP PRESS offers a variety of books on technical and business related topics for the SAP user. For further information, please visit our website: *www.sap-press.com*.

Norbert Egger, Jean-Marie R. Fiechter, Jens Rohlf
SAP BW Data Modeling
2005, 437 pp., ISBN 1-59229-043-4

Norbert Egger, Jens Rohlf, Jörg Rose, Oliver Schrüffer, Jean-Marie R. Fiechter
SAP BW Reporting and Analysis
2006, approx. 550 pp., 1-59229-045-0

Roland Fischer
Business Planning with SAP SEM
2004, 403 pp., ISBN 1-59229-033-7

Steffen Karch, Loren Heilig
SAP NetWeaver Roadmap
2005, 312 pp., ISBN 1-59229-041-8

Norbert Egger, Jean-Marie R. Fiechter, Robert Salzmann,
Ralf Patrick Sawicki, Thomas Thielen

SAP BW
Data Retrieval

Mastering the ETL process

Galileo Press

Bonn • Boston

Contents

3 Sample Scenario 67

4 Extractors: Overview of the Techniques 77

5 ETL Process: Master Data 163

6   ETL Process: Transaction Data   259

7   SAP Business Content   387

A Abbreviations — 407

B InfoSources — 409

C ODS Objects — 421

D InfoCubes — 425

E Update Rules — 435

F Transaction Codes — 479

G Metadata Tables 483

H Glossary 487

I Literature 537

J Authors 539

Index 542

Preface

Who hasn't experienced this? You're driving to a party and your passenger, with directions in hand, acts as the navigator: "… then the third left … first … second … oh, closed due to construction, please follow detour." What happens next? Where will this detour take you? The directions contain only the basic "right/left information." If only you had the street names. Then, you would have a starting point and you might be able to reach your destination. However, if you only have "delta directions" available that lack any kind of synchronization, a successful journey is a remote possibility.

I never would have thought that such topics as data extraction, data transformation, and data loading could have filled an entire book. The current volume by Norbert Egger's team of experienced authors proves just the opposite. This book's simple description of data retrieval, and its numerous examples, is a pleasure to read, especially because all too often a considerable amount of an already limited budget is consumed by this process. Therefore, the project manager, for example, must deal with data retrieval as efficiently as possible. After all, what good is a data warehouse without data? The many hints and examples in this book emphasize what is described on a conceptual level, whether it involves the delta processes in data extraction, which is explained earlier in this preface, or the design of aggregates for performance optimization.

Business intelligence has been a topic of discussion for quite some time now. However, the implementation of this concept highlights, for the first time in large global businesses, how useful the company data is and this increases its perceived value dramatically. However, in an almost relentless manner, the system shows us how this data is often structured heterogeneously. Therefore, we must pay particular attention to such concepts as "data hygiene," data quality, and data economics in order to achieve the company-wide consistency of business views required for global management decision support.

By addressing these topics, this second volume ranks as a valuable and welcome edition to the *SAP BW Library*. It is, as expected, a complete and long overdue documentation of data warehouse techniques designed specifically for the implementation of SAP BW. Planning and designing the cultivation of "data warehouses" should help you to provide an organized product offering, unlike those bargain basement sales where it is difficult to distinguish what you want because of the sheer quantity of items that you have to sift through.

I hope all readers enjoy this book and, to all those who like me do not want to or do not have to travel the long-suffering road to implementation, I hope you find it to be a useful guide and helpful navigator that enables you to reach your own *ETL milestone*.

Leverkusen, Germany, December 2005
Lothar Burow
Director of Business Intelligence Services
Bayer MaterialScience AG

Foreword

When Wiebke Hübner, then an editor at SAP PRESS, asked me in December of 2002 if I wanted to write a book on SAP BW, I scoffed at the idea. Such a book would have to be too voluminous to provide an adequate presentation of the topic. I also believed that there would not be sufficient demand for this type of book, so as to make the effort worthwhile. Fortunately, she persisted, which resulted in *SAP BW Professional*, our first book on SAP Business Information Warehouse. I paid particular attention to the rapid development of the reporting functionality in SAP BW 3.x and other topics in that book.

Background

Writing the book not only proved to be enjoyable, but the collective interest generated by this subject came as a welcome surprise. That's why I'm so pleased to thank you, the readers, in the foreword of this book for your support and invaluable feedback. Furthermore, because of this mounting interest in SAP BW, a second edition of the first book was published in several languages.

Thanks to the readers

I hope to contribute to enabling companies to meet the challenges of adequate information acquisition and usage. That includes the successful use of business intelligence tools. With SAP BW, SAP has been offering a very powerful tool for several years now. However, implementations often fail to reach an appropriate standard, so that the ability of such a product to function in real-world situations remains questionable. My goal is to increase the public's awareness of the functionality of business intelligence tools and the options that are available, so that future implementations and the operation of these solutions are more successful and beneficial.

My vision

Based on the great interest shown in the first book, the rapid development of SAP Business Intelligence components, and the welcome growth of our company, the management of the CubeServ Group decided to approach the topic even more comprehensively in collaboration with SAP PRESS. This led to the idea of offering a progressively, comprehensive compendium—a compendium that would describe the functionality of SAP BW in even greater detail.

The idea of a compendium

It became readily apparent that it would take more than one book and one individual involved in the life of a project to complete such a task: The functionality (luckily) is too vast and such a book would be too comprehensive. Therefore, we needed to create a multivolume work that would focus on specific aspects, such as data modeling, extraction, trans-

The SAP BW Library

formation, and loading (ETL) processes, reporting, or planning. The notion of a new series, the *SAP BW Library*, began to take shape.

Because our wonderful CubeServ team consists of many highly motivated coworkers, we were quickly able to form a team of authors that was willing to distribute the work and produce a book on each topic.

Volume 1: SAP BW Data Modeling Volume 1 of the *SAP BW Library*, an introduction to data modeling using SAP BW, was published a few months ago and, to our delight, met with a remarkable response.

Volume 2: SAP BW Data Retrieval It gives me great pleasure to be able to present the second volume of the *SAP BW Library* with an introduction to data retrieval with SAP BW. As data acquisition becomes more difficult due to a variety of data quality problems, a stable and flexible solution to ETL processes becomes increasingly more important. Without a suitable data model or consistently operable ETL processes, business intelligence solutions are destined to fail. Our goal with this current volume is to support you in finding the right path to mapping ETL processes using SAP BW.

Because several authors are already working on the forthcoming volumes, I'm confident that, step by step, this series will offer you a comprehensive description of the functionality of SAP BW. And, if interest continues to remain high, additional books will appear after the first four volumes and address SAP Business Intelligence tools in even greater detail.

Jona, Switzerland—December 2005
Norbert Egger

Introduction and Overview

The first step in a closed-loop business analytics process is data acquisition, which consists of extraction, transformation, and loading (ETL), as well as data quality assurance and metadata administration. This has proven to be the most important step in the model, because it lays the foundation for the success of all subsequent analytical tasks. If correct and reliably functioning ETL processes are not successfully implemented, the user's trust in business intelligence tools wanes, which ultimately results in the user's active or passive refusal to work with an analysis tool.

Introduction

This book is the second volume of a new series, the *SAP BW Library*; all its authors are considered experts in business intelligence and work at CubeServ Group.[1] This volume examines the fundamentals of *data retrieval*; the forthcoming volumes of the SAP BW Library address other topics, which include *data modeling*, *reporting and analysis*, and *planning and simulation*.

Volume 2 of the SAP BW Library

To enable easy access to the complex subject matter of SAP Business Information Warehouse, we have decided to work as close to actual practice and with as many examples as possible in all volumes of the *SAP BW Library*. Therefore, the foundation for our books is a uniform case study developed by the authors: a virtual company (CubeServ Engines). This case study is used to present and communicate all the important requirements of business intelligence applications in a manner that closely reflects real-world situations.

Comprehensive case study

The first goal of this book is to introduce the basic concepts (behind data warehousing as well as the ETL process) of SAP BW. Furthermore, the individual steps to a successful implementation of ETL processes with SAP BW will also be systematically detailed in sequence. Our case study will serve as an unbroken thread as you go through the material.

Goal of this book

The detailed description of the components and implementation steps will enable the various groups within a company that deal with SAP BW

---

1 You can find an overview of future volumes of the *SAP BW Library* in Appendix I of this book.

to comprehend the material even if they lack a deep understanding of IT. Our intention in using this procedure is to make SAP BW projects more successful so that employees of user and IT departments, application experts, and consultants can gain a profound knowledge of SAP BW and reach a common understanding of SAP BW's concepts and terms.

Structure of the Book

Four topic areas

This book can be divided into four essential areas:

1. Background and theoretical basics of SAP BW data retrieval (Chapters 1–2)

2. Presentation of the case study (Chapter 3)

3. Detailed presentation of four major topic areas: Extractors, Master data, Transaction data, and SAP Business Content (Chapters 4–7)

4. Additional supporting information (Appendices)

Chapter 1: Data warehouse principles

Chapter 1 gives you an overview of the basic concepts and architecture of data warehouse systems as well as an overall understanding of the functionality of SAP BW.

Chapter 2: ETL concepts and their implementation

Chapter 2 provides you with an overview of ETL concepts and their implementation with SAP Business Information Warehouse. You will develop an insight into data retrieval in the data warehouse environment and the data acquisition components of SAP.

Chapter 3: Sample scenario

Chapter 3 gives you an overview of the basic elements of the case study used in all volumes of the SAP BW Library. In light of the subject matter of this book, the chapter then examines specific aspects of *data retrieval* in detail.

Chapter 4: Extractors

Chapter 4 provides you with an overview of the consolidation and homogenization functions of data from heterogeneous systems. In this chapter, we introduce various SAP BW extraction mechanisms.

Chapter 5: Master data

Master data forms the basis of analytical applications, whose quality is critical for successful transactions and analytical processes in the company. *Chapter 5* shows how master data is acquired for SAP BW.

Chapter 6: Transaction data

The timely and accurate provision of transaction data is crucial for the productive usability of business intelligence solutions. *Chapter 6* introduces you to the basics of transaction data acquisition for SAP BW.

Chapter 7 describes the preconfigured solution, SAP Business Content, which SAP delivers with SAP BW. In particular, this chapter outlines the solution's strengths and weaknesses, and recommends how you can leverage Business Content for data retrieval to meet your requirements.

Chapter 7: SAP Business Content

The *appendices* provide additional assistance for your daily work: overviews, documentation on various data models, and, in particular, a comprehensive glossary.

Appendices: Overviews and glossary

Working with This Book

The goal of this book is to offer SAP BW users—from various areas and with differing levels of knowledge—a strong foundation for acquiring data with SAP BW.

This book is readily accessible to readers with varying levels of knowledge and individual information requirements:

What do you want to know?

▶ Readers who want to study SAP Business Information Warehouse starting from its conceptual design should begin by reading the theoretical approach in Chapter 1, *Data Warehousing and SAP BW*.

▶ Those readers who mainly want a quick overview of the ETL process should begin with Chapter 2, *Data Acquisition: ETL Concepts and Their Implementation in SAP BW*, and then, as needed, look at the details in the subsequent chapters.

▶ Chapter 1 (*Data Warehousing and SAP BW*), Chapter 2 (*Data Acquisition: ETL Concepts and Their Implementation in SAP BW*), and Chapter 7 (*SAP Business Content*) are especially appropriate for readers who want an overview of the specific topic mentioned.

▶ Readers interested in individual aspects, such as extract structures, LO Customizing Cockpit, update rules, data flow, and so on, can and should use this book as a reference guide. They can find information on specific topics by using the table of contents, the index, and the glossary.

To make it even easier for you to use this book, we have adopted special symbols to indicate information that might be particularly important to you.

Special symbols

▶ **Step by step**
An important component of this book is to introduce complex work with SAP BW step by step and explain it to you precisely. This icon points to the beginning of a step-by-step explanation.

▶ **Note**
Sections of text with this icon offer you helpful hints and detailed information in order to accelerate and simplify your work.

 ▶ **Recommendation**
This books offers tips and recommendations that have been proven in our daily consulting work. This icon indicates our practical suggestions.

 ▶ **Caution**
This icon indicates tasks or steps that require particular attention. The accompanying text indicates when you should exercise particular caution.

After You've Read the Book ...

Even after you've read the book, we'd like to continue to assist you if you need advice or help. We offer the following options:

▶ **Email to CubeServ**
If you have additional questions, you're invited to send them to the authors directly by email. See Appendix J, *Authors*, for their email addresses.

▶ **Information on the CubeServ website**
You can also receive additional information from the CubeServ Group via email. You can register for this service by sending an email that contains your personal registration code for this book to *bw-books @cubeserv.com*.

Acknowledgements

Books are never produced without the support and collaboration of many. That's why we'd like to express our special thanks to the following people for their collaboration, help, and patience.

Norbert Egger

Because various members of our CubeServ team are creating the SAP BW Library, I'd like to thank all the authors sincerely for their participation. Without them, work on this book would have been impossible, because it requires comprehensive and specialized knowledge. Acknowledgement is also due to all other colleagues in the CubeServ Group, especially since I had less time than usual to devote to them and my own work as well, while working on this volume. On behalf of all the authors of this volume,

I would especially like to thank Wiebke Hübner, who made this book possible thanks to her great dedication and immense creativity. I would also like to thank my publisher Galileo Press for the cooperation and patience with me. Above all, I thank my family, especially my beloved wife. Despite all my writing efforts, we were married last year. She supported me during the writing of this book by assuming all the tasks inherent in managing a family, and she did so with a great deal of fortitude and care.

Jean-Marie R. Fiechter

This volume would not have been possible without various sources of help. Thanks is due to all those who helped me. I would especially like to thank my wife Karin and my children, Patrick and Oliver, for their support and encouragement. As a third-generation author, I would like to dedicate this book to my role models: my father, the historian and author Jean-Jacques Fiechter, and my grandfather, the poet Jacques-René Fiechter.

Robert Salzmann

First, I would like to thank my boss and mentor Norbert Egger, who, by example, always motivated our team to achieve as much as possible. I would also like to thank my wife and our children whose patience was often tested. Furthermore, I would like to thank our customers, whose requests and requirements brought to light the problems for which we provide solutions on a daily basis. These solutions constitute the topics for this series of books.

Ralf Patrick Sawicki

I would like to thank the entire team at CubeServ Group for their support and feedback, especially Wiebke Hübner, who was always there when I needed advice or help. I would also like to thank my colleagues for their patience and for understanding that my time was limited while I was writing this book. I wish to dedicate this book to my parents Luzian and Karin Sawicki.

Thomas Thielen

First, I would like to thank Norbert Egger for his advice and help, which he provided to all his colleagues—any time, day or night. Furthermore, I would like to thank my partner Susann, for her patience with me and my work, and my family, the one constant throughout my life. A special thanks goes to my two sons Kevin and Fabian; you are my heroes.

Jona (Switzerland) and Flörsheim am Main (Germany)—October 2005
Norbert Egger
Jean-Marie R. Fiechter
Robert Salzmann
Ralf Patrick Sawicki
Thomas Thielen

1 Data Warehousing and SAP BW

Data warehouse systems enable efficient access to data from heterogeneous sources of information, customized storage, and a convenient display of the information gathered for the end user. This chapter gives you an overview of the basic concepts and architecture of data warehouse systems.

1.1 Introduction

The structure of a data warehouse and the formatting of data in a format specific to and optimized for the end user serve one main goal: to provide information that supports decision-making and generates knowledge and therefore enables actions beneficial to the business (the term "actionable knowledge" is widely used).

In this chapter, we describe the main features of the concepts *Data Warehouse (DWH)* and *Online Analytical Processing (OLAP)* and how these concepts are implemented in SAP Business Information Warehouse (SAP BW). Our goal in doing so is to provide you with a sufficient introduction to the basics, which should act as a foundation on which to base your understanding of the extraction, transformation, and loading (ETL) process of SAP BW. **Data warehouse and OLAP**

For several years, two terms have become preeminent in the area of information retrieval: **Reminder**

▶ **Data Warehouse (DWH)**
As a data pool to retrieve consolidated, historical, and consistent information

▶ **Online Analytical Processing (OLAP)**
As a description for the multidimensional analysis concept

SAP Business Information Warehouse is described as a comprehensive tool for analytical applications that contains all required data warehouse components.

You will find more detailed descriptions of data warehousing and its conceptual foundations in volume 1 of the SAP BW Library.[1]

---

1 Egger, Fiechter, Rohlf: *SAP BW Data Modeling*. SAP PRESS 2005.

1.2   The Data Warehouse Concept

Main benefit The main benefit of a data warehouse system lies in its ability to derive required information from data, which, in operational systems, is available only in a form that is inappropriate for analysis.

Such a system merges fragmented information from the most important systems across the whole value chain in a manner that enables quick and targeted decisions at all company levels. The data warehouse unifies information on vendors, products, production, warehouse stocks, partners, customers, sales and so on into a holistic view and does so independently of the data's source platform.

Example The derivative of warehouse (that is, "Warenhaus" or department store) is an apt analogy. A data warehouse can also be described as a self-service store for information. In fact, many characteristics of a data warehouse are identical to those of a traditional department store. The data warehouse is the central storage point for data (which primarily offers read access) and guarantees the formatting and availability of all required information. As is the case in a self-service store, end users (customers) independently take a product, in this case information, from the shelves and put it into their shopping cart. The shelves are arranged by product; the supply of goods is customer-oriented. Similar goods from various sources are located next to each other.

Typical characteristics According to Inmon,[2] the information in a data warehouse differs from the data in operational systems and exhibits the following characteristics:

▶ **Subject-orientation**
The data warehouse is organized according to the subjects to be analyzed, and not according to the operational application structure. Therefore, the data warehouse concept is based on the concentration on object and subject areas, such as products and customers. Operational data that is important only for running operational processes and is not involved in the process of supporting decision-making does not belong in a data warehouse.

Example If we return to the department store metaphor, this approach means that a buyer preselects goods and then places on the shelves only those goods for which demand likely exists. The buyer tries to avoid shelf-warmers.

---

2 Inmon, 2002.

► **Integration**

There are no syntactical and semantic data inconsistencies in the data warehouse. One of the central characteristics of a data warehouse is that when data is collected from the operational systems, it is brought to a consistent level in terms of both syntax and semantics. This uniformity comprises many different aspects and often refers to the formats, units, and coding. In addition, designers must agree on the characteristics stored in the data warehouse, because the various operational systems often describe the same concept with different characteristics and various subject areas with the same characteristics.

The goal of this uniformisation is to achieve a consistent set of data that represents "one source of the truth," even when the data sources are heterogeneous.

In terms of the department store example, this means that the goods must undergo an inspection when they arrive. This control sorts out unusable goods from partial deliveries and then formats and standardizes the remaining goods. Example

► **Time variance**

To enable time-series analyses, the data warehouse stores information over longer periods. But this apparent deficit of the data warehouse approach results from the way it is used. Views of long- and mid-term periods (annual, monthly, or weekly examinations) are the focus of DWH reports. That's why information that might not be completely up-to-date is fully acceptable for these evaluations. The data warehouse is updated at defined intervals (hour, day, or month), depending on the requirements for timeliness. Once stored, information is not typically modified or removed from the data warehouse.

The time variance also means that data in the data warehouse is valid only at a specific time for a specific interval. This *validity period* is recorded as part of the key for all the relevant data in the data warehouse. Temporal analyses (historical views of the changes over a given period) are possible because the data that is already in the data warehouse is not modified, however, updated data is added to it with a new validity period. Validity period

Example

The goal of our "department store" is not to follow the latest trends all the time, but to maintain an established supply of goods over the long term with periodic deliveries of goods. New models don't replace existing models; rather, they supplement existing models.

► **Non-volatility**
The storage of data over long periods requires well planned processes, tailored system landscapes, and optimized storage procedures to minimize the scope of the information to be stored and the runtime of individual analyses and reports. By contrast data of operational applications ultimately remains in those systems only until the processing of a specific transaction is completed. Then, the data is archived or deleted so that the performance of the system is improved and unacceptable response times are avoided.

The optimization of data access and the loading of data are important issues in modeling data warehouses. Updating data (modifying contents) is also not recommended, because the data of a data warehouse has a documentary character.

Example

In our example, the requirement of non-volatility would mean that the department store has an extensive storage capacity and ensures the availability of goods over the long term.

1.3 Basic Characteristics of a Data Warehouse Solution

Overall goal The overall goal of a good data warehouse architecture should be to describe an integrated data warehouse environment that meets the requirements of a company and that can be implemented iteratively.

This integrated environment covers all aspects of the data warehousing process: data acquisition, data storage with detailed data, lightly and heavily aggregated data, and the provision of analyses and reports (see Figure 1.1). All layers provide administrative functions that are supported by a comprehensive and consistent metadata repository. The repository contains information on the data stored in the data warehouse.

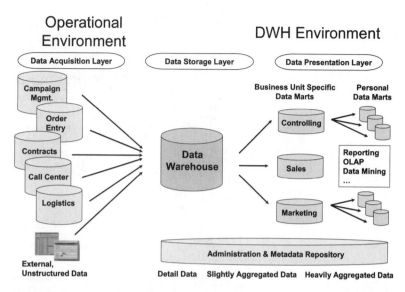

Figure 1.1 The Layers of an Integrated Data Warehouse Environment

A logical data warehouse architecture can be divided into three main layers.

▶ Data acquisition layer

▶ Data storage layer

▶ Data presentation layer

We will now introduce these layers.

1.3.1 Data Acquisition Layer

The function of the data acquisition layer is to extract data from various (operational) source systems through interfaces, to transform it, and to load it into the data warehouse. The main focus of the book is on this layer, so we will only briefly refer to it here.

The data acquisition layer (also called the ETL layer) is broken down into the following three process steps:

▶ **Extraction**
Filtering of the required data from the operational data sources

▶ **Transformation**
The syntactic and semantic data preparation thru data cleansing, data homogenization, and data quality assurance

▶ **Loading**
Inserting data into the data warehouse

Scheduling and metadata management round out these functions (see Figure 1.2).

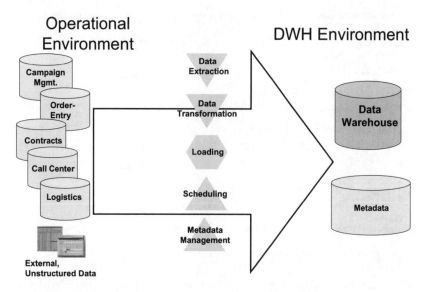

Figure 1.2 The ETL Process

1.3.2 Data Storage Layer

In simple terms, the data storage layer of a data warehouse consists only of the data and its relationships. The relationships are derived from the corresponding relationship in the source system and stored permanently. In terms of the database technology, *materialized views* are used to depict these relationships. Operational systems, however, usually use *virtual* (also called "normal") *views* that store only the definition of a query, so that the result must be recalculated at each new access.

Materialized views Materialized views mean that the results don't have to be recalculated for each query; they can be precalculated, resulting in a significant improvement in performance. However, the modified data from the affected relationships in the source systems must be loaded into the data warehouse at regular intervals.

Because a data warehouse rarely uses *real-time data*, materialized views don't have to be updated every time the data in the source system is modified. A deferred update at regular intervals is usually satisfactory.

Because a data warehouse should also ensure seamless access to integrated and historical data, it must sometimes deal with huge volumes of data (several gigabytes up to tens of terabytes). Such large volumes of data require special techniques for the efficient processing of queries.

The following section looks at the two most common options for query optimization: the use of aggregates and special indexing procedures.

Query Optimization

Aggregates

In addition to materialized views, *aggregates* (also called *aggregation tables* or *preaggregations*) are built in the data warehouse to optimize queries. Such aggregates are simply materialized views that usually contain the data being used in a preaggregated form. These aggregates allow you to respond to user-defined queries directly from the preaggregated values instead of having to calculate them from the detailed data each time.

The only drawbacks of these aggregates are the increased need for memory and the additional effort involved during the loading of the data warehouse.

Two challenges arise from the use of aggregates:

1. The correct choice of the aggregates to be built (considering the need for memory and the effort required in an update) and the expected use of these aggregates to process queries. The need for additional memory and the effort involved in the update make it impossible to calculate all combinations of aggregates. In addition, only a few of these combinations are actually used. Good data warehouse systems offer tools to determine the optimal combinations of aggregates.

2. The automatic (transparent to the end user) use of the available aggregates (if appropriate). This option is also characteristic of a good data warehouse.

Figure 1.3 illustrates the inner structure of a data warehouse and the distinction between detail data and aggregated data.

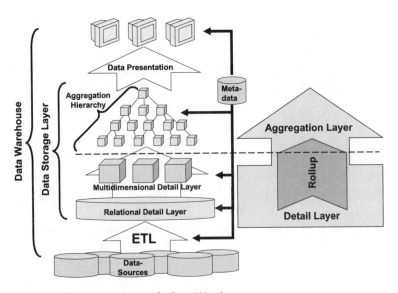

Figure 1.3 The Various Layers of a Data Warehouse

Relational detail data layer   The materialized views fed directly from the source system are assigned to the relational detail data layer of the data warehouse. These tables serve as a consistent foundation for the other layers in the data warehouse. To prepare for future modifications that might be wanted and to contribute to the greater flexibility of the data warehouse, the relational detail data is often stored at a greater level of detail than is currently required.

Aggregation layer   The multidimensional detail layer forms the basic layer for processing queries; the aggregation layer above contains aggregates for the efficient processing of the queries.

Aggregation hierarchies   *Aggregation hierarchies* are created when aggregates are built on the basis of other aggregates. The terms *upflow* or *rollup* are often used to describe the flow of information within such aggregate hierarchies.

The division into a relational detail data layer and various multidimensional aggregation layers above it also allows you to meet simultaneous requirements for different types of updating, and does so without jeopardizing the consistency of the data warehouse.

Indexing schemes

In addition to aggregates, indexing schemes are often used to accelerate the execution of queries. Studies of data warehouses over several years have shown that, besides the usual indices, two specific indexing schemes are particularly appropriate: the *bitmap index* and the *join index*.

Bitmap indices allow for a very efficient determination of the attribute properties of a data record. For example, a bitmap index for the four points of the compass would contain a two-bit vector with the following values: 00 for north, 01 for east, 10 for west, and 11 for south. The selection of all data records with the south attribute would therefore require a Boolean comparison with the value of 11. Such a task can be realized in a computer extremely efficiently.

Bitmap index

In addition, a bitmap index requires relatively little memory because only bit vectors are stored. And Boolean operators (AND, OR, and XOR) can calculate intersections and set unions of bitmap indices very efficiently

But there's also a downside to using bitmap indices, namely, they are only appropriate for attributes with a relatively small number of value properties (i.e., for attributes with a high cardinality).

A join index, however, maps the connection between relationships in terms of a common key; traditional index structures refer to a single table. To implement a join index, the references to all records (and the foreign key of the second table) are stored for each primary key of the first table. This approach permits an extremely efficient calculation of joins between two tables.

Join index

The literature also uses the term *star index* for the enhancement of the join-index concept into a multidimensional model (star schema). A star index permits the storage of all relationships between a fact table and dimension tables that belong to it so that it can very efficiently determine the records that belong to one or more dimension table elements.

Star index

Data Modeling

To differentiate data modeling from data handling by transaction-oriented systems, we usually refer to *online analytical processing (OLAP)* in this context. The OLAP model can best be described as a Rubik's cube (see Figure 1.4).

▶ The quantitative data (*key figures*, such as sales and distribution, also described as *variables*, or *measures*) builds the cells inside the cube.

Quantitative data (key figures)

▶ The desired approaches and aspects (*characteristics*, such as sales organization, products sold, time, that make up the qualitative data) are mapped on the dimensions (axes) of the cube.

Qualitative data (characteristics)

The result is a multidimensional data structure, also called a *hypercube* or *data cube*. Even if, strictly speaking, the metaphorical use of the cube is valid for only a three-dimensional model, we still speak of a cube, even with "n" dimensions.

Fact tables Key figures are usually stored in *fact tables* in OLAP implementations. The fact tables form the foundation of an OLAP data structure.

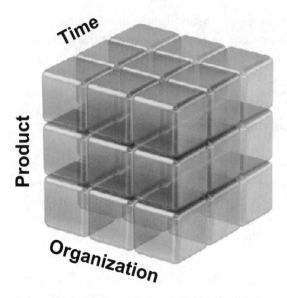

Figure 1.4 OLAP Data Model: Sample Cube

Dimension Hierarchy

Another important function of a data warehouse is the storage of aggregate data. That's why you can aggregate dimension elements at multiple levels and create dimension hierarchies or *consolidation paths*.

Normally, a *total aggregation* forms the highest level within a dimension. In our example, it allows you to evaluate key figures by organization and time, independently of the product. The lowest characteristic level within a dimension provides the granularity of the data and thus also determines the data set stored in the cube.

You define how aggregation is to occur individually for each key figure. In our day-to-day work, we often encounter key figures whose totals don't yield the desired results, or even lead to an incorrect result. For example, stock key figures (such as inventory stock) cannot be totaled. Totaling cumulative value key figures along certain dimensions (such as a data type dimension with plan, budget, and actual figures) is not very sensible. The system must offer alternate aggregation forms here: "last value," "average," "maximum," "no aggregation," and so on.

1.3.3 Data Presentation Layer

In order to convert the data collected in a data warehouse into information that is relevant to the business, the data must be formatted accordingly before it can be presented properly to a target group. The extremely varied needs of users are the most important consideration here. Because of these differences, it is imperative that business-relevant information and facts that are necessary for decision-making be made available in diverse forms. The main categories include the following:

▶ Data mining

▶ Reporting

▶ Ad-hoc analyses

▶ Business Planning and budgeting

Subsets (organizational, geographical, temporal, and so on) of data from the data warehouse are usually sufficient to mine the desired information. To accelerate and simplify the work of the analysis and presentation tools, the required data is often extracted from the detail layer of the data warehouse and stored in a specific and optimal format for the target tool (*data marts*).
Data marts

Data marts are specific (often organizational or geographical) subsets of a data warehouse. They enable an iterative implementation of data warehouse systems. Data marts built on a central data warehouse enable the extraction of subject-specific data (from the underlying data warehouse) for individual groups of decision-makers (see Figure 1.5).

The data presentation layer usually consists of one or more data marts that provide the required (multidimensional and tabular) structures for front-end applications and presentation tools.

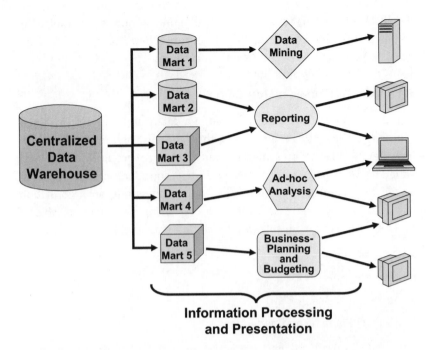

Information Processing
and Presentation

Figure 1.5 Various Target Groups and their Influence on the Provision of Data

1.4 Architecture of SAP BW: Overview

Comprehensive
data warehouse
solution

A good example of an integrated DWH environment is the SAP Business
Information Warehouse. SAP BW provides analytical applications as
defined in the data warehouse and OLAP concepts; it also builds the core
of the SAP NetWeaver Business Intelligence components.

It contains all the components required for the data warehouse process.
The following lists the core elements of SAP BW:

▶ **Functions for the ETL process**
Extraction of data from source systems and the corresponding data
processing

▶ **Components for data storage**
For data storage and data provision there is a central management
tool—the Administrator Workbench—which enables the structure,
maintenance, and operation of the data warehouse.

▶ **Tools for analyses and reports**
SAP Business Explorer with the browser-based SAP Web reporting and
the Excel-based Analyzer

Besides these core elements, SAP BW offers the required additional components, with tools for customizing (to set up and configure customer-specific applications), for administration, monitoring, scheduling, performance optimization, open hub components, and so on. All elements of SAP BW are based on consistent metadata, and you can manage the metadata with the Administrator Workbench.

Additional components

The data warehouse components of SAP BW—including innovations, updates, and improvements of the current SAP BW Release 3.5—are shown in Figure 1.6.

SAP BW Release 3.5

Figure 1.6 The Integrated Data Warehouse Architecture of SAP BW (Source: SAP AG)

The functionalities of SAP Business Information Warehouse shown above are those of the key processes of analytical applications: data acquisition, data storage, and data presentation. Numerous other components are also available, but addressing them here exceeds the scope of this introduction. We'd simply like to mention the following additional components and functionalities:

▶ The powerful and mature basic functions available as part of SAP R/3 Basis technology: job control, role and printing functionality, user management, and so on

▶ SAP BW components such as SAP BW-specific functions to control authorizations, based on core functions in SAP R/3 or the integration of documents in the reporting

The core element for the administration of a data warehouse is a central metadata repository.[3] It contains all relevant information on the data stored in the data warehouse.

SAP BW Business Content   With the SAP BW Business Content, SAP offers a variety of predefined analytical solutions directly supplied with SAP BW. These predefined models greatly help to reduce the time and effort required to set up and implement SAP BW, because they contain all the necessary components—from extraction to the data model to reports.

Thus, as part of a new SAP BW installation, Business Content allows for much shorter setup times, even if it is being used only as a template. However, you should not accept the predefined solution unquestioningly, even with all its benefits. This is because the solution frequently doesn't adequately fulfill the requirements of a real-world company. You should always check whether you can use the Business Content directly 'as is,' or whether it would be preferable to use it as a template for creating your own objects. For additional tips and advice on this subject, see Chapter 7, *SAP Business Content*.

A look ahead   In the following sections, we provide you with a brief overview of the most important elements and concepts of SAP BW. A more in-depth description of the data acquisition process (ETL) is provided in the chapters that follow. For additional information, we suggest that you refer to the other volumes of the SAP BW Library.[4]

1.4.1 Data Acquisition in SAP BW

SAP source systems   SAP BW runs on its own installation, that is, its own client/server architecture, which is why SAP BW has functions that enable it to communicate with other systems. Various technologies are used for communica-

---

3 In principle, metadata is data on data. Metadata is used to describe both technical and business-relevant characteristics of data.

4 Volume 1: Egger, Fiechter, Rohlf: *SAP BW Data Modeling*. SAP PRESS 2005.
   Volume 3: Egger et al.: *SAP BW Reporting and Analysis*. SAP PRESS 2006.
   Volume 4: Egger et al.: *SAP BW Business Planning and Simulation*. SAP PRESS 2006.

tion: Application Link Enabling (ALE, the proprietary SAP technology similar to EDI for communication between systems) for the exchange of metadata and data acquisition, and transactional Remote Function Calls (RFCs), the SAP interface protocol, for the extraction of data from SAP R/3.

SAP BW also handles connections to non-SAP source systems. Such connections can use the XML protocol or third-party extraction tools to exchange metadata. You can collect data with DB Connect, UD Connect, interface files, third-party extraction tools, or the XML protocol.

Non-SAP source systems

For the data acquisition for SAP BW, data from almost any source can be used (see Figure 1.7 and Chapter 2, *Data Acquisition: ETL Concepts and Their Implementation in SAP BW*).

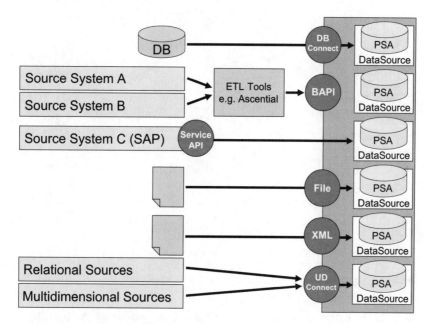

Figure 1.7 Integration of the ETL Process into the BW Architecture

1.4.2 Data Storage in SAP BW

InfoObjects

InfoObjects provide the basis of the data model in SAP Business Information Warehouse. SAP calls these InfoObjects *business evaluation objects*.

You can edit InfoObjects under InfoObjects in the modeling view of the Administrator Workbench, the SAP BW tool for the configuration, control, monitoring, and maintenance of all the processes involved in data acquisition, processing, and storage (see Figure 1.8).

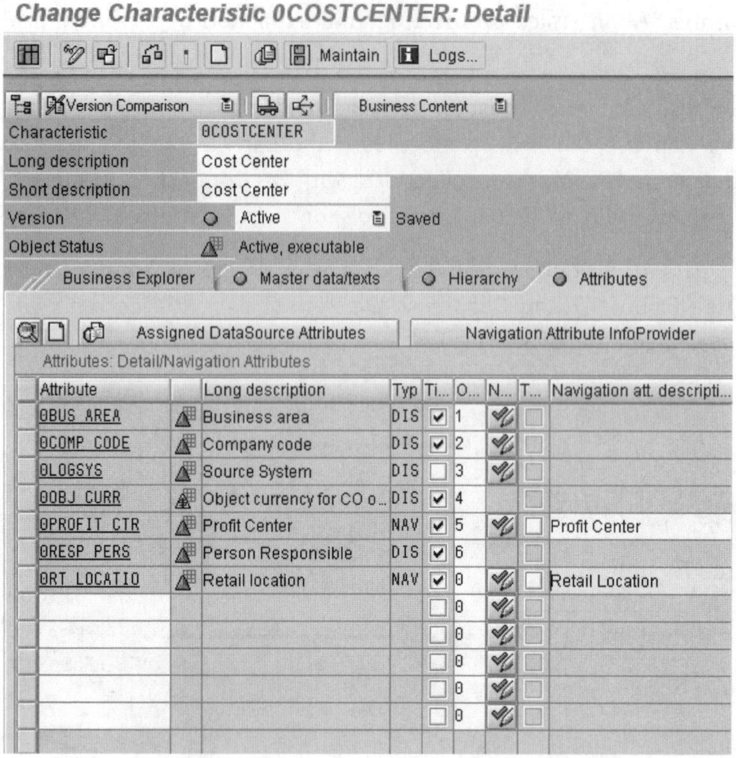

Change Characteristic 0COSTCENTER: Detail

Attribute	Long description	Typ	Ti...	O...	N...	T...	Navigation att. descripti...
0BUS_AREA	Business area	DIS	✓	1			
0COMP_CODE	Company code	DIS	✓	2			
0LOGSYS	Source System	DIS	☐	3			
0OBJ_CURR	Object currency for CO o...	DIS	✓	4			
0PROFIT_CTR	Profit Center	NAV	✓	5		☐	Profit Center
0RESP_PERS	Person Responsible	DIS	✓	6			
0RT_LOCATIO	Retail location	NAV	✓	0		☐	Retail Location
			☐	0			
			☐	0			
			☐	0			
			☐	0			
			☐	0			

Figure 1.8 InfoObjects are the Basis of the SAP BW Data Model

InfoObjects are divided into *key figures* and *characteristics*:

Key figures ▶ Key figures provide the values (amounts, quantities, counters, dates, and time) to be analyzed.

Characteristics ▶ Characteristics represent the business events and create relationships. SAP provides the following types of characteristics:

> ▶ Business characteristics (sold-to party, cost center, company code, and so on)

> ▶ Units (currency and quantity)

> ▶ Time characteristics (calendar day, calendar year, and fiscal year)

▶ Technical characteristics (number of a data load procedure, for example)

You can store master data, texts, and hierarchies for InfoObjects of the "characteristic" type. This data is then available for reporting on master and transaction data.

Master data and texts

SAP BW thus offers an opportunity to map very powerful key figures and characteristics. Examples include:

Complex key figures and characteristics

▶ Non-cumulative key figures built by opening and supporting postings

▶ Complex, time-dependent texts (short and medium-length texts) attributes (profit center and person responsible, for example)

▶ Hierarchies-based characteristics

▶ Characteristics compounded to a cost area

InfoObjects are contained in *InfoObjectCatalogs*, which, in turn, are grouped by application area into InfoAreas.

InfoObject-catalogs and InfoAreas

InfoProviders

All reportable objects (those that can be evaluated with *SAP Business Explorer*, the standard reporting tool of SAP BW) are called *InfoProviders*.

The SAP BW InfoProviders can be found under "InfoProvider" in the modeling view of the Administrator Workbench (see Figure 1.9). InfoProviders include the following objects:

▶ Objects that physically contain data; SAP BW stores the data for these objects in their database tables. The group of objects that physically contain data includes InfoCubes, operational data store (ODS) objects, and InfoObjects that contain master data.

▶ Logical views; objects whose data is stored in another system (such as SAP R/3) or in other physical objects. The group of logical views includes InfoSets, RemoteCubes, SAP RemoteCubes, virtual InfoCubes with services, and MultiProviders.

The Basic InfoCubes that contain data consist of several relational tables that organize the InfoObjects they contain according to the enhanced star schema, which enables the mapping of complex data models (see Volume 1 of the SAP BW Library).[5]

InfoCubes

---

5 Egger, Fiechter, Rohlf: *SAP BW Data Modeling*. SAP PRESS 2005.

Figure 1.9 InfoCubes Create a Suitable Foundation for Queries with OLAP Functionality

ODS objects
: Technically, ODS objects are simple tables that contain a number of key fields and a number of data fields. Note the following (possible) limitations to this approach: The number of key fields is limited to a maximum of 16. The arrangement of all key and non-key characteristics with the key figures in one data record can lead to extremely long records. The options for optimizing performance are much more limited here than they are with InfoCubes.

InfoObjects as InfoProviders
: Master-data-bearing characteristics as InfoProviders provide reporting with the master data tables of the attributes and texts of the particular characteristic involved.

SAP RemoteCube, RemoteCube, and virtual InfoCube
: Additional InfoProviders, objects in SAP BW that do not contain data, include the following: *SAP RemoteCubes* (access to transaction data in other SAP systems, based on an InfoSource with flexible update rules,

RemoteCubes (access to data from another system over BAPIs), and *virtual InfoCubes* (access to data from SAP and non-SAP data sources via a user-defined function module). All these InfoProviders enable flexible reporting.

Like InfoObjectCatalogs, InfoProviders are grouped into InfoAreas. **InfoAreas**

MultiProviders

MultiProviders combine data from various InfoProviders (see Figure 1.10). One possible use of a MultiProvider would be the combination of an InfoCube with sales data with an additional InfoCube with headcount data. This approach would enable reports that calculate "per capita sales." Another possible use enables the combination of InfoCubes with sales with an InfoProvider type of InfoObject Material to display materials without sales. Note that MultiProviders are not based on a join operation, but on a union operation (a union of the tables involved).

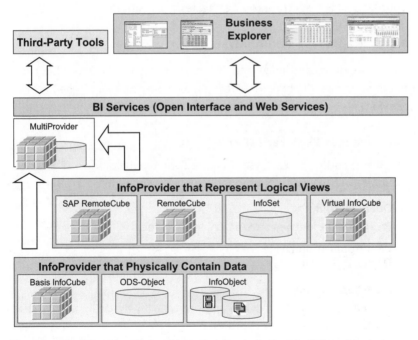

Figure 1.10 MultiProviders Make Objects that Physically Contain Data and Logical Views Available for Reporting

InfoSets

InfoSets form a semantic layer above the data sources, such as ODS objects and master data. With InfoSets, you can use all database techniques, including joins. The ability to use this technology greatly increases your flexibility in SAP Business Explorer.

For all objects, however, note that storing data in other systems and remote access generally precludes you to influence the system behavior, especially in terms of performance. Accordingly, you should use these objects only after careful consideration. One use that has been proven effective is for data checking: a SAP RemoteCube enables access to a source system; a MultiCube links the SAP RemoteCube to a BasicCube. A deviations analysis determines whether the data in the source system is consistent with the data in SAP BW.

Performance Optimization and Aggregates

You can use various functions to optimize performance. One of the main functions is the ability to model *aggregates*. Like InfoCubes, aggregates are modeled objects with a reduced volume of data or improved access options; SAP BW synchronizes aggregates automatically.

1.4.3 Reporting and Analysis Tools

Various reporting and analysis tools can be used with SAP BW. A basic differentiation exists between SAP tools and third-party tools. The SAP BW standard reporting tool is the *SAP Business Explorer (BEx)*.

SAP Business Explorer (BEx)

SAP BW reporting and analysis tools are components of the SAP Business Explorer. SAP BEx consists of the following components:

Components of SAP BEx

▶ **Query Designer**
Tool to define queries on SAP BW InfoProviders

▶ **Web Application Designer**
Tool to create Web-reporting applications

▶ **Web Applications**
The environment for running reports and analyses in a Hypertext Markup Language (HTML) browser

▶ **Analyzer**
The environment for running queries in MS Excel

▶ **Information Broadcasting**
The option to make objects with business-intelligence content available to a wide group of users

► **Additional functions**

Personalization and mobile reporting components and functions to integrate SAP BEx Web applications into SAP Enterprise Portal

Reporting Agent

The *Reporting Agent* supplements the functions of SAP Business Explorer. The reporting agent offers background and additional functions:

► Evaluation of exceptions with alternate follow-up actions, such as "sending messages" (email) or "creating entries in the alert monitor"

► Printing queries

► Precalculation of Web templates and value sets for characteristic variables

► Managing bookmarks

► Functions for third-party tools

Third-Party Tools

You can also use a variety of third-party tools to access data in SAP BW. Up to now, the primary means of doing so was to run an SAP Business Explorer query from a front-end tool supplied by a third party. Nowadays, you can also use various additional SAP interfaces to access queries:

► The ODBO[6] interface

► The XMLA[7] interface

► The BAPI[8] interface

These are standardized programming interfaces that enable external access to business processes and data of the SAP system.

---

6   OLE DB for OLAP
7   XML for Analysis
8   Business Application Programming Interface

2 Data Acquisition: ETL Concepts and Their Implementation in SAP BW

This chapter will give you an overview of the most important and most difficult step in the data warehousing process: data acquisition. You will learn about data acquisition in the data warehouse environment and the data acquisition[1] components of the SAP Business Information Warehouse.

2.1 Introduction

The first step in a *closed-loop business analytics process*[2] is the acquisition of data, which consists of the extraction, transformation, and loading of data (ETL), as well as data quality assurance and metadata administration. This has proven to be the most important step in the model, since the success of all subsequent analytical tasks depends on this step.

Most of the data quality assurance measures are implemented in this step in order to avoid the infamous "garbage in, garbage out" syndrome. If these basic and (visible) data quality assurance measures are not performed, the end users' faith in the data and their readiness to work with business intelligence tools diminishes quickly.

The following quote also emphasizes the importance of creating a clean foundation for the data warehouse:

Historically, the ETL process has been the most time-consuming, labor-intensive, and expensive process in data warehousing implementation projects, consuming upward of 70% of the budget and time. ETL is also one of the most resource-intensive processes for ongoing data warehouse maintenance. The constant addition of data into the data warehouse and changes, additions, or deletions to source systems keep the IT staff con-

Closed-loop business analytics process

---

1 In general Data Warehousing literature, the accepted terms for the ETL (extraction, transformation & loading) process are *data acquisition* and *data collection*. *Data retrieval* is used for the part of the DWH process that gets the data out of the DWH for analysis and reporting. SAP, on the other hand, uses the term *data retrieval* for the ETL process. In this book, we will stick to the commonly used term *data acquisition* to represent the ETL process in the general introductory chapters, and revert to the term *data retrieval* in the BW-specific chapters.

2 A *closed-loop business analytics process* allows you to transform operational data into analyzable information, and then generate *actionable knowledge* in order to finally impact the operational systems.

tinuously engaged. Adding to the data integration challenge, mergers and acquisitions increase the rate at which new data sources must be absorbed.[3]

Now we'll take a closer look at the process steps in the data acquisition layer.

2.2   Process Steps in the Data Acquisition Layer

As we already described in Chapter 1, *Data Warehousing and SAP BW*, the process steps of the ETL process can be broken down as follows (see Figure 2.1):

The ETL process

▶ **Extraction**
Filtering the required data from the operational data sources

▶ **Transformation (data cleansing)**
Syntactic and semantic data formatting

▶ **Loading**
Transferring data into the data warehouse

Scheduling and metadata management round out these steps.

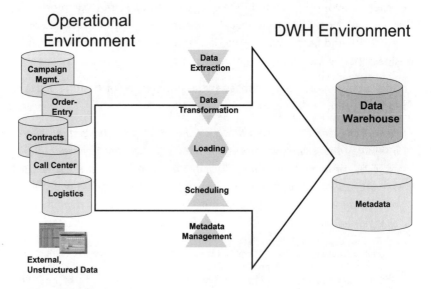

Figure 2.1 The ETL Process

---

3 Dan Vesset, Research Director, Analytics and Data Warehousing, IDC, 2003.

2.2.1 Extraction from Source Systems

In the extraction process step, the data needed by users is collected from the different heterogeneous operational data sources so that it can then be stored in the data warehouse. After the initial data import (*initial load*), the data warehouse must be reloaded with new data according to user-defined requirements for timeliness and consistency. Users have two methods for a reload:

Loading from heterogeneous data sources

▶ **Reloading, Full Load**
The complete reloading of all data

▶ **Incremental Load, Delta Load**
Incremental data acquisition. Instead of deleting and reloading a section of the data in the data warehouse, during an incremental data acquisition only the changes to the operational data are loaded into the data warehouse.

The initial load, as well as the complete reload of the data, does not pose any specific data acquisition problems.

However, for an incremental data import, you must first extract the changes relevant to the data warehouse from the operational systems. Depending on the operational application, you have the following various options from which to choose:

Obstacles to incremental loading

▶ **Triggers**
If the operational database supports the use of SQL triggers, you can use them to retrieve the data. Triggers allow the definition of database operations that are executed automatically based on specific events. For the extraction of data, Triggers are used that run at each modification of the operational data set and store the modifications in an appropriate modification table. The data records in the modification table can then be transferred to the data warehouse at regular intervals.

▶ **Log files**
You can often use the log files of the operational database systems for extraction. Most database systems support log files to recreate a consistent state for the database (*recovery*) after a system failure. Special programs can evaluate log files and extract the data manipulation operations contained therein. The data is then transferred into the data warehouse.

▶ **Monitor programs**
In some circumstances, neither triggers nor log files can be used to extract data, so that the only remaining option is access to the operational data set. In this case, you can use special monitor programs to extract the relevant modifications. Such programs periodically generate a snapshot of the data and then calculate the difference between the current snapshot and the previous one (*differential snapshot algorithm*).

▶ **Modification of the operational application systems**
If the operational system storing the data does not support triggers or log files, and you cannot use a monitor program, you must modify the operational system so that it logs every modification that it executes in a separate database. Then, you can transfer the relevant modifications into the data warehouse periodically. Some manufacturers of operational application systems have adjusted their software in order to enable the automatic transfer of differential data to specific data warehouse systems. One example is the integration of the ERP application, SAP R/3, with SAP Business Information Warehouse.

In some circumstances, an update of the data warehouse requires both the filtering of the relevant modifications and executing queries and transformations on the operational data to reduce the number of data records to be transferred.

2.2.2 Transformation, Data Cleansing, and Data Quality Assurance

Transformation
A unified data schema is set for the data warehouse during the development phase. The data from the various operational systems must then be transformed into the data warehouse format during loading. In addition, the heterogeneity of the data sources and the operational systems frequently leads to inconsistencies and even to erroneous data.

For example, the following problems can occur:

▶ The use of different attribute values for the same attributes

▶ Missing values

▶ Different formatting of the data

Data quality assurance
These problems must be eliminated to create a clean and consistent data warehouse. This is where data quality assurance measures come into play. The data quality management process can be broken down into four steps:

1. **Data Auditing and Standardization**

   Rules and relationships between the data are identified in the data auditing step. Frequencies, minimums, maximums, unambiguous values, and missing values are listed. Non-standard data and formats are made visible through clustering processes. The tools then check whether the rules have been violated. It's impossible to determine with absolute certainty whether an error exists; therefore, the tools simply notify you about possible errors, which you must then correct manually. The data cleansing rules are also defined during this step together with the user departments.

2. **Data Linking and Consolidation**

   Have you ever received five copies of the same advertisement (each copy with a slightly different name or address)? Did you find this annoying? Differences that are obvious to a person are often not identified by a computer. In the consolidation step, area-specific knowledge and the most modern analysis technologies (for example, fuzzy logic and neural networks) are combined in order to standardize data and eliminate redundant records. Records from heterogeneous data sources that belong together are also linked.

3. **Data Enhancement (Data Enrichment)**

   In this step, exisiting data is enriched with additional information in order to make it more useful. Examples include the enrichment of supplier data with DUNS numbers (from Dun & Bradstreet) or the grouping of customers in households (householding). This data comes primarily from external sources. Because the format of the external data cannot be manipulated, combining this external data with internal data will require some clever processing.

4. **Data Cleansing**

   Data from different data sources is adjusted and standardized here. Data is transformed, corrected, and modified so that it is consistent with the target format. In addition, the data can be verified. For example, addresses can be checked and corrected by using a table of all ZIP codes and the corresponding town and street names.

Figure 2.2 illustrates that these data quality assurance measures are not simply implemented once, but rather, they are part of a larger continual process to ensure quality.

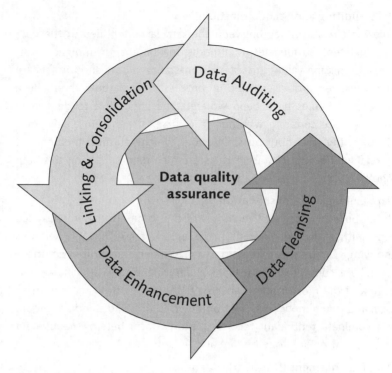

Figure 2.2 The Data Quality Assurance Process

Data cleansing tools The data cleansing tools on the market can be subdivided into the following groups:

▶ **Data migration tools**
This category of data cleansing tools permits the definition of simple transformation rules to transform the data from the source systems into the target format (for example, transformation of the attribute value "male" to "m" or "1").

▶ **Data scrubbing and data cleansing tools**
Data scrubbing tools use area-specific knowledge to cleanse the data from the operational sources. For example, they might use a table of all postal codes, localities, and street names to check and correct addresses. In terms of technology, these tools frequently use fuzzy logic and neural networks.

▶ **Data auditing tools**
Data auditing tools can recognize rules and relationships between data. The tools then check whether the rules have been violated. Since it is almost impossible to determine with absolute certainty whether or not an erroneous state exists, the tools simply notify you of possible

errors, which you must then correct manually. Such tools can use statistical evaluations to determine that the discrepancies between specific values might indicate the presence of incorrect entries. This type of data analysis is usually based on data mining techniques.

There are also tools that cover several (or even all) categories (which would definitely be a more sensible alternative).

It is essential that the data quality assurance measures be seamlessly and transparently integrated into the transformation step.

Although these measures should work automatically and transparently, they must be made visible and understandable to the end user through adequate documentation to increase their trust in the data.

The key to a successful implementation and operation of business intelligence applications is not in the successful implementation of certain data quality tools, but rather in managing the data quality process, which is a continuous task.

The data quality determines the data consistency and the end user's faith in the data, and is ultimately responsible for the success of a closed-loop business analytics process. Feedback from the business intelligence system to the operational systems is only possible if adequate data quality and consistency are achieved.

The importance of data quality

However, data quality assurance remains one of the main challenges when implementing business intelligence solutions. Unfortunately, data quality, in spite of its importance, has long been relegated to the background, primarily because it requires much discipline and dedicated resources (which are almost always lacking), in order to master this challenge.

However, our experience shows that neglecting the data quality in an environment that demands ongoing increased productivity in all processes is not a viable alternative.

2.2.3 Inserting Data in the Data Warehouse

The actual inserting of the data into the data warehouse occurs after the extraction of the required data from the source systems and the subse-

Loading

quent data cleansing. Most systems also perform the following tasks concurrently:

- ▶ Checking the integrity constraints
- ▶ Calculating aggregations
- ▶ Generating indices

Using ODS To reduce the load on the operational systems to a minimum, you can decouple the actual inserting of data into the data warehouse from the transmission of data from the operational systems. You would use *operational data stores (ODS)* to do so. An ODS stores data from the operational systems in an almost unmodified form until it can be inserted into the data warehouse. To reduce the length of the load process, you can execute data cleansing and aggregation operations within the ODS tables.

Updating Data is loaded to the data warehouse based on user-defined timeliness and consistency requirements. To avoid inconsistent results from queries, you cannot access the data in the data warehouse during the update. However, a "query copy" of the data can be made available during the update. For this reason, most data warehouses are updated when few queries on the data occur, namely, at nights and on weekends.

In addition to updating the actual data warehouse, you must also, while loading the data, update the data basis of the data mart system used. For relational data mart systems, this data basis is usually identical to the data warehouse. However, multidimensional data mart systems (OLAP systems) are based on specific multidimensional database systems that must also be brought up-to-date.[4]

2.3 Metadata Management

During the Data Acquisition phase, you must also consider the relevant metadata. This includes the management of all types of metadata (technical, administrative, business-relevant, and so on).

Metadata Repository A central, integrated Metadata Repository is a condition sine qua non for the efficient and user-friendly administration of a data warehouse. It enables the transparent and unified access from all components of the business intelligence solution to all data. In this way, changes in one pro-

---

4 You can find detailed information on the various OLAP technologies in Chapter 1 of the first volume of the SAP BW Library; see Egger, Fiechter, Rohlf: *SAP BW Data Modeling*. SAP PRESS 2005.

cess (for example, ETL) can be seamlessly passed along to all other processes (for example, to the end-user analysis tools).

This is an essential capability for the IT department as well as for the user
departments. For IT, it allows a better understanding of the effects of
changes in the data and in the data flow, as well as the development of
consistent, analytical applications. It also provides the user departments
with a transparent and seamless access to information, regardless of the
analysis tools used.

In general, we differentiate between technical and business metadata.   **Types of metadata**

Technical metadata

This type of metadata contains all the technical information needed for
the development, operation, and use of a data warehouse. This metadata
can be further distinguished by the time of its creation:

▶ **Administrative metadata**
This group of metadata contains all the information created during the
development and use of the data warehouse. Examples include:

  ▶ Definition of the data warehouse and OLAP schema with the corre-
    sponding key figures, characteristics, attributes, dimensions, and
    hierarchies

  ▶ Description of the data sources, time of data loading, data cleansing
    and transformation rules

  ▶ Description of the indices and aggregates used

  ▶ Characteristics of predefined reports and queries

  ▶ User profiles and roles with the corresponding authorizations

▶ **Operational metadata**
Operational metadata is created during the operation of the data warehouse. Examples of this data include:

  ▶ Monitoring data for the ETL process (extractions, transformations,
    data cleansing, and data loading) and modifications of the source
    system

  ▶ The state of archiving and backup jobs and monitoring of memory
    usage

  ▶ User statistics and requests that contain errors

Business metadata

This type of metadata contains all the required information on the business environment in the company. It includes the definition of relevant field contents, nomenclature (synonyms and homonyms), and glossaries. It also stores the rules for semantic interpretation, derivations, and calculations.

2.4   ETL Components of SAP BW

SAP BW provides great functionality and flexibility for the entire ETL process. SAP BW Release 3.5 provided additional innovations and enhancements for the data acquisition area. Figure 2.3 gives an overview of the BW architecture for Release 3.5.

Figure 2.3 The Integrated Architecture of SAP Business Information Warehouse (Source: SAP AG)

2.4.1   Data Sources and their DataSources

You can load data from almost any source into SAP BW. Note the differentiation among the following main groups (see Figure 2.4):

► **SAP systems**
SAP R/3, mySAP CRM, SAP APO, and SAP SEM

► **Structured interface files**
So-called *flat files*

► **XML data (via standard SOAP protocol)**
Enables you to implement cross-system business processes directly or
use SAP Exchange Infrastructure (SAP XI). Within the overall architecture of SAP NetWeaver, SAP XI handles the task of process integration.

► **Relational database systems**
Enables you to establish a connection via DB Connect

► **Universal data connect (UD Connect)**
Permits access to practically all relational and multidimensional data
sources

► **Third-party systems**
Enables you to use *staging BAPIs* to load data and metadata into SAP
BW (for example, Ascential Datastage and Informatica PowerCenter)

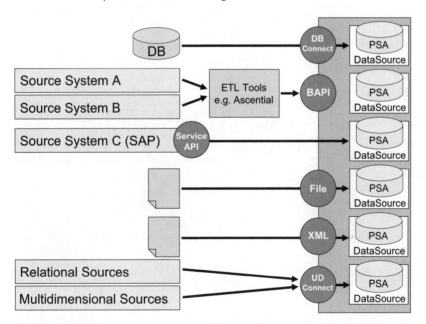

Figure 2.4 Integration of the ETL Process into BW Architecture

Ultimately, the source systems make the data available, usually through
DataSources. Upon request, SAP BW starts to transfer the data. With
source systems such as SAP systems, database systems (with UD Connect
and DB Connect), and third-party systems (linked via BAPIs), the connec-

DataSources

tion is highly integrated. SAP BW reads the data directly from the source system and then imports it according to the selected procedure.

You can maintain source systems under **Source Systems** in the modeling view of the Administrator Workbench (see Figure 2.5). For each source system, the known DataSources can be displayed.

You can use DataSources for all objects that contain data: master data (texts, attributes, and hierarchies on InfoObjects) and transaction data.

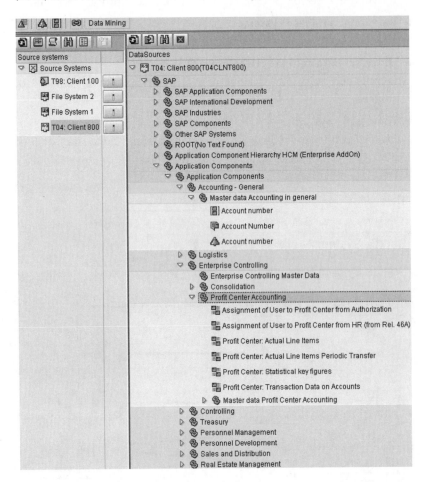

Figure 2.5 DataSources of SAP and Non-SAP Systems in the Administrator Workbench

Transfer structure The structure for transferring data from a DataSource to SAP BW is called a *transfer structure*. If new DataSources are added later, they become available with a subsequent metadata upload. SAP R/3 systems provide a number of SAP Business Content DataSources that you can use immediately.

2.4.2 InfoSources

An *InfoSource* is a data set of logically related information that is combined into a unit. You can maintain InfoSources under **InfoSources** in the modeling view of the Administrator Workbench (see Figure 2.6). One or more DataSources for each selected source system are assigned to a specific InfoSource. Each DataSource then makes its transfer structure available to that InfoSource.

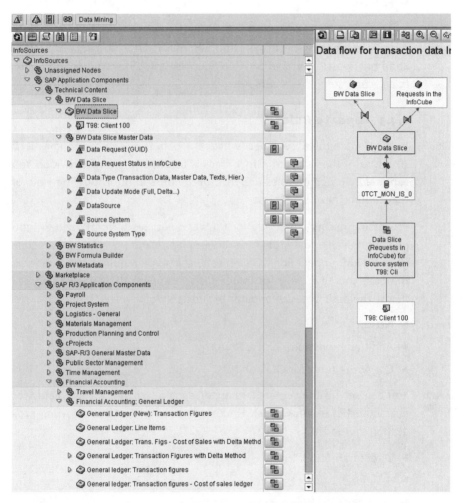

Figure 2.6 Configuration of Data Acquisition from Connecting the DataSource to Posting the Data to the Data Target (here: InfoCubes) in the Administrator Workbench

A *communications structure* contains the InfoObjects into which an Info-Source is to transfer data (for master data, characteristic values, language key, and long text, for example).

Transfer rules You use *transfer rules* to convert the data delivered in the transfer structure to a form that is appropriate to SAP BW in the communications structure. The transfer can occur in any of the following ways:

▶ Direct transfer (1:1 rule)

▶ Assignment of a constant value

▶ Routines (ABAP/4 program coding)

▶ Formulas

You can use the mechanisms described here to update master data directly in the InfoObjects. For InfoProviders (transaction data and, as an additional possibility as of SAP BW 3.0, also InfoObjects), posting occurs in a second step, the *update rules*.

2.4.3 Update Rules

Definition In the update rules, you specify how the data from the communications structure of the assigned InfoSources is inserted in an InfoProvider. You can maintain update rules under **InfoProviders** in the **Modeling** view of the Administrator Workbench.

Processing occurs differently for the various types of InfoProviders: You must define an update rule for every key figure and the related characteristics for InfoCubes. For ODS objects, the same requirement applies to the data and key fields; for InfoObjects, it applies to attributes and key fields. The basic types of updates include the following:

Rules for each data field

▶ No update

▶ Addition, minimum, or maximum

▶ Overwrite (only for ODS objects)

Rules for each key field You can set up the required rules for each key figure for key fields (or characteristics in InfoCubes). Here, too, you can use the following processing methods:

▶ Direct transfer (1:1 rule)

▶ Assignment of a constant

▶ Routines (ABAP/4 program coding)

▶ Formulas

In general, we recommend that you use the transfer rules to create adequate cleanliness of the data and the update rules to create logical transformations. Although SAP does not require that you adhere to this approach, it has the advantage of cleansing the data as soon as it "enters" SAP BW. It also allows you to dispense with (possibly) redundant cleansing functions and avoid the danger of not cleansing at all the required locations, which would result in inconsistent and incorrect data for reporting.

2.4.4 Requesting the Data Transfer and Monitoring

You use the scheduler to request transfer of the data into SAP BW. Configuration occurs in *InfoPackages* that you maintain under **InfoSources** in the **Modeling** view of the Administrator Workbench.

InfoPackage

InfoPackages define the selection, processing, and scheduling criteria for a DataSource assigned to an InfoSource. Customizing of the InfoPackages offers the settings required by the DataSources for various types of source systems:

▶ For interface files, you select the location of a flat file.

▶ For delta-capable SAP R/3 DataSources, you choose the full or delta upload option.

▶ For third-party tools, you select the parameters specific to the tool.

As of SAP BW 3.0, you can use process chains to configure complex processes (defining the sequence and criteria according to which data requests are to be processed).

Process chains

You can observe the load in progress with the monitor. The monitor offers an overview screen, as well as detailed information on the status and result of the load process (see Figure 2.7).

Monitor

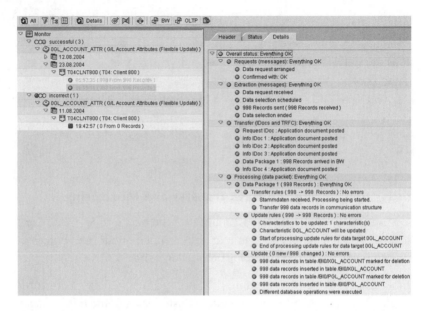

Figure 2.7 The Monitor Allows for Cross-System Monitoring of Data Acquisition and Supports Error Analysis.

2.4.5 Persistent Staging Area (PSA)

PSA When using the relevant transfer methods, the *persistent staging area (PSA)* allows you to store the data in SAP BW as it was delivered by the source system (except for technical conversion, such as the "date" type). Transparent tables are used to store the data.

Systematic reorganization of the PSA: Note that when you use the PSA transfer method, the data is stored in the PSA by default. This feature means that the PSA can quickly reach a size many times larger than that of the actual reporting-relevant objects. We therefore strongly recommend that you monitor the size of the PSA and subsequently reorganize the PSA as needed.

2.5 Data Transfer into SAP BW: Components and Options

2.5.1 Transferring Data Using SAP XI

The starting point for every kind of business software is a process culled from the real business world, which must be automated in order to accelerate business processes and reduce costs. The SAP Exchange Infrastructure

(SAP XI) enables cross-system business processes. Within the overall architecture of SAP NetWeaver, SAP XI handles the task of process integration.

The implementation of a collaborative process with SAP XI is divided into three phases:

Implementation with SAP XI

▶ **Design**
The entire collaborative process is devised during the design phase and the required interfaces are derived from this process. You can either define new system-independent interfaces for implementation at a later stage (outside-in development), or you can use existing functions in the systems (inside-out development). The logical collaborative process is designed in this phase, in which the message exchange between application components in a specified role is described. This description is still independent from the actual systems in use.

▶ **Configuration**
During the configuration phase, the collaborative processes for a specific system landscape are implemented. Therefore, you can establish conditions suitable for the message flow and select the design objects that you want.

▶ **Runtime**
The configuration data is evaluated during runtime and this data controls the communication. The message flow can be monitored via a centralized monitoring.

These three phases are quite apparent when you look at the SAP XI architecture (see Figure 2.8).

The design and configuration phase each have their own central storage area—the *Integration Repository* or the *Integration Directory*—providing an overview of all data that is relevant for a cross-system process. This data is processed by a shared tool, the *Integration Builder*. The content of the Integration Repository and the Integration Directory is referred to as *collaboration knowledge*.

Collaboration knowledge

During runtime, the *Integration Server* is the central "distribution engine" for messages in the SAP Exchange Infrastructure. All systems that communicate with each other via SAP XI exchange messages through this server. The technical systems or communication partners of a specific system landscape are what are referred to as *business systems* on a logical level. The configuration data from the Integration Directory indirectly determines which recipients the Integration Server transfers the message to and whether mapping will be performed prior to the transfer.

Collaborative business processes

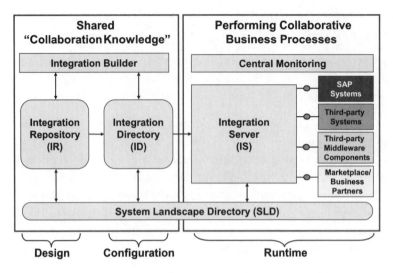

Figure 2.8 The Architecture of SAP XI

The integration of SAP XI and SAP BW enables you to send data from various sources via SAP XI to the delta queue in SAP BW. This provides a range of advantages:

▶ **Central maintenance of the message flow between the logical systems of a system landscape**

▶ **Options to transform message content between sender and recipient**
By using mappings, the values and structures of the messages can be adjusted for the recipient. This enables data of various types to be transferred into a SAP BW system via interface mappings.

However, the data must always be transformed so that it arrives in a flat structure in SAP BW, so as to be compatible with the interface of the function module generated and used for data transfer in SAP BW.

▶ **Utilizing Proxy communication with SAP BW**
Proxies are executable interfaces generated in application systems for communication with SAP XI Integration Server.

To communicate with SAP BW we recommend the use of proxies as they guarantee *full quality of service* (exactly once in order). This ensures that the data is transferred only once and in the right sequence. The SAP XI integration server maintains the serialization as it was established by the sender.

2.5.2 Transferring Data with UD Connect

Universal Data Connect (UD Connect) enables the reporting and analysis of SAP and non-SAP data by utilizing the SAP Web AS J2EE[5] connectivity. UD Connect allows you to access almost all relational and multidimensional data sources and it transfers data as two-dimensional (flat) data. When using UD Connect, multidimensional data is flattened (into a two-dimensional format) for transfer. Figure 2.9 illustrates the architecture of UD Connect.

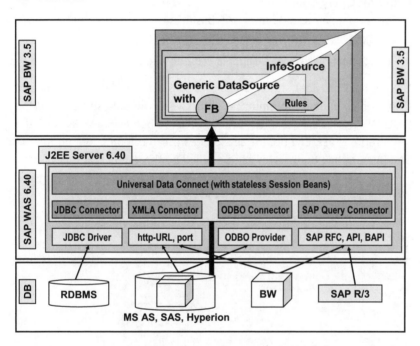

Figure 2.9 SAP UD Connect Architecture

UD Connect Architecture

UD Connect consists of two essential parts: The Java components are contained in SAP Web Application Server (Web AS) and are responsible for communication between data sources and SAP BW. The ABAP components are part of SAP BW. A connection to the SAP Web AS J2EE Engine is established for the data sources with their source objects.

---

5 Java 2 Platform, Enterprise Edition (see also *http://java.sun.com/j2ee/*)

The data sources and the existing source objects are addressed (as resource adapters) via the JCA[6]-capable BI Java Connectors,[7] which are available for various drivers, protocols, and providers.

▶ **BI JDBC[8] Connector**
For connecting to relational JDBC data sources

▶ **BI ODBO[9] Connector**
For connecting to OLE DB for OLAP-capable data sources

▶ **BI SAP Query Connector**
For connecting to data from SAP business applications

▶ **BI XMLA[10] Connector**
For connecting to XMLA-capable DataProviders

UD Connect provides stateless session beans via the SAP Java Connector (JCo), which enables communication between the data sources and the SAP BW server. Because of the RFC connection between SAP BW and the SAP Web AS J2EE Engine, the session beans can call function modules in SAP BW or, they themselves can be called by those function modules.

Figure 2.10 Calling the UD Connect Wizard in InfoSource Maintenance

---

6 J2EE Connector Architecture
7 You can get more information on BI Java Connectors from SAP Help Portal at *http://help.sap.com/saphelp_nw04/helpdata/en/a6/c0e51914e842e19bda39dbbe4fe78c/content.htm*
8 Java Database Connectivity
9 OLE DB for OLAP—an industry standard initiated by Microsoft for accessing multidimensional structures.
10 XML for Analysis (see also *http://www.xmla.org*)

SAP BW contains a wizard in the InfoSource maintenance that can be used to create a generic DataSource with a source-specific function module that reads and transfers data into SAP BW (see Figure 2.10). RFC destinations, UD Connect sources, and source objects are set there and a connection between source object elements and BW DataSource fields are established (see Figure 2.11). The use of this UD Connect DataSource is then similar to the use of any other DataSource type in SAP BW.

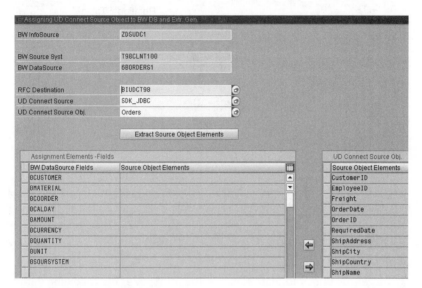

Figure 2.11 UD Connect DataSource Wizard

2.6 Data Transfer out of SAP BW: Components and Options

The *Open Hub Service* enables the distribution of data from a SAP BW system to SAP and non-SAP data marts, analytical applications, and other applications. This ensures the controlled distribution across multiple systems. The central object for data export is the *InfoSpoke*. The InfoSpoke defines the object from which data is retrieved and to which destination it is forwarded.

The Open Hub Service makes SAP BW the hub of an enterprise data warehouse. In turn, a centralized monitoring in the SAP BW system makes the distribution of the data manageable.

SAP BW objects such as *InfoCubes*, *ODS objects*, and *InfoObjects* (attributes or texts) can serve as open hub data sources (see Figure 2.12). You can select database tables or flat files as an open hub destination.

There is both a full or a delta extract mode available as an extraction mode.

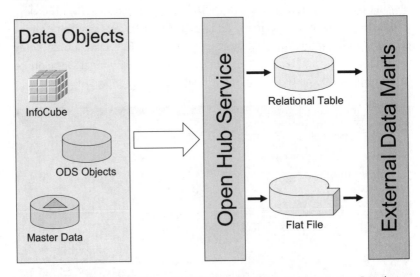

Figure 2.12 As of SAP BW Release 3.0, You Can Use Open Hub Services to Distribute Data from SAP BW into Other SAP and Non-SAP Systems.

The Open Hub Service consists of the following objects:

▶ **InfoSpoke**
The central object for data export is the InfoSpoke. The following items are defined in the InfoSpoke:

▶ The *Open Hub Data Source* from which the data is extracted

▶ The *Extraction Mode* used for extraction

▶ The *Open Hub Destination* to which the data is delivered

You can also select which data selection is to be extracted from the respective InfoProviders. By making this selection, you ensure that a destination can be provided with data for various selection criteria at different times from the same InfoProvider by delta. You can only freely set the selection before extraction has occurred in the delta mode. After that, it is no longer possible.

▶ **Open Hub Data Source**
The BW objects InfoCube, ODS object, and InfoObject (attributes or texts) can act as open hub data sources.

▶ **Extraction Mode**
You can use both full and delta extract modes as extraction modes.

▶ **Open Hub Destination**

You can select database tables or flat files as open hub destinations. Data can be transferred from the database via APIs (by a third-party tool) to a non-SAP system. The open hub destination contains all information about a destination system for the data from an InfoProvider: the type of the destination, the names of the flat file or the database table, and so on. It also contains a logical target system that helps to organize the individual open hub destinations in the open hub monitor. The open hub monitor groups the requests according to the logical target system, open hub destination, and InfoSpoke. You can ensure a better overview of the individual open hub requests by specifying a logical target system.

2.7 Data Transfer and Application Development with SAP BW: BI Java SDK

Analytical applications can be developed with the BI Java SDK[11], which enable you to access, process, and display multidimensional data (Online Analytical Processing or OLAP) as well as relational data in tabular form.

The APIs of the BI Java SDK are implemented by the BI Java Connectors, which also enable the connection of the applications that were developed with the SDK to various data sources.

Characteristics of the SDK Architecture

The SDK components facilitate the integration of data from various data sources through a uniform metadata model and a common access interface. Open standards such as the *Java Metadata Interface (JMI)* and the *Common Warehouse Metamodel (CWM)* are used to support access to and the display of metadata. This approach hides the complexity and details of the underlying communication and access protocols, thus allowing you to concentrate on business requirements.

Open standards

By implementing this approach, you'll only have to write applications once for different types of data sources and operating systems. A batch of connectors, *BI Java Connectors*, is used in this driver-based architecture to connect applications with SAP and non-SAP data sources.

Another characteristic of the SDK architecture is the use of OLAP and relational query models. These models provide a simplified command processor as an interface, which can be used to define multidimensional

---

11 Software Development Kit

and relational queries so that the complexity and the details of the query language it contains remain hidden.

Common Warehouse Metamodel

The *Common Warehouse Metamodel (CWM)* is a standard of the *Object Management Group (OMG)*, which provides a framework for presenting metadata in the data warehousing, business intelligence, and knowledge management areas.

Since BI applications are mainly controlled by metadata, the CWM[12] is of particular significance for the BI Java SDK. The OLAP and relational metadata models of the SDK are provided completely by the CWM as a consistent metadata model, whose architecture is based on a solid, standardized metadata approach. There are other reasons why the SDK uses the CWM metadata model:

▶ The CWM complies with the MOF[13] standard. This standard enables the SDK to provide a standard API by using JMI[14] mappings to process and navigate instances of the model.

▶ The CWM metadata model allows you to model a variety of OLAP and relational providers that are generic and extensible in terms of their content and structure. In addition, they are not affected by any implementation plans. This is of particular relevance for the SDK, because in it there are many different providers mapped in a standard metadata model.

▶ The CWM provides a complete, relational metadata model based on the SQL standard. Therefore, it is easy to define a relational metadata service for access to tabular data providers such as JDBC.

▶ The CWM provides an OLAP metadata model, which contains most of the OLAP concepts that are implemented by the most important OLAP systems.

Significance for BI Java SDK

---

12 Common Warehouse Metamodel (see also *http://www.omg.org/cwm*), a standard of the OMG (= Object Management Group, see *http://www.omg.org*)
13 Meta-Object Facility (see also *http://www.omg.org/cwm*)
14 Java Metadata Interface

3   Sample Scenario

This chapter introduces you to the case study that will be used in the following chapters to illustrate typical scenarios that you might encounter in your everyday work. It describes the structure of CubeServ Engines, the model company, its analytical and planning requirements, and the SAP components included in the solution.

To enable you to understand the complex subject matter of SAP Business Information Warehouse (SAP BW), we've decided to work as closely to real-world situations and with as many examples as possible in all volumes of the *SAP BW Library*.

Therefore, the basis for our books is a uniform case study developed by the authors: a virtual company (CubeServ Engines). We will use this case study to describe all the important requirements of business intelligence applications in a manner that parallels the everyday context of your work.[1]

This chapter provides an overview of the basics of the case study. Because the focus of this book is data retrieval, this chapter also contains a detailed description of the extraction, transformation, and loading (ETL) requirements to be implemented.

3.1   The Model Company: "CubeServ Engines"

3.1.1   Company Structure

The model company, CubeServ Engines, operates internationally: It includes various subsidiaries as legal units. Subgroups combine the subsidiaries, and CubeServ Engines (Holding) runs the subgroups. CubeServ Engines consists of the following subgroups (see Figure 3.1):

Businesses and subgroups

▶ The CubeServ Engines AMERICAS subgroup incorporates the American subsidiaries.

▶ The CubeServ Engines ASIA subgroup incorporates the Asian subsidiaries.

---

1 Upcoming volumes of the *SAP BW Library* will develop and modify the case study as needed to examine *reporting and analysis* and *planning and simulation*.

▶ The CubeServ Engines EUROPE subgroup incorporates the European subsidiaries.

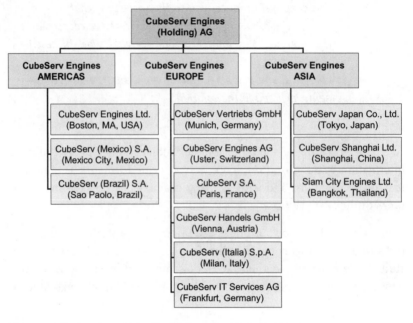

Figure 3.1 The Structure of the Model Company: CubeServ Engines

3.1.2 Infrastructure

Specializations The various elements of the company are specialized:

▶ The following list contains companies involved only in sales:

  ▶ CubeServ Engines Ltd. (Boston, MA, USA)

  ▶ CubeServ (Brazil) S.A. (Sao Paulo, Brazil)

  ▶ CubeServ Vertriebs GmbH (Munich, Germany)

  ▶ CubeServ Handels GmbH (Vienna, Austria)

  ▶ CubeServ Japan Co., Ltd. (Tokyo, Japan)

  ▶ Siam City Engines Ltd. (Bangkok, Thailand)

▶ The following list shows the production companies that also perform sales tasks:

  ▶ CubeServ (Mexico) S.A. (Mexico City, Mexico)

  ▶ CubeServ Engines AG (Uster, Switzerland)

  ▶ CubeServ S.A. (Paris, France)

- ▷ CubeServ (Italia) S.p.A. (Milan, Italy)
- ▷ CubeServ Shanghai Ltd. (Shanghai, China)
- ▶ The following businesses provide shared services:
  - ▷ CubeServ Engines (Holding) AG
  - ▷ CubeServ IT Services AG (Frankfurt, Germany)

The Euro is the group currency. The various company codes use the following local currencies:

Currencies

- ▶ US dollar
  CubeServ Engines Ltd. (Boston, MA, USA)
- ▶ Mexican peso
  CubeServ (Mexico) S.A. (Mexico City, Mexico)
- ▶ Brazilian real
  CubeServ (Brazil) S.A. (Sao Paulo, Brazil)
- ▶ Euro
  (CubeServ Vertriebs GmbH, Munich, Germany; CubeServ IT Services AG, Frankfurt, Germany; CubeServ Handels GmbH, Vienna, Austria; CubeServ S.A., Paris, France; and CubeServ (Italia) S.p.A., Milan, Italy)
- ▶ Swiss franc
  CubeServ Engines AG (Uster, Switzerland)
- ▶ Japanese yen
  CubeServ Japan Co., Ltd. (Tokyo, Japan)
- ▶ Chinese renminbi (yuan)
  CubeServ Shanghai Ltd. (Shanghai, China)
- ▶ Thai baht
  Siam City Engines Ltd. (Bangkok, Thailand)

The model company's fiscal year corresponds to the calendar year with four special periods.[2]

Fiscal Year Variant

CubeServ Engines uses four different operational systems: It uses SAP R/3 and the products of other software manufacturers for IT support of its transactional processes.

IT systems

---

2 See also the explanations on the fiscal year variant in Egger, Fiechter, Rohlf: *SAP BW Data Modeling*. SAP PRESS 2005.

3.2 Requirements of the Case Study

CubeServ Engines is planning some changes: The existing analytical and planning applications (MS Excel, Hyperion, Cognos, and Crystal Reports) are to be replaced with a uniform and professional IT solution based on SAP NetWeaver, particularly SAP Business Information Warehouse (SAP BW) and SAP Enterprise Portal (SAP EP). Integration with legacy systems is not required: The transfer of data from legacy systems will occur over a file interface.

The overriding need for analysis and planning at CubeServ Engines involves sales, profitability analysis, and financial reporting (general ledger accounting and consolidation). The company also requires data from all the analytical applications to be mapped for comprehensive management reporting. Such mapping demands integration with a link to aggregated information from sales and profitability analysis, along with financial key figures.

3.2.1 Requirements of the Analytical Applications

Basic requirements

The first step in implementing comprehensive business intelligence solutions includes mapping analytical applications (Sales & Distribution and Profitability Analysis), financial reporting for management, and operational processing.

All analytical applications must provide comparisons with the previous year and periods and time-series analyses. Both involve the use of hierarchies (characteristic and key figure hierarchies). A comprehensive consideration of the data requires currency conversion. All analytical applications contain tabular and graphical presentations.

Additional requirements

The following special requirements apply to individual analytical applications:

▶ **Sales & Distribution**
Additional document reporting and automatic alerting (for late deliveries, for example)

▶ **Profitability Analysis and Financial Reporting**
Additional plan–actual comparisons and structure analyses (the structure portion of profitability analysis items, for example)

▶ **Management Reporting**
Additional plan–actual comparisons, geographical reporting (map graphics), and alerting (overviews according to information clusters, such as traffic lights for the analysis of goals reached)

For the requirements from the Sales & Distribution area, the model company requires information from various sales documents (sales orders, deliveries, and invoices) as well as sales order stock.

Lists of customers and customer orders must be mapped first in order to meet this requirement. This includes data from the sales order (sold-to party, for example), the sales order item (material, order quantity, and value, for example) and delivery scheduling (confirmed quantity and dates, for example) at the document level.

Additional phases of the implementation will map the following additional information:

▶ **Deliveries**
Data on the delivery (ship-to party, for example) up to the delivery item (such as material and delivery quantity) at the document level

▶ **Invoices**
Billing data (such as payer) up to the invoice item (such as material, billed quantity, and value)

The following levels of detailed key figures must be mapped to meet the analytical requirements of profitability analysis.

▶ **Determining Net Revenue**
Revenues minus revenue reductions

▶ **Determining the Profit Margin II**
Net revenue minus full costs of production

▶ **Determining the Profit Margin III**
Profit margin II plus or minus price and quantity deviations

▶ **Determining the Profit Margin IV**
Profit margin III minus area fixed costs

▶ **Determining the Profit Margin V (= Operating Profit)**
Profit margin IV minus company fixed costs

The analyses of profit margins must be enabled as local solutions (the non-consolidated view of individual entities in the company) and as consolidated solutions (with the elimination of revenues and costs between subsidiary companies).

Information from general ledger accounting and consolidation is required to meet requirements in the area of financial reporting:

▶ Legal balance sheet and profitability accounting

▶ Consolidated balance sheet and profitability accounting

Management reporting

Data from all analytical applications is used to map comprehensive management reporting. The first step involves storing the complete data from the previous year and the periods of the current year. In the case study, this step includes the actual data of 2003 up to and including the data of September 2004.

3.2.2 Planning Requirements

Rolling planning requires the integration of sales, revenue, and profit margin planning with plan profitability analysis. The plan data of sales, revenue, and full cost of manufacturing planning is to be transferred to plan profitability analysis.

Planning horizon

Plan data is also available as of 2003. Planning involves September 2004 as the current planning point with plan data from October 2004 up to and including December 2005. Rolling planning occurs quarterly with a timeframe of 12 periods.

Planning functions

The planning process includes the transfer of actual data (sales quantities) with extrapolation to the entire year as an annual value. Distribution to the individual periods of the planning period is based on seasonal factors that you can enter. Variable, percentage-based revaluation is available for selected key figures. Revaluation of the sales quantities occurs on the basis of plan prices and plan cost rates; revenue reductions should be planned as devaluation percentages.

Key figures to be planned and granularity

To meet the planning requirements, you must ensure that aggregated key figures are mapped:

▶ The key figures for sales, revenue, and the full cost of manufacturing are to be mapped to the level of product hierarchy 2, customer country, company code, currency type, version, value type, transaction type, and period/year.

▶ Plan prices are to be mapped to the level of product hierarchy 2, customer country, company code, currency type, version, value type, transaction type, and period/year.

▶ Plan CGM/FC is to be mapped as consolidated manufacturing costs at the level of product hierarchy 2, version, value type, and period/year.

▶ Plan profitability analysis is to be mapped at the level of the company code, plan item, period/year, currency type, version, and value type.

3.3 Procedure and the SAP Components Involved

CubeServ Engines also requires coverage of the following SAP components:

SAP R/3 upstream systems

▶ **Sales & Distribution**
SAP R/3 SD (Sales & Distribution)

▶ **Profitability Analysis**
SAP R/3 CO-PA (Controlling — Profitability Analysis)

▶ **General Ledger Accounting**
SAP R/3 FI-GL (Financial Accounting — General Ledger Accounting)

▶ **Consolidation**
SAP R/3 EC-CS (Enterprise Controlling — Consolidation) and SAP SEM-BCS (Strategic Enterprise Management — Business Consolidation)

The project must implement the corresponding data targets (InfoCubes and InfoObjects, for example) and the ETL process for these components.

Components of SAP Business Content (SAP BCT) are also used as much as possible to improve understanding. If needed, the components of SAP BCT can be expanded and modified. The project must define its own objects if no components of SAP BCT are available.

Use of SAP Business Content

Integrated data retrieval with extractors is used to link upstream SAP R/3 systems. Four extraction methods are used for the ETL process from SAP R/3 upstream systems:

Extraction methods

▶ The transaction data of the Profitability Analysis is retrieved with application-specific extractors of profit and market segment accounting at the line items level.

▶ The transaction data of Sales & Distribution is retrieved with an application-specific extractor of the *logistic extract structure customizing cockpit* at the document level.

▶ The transaction data of the general ledger and master data is retrieved with Business Content extractors.

▶ Business Content and application-specific extractors map unmapped SAP R/3 source data with generic DataSources.

Universal Data Connect (UD Connect) will link external systems. File uploads and XML interfaces retrieve additional data.

Linking external systems

| Use of SAP BW data targets | In general, the reporting components in SAP BW use InfoCubes and MultiProviders. The planning applications write their data back to transactional InfoCubes. An operational data stores (ODS) layer is used to store document data. Other types of InfoProviders are used for dedicated applications in later steps of the implementation. |

| Reporting tools | Business Explorer (BEx) Web applications are used as the standard medium to map analytical requirements. The BEx Analyzer is used for specific requirements. |

| Planning interface | Web interfaces are generally used as the standard medium to map planning requirements. |

3.4   Details of ETL Requirements

Master data provides the core of the data both in transactional applications and in Online Analytical Processing (OLAP) applications. Therefore, master data must be retrieved from the transactional upstream systems for the analytical applications of our model company.

While the master data forms the basis for the analysis, the main part of the analyses is generally based on *transaction data*. Thus, the timely and accurate provision of transaction data is critical for the productive usability of business intelligence solutions.

3.4.1   Master Data

| Texts, attributes, and hierarchies | For the InfoObjects that contain master data of the analytical applications,[3] according to the InfoObject properties, you must load master data texts, master data attributes, and master data hierarchies from the transactional upstream systems for the corresponding InfoObjects of SAP BW. |

Chapter 5, *ETL Process: Master Data*, describes the various SAP BW-side ETL components and their interaction.

| Data retrieval for the "company code" characteristic | In our example, the implementation of the ETL process for master data texts and attributes takes place for the "company code" characteristic (0COMP_CODE) for the source systems "SAP R/3" and "file." In this context, the following components will be described individually: |

▶ DataSource in the SAP Online Transaction Processing (OLTP) source system

▶ InfoSource with transfer structure, transfer rules, and communications structure

---

3   See Egger, Fiechter, Rohlf: *SAP BW Data Modeling*. SAP PRESS 2005.

- ▶ Update rules
- ▶ InfoPackage

For data quality, you must use start and transfer routines and forms in order to ensure that the data is clean.

As an example, we'll demonstrate the implementation of the ETL process for the master data hierarchy for the "cost center" characteristic (0COSTCENTER) for the source system "SAP R/3" with the following components:

Data retrieval for the "cost center" characteristic

- ▶ Connection to SAP R/3 DataSource
- ▶ Setup of the InfoSource with transfer structure, transfer rules, and communications structure
- ▶ InfoPackage

3.4.2 Transaction Data

The general requirements for implementing the ETL process for transaction data include the following:

General requirements

- ▶ In general, for all applications, the InfoSources must be set up with transfer structure, transfer rules, communications structure, update rules, and InfoPackages.
- ▶ Basically, incremental data retrieval (delta upload) must be enabled.
- ▶ Also, the identification of the harmonized (reporting) version[4] and source system information is required.
- ▶ Some of these requirements can be mapped by routines in transfer or update rules.

The requirements of our model company, in terms of the ETL process, are particularly dependent on the specifics of the individual applications.

Application-specific requirements

Profitability Analysis

Data can be retrieved in different ways for profitability analysis:

Flat file upload, SAP R/3 connection, and UD connect

- ▶ From interface files (for example, for CubeServ Engines ASIA)
- ▶ By using an application-specific DataSource from SAP R/3 (for example, for CubeServ Engines EUROPE)
  For this, the application-specific DataSource must be configured in the SAP R/3 source system.

---

4 See Egger, Fiechter, Rohlf: *SAP BW Data Modeling*. SAP PRESS 2005.

> ► By using UD Connect from a SQL database (for example, for CubeServ Engines AMERICAS). You have to create the UD connect DataSource that reads from a table in a SQL database in SAP BW.

You can retrieve the data through an ODS object in an InfoCube.

Sales Order Stock

Using the ODS object for stock updates

The ODS object posted for Profitability Analysis also acts as a source for sales order stock analysis: The order entries are to be posted as increasing sales order stock and the invoices are to be posted as events that decrease sales order stock.

Financial Reporting

Using SAP Business Content DataSources

In the first implementation phase, the SAP R/3 general ledger data is loaded as a basis for the balance sheet and profitability accounting. This data retrieval process can be performed by utilizing an SAP Business Content DataSource and Business Content ETL components in SAP BW. You should also carry out the ETL process here via an ODS object in an Info-Cube.

Sales Documents: Sales Order

Using the logistic extractors on the document level

The sales order data is required on the document level. The logistic extractors for the sales orders are used to this end. You must configure the extractors in the SAP R/3 source system and from there, you can use them with the customer-specific characteristics for the ETL process in SAP BW. You must also collect the sales order data in ODS objects and then transmit this data to the InfoCubes.

3.5 A Look Ahead: Additional Steps in the Implementation

As noted, the case study used in the first volume of the SAP BW Library will be further developed as necessary for the various topic areas.

The first step of the implementation of our model company's requirements occurs in the first volume of the SAP BW Library.

Additional requirements will be developed for later implementation steps in the volumes of the SAP BW Library that follow.

► HR reporting

► Logistics

► Competitors

4   Extractors: Overview of the Techniques

One of the most important processes in data warehousing is the consolidation and homogenization of data from heterogeneous systems. The SAP Business Information Warehouse (SAP BW) addresses this task. As a modern data warehouse, it provides techniques and programs that simplify data retrieval from the data sources. In this chapter, we introduce various SAP BW extraction mechanisms.

4.1   General Overview

4.1.1   Extractor Types

In looking at the historical development of information technology, you will notice that there are many different kinds of data sources. Flat files, ERP systems, relational and multidimensional databases, and XML files are just a few examples of the wide variety of data sources. Furthermore, because data sources differ considerably in their structure, so too must there be different extraction mechanisms for high-performance data retrieval.

Data sources from an historical perspective

It is not surprising that SAP, being a successful provider of ERP systems, provides various extractors for its own range of products, so that the different applications use their own particular extractors. The large number of extractors can also be traced back to the historical development of individual modules. For example, standard SAP R/3 systems don't contain the BW-relevant source system functions, extractors, and DataSources. These are supplied as a component of the service application program interface (API) via plug-ins.

SAP source systems

The service API can be considered as a framework for SAP R/3, mySAP Customer Relationship Management (mySAP CRM), and SAP BW systems, which, in addition to the administration of DataSources and the implementation of its own DataSources, comprises even more components. These include:

Service API

▶ The configuration of source system connections

▶ Delta handling

▶ Controlling data extraction by exchanging messages between the systems

▶ RemoteCube technology

Figure 4.1 shows some of the most important extractors that are used for data retrieval from SAP source systems.

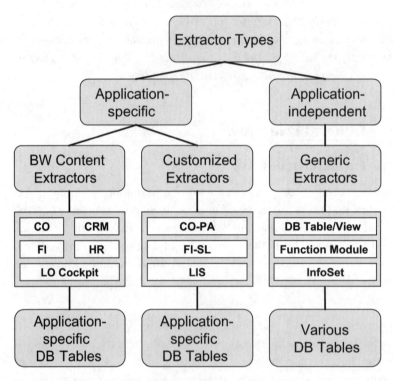

Figure 4.1 Extractor Types for SAP Source Systems

Application-specific extractors
An essential characteristic that differentiates these extractors is that they are part of a specific application. Extractors that extract data from a specific module or a specific component of an SAP source system are called *application-specific extractors*. Such modules include, among others, the sales, accounting and finance, or controlling modules. Due to the structure of individual modules and components, it is necessary to further break down the application-specific extractor types into subgroups.

BW Content extractors
On the one hand, there are extractors that collect data from components that are statically predefined in the SAP source system when it is supplied. These extractors include applications such as the SD (sales) or MM (materials administration) modules, which are supplied with standard tables and standard fields. Smaller customer-specific adjustments to the

tables—made by inserting customer-specific fields—are not considered to be differentiating factors between extractor types. Due to this constantly recurring structure, SAP provides DataSources that can be activated with programmed extraction mechanisms in Business Content.

In contrast to this, however, SAP source systems also contain components, whose tables are created on-site and adjusted to meet the customer's requirements. Some of these applications would include CO-PA, the profitability analysis. The table fields can also be customized.

Therefore, you must have the option to generate customer-defined Data-Sources with extraction mechanisms. These are referred to as *generic extractors*, that is, extractors that don't know from which tables the extractor is supposed to read the data into a specific structure until the name of the DataSource is called.

Application-independent extractor types similarly contain generic extractors. These extractors can be defined as required. In this case, specific DataSources are generated on the basis of any data sources required. These data sources can be SAP database tables for instance, customer-specific tables, or even Views to tables of an SAP source system. The generic DataSources are applied if the Business Content doesn't contain any extractors or, the implementation in Business Content is insufficient.

4.1.2 Enhancing Extractors

Many of the DataSources supplied by SAP in Business Content can be used for data retrieval from SAP source systems. This often requires changes to the extract structures as each customer has his or her own requirements that are necessary to retrieve the data and which the extractor is supposed to supply. An adjustment can then be required if additional SAP fields or customer-specific fields are to be integrated into the data- warehousing process.

For this reason, SAP enhances standard extract structures via append structures. The individual fields of the extract or append structure are described through data elements for each respective data dictionary. When creating append structures, you should note that the attached fields begin with ZZ or YY, that is, they are in the customer name sphere and you can assign an append structure to only one table or one structure, although several append structures can be assigned to a table or structure.

Customer-specific extractors

Generic extractors

Append structures

Creating append structures

After you have called the data dictionary (Transaction code SE11) in the SAP source system, you must select the table or structure that you want to enhance and then display it in the change mode. For our example, we selected the MC11VA0ITM structure as a data type in the dictionary, which is an extract structure for sales documents on the items level. In this case, when calling in the change mode, you receive a message that it refers to an SAP-specific structure, which cannot be changed.

- ▶ Confirm this message and the MC11VA0ITM structure is displayed (see Figure 4.2).

- ▶ When you click on the **Append Structure** button (see Figure 4.2, Step 1), you are prompted to assign a name to the append structure.

- ▶ Accept the suggested name ZAMC11VA0ITM (Step 2). The append structure is now displayed in maintenance (Step 3).

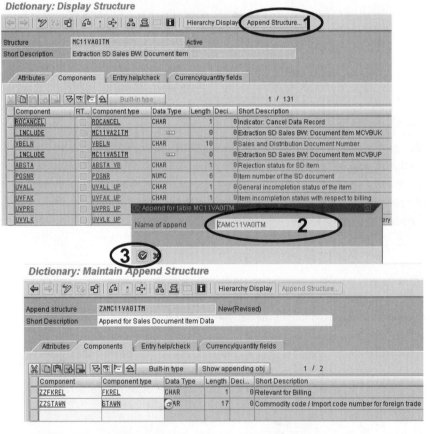

Figure 4.2 Creating Append Structures in the Data Dictionary

▶ Enter the individual components and their types. The *Component* stands for the field name that should begin with ZZ or YY. You must assign a corresponding data type to a component type, for example, MATNR for a material number with an 18-digit character field.

▶ After you have inserted the fields that you want, save and activate the append structure.

▶ The individual fields of the append structures, which have been attached to an extract structure, can now be populated with data via function enhancements. Call Transaction code CMOD to display the function enhancements.

Function modules in the SAP source system

▶ Here, you must first create a project to which you add the SAP enhancement RSAP0001. This exit then provides the following function modules that must be programmed using ABAP:

  ▶ EXIT_SAPLRSAP_001 for the enhancement of transaction data

  ▶ EXIT_SAPLRSAP_002 for the enhancement of attributes and text

  ▶ EXIT_SAPLRSAP_004 for the enhancement of hierarchies

The function module EXIT_SAPLRSAP_003 is used only for a data request for SAP BW Release 1.2B. Originally, it was used to expand texts; however, these texts were integrated into EXIT_SAPLRSAP_002. Figure 4.3 shows the different function modules.

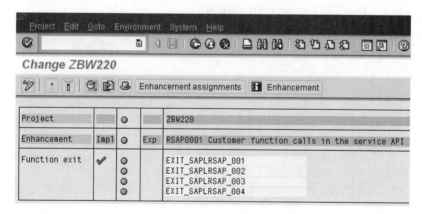

Figure 4.3 Function Enhancements in the SAP Source System

4.2 SAP BW Content Extractors: Extraction of SD Transaction Data with the LO Customizing Cockpit

4.2.1 Requirements from the Case Study

In our case study, sales data is to be extracted from an SAP R/3 source system and provided for analysis in SAP BW. In the functional specification, the sales data consists of the following transaction data:

▶ Sales orders down to the allocation level

▶ Deliveries down to the items level

▶ Invoices down to the items level

LO Customizing Cockpit
Additional transaction data from sales such as requests and offers doesn't have to be considered at this time. In the Business Content installed in SAP R/3, SAP BW provides its own extractors, which are used to extract this SD transaction data. The extract structures and DataSources that provide the document data to SAP BW can be processed and maintained along with other extractors from the logistic area in the *Logistic Extract Structures Customizing Cockpit* (often referred to as the *LO Customizing Cockpit* or the *LO Cockpit*).

4.2.2 The SD Extraction Concept

Sales applications
The SD transaction data is extracted from the SAP R/3 system via special logistics extractors. For extractions that pertain to sales orders, deliveries, and invoices, the following three applications are available:

▶ Application 11: SD Sales BW

▶ Application 12: LE Shipping BW

▶ Application 13: SD Billing BW

You create, change, and delete documents online in these SAP R/3 applications. For sales orders for instance, you carry out document processing using Transaction codes VA01 (creating an order) and VA02 (changing or deleting an order).

DataSources for header data, items, and allocations
Similar to data storage in SAP R/3, you design the LO DataSources from sales. In SAP R/3, you save the data in normalized form, that is, for sales orders, there are tables for header data, item data, and allocation data. This form of normalized data storage has also been implemented for SD transaction data. Here, you can also find DataSources for header, item, and allocation data.

The following problems with LIS DataSources may appear obvious, but it is still worth mentioning them. If reporting is to be implemented on the basis of header data, then you wouldn't need to transfer additional data to the item or allocation levels. As well as having to deal with reduced performance due to the variety of data, you would also require additional storage space. These and other issues led SAP to replace LIS Data-Sources—which had originally been installed, such as 2LIS_01_S260 for the complete sales order—and their extraction mechanisms with new, distributed logistics DataSources that contain new extractors.

Problems with LIS DataSources

Since many documents accrue over the course of time, and because it makes no sense in terms of performance and in terms of an historic view of the data to constantly reload all data on a daily or weekly basis, all LO DataSources for SD transaction data are delta-capable. This property ensures that only those data records that have changed since the last delta initialization or the previous delta, as well as new data records, have to be transferred.

Delta-capable DataSources

Figure 4.4 illustrates the data flow. The data records originate online in the individual applications. In addition to the physical storage in database tables of the SAP source system, the data is also provided in the individual LIS communications structures, in other words, in the memory. These LIS communications structures, a relic from the era of LIS DataSources, function as interfaces between the logistics applications and the DataSources for logistics transaction data.

LIS communications structures

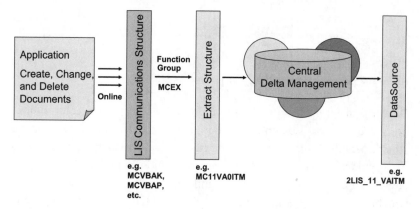

Figure 4.4 Data Flow to the Central Delta Management in SAP R/3

The data from the LIS communications structures is transferred to a central delta management via extraction modules and extract structures. Depending on the selected update method, this transfer can be carried

Central delta management

out at the same time as the document posting takes place in the applications, or independently of it (see Section 4.2.5). The central delta management buffers the data that you can request by using delta requests from SAP BW. However, if the data is transferred using a full update request, then delta management is not involved.

Push mode Because the extractors, in this case, the function group MCEX with the function module MCEX_BW_LO_API, are virtually called from the SAP source system itself and not from SAP BW, in BW jargon, you refer to this as a *Delta transfer in the push mode*.

Reconstruction of document data Since it is possible for older document data to exist in the SAP source system at the time that SAP BW is implemented, either because of the existing R/3 operation or due to a data transfer in the context of an R/3 migration, you must provide a mechanism that extracts these old documents as well. This is referred to as a *reconstruction of document data*. This reconstruction is performed by an ABAP program (see Figure 4.5).

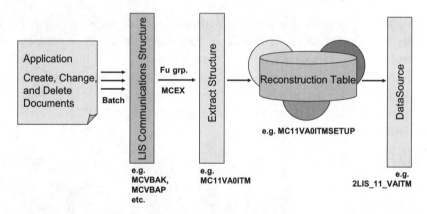

Figure 4.5 Data Flow During Delta Initialization (in SAP R/3)

Data is transferred from the application tables into the LIS communications structure via a batch job and, in turn, it is transmitted to a reconstruction table using extraction modules and an extract structure. For each extract structure, there is a reconstruction table, whose name is composed of the extract structure and the "setup" suffix. These reconstruction tables are cluster tables. The display of data in the source system is enabled by the *Extractorchecker* (Transaction code RSA3), which is also supplied as a component of the service API (see Figure 4.6).

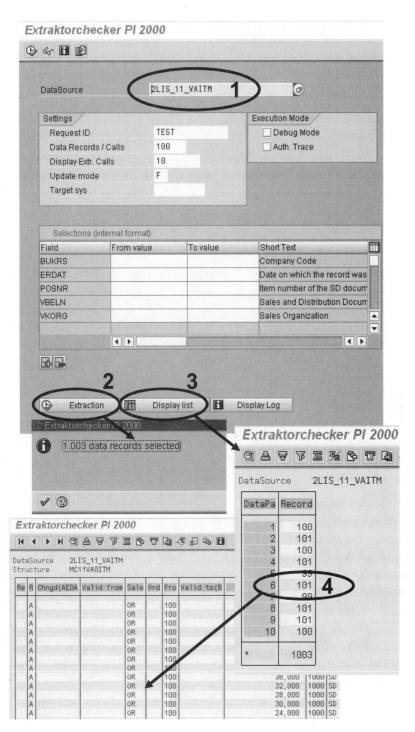

Figure 4.6 Extractorchecker

After the legacy data has been supplied to the tables, you can transfer this data to SAP BW by initiating either a full update request or a delta initialization request with data transfer. If you want to begin operating SAP BW while running the SAP source system, and thus during the generation of new documents or while document changes are occurring, you should select the **Early Delta Initialization** function in the InfoPackage maintenance.

After the reconstruction, we recommend that you delete the reconstruction tables, since these tables will serve no purpose in subsequent operations and further reconstruction will have to occur with each new document.

4.2.3 Structure of the Extract Structures

Extract structures are DDIC structures. Most fields contained in the extract structures are populated from the field content of the LIS communications structures, before the field contents of the extract structures are transferred via the DataSources to SAP BW. However, some fields cannot be filled from the LIS communications structures. Special function modules are provided for populating these structures.

A particular characteristic of the extract structures is that they contain the fields from the LIS communications structures in the form of include structures. To ensure that the field names are unique, you cannot use a field name more than once in an extract structure. Inserting additional include structures with customer-specific fields is enabled by using the append technique.

As already mentioned, there are several DataSources in the logistics extractors and also several extract structures for different document levels such as header or item data. If the DataSources are poorly designed, this can lead to incorrect key figure values in SAP BW, if the same key figure provides its values from both the header and items levels. For this reason, the fields of the extract structures were established in such a way that they could provide only attribute values to fields on the same level, and not key figure values of superordinate levels. Obviously, detailed fields of subordinate levels cannot be provided. The rules regarding which communications structure the fields can be inserted into are described in the TMCEXCFS control table of the SAP source system. When customizing the individual extractors, the fields available depend on the settings.

You will now get a brief overview of which DataSources, extract structures and communications structures belong together and interact with each another.

- ▶ Sales orders at the header level
  - ▶ DataSource 2LIS_11_VAHDR
  - ▶ Extract structure MC11VA0HDR
  - ▶ Communications structures MCVBUK, MCVBAK
- ▶ Sales orders at the items level
  - ▶ DataSource 2LIS_11_VAITM
  - ▶ Extract structure MC11VA0ITM
  - ▶ Communication structures MCVBUK, MCVBUP, MCVBAK, MCVBAP, MCVBKD
- ▶ Sales orders at the allocation level
  - ▶ DataSource 2LIS_11_VASCL
  - ▶ Extract structure MC11VA0SCL
  - ▶ Communication structures MCVBUK, MCVBUP, MCVBAK, MCVBAP, MCVBEP, MCVBKD
- ▶ Deliveries on the header level
  - ▶ DataSource 2LIS_12_VCHDR
  - ▶ Extract structure MC12VC0HDR
  - ▶ Communications structures MCVBUK, MCLIKP
- ▶ Deliveries on the items level
  - ▶ DataSource 2LIS_12_VCITM
  - ▶ Extract structure MC12VC0ITM
  - ▶ Communications structures MCVBUK, MCVBUP, MCLIKP, MCLIPS
- ▶ Invoices at the header level
  - ▶ DataSource 2LIS_13_VCHDR
  - ▶ Extract structure MC13VD0HDR
  - ▶ Communications structures MCVBUK, MCVBRK
- ▶ Invoices at the items level
  - ▶ DataSource 2LIS_13_VDITM
  - ▶ Extract structure MC13VD0ITM
  - ▶ Communications structures MCVBUK, MCVBUP, MCVBRK, MCVBRP

Application 11— sales

Application 12— delivery

Application 13— invoices

Extraction of conditions	Readers with knowledge of the SD module might have noticed that in the logistics DataSources for SD transaction data described so far, there has been no mention of the communication structure MCKOMV for conditions. Until Plug-in Release 2004_1, a clean extraction of conditions was only possible via laborious measures. Since this release, however, there are DataSources specifically designed for SD conditions: 2LIS_11_VAKON for sales order conditions and 2LIS_13_VDKON for invoice conditions. Both DataSources are delta-capable.

4.2.4 Delta Update in SAP SD

Service API and delta queue	Delta update is an important aspect in the context of SD extraction. If a sales order is changed in the SD module, by increasing the sales quantity, for example, and the document status is changed during the document flow, this information must also be reflected in SAP BW. This correct transfer of delta information is carried out commonly by the service API—a layer in the source system that sends requests and starts extractors—and the delta queue, which is the storage area for new and modified (delta) records in the SAP system.
Delta process	The way in which the data records with the delta information are transferred depends on a specific property of the extractor—the *delta process*. The delta process used is saved as an attribute of the DataSource and can therefore be identified in the SAP source system via table ROOSOURCE (Transaction code SE16 and entry of the table name). For DataSource 2LIS_11_VAITM for the sales order items, the delta process is used with the technical name ABR (see Figure 4.7, **DV** field).

For each occurrence of the delta process, we must determine how the data of the DataSource is transferred to the data destination. Consequently, we can also determine whether an update in an ODS or a Basic-Cube is allowed, what kind of update occurs, and whether a serialization per data package or per request is necessary.

This detailed information on the individual delta processes is also stored in a table in the SAP source system where it can be requested as required. Figure 4.8 shows the RODELTAM table where this information is stored.

Example	We will now explain the functionality of the ABR delta process, which is valid and is used for the SD DataSources referred to in the case study for sales contracts, deliveries, and invoices, by using a short sample scenario.

Data Browser: Table ROOSOURCE Select Entries   2.825

DataSource	OLTP Source Version	DataSource Type	Appl. component	Inter...	DV	Da...	Ind.	Ind.	Ind.	Delta Test Pos...
2LIS_08TRTK	A	TRAN	SD		ABR					
2LIS_08TRTK	D	TRAN	SD		ABR					
2LIS_08TRTLP	A	TRAN	SD		ABR					
2LIS_08TRTLP	D	TRAN	SD		ABR					
2LIS_08TRTS	A	TRAN	SD		ABR					
2LIS_08TRTS	D	TRAN	SD		ABR					
2LIS_11_VAHDR	A	TRAN	SD		ABR					X
2LIS_11_VAHDR	D	TRAN	SD		ABR					X
2LIS_11_VAITM	A	TRAN	SD		ABR					X
2LIS_11_VAITM	D	TRAN	SD		ABR					X
2LIS_11_VAKON	A	TRAN	SD		ABR					X
2LIS_11_VAKON	D	TRAN	SD		ABR					X
2LIS_11_VASCL	A	TRAN	SD		ABR					X
2LIS_11_VASCL	D	TRAN	SD		ABR					X
2LIS_11_VASTH	A	TRAN	SD		ABR					X
2LIS_11_VASTH	D	TRAN	SD		ABR					X
2LIS_11_VASTI	A	TRAN	SD		ABR					X
2LIS_11_VASTI	D	TRAN	SD		ABR					X
2LIS_11_V_ITM	A	TRAN	SD		ABR					X
2LIS_11_V_ITM	D	TRAN	SD		ABR					X
2LIS_11_V_SCL	A	TRAN	SD		ABR					X
2LIS_11_V_SCL	D	TRAN	SD		ABR					X
2LIS_11_V_SSL	A	TRAN	SD		ABR					X
2LIS_11_V_SSL	D	TRAN	SD		ABR					X
2LIS_12_VCHDR	A	TRAN	SD		ABR					X
2LIS_12_VCHDR	D	TRAN	SD		ABR					X
2LIS_12_VCITM	A	TRAN	SD		ABR					X
2LIS_12_VCITM	D	TRAN	SD		ABR					X
2LIS_12_VCSCL	A	TRAN	SD		ABR					X
2LIS_12_VCSCL	D	TRAN	SD		ABR					X
2LIS_13_VDHDR	A	TRAN	SD		ABR					X
2LIS_13_VDHDR	D	TRAN	SD		ABR					X
2LIS_13_VDITM	A	TRAN	SD		ABR					X
2LIS_13_VDITM	D	TRAN	SD		ABR					X
2LIS_13_VDKON	A	TRAN	SD		ABR					X
2LIS_13_VDKON	D	TRAN	SD		ABR					X
2LIS_17_I0ACTY	A	TRAN	PM		ABR					X
2LIS_17_I0ACTY	D	TRAN	PM		ABR					X
2LIS_17_I0CAUSE	A	TRAN	PM		ABR					X
2LIS_17_I0CAUSE	D	TRAN	PM		ABR					X
2LIS_17_I0ITEM	A	TRAN	PM		ABR					X
2LIS_17_I0ITEM	D	TRAN	PM		ABR					X

Figure 4.7 Table ROOSOURCE

Data Browser: Table RODELTAM Select Entries   20

Table: RODELTAM
Displayed fields: 5 of   5 Fixed columns: ⫪ List width 0250

Delta Process	FullUpdate Only	Before-Image	After-Image	Long description
	X			Delta only with Full Upload (ODS or InfoPackage Selection)
A			X	ALE Update Pointer (Master Data)
ABR		X	X	Complete Delta with Deletion ID Using Delta Queue (Cube-Cap.)
ABR1		X	X	As 'ABR' Procedure, but Serializatn only Request by Request
ADD				Additive Extraction Using Extractor (e.g.LIS-InfoStructures)
ADDD				As 'ADD' but via Delta Queue (Cube Enabled)
AIE			X	After Images Using Extractor (FI-GL/AP/AR)
AIED			X	After-Images with Delete Indicatr via Extractr (FI-GL/AP/AR)
AIM			X	After Images Using Delta Queue (e.g. FI-AP/AR)
AIMD			X	After Images with Deletion ID Using Delta Queue (e.g. BtB)
CUBE				InfoCube Extraction
D				Unspecific Delta Using Delta Queue (Not ODS-Capable)
E				Unspecific Delta Using Extractor (Not ODS-capable)
FIL0			X	Delta Using File Import with After Images
FIL1				Delta Using File Import with Delta Images
NEWD				Only New Records (Inserts) via Delta Queue (Cube Enabled)
NEWE				Only New Records (Inserts) via Extractor (Cube Enabled)
O		X	X	
ODS		X	X	ODS Extraction
X				Delta Unspecified (Do Not Use!)

Figure 4.8 Table RODELTAM

After image	In SAP R/3, a sales order with an item is created. The order quantity for article A at this item is 5. A data record now exists in the LIS communications structures that acts as a so-called *after image*. An after image is a newly created record, or a record that has been changed that fits with the "after image" idea more closely.
Before image	In the next step, the order quantity is reduced to three items and article A is replaced by article B. Now there are two more records in the LIS communications structures that are loaded into BW: Article A as a before image (old data record) and a new after image that contains article B and the new order quantity of three items. To ensure the correct cumulative key figure update, the order quantity from the before image is transferred into SAP BW with the opposite algebraic sign. This summation virtually books out the old quantity, and the correct order quantity, which is supplied via the after image, is made available for reporting. Depending on whether the delta process allows overwriting or adding to the data target, article A can be replaced by article B or, by serialization, article B can be provided in a new record.
Reverse image	If the order is cancelled, a reverse image is delivered. The reverse image also sends the record with a reversed algebraic sign and marks this data record for deletion.
0RECORDMODE	The description of the record content—that is, whether the record is an after image, a before image, or a reverse image—is provided in the extract structure by the ROCANCEL field or, in SAP BW, by the technical InfoObject 0RECORDMODE.
Returns and credit notes	There is another characteristic of the algebraic sign logic—in the context of extraction from the SD module—that you should note: Do not preface the key figures for newly created orders (and invoices) transferred into SAP BW with a plus sign. In terms of business administration, return or credit note items are different than a standard customer order. Therefore, the quantities and values are transferred into SAP BW with negative algebraic signs. This happens if the debit/credit flag in the item is set. In R/3, this flag is provided by the SHKZG field. The equivalent to this in SAP BW is the 0DEB_CRED InfoObject. However, if you still want to transfer these figures with a plus sign, you can do this in the update rules via InfoObject 0DEB_CRED instead of customizing the order item types in the SD module.

4.2.5 An Overview of Update Methods

Depending on the plug-in release status of the LO Customizing Cockpit, the following update methods maybe available:

▶ Serialized V3 update

▶ Direct delta

▶ Queued delta

▶ Unserialized V3 update

Up to and including PI 2001.2, only the serialized V3 update was available for all logistics applications in the Cockpit. However, because this method can cause errors in the update process, it is no longer supplied as of PI 2003.1. Therefore, you should use one of the three alternative update methods instead.

Serialized V3 update

The functionality of the serialized V3 update is illustrated in Figure 4.9: A document is created in one of the logistics applications SD, MM, or PP. In addition to the usual method of storing document data in the database via the V1 update, another V3 function module that creates the data in R/3 update tables is called. From there, the document data can be collected by a periodically planned V3 collection run and provided in the form of an LUW (Logical Unit of Work) in the BW delta queue. An LUW can either be an individual document or an individual document item, or a collection of documents or document items. The data is collected from the queue via a delta request and transferred into SAP BW.

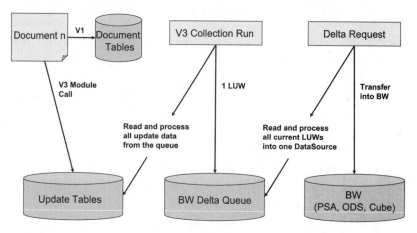

Figure 4.9 Schematic Data Flow During a Serialized V3 Update

As already mentioned, there are problems with this update method, which can lead to errors in the update and also to data inconsistencies in SAP BW. We should point out a few of the more significant problems.

In the V3 collection run, only the posting entries of one language are transferred with a process call from the update table VBHDR into the BW delta queue. Therefore, several process calls must be made for the documents if they were created in several logon languages. In this case, the data records of an update table are always read sequentially, that is, if a new language appears, the process ends and a new one starts. If there are many records, the process of reading a record can take longer than inserting new or changed records from the running operation.

Data serialization is only possible if the times are precisely synchronized on all the instances of a system. This is necessary because the update data is sorted only after the update request is created.

Another equally serious problem emerges if posting errors exist in the V2 update of a transaction. The V3 update can only take place if the V2 update was successful. For this reason there can very easily be inconsistencies between the R/3 system and the BW system.

It is precisely because of the problems that we refer to here that additional update methods were developed, which we will now introduce. One of these methods is *direct delta*. In this update method, a function module is called at the same time that the V1 update process to the document tables is started; this function module writes the data record as an LUW into the delta queue (see Figure 4.10).

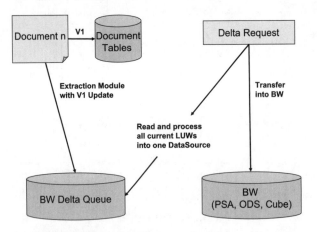

Figure 4.10 Schematic Dataflow in Direct Delta

Serialization is ensured due to the direct use of the delta queue. In addition, this method is independent from errors in the V2 update and it is no longer necessary to schedule a collection run. However, the disadvantage of this update method is that the V1 update has a heavier load and an LUW is created for every data record in the delta queue. With a large number of documents, that is, more than 10,000 documents in the queue, you cannot ensure that all data records are correctly transferred to BW.

An alternative to direct delta is the more flexible update method known as *queued delta*. In this method, document serialization takes place by populating the extraction queue from the V1 update. The documents accumulated are read out from the extraction queue by a periodically scheduled extraction collection run, and then combined into an LUW. Lastly, they can be requested from the BW via a delta request (see Figure 4.11).

Queued delta

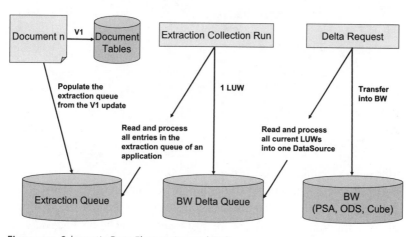

Figure 4.11 Schematic Data Flow in Queued Delta

This update method is advisable if serialization is important and there is a high occurrence of documents. Additionally, the collection run is much more efficient than the serialized V3 update and subsequent processes can be scheduled, since an event is automatically triggered on completion of a collection run of an application.

The fourth update method is the unserialized V3 update. Although no serialization is actually implemented here, this method is comparable to the serialized V3 update. The update tables are also used here and are read out using an update collection run. Furthermore, this update can

Unserialized V3 update

lead to inconsistencies in BW, especially when update errors occur during the V2 update of a transaction in the SAP source system.

4.2.6 Installing the DataSources from the Business Content

Installing Business Content with RSA5

Before the SD DataSources can be maintained, you must install these Data-Sources that come from the Business Content into the SAP source system. Incidentally, this is necessary for all DataSources that have been supplied with SAP Business Content. You can install these DataSources directly via Transaction code RSA5 or by calling them via the BW customizing menu (Figure 4.12), which you can access through Transaction code SBIW.

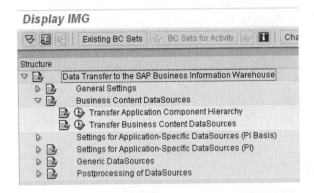

Figure 4.12 Path for Installing DataSources

Application components hierarchy

After calling the transaction, you can access the installation screen. Here, you must select and transfer the required DataSources (see Figure 4.13, Steps 1 and 2). You can find the sales transaction data under the SD application component. In certain circumstances, it might be necessary to install the application components hierarchy straightaway.

A Version and post-processing

During the transfer, *A versions* of the selected DataSources are created from the D version of the DataSources supplied. Now these DataSources undergo a post-processing, for example, in order to maintain the extract structure. With logistics transaction data, the post-processing takes place in the LO Customizing Cockpit; the other DataSources can be maintained by using Transaction code RSA6.

Comparison function

Another interesting feature in Transaction RSA5 is the comparison function. This function enables you to determine whether an A version of the DataSource has already been generated and if it has, whether deviances exist between the D version and the A version.

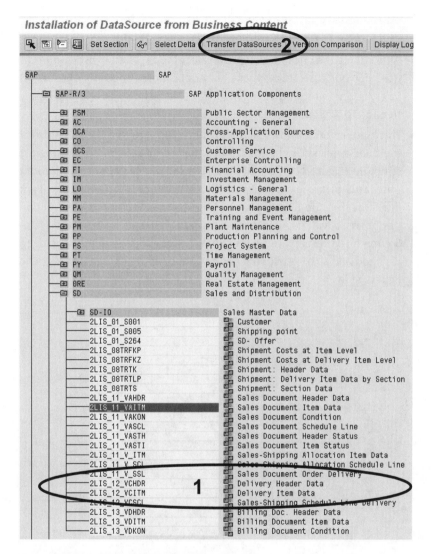

Figure 4.13 Transferring SAP Business Content DataSources

4.2.7 Settings in the LO Customizing Cockpit

As previously described, the settings of the DataSources are established in the Logistics Extract Structures Customizing Cockpit (LO Customizing Cockpit).

▶ The LO Customizing Cockpit can be called directly in the SAP source system using Transaction code LBWE. Alternatively, you can also call the LO Customizing Cockpit through the BW-specific hierarchy tree in customizing (Transaction code SBIW), which is installed during the BW plug-in installation (see Figure 4.14). You can also access this BW hierarchy tree via SAP R/3 Customizing (Transaction code SPRO).

▶ After calling the cockpit, you must select the required logistics application. For our case study, these are applications 11 to 13, that is, SD Sales, LE Shipping, and SD Billing. Figure 4.15 shows an open hierarchy tree for application 11, SD Sales.

Status display by traffic lights
▶ This hierarchy tree shows all the extract structures that are available for the sales application. In addition to the technical name of the extract structure (Figure 4.15, marked as 1), a traffic light notifies you about the status of the extractor and the DataSource. A green traffic light indicates that the DataSource has been generated and the extraction has been activated. A yellow traffic light indicates a generated DataSource but a deactivated extraction. If the extract structure has been changed and the DataSource has not yet been regenerated, the traffic light is red.

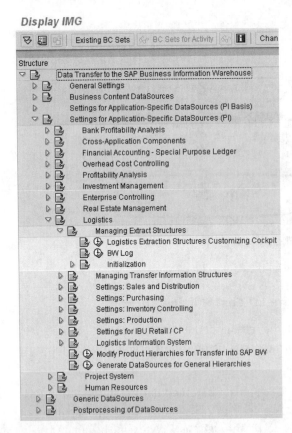

Figure 4.14 Path to the LO Customizing Cockpit

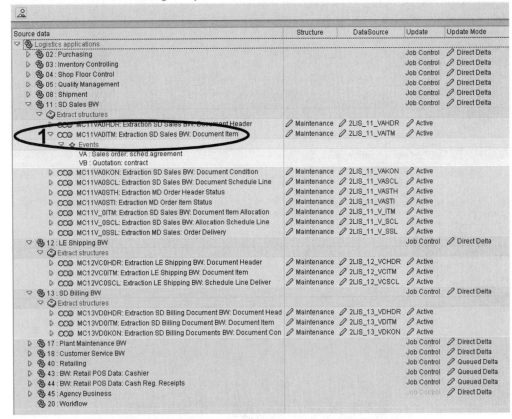

Source data	Structure	DataSource	Update	Update Mode
▽ 🔲 Logistics applications				
▷ 🏵 02 : Purchasing			Job Control	🖉 Direct Delta
▷ 🏵 03 : Inventory Controlling			Job Control	🖉 Direct Delta
▷ 🏵 04 : Shop Floor Control			Job Control	🖉 Direct Delta
▷ 🏵 05 : Quality Management			Job Control	🖉 Direct Delta
▷ 🏵 08 : Shipment			Job Control	🖉 Direct Delta
▽ 🏵 11 : SD Sales BW			Job Control	🖉 Direct Delta
▽ ◯ Extract structures				
▷ ◯◯◯ MC11VA0HDR: Extraction SD Sales BW: Document Header	🖉 Maintenance	🖉 2LIS_11_VAHDR	🖉 Active	
▽ ◯◯◯ MC11VA0ITM: Extraction SD Sales BW: Document Item	🖉 Maintenance	🖉 2LIS_11_VAITM	🖉 Active	
▽ ✿ Events				
VA : Sales order: sched.agreement				
VB : Quotation: contract				
▷ ◯◯◯ MC11VA0KON: Extraction SD Sales BW: Document Condition	🖉 Maintenance	🖉 2LIS_11_VAKON	🖉 Active	
▷ ◯◯◯ MC11VA0SCL: Extraction SD Sales BW: Document Schedule Line	🖉 Maintenance	🖉 2LIS_11_VASCL	🖉 Active	
▷ ◯◯◯ MC11VA0STH: Extraction MD Order Header Status	🖉 Maintenance	🖉 2LIS_11_VASTH	🖉 Active	
▷ ◯◯◯ MC11VA0STI: Extraction MD Order Item Status	🖉 Maintenance	🖉 2LIS_11_VASTI	🖉 Active	
▷ ◯◯◯ MC11V_0ITM: Extraction SD Sales BW: Document Item Allocation	🖉 Maintenance	🖉 2LIS_11_V_ITM	🖉 Active	
▷ ◯◯◯ MC11V_0SCL: Extraction SD Sales BW: Allocation Schedule Line	🖉 Maintenance	🖉 2LIS_11_V_SCL	🖉 Active	
▷ ◯◯◯ MC11V_0SSL: Extraction MD Sales: Order Delivery	🖉 Maintenance	🖉 2LIS_11_V_SSL	🖉 Active	
▽ 🏵 12 : LE Shipping BW			Job Control	🖉 Direct Delta
▽ ◯ Extract structures				
▷ ◯◯◯ MC12VC0HDR: Extraction LE Shipping BW: Document Header	🖉 Maintenance	🖉 2LIS_12_VCHDR	🖉 Active	
▷ ◯◯◯ MC12VC0ITM: Extraction LE Shipping BW: Document Item	🖉 Maintenance	🖉 2LIS_12_VCITM	🖉 Active	
▷ ◯◯◯ MC12VC0SCL: Extraction LE Shipping BW: Schedule Line Deliver	🖉 Maintenance	🖉 2LIS_12_VCSCL	🖉 Active	
▽ 🏵 13 : SD Billing BW			Job Control	🖉 Direct Delta
▽ ◯ Extract structures				
▷ ◯◯◯ MC13VD0HDR: Extraction SD Billing Document BW: Document Head	🖉 Maintenance	🖉 2LIS_13_VDHDR	🖉 Active	
▷ ◯◯◯ MC13VD0ITM: Extraction SD Billing Document BW: Document Item	🖉 Maintenance	🖉 2LIS_13_VDITM	🖉 Active	
▷ ◯◯◯ MC13VD0KON: Extraction SD Billing Documents BW: Document Con	🖉 Maintenance	🖉 2LIS_13_VDKON	🖉 Active	
▷ 🏵 17 : Plant Maintenance BW			Job Control	🖉 Direct Delta
▷ 🏵 18 : Customer Service BW			Job Control	🖉 Direct Delta
▷ 🏵 40 : Retailing			Job Control	🖉 Queued Delta
▷ 🏵 43 : BW: Retail POS Data: Cashier			Job Control	🖉 Queued Delta
▷ 🏵 44 : BW: Retail POS Data: Cash Reg. Receipts			Job Control	🖉 Queued Delta
▷ 🏵 45 : Agency Business			Job Control	🖉 Direct Delta
🏵 20 : Workflow				

Figure 4.15 LO Customizing Cockpit

▶ Various events are listed underneath the extract structure. This is completely informal and there are no underlying functionalities. The individual events provide an insight into when in the Online Transaction Processing (OLTP) system data can be transferred into SAP BW.   **Events**

Maintaining the Extract Structure

The **Maintenance** item in the **Structure** column, on the other hand, is much more interesting.

▶ You can access the maintenance screen for the extract structure by clicking on the corresponding link (Figure 4.16, Step 1).

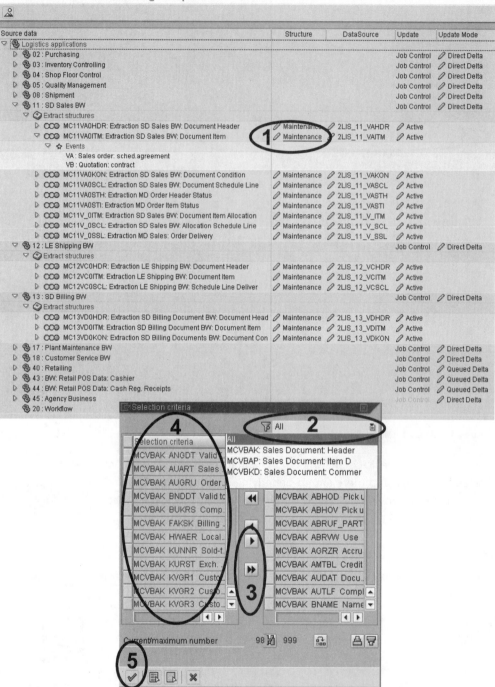

Figure 4.16 Maintaining the Extract Structures

- By using the drop-down box (Figure 4.16, Step 2), you can filter the individual LIS communication structures and display the available fields.

- The required fields can be transferred or deleted again, as required, by selecting them in the right-hand column and clicking on the arrow key in the selection list (Step 3).

- The fields in the selection pane form the extract structure of the Data-Source (Step 4). The settings are transferred using the **Confirm** button (Step 5).

Maintaining the DataSource

- You can access the DataSource maintenance by calling the **DataSource** link (see Figure 4.17, Step 1). Each time this menu item is called, the DataSource is regenerated. Later, you must replicate the DataSource again into BW even if you are not carrying out any changes, since the OLTP DataSource timestamp is different from the timestamp in BW because of the regeneration.

- You can find the technical name for the extract structure of the Data-Source in the maintenance screen and determine whether the Data-Source is delta-compatible (Step 2).

- You can determine which fields should be available for a selection later in the InfoPackages and whether individual fields of the extract structure should be hidden later in the BW DataSource (Steps 3 and 4). We strongly recommend that you use caution with both of these functions. When using the delta uploads, restrictive selections are useful only if the data records excluded will no longer be needed in the BW system. Hiding the fields can also result in the incorrect updating of data in BW, especially if important fields in the transfer structure and the transfer rules are not available.

- Step 5, where the inverted key figures are set is also interesting. These signs are already correctly set by default so that the key figures can be transferred according to the respective business requirements with positive or negative algebraic signs into BW.

- When making a change, we recommend that you regenerate the Data-Source (menu items **DataSource** and **Generate**).

- Click on **Save** to exit the maintenance screen.

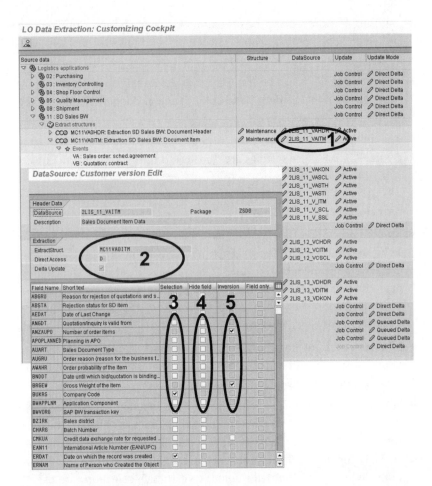

Figure 4.17 Maintaining the DataSource

Selecting the update method

▶ When the DataSource has been generated, an update method can be selected for it. In the context of an SD Extraction, the **Queued Delta** update method is selected (see Figure 4.18). Because this is a global setting on the application level, the selection of the update mode is made directly in application 11 (SD Sales BW).

▶ After the update method has been selected, you should click on the mouse to activate the update (see Figure 4.19).

▶ If you want to deactivate the update, click on the mouse again.

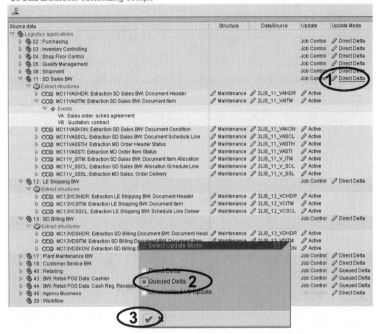

Figure 4.18 Selecting the Update Method

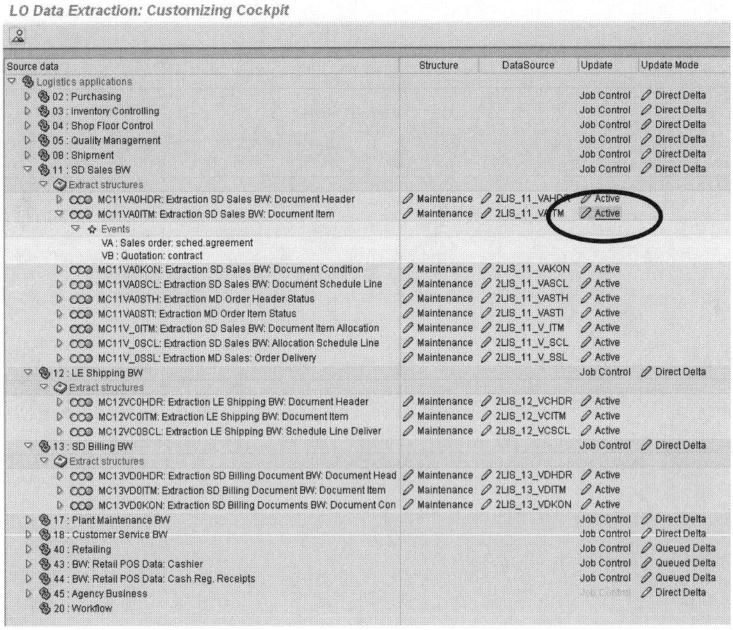

Figure 4.19 Activating the Update

Replicating the DataSource

After the settings for the DataSource have been successfully activated for the DataSource in the OLTP system, the DataSource can be replicated into SAP BW.

► In the Administrator Workbench (Transaction code RSA1) of SAP BW, navigate to the **Source systems** area.

► Then, select the SAP source system and its application component hierarchy by double-clicking on it.

► To avoid replicating all DataSources, which can sometimes take several hours, you can choose to replicate only the required DataSource by using the context menu on the DataSource (see Figure 4.20).

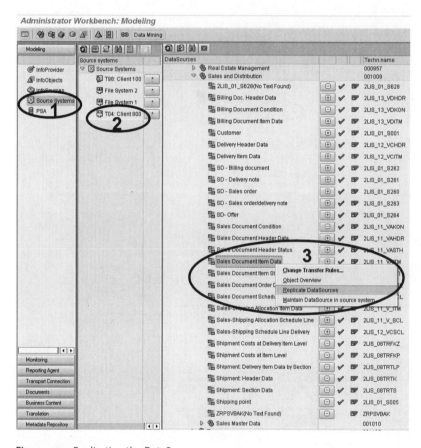

Figure 4.20 Replicating the DataSource

4.2.8 Initializing the Transaction Data

Since the implementation of SAP BW and the extraction of SD transaction data often occur after the OLTP system has gone live, you must also be able to extract existing document data. This is referred to as *reconstructing* or *initializing* transaction data.

Reconstructing

When reconstructing this transaction data, existing documents are provided in reconstruction tables in the OLTP system.

▶ The transaction for reconstructing SD sales orders is called OLI7BW. Use OLI8BW or OLI9BW as transaction codes to reconstruct LE deliveries or SD billing documents. As you can see in Figure 4.21, the required application can be called via the SBIW menu in the SAP source system.

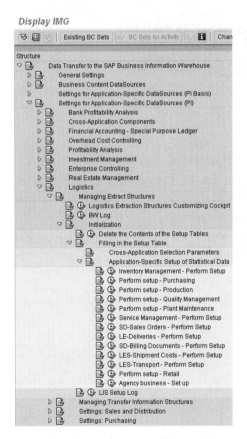

Figure 4.21 Path to Reconstruct the Transaction Data

▶ Since the reconstruction is once again carried out according to the specific application, you don't need to import all logistics transaction data. Instead, you can select the relevant applications. Figure 4.22 shows the possible settings that you can use to reconstruct the sales orders.

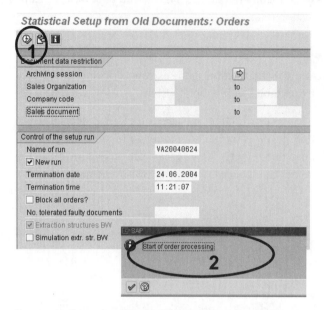

Figure 4.22 Reconstructing the Sales Orders

Reconstruction simulation

▶ During the reconstruction, you should not carry out any document postings in the OLTP system. This ensures that all current documents are actually extracted and made available in the reconstruction tables. A simulation of the extraction can be used if you want to calculate the approximate total runtime of the extraction.

Reconstruction protocol

▶ You can view the result of the transaction data reconstruction via the LIS setup log by using Transaction code NPRT (see Figure 4.23). This log is application- and user-dependent.

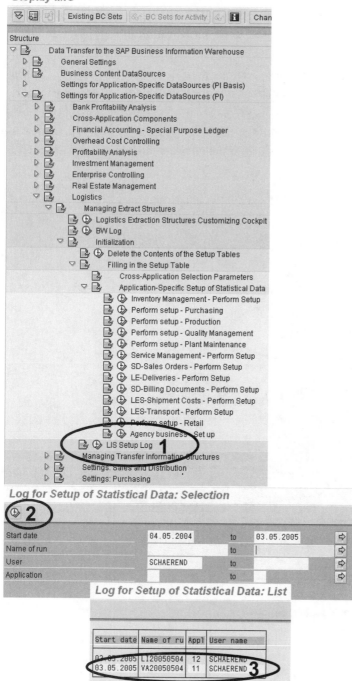

Figure 4.23 LIS Setup Log

Delta Initialization

▶ When the reconstruction has been successfully performed, you can start an InfoPackage with **delta initialization** in SAP BW (see Figure 4.24, Step 1).

▶ Consequently, the BW delta queue related to the DataSource is initialized. This is done via Transaction code RSA7 in the source system (Step 2).

▶ If you initialize the delta process with data transfer, you will receive a message in the monitor of the Administrator Workbench upon successful initialization similar to the one illustrated in Figure 4.24, Step 3.

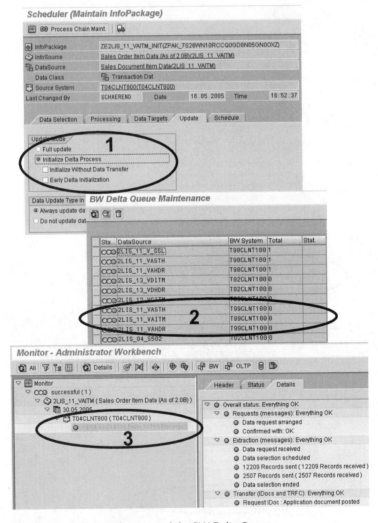

Figure 4.24 Delta Initialization and the BW Delta Queue

The data is available in central delta management only upon a successful delta initialization. Then, document processing in the OLTP can continue.

4.2.9 Extracting SD Transaction Data in Action

Once the SD transaction data has been successfully initialized, you can start or continue the order processing in the source system. In order to demonstrate the BW delta queue, we will now create a new sales order in the SAP R/3 source system. Use Transaction VA01.

Creating a Sales Order

▶ After you have selected the order type, sales organization, division, and sales channel in the VA01 entry screen, you are in the actual order maintenance.

▶ As you can see in Figure 4.25, you must first enter a sold-to party (Step 1).

▶ If the recipient of the goods is the same person, this is automatically entered during customizing of the SD partner roles (Step 2).

▶ You must then enter the PO number in the order header (Step 3).

▶ Enter the product ordered and the order quantity at the items level (Step 4).

▶ The process can vary according to the settings in customizing, since you can mark additional fields as mandatory, which means that additional entries would be necessary as well.

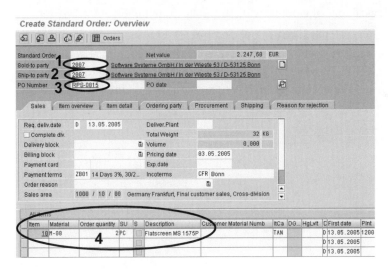

Figure 4.25 Creating a Sales Order

Update Collection Run

The next step involves preparing the data transfer to the BW. In the **queued delta** update method, you must start an update collection run. Typically, you should schedule this job at regular intervals. No more than 10,000 documents should accumulate per time interval, that is, if a large number of documents occurs, we recommend that you do an hourly collection run.

▶ The update collection run is also started via the logistics extract structures customizing cockpit (see Figure 4.26, Step 1).

▶ First select a start date for the job (Step 2). You can schedule this for a specific date and a specific time, or after another job or a specific event.

▶ You should execute the job periodically during production hours (Step 3).

▶ The print parameters must also be maintained (Step 4).

▶ Please ensure that the output device attached is not a local printer connected to the client, which would mean the job would not be executed (Step 5).

▶ Once all the settings are done, the job is scheduled (Step 6) and the sales orders are read out from the extraction queue and placed into the BW delta queue. You can track the status in the job overview.

LUWs in the BW delta queue

▶ As the update collection run is dependent on the application, all three active SD sales order DataSources (header, position, and schedule line delivery data) in the BW delta queue of the SAP source system contain a logical unit of work (LUW). This is illustrated in Figure 4.27, Step 1.

▶ If you now take a look at the data records of this LUW (Steps 2 and 3), you can see that two orders were created and summarized into this one LUW. However, this only occurs with **queued delta.** If you had chosen **direct delta** as an update method, you would have gotten two LUWs—one for each order.

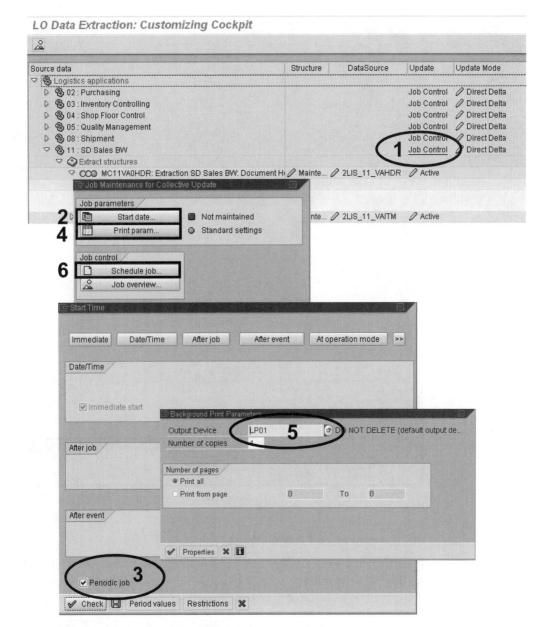

Figure 4.26 Scheduling the Update Collection Run

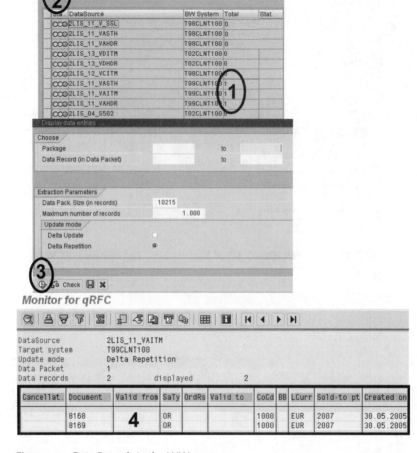

Figure 4.27 Data Records in the LUW

qRFC Monitor and BW Delta Queue

Technically speaking, queued Remote Function Calls (qRFC) are the basis for the BW delta queue. The BW delta queue reads from the qRFC queue without changing the status of the delta queue.

▶ You can access the qRFC monitor (see Figure 4.28) with Transaction code SMQ1 and it displays basically the same data as the BW delta queue, only somewhat less concisely (Step 3).

▶ You must use the internal queue name, which consists of the prefix "BW," the client, and the short name of the DataSource, in order to make a selection on the entry screen of the qRFC monitor (Step 1). For

DataSources whose names contain 19 characters or less, the short name is the same as that of the DataSource. For DataSources whose names are longer than 19 characters, the short name is assigned in Table ROOSSHORTN.

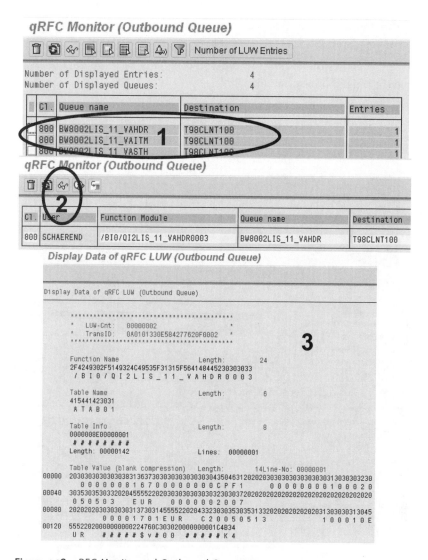

Figure 4.28 qRFC Monitor and Outbound Queue

Experienced BW administrators also find the RSC1_DIAGNOSIS diagnosis program very helpful, because the most important information on the status and state of the delta queue for a specific DataSource is provided by these programs: For example, an analysis of ARFCSSTATE is made

Diagnosis program for BW delta queue

available, which allows you to see whether there are obvious inconsistencies in the delta queue.

Delta request

▶ The data can then be collected via a delta request (Figure 4.29, Step 1) from the BW delta queue of the SAP R/3 system.

▶ You must confirm the message that appears after scheduling the request (Step 2).

▶ Step 3 shows the monitor where you can verify that two data records were indeed transferred into BW.

▶ You can also display the content of both of these records in the Persistent Staging Area (PSA) (Steps 4 and 5).

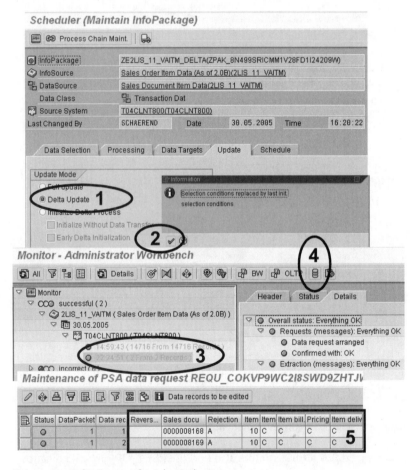

Figure 4.29 Delta Request for Sales Order Items

Resetting the LUW

If you look at the BW delta queue in the SAP R/3 system again, you will notice that, despite the correct data transfer into BW, there is still an

LUW in the SD sales order DataSource. This is not a bug. On the contrary, it is absolutely correct. If unexpected errors occurred during the data transfer, the data can once again be requested by repeating the delta. Only another delta request will remove the LUW from the BW delta queue, provided the data records were correctly transferred earlier.

4.3 Customer-Specific Extractors in the Example of SAP CO-PA

4.3.1 Requirements from the Case Study

In our case study, data will also be extracted from CO-PA (Controlling—Profitability Analysis), the profitability analysis tool of SAP R/3 that ensures that profit margins analyses can be implemented later with SAP BW. You can retrieve the CO-PA transaction data from the individual items level. Due to the customer-specific structure of CO-PA, you cannot use standard DataSources from Business Content here; instead, you must create customer-specific DataSources.

4.3.2 Principles of SAP CO-PA

Profitability Analysis (PA) is concerned with questions such as "In which of our divisions, with which product group, and for which target group will we aim for the greatest sales and profit margin?" It's already apparent from this question that CO-PA deals with an area of the SAP R/3 system that collects its data from several modules. As a matter of fact, revenues and discounts go from the SD into the profitability analysis just as well as standard production costs from Product Cost Controlling, or data from Overhead Cost Controlling.

Various data sources

While Overhead Cost Controlling (CO-OM) copies many postings from the FI module (Financial Accounting), Product Cost Controlling (CO-PC) gets its information from the material master of the MM module (materials management) and the item lists and work plans from the PP module (Production Planning). In contrast to CO-OM and CO-PC, where the data structures are delivered with the SAP R/3 system, CO-PA requires that all fields are derived from the master data, and you must define them yourself. Since it is very unlikely that different companies use the same master data, this stipulation does make sense. Therefore, you must be able to create a DataSource for the CO-PA extraction that is suitably flexible and yet company-specific.

Company-specific data structures

You can specify these company-specific data structures of CO-PA by defining an operating concern. The operating concern, in turn, consists of *characteristics* and several *value fields* (in costing-based profitability analysis). If an account-based profitability analysis is used, the operating concern consists of *characteristics*, an *amount*, and a *quantity*, as well as several *G/L accounts*.

Possible characteristics of CO-PA are "customers," "company code," or "material." These characteristics have their own properties, the so-called *characteristic values*, such as "company code DE01" for Germany, or "company code CH01" for Switzerland. If you combine the individual characteristic values, you get what is referred to as a *profitability segment*, which gives you a specific view of the data.

The key figures in CO-PA are referred to as *value fields*. The characteristics and value fields for CO-PA are supplied by SAP. They can, however, also be created as customer-specific. After these definitions are established, the operating concern must be recreated or regenerated.

The basis for data storage is the actual line-item Table CE1xxxx, where xxxx stands for the name of the operating concern. This table is generated from the previously defined characteristics and value fields and contains all data at a most detailed level. A line item corresponds to an invoice or billing item from the SD module. Saving the CO-PA data in the actual line-item table is comparable to saving data in an ODS on the BW side: All the data is stored in a large relational table.

In addition to the line-item table, you can also store plan data at the line-item level. This is done via Table CE2xxxx.

The line items contain some information at the document level, which is usually too detailed a view for analysis purposes. Consequently, CO-PA uses a condensed view of the data. Figure 4.30 shows how this condensed view is structured. First, attributes that describe a particular business object are removed from the line-item table and stored with a unique profitability segment number in a separate Table CE4xxxx, the so-called *object table*.

The value fields are also condensed here. Here cumulative values for the period are created per profitability segment number, which are stored in the table that contains the object levels, Table CE3xxxx. In order to ensure that it is possible to assign a value to a profitability segment in the CO-PA application later, the value fields are condensed on the profitability segment number level, on a period level, as well as on a process level for characteristics such as plan-actual flag, record type, and plan version.

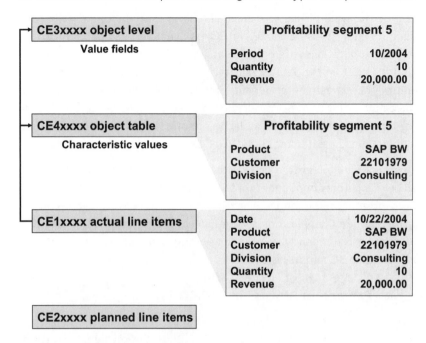

Figure 4.30 Database Structures in CO-PA

4.3.3 Requirements to the Extractor

Given the previous explanations and overall principles of CO-PA, it should be apparent that there can be no standard DataSources in Business Content. Like the application itself, these DataSources must be customized and generated by the user. In addition to the characteristics and value fields, DataSources for CO-PA consist of other important information, such as the name of the operating concern, the client, update status, and a timestamp that can be used to establish what data has already been loaded into SAP BW.

For the data retrieval requirements for our case study, the extractor will read out its data later from the line-item Table CE1xxxx. The extractor accesses this table once a field is extracted on the line-item level, except for the **Record Currency** field (REC_WAERS), which is always checked.

Realignments in CO-PA

What is surprising is that the extractor also reads the object table when it extracts on the line-item level. The reason behind this is that information on status changes in CO-PA is stored only in Table CE4xxxx. If you only read data from Table CE1xxxx, you will not get any information on the status changes in OLTP, which would cause the invalidation of the Data-Source delta status.

Delta with pull mode

In order to avoid having to extract all records every time, the delta handling function is also available in CO-PA DataSources. .Contrary to the logistics applications where the new data must be placed in the queue by a push, in CO-PA the data is read at the time of extraction by a pull mechanism. The extractor—the function module RKE_BIW_GET_DATA_API is the extractor for CO-PA—is called from BW via a delta request and reads the data from the line-item table. The information is written to the BW delta queue and extracted from there into SAP BW via the service API.

Safety delta

To ensure data integrity, a delta initialization or a delta request replicates all new line items from line-item tables at point t, which had been previously posted (t=30 minutes). The reason for this process is that the timestamp of different application servers can easily differ from one other. This 30 minutes is frequently referred to as *safety delta* because only data that is older than 30 minutes is extracted.

4.3.4 Extraction Process in SAP CO-PA

Assigning key figures

The key figures are assigned in the first step (see Figure 4.31). In this context, you can assign a value field from CO-PA to the key figures, as is the case with revenue in our example. It is also possible to assign elements from a key figure scheme to some key figures that were predefined in CO-PA, or to calculate these key figures via a function module. Later, you can incorporate these fields in the DataSources.

A basic advantage of this step is that calculated key figures don't have to be redefined later in SAP BW queries; rather, the same formula from the SAP R/3 source system can be used with this key figure. This means that the business context remains identical in both the data retrieval process and reporting.

However, you should use the key figure scheme with caution. We recommend that you carry out detailed checks on the formula on which the key figures are based since they do not always provide the desired result. For this reason, you can change existing key figure schemes and add new ones.

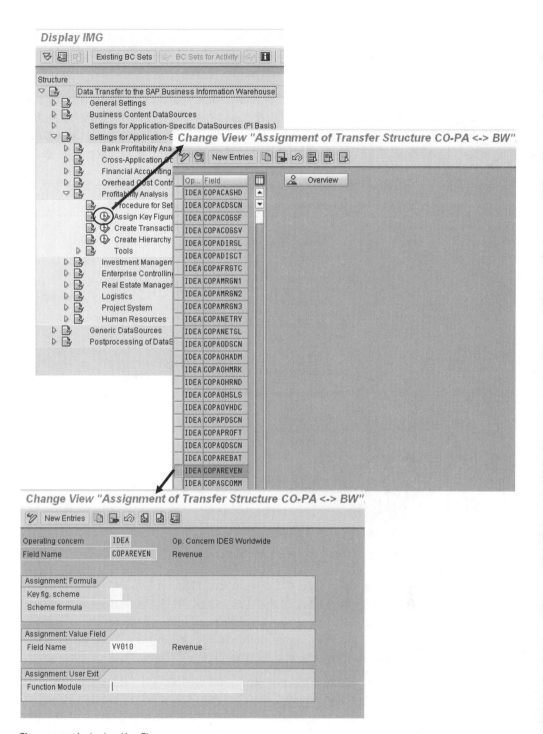

Figure 4.31 Assigning Key Figures

Creating DataSources

The DataSource for the CO-PA extraction must first be created in the SAP R/3 system and then replicated in SAP BW.

 To do this, select **Settings for Application-Specific DataSources** in the BW-specific hierarchy (Transaction code SBIW), as shown in Figure 4.32, then **Profitability Analysis,** and lastly, select **Create Transaction Data Data-Source.** This function can also be called directly by Transaction code KEBO.

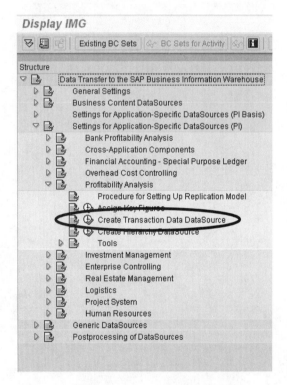

Figure 4.32 The Path to the CO-PA DataSource

▶ You are now in the first dynpro (see Figure 4.33), where you must set the basic properties of the DataSource. The system suggests the seemingly cryptic text 1_CO_PA<%CL><%ERK> for the technical name of the DataSource. The characters contained in the tags (< >) are placeholders for the client and the operating concern.

▶ CO-PA DataSources are always defined on the client and operating concern levels. As an option, you can add <%SYS> for the system ID. In our case example, we will replace the DataSource later with the current client and the selected operating concern. Therefore, no entry or replacement is required at this point.

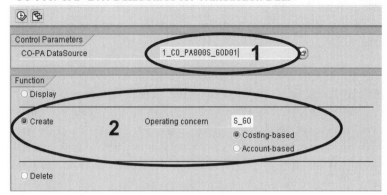

CO-PA / SAP BW: DataSource for Transaction Data

Control Parameters
CO-PA DataSource   1_CO_PA800S_60D01| **1**

Function
○ Display

● Create   **2**   Operating concern   S_60
                                              ● Costing-based
                                              ○ Account-based

○ Delete

Figure 4.33 The Technical Name of the CO-PA DataSource

▶ However, as this is a standard suggestion, we will also add the Postfix D01 so this CO-PA DataSource can be differentiated from other CO-PA DataSources in the source system (see Figure 4.33, Step 1).

The client and the operating concern are optional entries and can also be omitted. However, the 1_CO_PA prefix is mandatory. But, we wouldn't advise that you use this because later a relatively simple recognition attribute of the origin of the DataSource would be lost.

▶ In the next step (Step 2), you should select the **Create** function. To do this, select the operating concern template Quickstart S_GO from the SAP R/3 system and set the type of the CO-PA DataSource to **Costing-based**.

▶ Finally, the DataSource is created by clicking on the **Execute** button, or by pressing the **F8** key.

Characteristics from Object Level and Object Table

As you can see in Figure 4.34, Step 1, the technical name of the DataSource has been created correctly. Later, after the DataSource has been replicated in SAP BW, an InfoSource is automatically created by SAP BW with the specified name.

▶ In Step 2, you must assign the descriptions for the short, medium, and long texts. These are more or less standard settings. But now the relevant characteristics and key figures will be transferred to create the required settings for the case study.

▶ The relevant key fields are already marked for the characteristics on the segment level (Step 3) and cannot be deactivated. It is not necessary to include the **Week** attribute at the object level because of the data model in BW.

At this point, it is worth mentioning that many fields are not transferred "as is" into SAP BW. The **PLIKZ** field in the OLTP system (values 0 and 1 for the value type) is later mapped to the BW InfoObject 0VTYPE with the values 010 or 020; the **PALEDGER** field (internal/external values 01/B0, 02/10, 03/B2, and 04/12) is allocated to the BW InfoObjects 0CURTYPE (values B0, 10) for the currency types, and 0VALUATION for the evaluation view (values 0, 2). The fiscal year variant **PERIV** is added to the fiscal year **GJAHR** to provide a better description of the period **PERIO**.

▶ You must transfer all suggested characteristics from the segment table (Step 4) to SAP BW, and therefore, they have to be activated. These characteristics include the characteristics maintained with Transaction code KEQ3 (profitability segment characteristics), which form the profitability segment.

▶ In the fields for units of measure (Step 5), the only field, the gross quantity unit, is already activated and you must also transfer this field, since a key figure with the corresponding unit must be transferred to SAP BW.

Excursus

In Figure 4.34, all characteristics, even the material and main material groups, are checked. This enables the extraction of the characteristic properties at the time of the update ("as updated") in the SAP R/3 system.

If, on the other hand, you want to make the current characteristic properties constantly available for reporting instead, you should select the main material group as a navigation attribute of "product," for example. In reporting, you can then navigate directly to the master data. If the attributes are also time-dependent, you can also retrace possible changes to the characteristic properties by using the query key date.

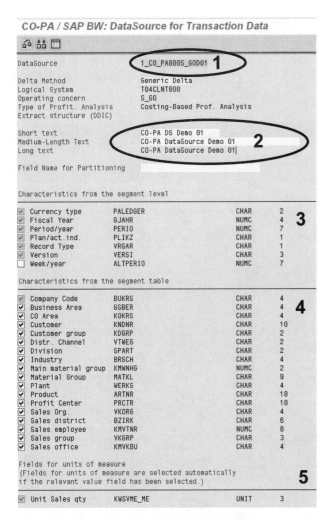

Figure 4.34 Description and Characteristics at the Object Level

▶ The attributes on the line-items level appear under the unit fields (see Figure 4.35, Step 1), as do the value fields (Step 2) and the calculated key figures from the key figure scheme (Step 3).

▶ In order for CO-PA reporting to be possible down to line-item level, you must select additional line-item fields in addition to the **REC_ WAERS – Record Currency** field, which is already selected by default. Here, the line-item fields contain those characteristics that were not selected for the operating concern in Transaction KEQ3, such as fields that are saved only in line items.

▶ You must also select the required fields for the key figures.

Characteristics from line items, value fields, and calculated key figures

- ▶ The only instance in which you don't need to select fields is in the case of calculated key figures, the reason being that the key figures calculated in CO-PA—in the different SAP R/3 systems, which this case study is based on—can be defined in various ways. Therefore, a standard definition of the calculated key figures is performed later in the SAP BW Query Designer.

- ▶ After the selection is made, you must adjust the InfoCatalog by clicking on the button in Step 4.

CO-PA / SAP BW: DataSource for Transaction Data

Characteristics from the line items

☑ Record Currency	REC_WAERS		CUKY	5
☑ Billing Date	FADAT		DATS	8
☑ Billing Type	FKART	**1**	CHAR	4
☑ Canceled doc.	STO_BELNR		CHAR	10
☑ Canceled item	STO_POSNR		CHAR	6
☑ Cost Element	KSTAR		CHAR	10
☑ Cost Object	KSTRG		CHAR	12
☑ Document number	BELNR		CHAR	10
☑ Goods issue	WADAT		DATS	8
☑ Item number	POSNR		CHAR	6
☑ Order	RKAUFNR		CHAR	12
☑ Partner Pr.Ctr	PPRCTR		CHAR	10
☑ Posting date	BUDAT		DATS	8
☑ Ref.doc.number	RBELN		CHAR	10
☑ Reference item	RPOSN		CHAR	6
☑ Sales Order	KAUFN		CHAR	10
☑ Sales ord. item	KDPOS		NUMC	6
☑ Sender BProc	PRZNR		CHAR	12
☑ Sender cost ctr	SKOST		CHAR	10
☑ WBS Element	PSPNR		NUMC	8

Value fields

☑ Administration Costs	KWGOHD		CURR	15 REC_WAERS
☑ Anticipd ship. costs	KWKLFK		CURR	15 REC_WAERS
☑ Bonuses	KWBONI	**2**	CURR	15 REC_WAERS
☑ Cash discount	KWSKTO		CURR	15 REC_WAERS
☑ Customer Discount	KWKDRB		CURR	15 REC_WAERS
☑ Direct mat. costs	KWMAEK		CURR	15 REC_WAERS
☑ Fixed prod. costs	KWFKFX		CURR	15 REC_WAERS
☑ Gross sales	KWBRUM		CURR	15 REC_WAERS
☑ Marketing division	KWMKDP		CURR	15 REC_WAERS
☑ Mat. overhead costs	KWMAGK		CURR	15 REC_WAERS
☑ Material discount	KWMARB		CURR	15 REC_WAERS
☑ Other overhead	KWSGEK		CURR	15 REC_WAERS
☑ Other variances	KWABSG		CURR	15 REC_WAERS
☑ Price variances	KWABPR		CURR	15 REC_WAERS
☑ Quantity discount	KWMGRB		CURR	15 REC_WAERS
☑ Quantity variances	KWABMG		CURR	15 REC_WAERS
☑ Research & Developmt	KWFOEN		CURR	15 REC_WAERS
☑ Sales commission	KWVKPV		CURR	15 REC_WAERS
☑ Sales costs	KWSOHD		CURR	15 REC_WAERS
☑ Sales quantity	KWSVME		QUAN	15 KWSVME_ME
☑ SalesSpecDirectCosts	KWVSEK		CURR	15 REC_WAERS
☑ Variable prod.costs	KWFKVA		CURR	15 REC_WAERS

Calculated Key Figures from the Key Figure Scheme

☐ Sales unit	COPASLQTU		UNIT	3
☐ Sales quantity	COPASLQTY		QUAN	15 COPASLQTU
☐ Revenue	COPAREVEN	**3**	CURR	15 REC_WAERS
☐ Cust. discnt	COPACDSCN		CURR	15 REC_WAERS
☐ Prod. Discount	COPAPDSCN		CURR	15 REC_WAERS
☐ Qty discount	COPAQDSCN		CURR	15 REC_WAERS

Figure 4.35 Characteristics from Line Items, Value Fields, and Key Figures

▶ After clicking on the **Adjust InfoCatalog** button, you must select the fields required for a later selection in the InfoPackages, as shown in Figure 4.36, Step 1.

▶ In the next step, save the settings (Step 2). Then, confirm the message stating that the DataSource was successfully created (Step 3).

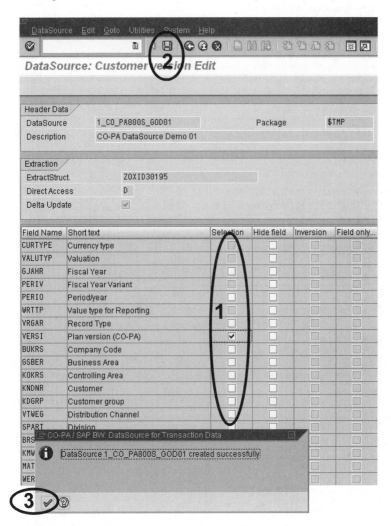

Figure 4.36 Selection Criteria and Adjusting the InfoCatalog

DataSource

Consequently, you will see the screen shown in Figure 4.37, where all the selected and unselected fields are displayed as read-only.

► The DataSource was generated when you saved your entries (see Figure 4.37, Step 1).

► If you consider the DataSource when post-processing the DataSources (Transaction code RSA6), you will notice that the DataSource was created in the SAP Application Components hierarchy under the **Profitability Analysis** node (Step 2).

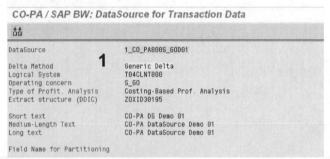

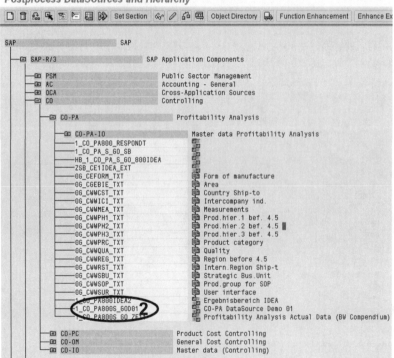

Figure 4.37 Generating DataSources

Your work on the SAP R/3 source system-side is now concluded, and you can replicate the DataSource in SAP BW via the Administrator Workbench

(Transaction code RSA1) in the **Source systems tab**. As you know from the previous step where the DataSource is located, we recommend that you only replicate the **Profitability Analysis** node of the SAP Application Components hierarchy by using the context menu (see Figure 4.38).

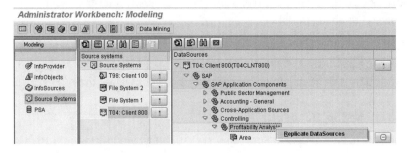

Figure 4.38 Replicating DataSources

If you want to enhance the CO-PA DataSource, using the standard functions of SAP BW alone is not sufficient. You must first delete the DataSource and then recreate it.

Enhancements to CO-PA DataSources

4.4 Further Application-Specific Extractors

4.4.1 Extracting SAP FI-GL Transaction Data

The G/L (general ledger) accounting from the Financial Accounting (FI) module represents the external accounting system of a company. This is where the daily business transactions of a company are entered, in the form of postings according to the relevant accounting and taxation regulations and laws. The characteristic properties of the general ledger include automatic posting of all items from the subledgers in the general ledger (referred to as *reconciliation accounts*) and evaluating and tracking documents, line items, and transaction figures at different levels.

General ledger accounting in the FI module

The base table for storing transaction figures from the general ledger accounting in the SAP R/3 system is Table GLT0. Transaction data can be extracted from Table GLT0 via application-specific SAP Business Content extractors.

Table GLT0

Depending on the Plug-in release used, there are various extraction options available, one of which is DataSource 0FI_GL_1. This DataSource is noteworthy for not being delta-capable. For a periodic or monthly extraction, this means that you must carry out a selective extraction. Therefore, you must select a specific period of a year via the InfoPackage and then load it into SAP BW. From an IT and business point of view, it

DataSource 0FI_GL_1

does not make sense to extract the entire table, because of the following reasons: First, the table would have greatly increased in size over time, which would further add to the extraction runtime; secondly, since periods are closed at a specific point in time (i.e., you are prohibited from posting during closed periods), you would always extract the exact same "frozen," unchanged data.

DataSource OFI_GL_6

DataSource OFI_GL_6 is another extraction option. It also extracts transaction figures from the general ledger, but unlike DataSource OFI_GL_1, this option is delta-capable and replaces the older DataSource OFI_GL_1.

Installing the DataSource

This transaction data DataSource must first be installed from the Business Content by using Transaction code RSA5, as shown in Figure 4.39.

▶ To do this, first select DataSource OFI_GL_1 (Step 1).

▶ Then click on the **Transfer DataSources** button (Step 2).

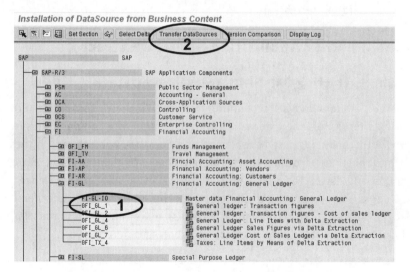

Figure 4.39 Installing the OFI_GL_1 Transaction Data DataSource

Post-processing the DataSource

The installed DataSource is now available for post-processing (see Figure 4.40).

▶ You can change the DataSource already selected (Step 1), in the usual way, by clicking on the pencil icon (Step 2): Select fields for selection, invert key figures, and so forth (Step 4).

▶ You will note in Step 3 that the DataSource is not delta-capable, that is, that there is no tick next to **Delta Update**, and that the extract structure of the DataSource is called DTFIGL_1.

▶ If you want to enhance this extract strucure with additional fields, you must click on the **Enhance Extraction Structure** button (Step 5).

If you consider the individual fields of the extract structure in more detail, you will notice that there are three key figures: **Total credit postings**, **Total debit postings** and **Accumulated balance**. A particular characteristic of extractor FBIW_DATA_TRANSFER_GL_1 is that it transfers all data records from Table GLT0, which has a column-oriented structure, to an account-oriented model adequate for SAP BW, and that it calculates the accumulated balance at the same time.

Cumulative key figures

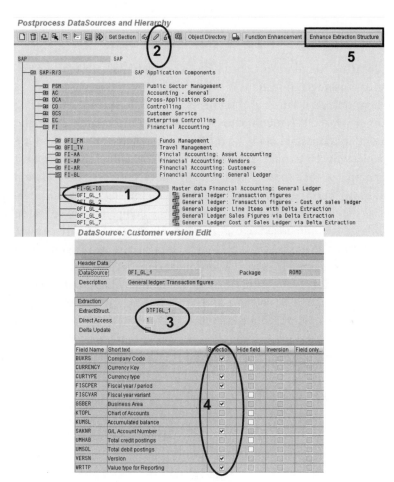

Figure 4.40 Post-Processing the DataSource

4.4.2 Extracting Master Data

Because you can extract the DataSources for master data delivered with the Business Content in the same way as was described in the previous section, we will avoid repeating the instructions here.

Delta-capability   With regard to master data, you must also differentiate between delta-capable DataSources and non-delta-capable DataSources. This varies from application to application and must be checked in each individual case. If a non-delta-capable extractor appears to be unnecessary, you can still use a generic extractor that fulfills the delta-capability.

An accumulation or calculation of the key figures by the extractor is a distinctive feature of certain DataSources for transaction data. For master data, however, this doesn't have much significance.

4.4.3 Extracting SAP EC-CS Transaction Data

Consolidation in the EC-CS module   Module EC-CS (Enterprise Controlling—Consolidation) is based on the individual business transactions of the external accounting and the corresponding individual financial statements of an independent accounting unit (in general, this is a company code), such as the balance sheet and the profit and loss statement. As soon as an individual entity within the company owns shares of at least another individual entity, and there exist cross-company code processes between these entities, consolidation functions will become necessary. Because a pure totaling of the individual financial statements gives a false picture of the company's consolidated accounts, the summarized gross-ups and eliminations are necessary, which clean up the aggregated balance sheets. In business jargon, these concepts are often referred to as a consolidation of investments, an elimination of IC payables and receivables, an elimination of IC profit and loss, and an elimination of IU revenue and expense. The entire area of intercompany consolidation is quite complex, as there are additional national and international business accounting principles that you need to consider and to which you must adhere.

Customizing the Extractors

As is the case for the transaction figures of the general ledger accounting, an installation of the DataSources is not possible for EC-CS transaction data.

▶ Instead, as described in Figure 4.41, you must navigate the BW-specific SPRO menu in the SAP R/3 source system Transaction code SBIW). Once there, you can define the customizing for the extractor by selecting the menu item **Enterprise Controlling**.

▶ You can now access the selection screen of the individual transaction data for EC-CS (see Figure 4.42). Here, you will encounter three Data-Sources: 3EC_CS_1 (outdated DataSource), 3EC_CS_1R (RemoteCube-capable DataSource) and 3EC_CS_1A, which replaces the old Data-Source 3EC_CS_1. Out of the three DataSources, we'll use DataSource 3EC_CS_1A.

**DataSource
3EC_CS_1A**

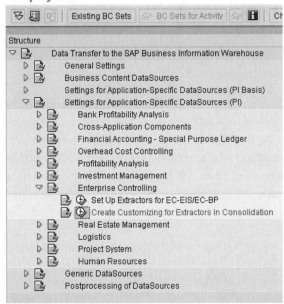

Figure 4.41 Customizing for Extractors in Consolidation

▶ You must therefore select this DataSource (Step 1) and then generate it (Step 2).

▶ If the DataSource generation was successful, you will also see the log entry displayed.

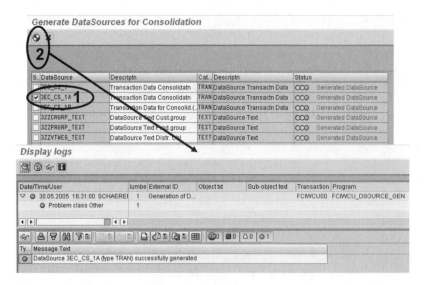

Figure 4.42 Generating DataSources for EC-CS

3EC_CS_1A
non-delta-capable

▶ If you now use Transaction code RSA6 to go to the maintenance mode of the DataSource (see Figure 4.43), you'll recognize the extract structure and the individual settings for the fields of the extract structure. You'll also notice that this DataSource 3EC_CS_1A is not delta-capable. As a solution here—similar to the transaction figures DataSource 0FI_GL_1—we recommend that you employ selective extraction (for example, via a period).

One of the basic requirements for extracting transaction data from the EC-CS is that the master data in the SAP R/3 system is properly maintained. Contrary to other DataSources, the extractor does not readily oversee missing properties of certain fields. If, for example, a consolidation unit is not assigned a fiscal year variant, the extractor cancels and generates an error message. Until you have solved this error in the source system, you will not be able to extract transaction data again. We also recommend that you load all master data before you start extracting the transaction data, in particular, any hierarchies for charts of accounts, consolidated entities, and consolidation units.

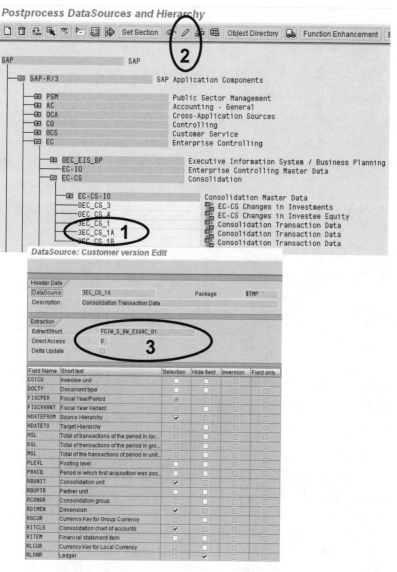

Figure 4.43 Post-Processing the EC-CS DataSource

Key figures are a special feature in extraction from EC-CS. As shown in Figure 4.44, there is a total of eight different key figures. In this context, the time variant of key figures is a distinctive feature. Four of the key figures represent the current value of a period, while the other four key figures represent a cumulative year-to-date value, which is the cumulative value up to and including the currently selected period. In addition, you

Cumulative and other key figures

can differentiate the key figures according to their functionality. There is a quantity key figure for transactions and three amount key figures in three different currencies:

▶ Currency from the document (transaction currency)

▶ Currency of the company or consolidation unit (local currency)

▶ Currency of the controlling area (controlling area currency)

This extractor also accumulates all values with certain characteristic properties from the R/3 Table ECMCA, so that period values originate from individual (daily) values.

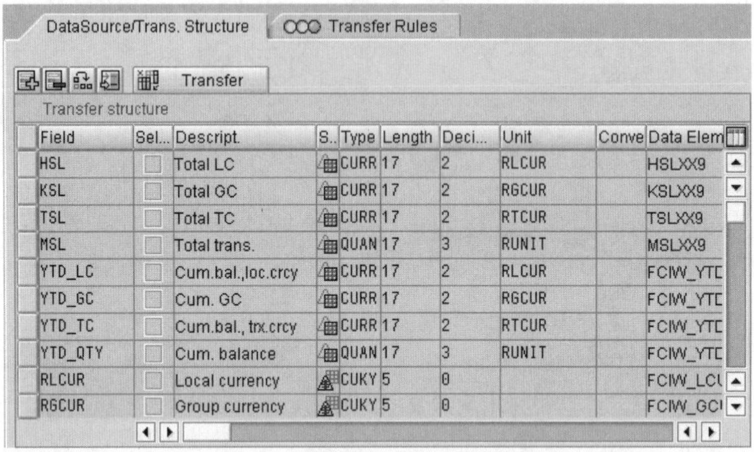

Field	Sel...	Descript.	S..	Type	Length	Deci...	Unit	Conve	Data Elem
HSL	☐	Total LC		CURR	17	2	RLCUR		HSLXX9
KSL	☐	Total GC		CURR	17	2	RGCUR		KSLXX9
TSL	☐	Total TC		CURR	17	2	RTCUR		TSLXX9
MSL	☐	Total trans.		QUAN	17	3	RUNIT		MSLXX9
YTD_LC	☐	Cum.bal.,loc.crcy		CURR	17	2	RLCUR		FCIW_YTD
YTD_GC	☐	Cum. GC		CURR	17	2	RGCUR		FCIW_YTD
YTD_TC	☐	Cum.bal., trx.crcy		CURR	17	2	RTCUR		FCIW_YTD
YTD_QTY	☐	Cum. balance		QUAN	17	3	RUNIT		FCIW_YTD
RLCUR	☐	Local currency		CUKY	5	0			FCIW_LCU
RGCUR	☐	Group currency		CUKY	5	0			FCIW_GCU

Figure 4.44 Replicated DataSource with Cumulative Key Figures

Further characteristics

There are some other points that distinguish this extractor from other extractors: Unlike other applications, data can be extracted from the EC-CS from period 0. This data is really the consolidated data, that is, the data after interunit (IU) and other eliminations. The balance sheet accounts are carried forward in period 0 as an opening balance. As is apparent, this is not the case for profit and loss accounts.

The amount of records transferred may be startling at first. If you select the month of May (period 5, if the fiscal year is identical to the calendar year), records for the following month are also transferred. The reason for this is that when reporting on the cumulative key figures occurs, the wrong value 0 does not appear; instead, the period value that was current during the last load process appears. If you want to carry out adjustment postings in a previous month such as April, for instance, you must extract the month again. This will change the cumulative value for April. If you allow May to remain unchanged now, in reporting, as expected, you'll get the old cumulative value, which is no longer valid. Therefore, all values for the months that follow the month to be extracted again (in this example April) must all be selectively deleted and extracted once again.

4.5 Application-Independent Extraction from SAP R/3

4.5.1 Requirements to the Extractor

In cases where extraction cannot occur through the Business Content DataSources because, for instance, dictionary tables that you have developed are to be extracted, or simply because no corresponding Data-Source is supplied with Business Content, you can define generic Data-Sources.

With regard to these generic extractors, you must distinguish between DataSources for transaction data, master data attributes, and texts. Data retrieval via a full update or a self-defined delta is also possible with the generic extractors.

In addition, the generic DataSources can be enhanced, if additional fields from other tables are to be read in, or corresponding derivations are to be performed in the source system.

4.5.2 Creating a Generic R/3 Extractor

To demonstrate the generic extractor, Table VBKA (see Figure 4.45), which contains contacts from the SD module, is to be extracted from the SAP R/3 system. In this case, a generic DataSource is necessary because no standard extractor is provided by SAP.

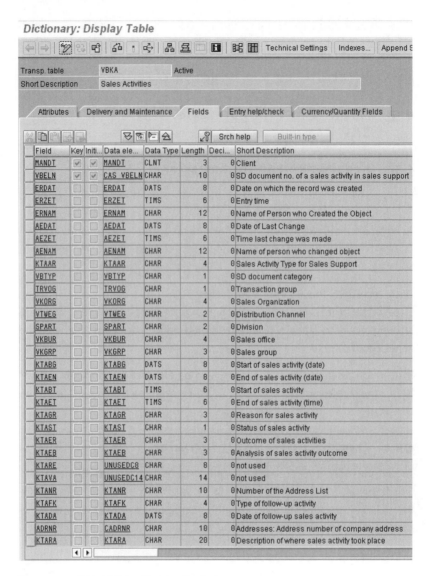

Figure 4.45 Table VBKA with Sales Contacts

Creating Generic DataSources

▶ The generic DataSource is maintained via Transaction code RS02 in the SAP R/3 source system, or, as shown in Figure 4.46, through the SBIW-specific menu.

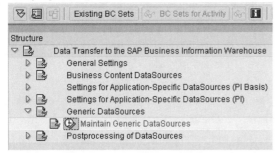

Figure 4.46 Starting Point for Generic DataSources

▶ Because the table data involves master data attributes, you must select **Master Data Attributes** as the DataSource type and assign a relevant technical name to this DataSource (see Figure 4.47).

DataSource type and technical name

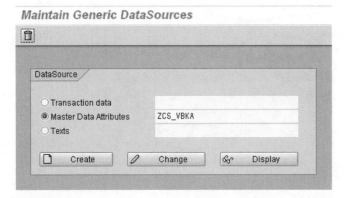

Figure 4.47 Technical Name for a Generic DataSource

▶ You are now in the maintenance screen for the generic DataSource. As you can see in Figure 4.48, the first step is to specify an application component, through which the DataSource is later to be created. In our example, the SD node for the sales module is selected (Step 1).

Basic settings for a generic DataSource

▶ For a data source, enter the technical name of the table, that is, VBKA (Step 2). For other scenarios, this could be the name of database views or function modules.

▶ Next, assign the descriptions for short, medium, and long texts (Step 3).

▶ To ensure that the DataSource is delta-capable, go to a modal dialog box by clicking on the **Generic Delta** button (Step 4), where you can set the delta-defining characteristic such as a date or a numeric pointer (for example, document number, counter). You can also use a security interval here to ensure that all the data records are extracted.

▶ In our example, it will suffice to set the calendar day with the change date AEDAT (Step 5). The current status of the delta attribute can be traced via the delta queue (Transaction code RSA7).

▶ Then, you must save the settings (Step 6).

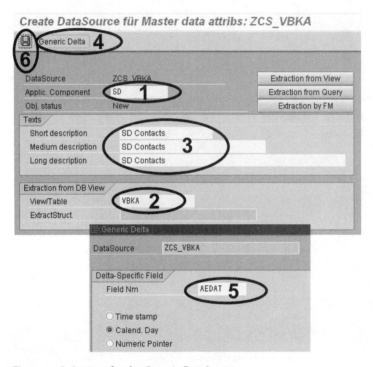

Figure 4.48 Settings for the Generic DataSource

Maintaining the Generic DataSource

You are now in the selection screen for maintaining the DataSource, which we have described many times already (see Figure 4.49).

Generating and replicating DataSources

▶ Here, you can again select fields for the selection method in the Info-Pakkages, hide fields, or invert key figures (Step 1).

▶ The contact number and the creation date are marked for the selection.

▶ When you save your entries again or when you use the **Generate DataSource** menu item (Steps 2 and 3), the DataSource is created in the selected node of the application components hierarchy, which you can trace by using Transaction code RSA6 (Step 4).

▶ You can now replicate the DataSource in the BW.

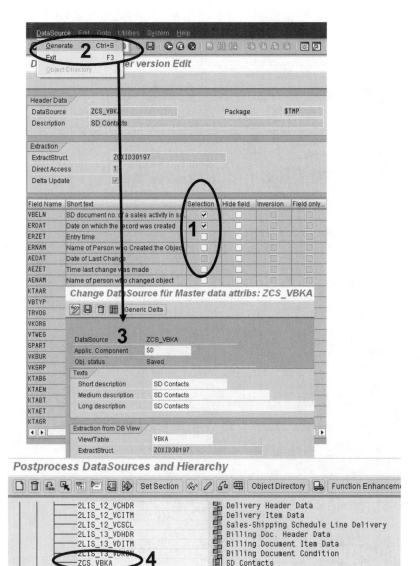

Figure 4.49 Maintaining and Generating a DataSource

Extractorchecker

You can also use the extractorchecker on the source system side for generic extractors.

▶ You can call the extractorchecker either through Transaction code RSA3 or directly via the generic DataSource menu (see Figure 4.50, Step 1).

▶ If you start the extraction and display the list of the extracted data records (Steps 2 and 3), you'll receive the correct result you had expected.

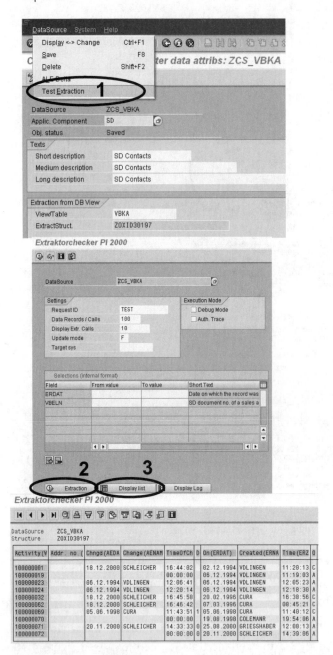

Figure 4.50 Extractorchecker for the Generic DataSource

4.6 Extraction from Interface Files

4.6.1 Requirements to the Data Source

In addition to the familiar DataSources and extractors for data retrieval from SAP source systems, SAP BW enables you to load data from other sources, such as files.

Data retrieval via the file interface is a flexible and simple way to load master data and transaction data from legacy systems into the SAP BW. You must, however, note that not all file formats can be used. For example, files with a hierarchical structure are not suitable for this purpose. This file interface supports only flat files in the CSV and ASCII formats.

CSV stands for *Comma Separated Values*. As the name suggests, data in this format is separated by a comma; however, this is not completely accurate. Other field separator characters are permissible, for example, in the first instance semicolons can be used and are even seen frequently. You must use the separator character correctly: If the separator character appears in the data and is not correctly identified, then the field structure is distorted, and data of different types is jumbled, resulting in inconsistent data because of an incorrect interpretation of the separator character. The individual data records are completed with a carriage return (CR).

CSV files

The following listing describes the sample structure of a CSV file:

Sample listing

```
K4;CH01;2500;2000;Tell;1740;CHF
K4;DE01;1000;3000;Maier;1050;EUR
K4;US01;2000;3400;Johnson;1690;USD
K4;DE01;1000;3200;Schulz;1650;EUR
```

ASCII stands for *American Standard Code for Information Interchange*. The distinctive feature of this file format is that fixed field lengths are used to differentiate the fields of the individual data records. The ASCII format is the more efficient than using the CSV format, but it can be more difficult to implement.

ASCII files

In the ASCII format, the example used for the CSV file would look as follows:

Sample listing

```
K4CH0125002000Tell       1740CHF
K4DE0110003000Maier       1050EUR
K4US0120003400Johnson     1690USD
K4DE0110003200Schulz      1650EUR
```

Fields that are not populated in a CSV file must be prepared in an ASCII format. Character fields, that is, fields of the character string type, are filled with blank characters, and numeric fields are filled with zero characters.

Conversion exits According to the conversion exit used, you must be aware of additional characteristics that exist in both file formats: For example, there may be an instance where leading zeros must either be entered or not entered, or an instance where the date format is different from the default format "YYYYMMDD."

Due to the flexible nature of the file interface, other functions are also available. The files may keep their column headings for the data, since the headings can be skipped over when loading. You can also customize decimal points and the thousand character (i.e., a comma or decimal point) as needed. The files can be loaded both directly from the application server and from any client workstation.

4.6.2 Field Definitions and Mapping for Interface Files

When compared with the extraction from SAP source systems, interface files lack DataSources and extractors in the source system. This is almost a given for files, because flat files are largely independent within their system and, due to their simple structure, they contain no additional BW objects. Therefore, in the context of data retrieval from interface files, the process focuses mainly on SAP BW.

In the transfer structure of the DataSource, you must first specify what structure the individual file has, that is, which fields from which type exist in which field length and between which fields and InfoObjects mapping occurs. Figure 4.51 shows a sample definition of a file DataSource.

You can also load transaction data, attributes, texts, and hierarchies here. When defining the fields and mapping transaction data, there is nothing specific that you have to bear in mind. You should merely ensure that the sequence of the field definition in the transfer structure is identical to the sequence in the file. For attributes, texts, and hierarchies, it may be necessary in certain circumstances to check the website *http://help.sap.com* for more information about extraction and interface files.

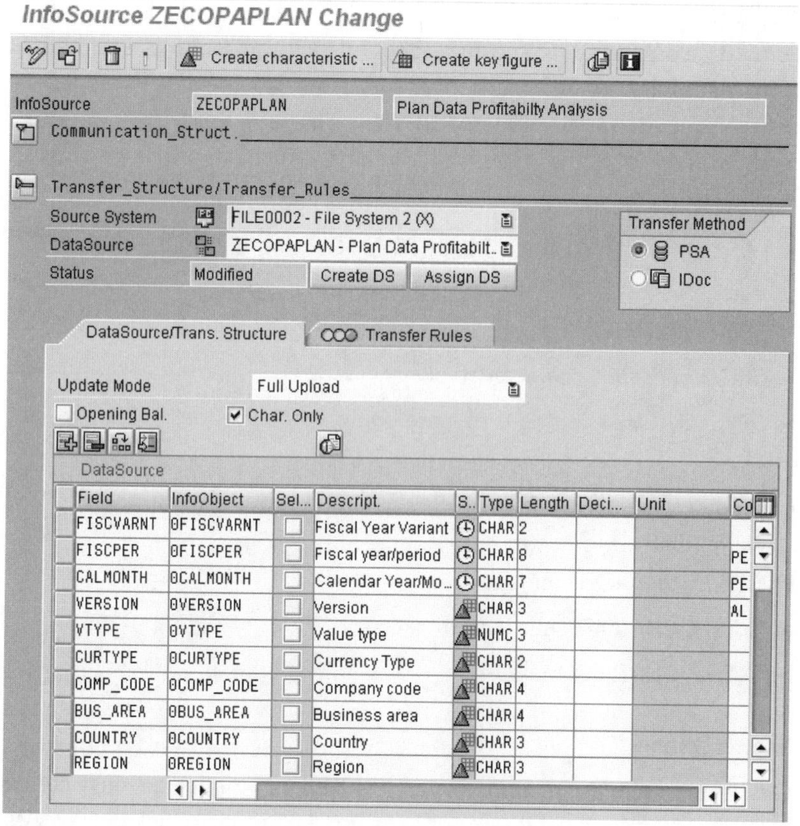

Figure 4.51 Definition of a DataSource for Interface Files

Attributes

When loading attributes, both compounding and the use of time-dependent master data can play an important role and indicate that additional fields are necessary.

▶ /BIC/<ZYYYYY>, key of the compounded characteristic (if a characteristic is available)

▶ /BIC/<ZYYYYY>, characteristic key

▶ DATETO, CHAR 8, valid-to date (only with time-dependent master data)

▶ DATEFROM, CHAR 8, valid-from date (only with time-dependent master data)

Texts

For texts, compounding and time-dependency can also make additional fields necessary. Furthermore, for texts, you can use language dependency for master data and to maintain different texts, that is, short, medium, and long texts. Therefore, a flat file for texts can have the following structure:

▶ LANGU, CHAR 1, Language key (D for German, E for English)

▶ /BIC/<ZYYYYY>, key of the compounded characteristic (if a characteristic is available)

▶ /BIC/<ZYYYYY>, characteristic key

▶ DATETO, CHAR 8, valid-to date (only with time-dependent master data)

▶ DATEFROM, CHAR 8, valid-from date (only with time-dependent master data)

▶ TXTSH, CHAR 20, short text

▶ TXTSH, CHAR 40, mid-length text

▶ TXTLG, CHAR 60, long text

Hierarchies

Classic examples for hierarchies are customer, product, or cost center hierarchies. There are two options for providing hierarchies in SAP BW: you can create hierarchies manually in SAP BW, or load hierarchies from external systems such as R/3 or interface files into the BW. This also enables you to maintain and enhance hierarchies after they have been created by loading subtree hierarchies.

In addition to the settings for attributes and texts described earlier, such as language dependency, validity period, and text length, other settings are also possible for hierarchies, for example, sorting within hierarchies and incorporating characteristics in the form of intervals under a hierarchy node.

The following list is a sample structure of the most complex hierarchy form. When defining this type of hierarchy, it is critical that you maintain a consistent sequence:

▶ NODEID, NUMC 8, node identification

▶ INFOOBJECT, CHAR 30, name of the InfoObject

▶ NODENAME, CHAR 32, node name

- LINK, CHAR 1, link character
- PARENTID, NUMC 8, higher-level node
- CHILDID, NUMC 8, first lower-level node (only for sorted hierarchy)
- NEXTID, NUMC 8, next lower-level node (only for sorted hierarchy)
- DATETO, CHAR 8, valid-to date (only for time-dependency)
- DATEFROM, CHAR 8, valid-from date (only for time dependency)
- LEAFTO, CHAR 32, interval to (only when using intervals)
- LEAFFROM, CHAR 32, interval from (only when using intervals)
- LANGU, CHAR 1, language key (only for language dependency)
- TXTSH, CHAR 20, description—short
- TXTMD, CHAR 40, description—medium
- TXTLG, CHAR 60, description—long

To provide a more vivid description of the structure of a flat file with hierarchy data, we will load the company structure of our model company *CubeServ Engines* for the InfoObject ZBUKRS in SAP BW. Figure 4.52 shows the structure of the company.

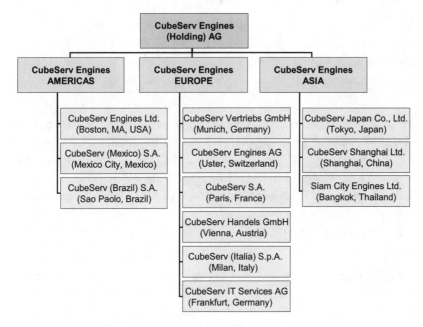

Figure 4.52 The Company Structure as a Hierarchy

For the sake of simplicity, the hierarchy should neither be sorted nor loaded with intervals. The time-dependency and language-dependency of the hierarchy is also not relevant here and therefore should not be included. This simplification results in the flat file structure shown in Figure 4.53.

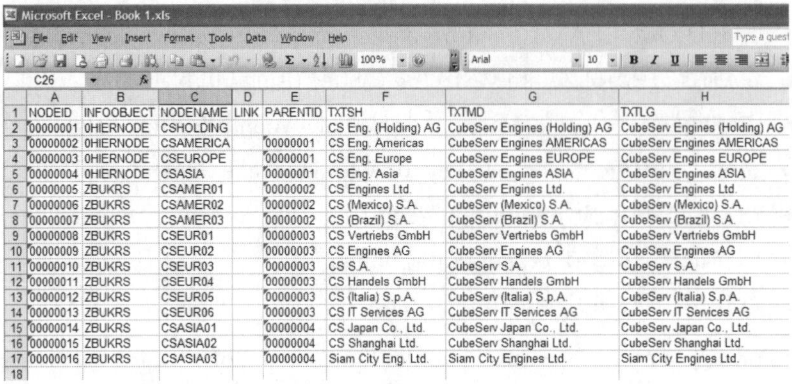

NODEID	INFOOBJECT	NODENAME	LINK	PARENTID	TXTSH	TXTMD	TXTLG
00000001	0HIERNODE	CSHOLDING			CS Eng. (Holding) AG	CubeServ Engines (Holding) AG	CubeServ Engines (Holding) AG
00000002	0HIERNODE	CSAMERICA		00000001	CS Eng. Americas	CubeServ Engines AMERICAS	CubeServ Engines AMERICAS
00000003	0HIERNODE	CSEUROPE		00000001	CS Eng. Europe	CubeServ Engines EUROPE	CubeServ Engines EUROPE
00000004	0HIERNODE	CSASIA		00000001	CS Eng. Asia	CubeServ Engines ASIA	CubeServ Engines ASIA
00000005	ZBUKRS	CSAMER01		00000002	CS Engines Ltd.	CubeServ Engines Ltd.	CubeServ Engines Ltd.
00000006	ZBUKRS	CSAMER02		00000002	CS (Mexico) S.A.	CubeServ (Mexico) S.A.	CubeServ (Mexico) S.A.
00000007	ZBUKRS	CSAMER03		00000002	CS (Brazil) S.A.	CubeServ (Brazil) S.A.	CubeServ (Brazil) S.A.
00000008	ZBUKRS	CSEUR01		00000003	CS Vertriebs GmbH	CubeServ Vertriebs GmbH	CubeServ Vertriebs GmbH
00000009	ZBUKRS	CSEUR02		00000003	CS Engines AG	CubeServ Engines AG	CubeServ Engines AG
00000010	ZBUKRS	CSEUR03		00000003	CS S.A.	CubeServ S.A.	CubeServ S.A.
00000011	ZBUKRS	CSEUR04		00000003	CS Handels GmbH	CubeServ Handels GmbH	CubeServ Handels GmbH
00000012	ZBUKRS	CSEUR05		00000003	CS (Italia) S.p.A.	CubeServ (Italia) S.p.A.	CubeServ (Italia) S.p.A.
00000013	ZBUKRS	CSEUR06		00000003	CS IT Services AG	CubeServ IT Services AG	CubeServ IT Services AG
00000014	ZBUKRS	CSASIA01		00000004	CS Japan Co., Ltd.	CubeServ Japan Co., Ltd.	CubeServ Japan Co., Ltd.
00000015	ZBUKRS	CSASIA02		00000004	CS Shanghai Ltd.	CubeServ Shanghai Ltd.	CubeServ Shanghai Ltd.
00000016	ZBUKRS	CSASIA03		00000004	Siam City Eng. Ltd.	Siam City Engines Ltd.	Siam City Engines Ltd.

Figure 4.53 A Flat File with Hierarchy Data

4.6.3 Delta Handling for Files

When creating a DataSource for interface files in SAP BW, you must set the delta-capability of the file in the transfer structure in addition to defining fields and mapping fields to the InfoObject. There are basically three options available for delta management that we will describe in the following sections.

Delta with status "new" only

For a delta with the sole status **New**, the file delivers only new records or the after image of a record. An after image is the result of a record that has been changed. If you choose this delta, the record must first be directed to an Operational Data Store (ODS) where it is newly created, or an existing record is overwritten with the corresponding key combination. Only then can the BasicCubes or another ODS be supplied with the additive data from this ODS.

Additive delta

When using the additive delta, either an additive image (the delta of a record change), or both images (a before and an after image), is delivered by the file. In this scenario, you can write the data directly into Basic-Cubes or ODS objects using the **Insert** setting.

Pseudo delta by deleting and inserting

During a pseudo delta, data is selectively deleted from a data target and then posted anew with its current status via a full upload. This process is not undertaken in order to delete the entire BasicCube or the entire ODS, but to remove only the data that can change. In practice, accounting periods are frequently used as an ID for changeable data because legal regulations prohibit back-dated postings.

4.7 Extracting XML Data

4.7.1 Technological Basics

XML (*Extensible Markup Language*) is an enhanced markup language, which was developed as part of a *Standard Generalized Markup Language* for use on the World Wide Web.

XML

Similar to the Web site description language HTML, XML also consists of markups/tags (<tag>), attributes (for example, <tag attr="value">), and data content. The most important and significant difference, however, is that in HTML, all tags and attributes are precisely defined, whereas in XML, the tags and attributes can be freely defined, which almost makes XML a metadescription language. With XML, you must ensure that the form is correct, that is, each opening tag must also own a closing tag; you must also ensure that the data is valid, that is, that you can use the data types of the data content. In recent years, XML has become a frequently used data exchange format that enjoys widespread acceptance in companies. One of the reasons for this high approval rating is that XML is very easy to learn and therefore, small XML files can be created very quickly.

Here's a simple XML example:

Sample listing

```
<?xml version="1.0"?>
<CubeServEnginesHoldingAG>
    <CubeServEnginesAMERICAS>
        <Company>CubeServ Engines Ltd.</Company>
        <Company>CubeServ (Mexico) S.A.</Company>
        <Company>CubeServ (Brazil) S.A.</Company>
    </CubeServEnginesAMERICAS>
    <CubeServEnginesEUROPE>
        <Company>CubeServ Vertriebs GmbH</Company>
        <Company>CubeServ Engines AG</Company>
        <Company>CubeServ S.A.</Company>
        <Company>CubeServ Handels GmbH</Company>
        <Company>CubeServ (Italia) S.p.A.</Company>
        <Company>CubeServ IT Services AG</Company>
    </CubeServEnginesEUROPE>
    <CubeServEnginesASIA>
```

```
      <Company>CubeServ Japan Co., Ltd.</Company>
      <Company>CubeServ Shanghai Ltd.</Company>
      <Company>Siam City Engines Ltd.</Company>
    </CubeServEnginesASIA>
</CubeServEnginesHoldingAG>
```

In order for the XML data to be transferred to SAP BW, there are two other important technologies that are noteworthy. On the one hand, there is Hyper Text Transfer Protocol (HTTP), the World Wide Web's standard protocol at the application level. On the other hand, there is Simple Object Access Protocol (SOAP) technology. Originally, SOAP was created to simplify information exchange as much as possible. However, because this process cannot be simplified to the degree that was initially intended and SOAP has relatively little to do with object access, SOAP has since been used as an independent concept. Furthermore, because SOAP is based on XML, it is language and platform-independent.

The structure of a SOAP message is somewhat more complex than the structure of a simple XML document. Basically, a SOAP document consists of the following three parts (see Figure 4.54):

▶ **SOAP Envelope**
The envelope contains the entire SOAP message. It is always the first element of a SOAP message and declares the document as a SOAP document. The envelope contains the details on the version of the message and identifies the rules used by the application to serialize data.

▶ **SOAP Header**
The header is optional and contains additional information such as details on authorizations or login information. The header is not used in the scope of SAP BW.

▶ **SOAP Body**
The body contains the actual data of the message.

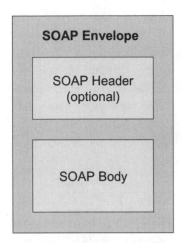

Figure 4.54 Structure of a SOAP message

```
<?xml version="1.0" ?>
<SOAP:Envelope xmlns:SOAP="http://schemas.xmlsoap.org/soa
p/envelope/">
<SOAP:Body>
<rfc:_-BIO_-QI6AZCUBESERVXML_RFC xmlns:rfc="urn:sap-
com:document:sap:rfc:functions">
<DATASOURCE>6AZCUBESERVXML</DATASOURCE>
<DATA>
    <item>
        <SALESORG>1000</SALESORG>
        <MATERIAL>3300-310</MATERIAL>
        <CUSTOMER>0000000110</CUSTOMER>
        <AMOUNT>150</AMOUNT>
        <CURRENCY>EUR</CURRENCY>
    </item>
    <item>
        <SALESORG>1000</SALESORG>
        <MATERIAL>BR-AS900</MATERIAL>
        <CUSTOMER>0000000482</CUSTOMER>
        <AMOUNT>145</AMOUNT>
        <CURRENCY>EUR</CURRENCY>
    </item>
</DATA>
</rfc:_-BIO_-QI6AZCUBESERVXML_RFC>
</SOAP:Body>
</SOAP:Envelope>
```

Sample listing

In addition to the missing header, there are some other specifics that characterize a SOAP message in SAP BW. The first line after the opening body tag contains an RFC-capable function module, which is required to load XML data into SAP BW. The next line contains DataSource 6AZCUBESERVXML for which the data is to be loaded. The actual data is contained in the <DATA> tag where each <ITEM> tag displays a new data record. For data retrieval of XML data for BW, only flat structures such as the one in the sample listing are allowed. More interleaved hierarchical markups cannot be used.

4.7.2 Extraction Concept

The basis for XML extraction is the SOAP service, which has been available since Release 6.10 of the SAP Web Application Server (SAP Web AS). Using this service, you can transfer XML data, which is compatible with the structure of the SOAP protocol, to SAP BW.

Push technique

Contrary to many other data warehouse applications, data extraction occurs from an external application. This application generates a SOAP file from the data to be extracted, which is transferred by a push technique via HTTP protocol to the SOAP RFC service (see Figure 4.55).

**RFC-capable
function module**

Calling this SAP Basis service can also be triggered by a URL. By specifying the RFC-capable function module and the DataSource in the SOAP message, this function module analyzes and parses the received data, converts it to the RFC tabular format, and stores it in the BW delta queue of the BW service API. From there, you can request the data via an InfoPackage and update it in the data targets.

This type of extraction is suitable for small as well as large data quantities. You should note, however, that for each individual data content the corresponding meta information must also be provided, which can inflate the entire size considerably. In some circumstances, this can cause a serious load on the network which is why you should consider splitting up the data quantity into several groups.

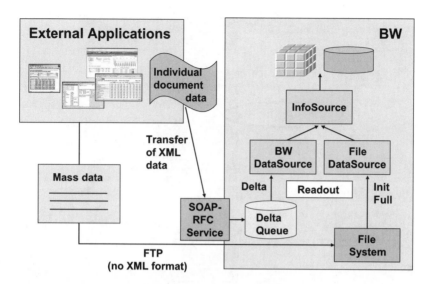

Figure 4.55 Schematic Flow of XML Extraction

4.7.3 Process for Extracting XML Data

Before data is sent to the SOAP RFC service, you should verify whether the service is active and to which port the data has been or will be transferred.

Controlling the Service

You can control the SOAP RFC service by using the *Internet Communication Manager (ICM)* monitor with Transaction code SCICM.

▶ After entering the transaction, select **Goto · Services** (see Figure 4.56, Step 1).

▶ Here you will find the port number (Step 2) and determine whether the service is active (Step 3).

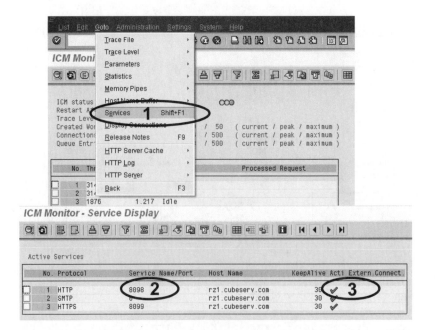

Figure 4.56 Controlling the SOAP RFC Service

Creating an InfoSource:

Before you create the XML DataSource, we recommend that you create an InfoSource.

▶ To create an InfoSource, open the Administrator Workbench (RSA1) and select the **InfoSources** tab.

▶ Select an InfoSource with flexible update (see Figure 4.57, Step 1). You must select this option, because data can only flow into the delta queue that can be flexibly updated.

▶ Insert the required InfoObjects into the communications structure (Step 2).

▶ Save the **InfoSource** structure (Step 3).

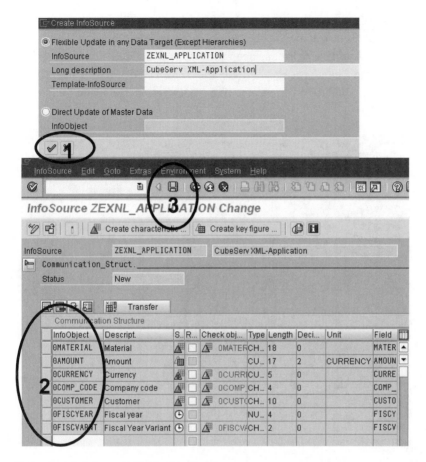

Figure 4.57 InfoSource with Flexible Update

Creating a File DataSource

Next, you will create a file DataSource. This process is somewhat awkward but necessary since you need this interface file to define the structure of the individual elements of the SOAP message

▶ Assign the file system as a source system to the InfoSource as shown in Figure 4.58, Step 1.

▶ When prompted to save the DataSource, click on **Yes**.

▶ SAP BW then suggests the transfer structure and transfer rules that you should adhere to (Step 2).

▶ Depending on whether the XML document will be created according to the SAP BW settings, or the extract structure should conform to the XML document, you may have to adjust the names in the extract structure. Contrary to the extraction from interface files, the sequence of the fields in the extract structure is not important here. If the update mode **Additive delta** has been set for the DataSource of the interface file, the delta process used for the XML DataSource is ABR (After, Before, Reverse); otherwise, the AIM(After Image-)delta process is used.

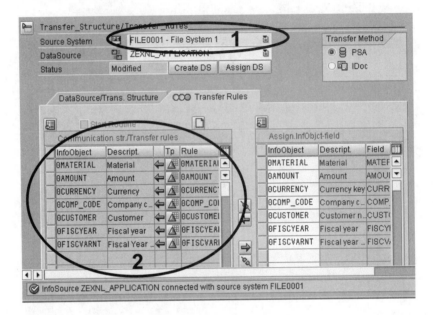

Figure 4.58 Creating a File DataSource

Creating an XML DataSource

The actual work on the XML DataSource begins in the next step.

▶ From the editing mode for InfoSources, open the **Extras** menu and select **Create BW DataSource with SOAP Connection** (see Figure 4.59, Step 1) or, alternatively, you can enter Transaction code GEN_DS.

▶ From the technical name of the DataSource the system now creates a new technial name for the XML DataSource, which is a combination of the prefix 6A as a dedicated namespace for XML DataSources, and the technical name of the file DataSource.

▶ Confirm the popup message that prompts you to save changes, and the following message as well in which the new DataSource is assigned to the MySelf system (Steps 2 and 3).

▶ Consequently, you will receive the XML DataSource (Step 4) which has the same structure as the interface DataSource. The transfer rules were copied as well.

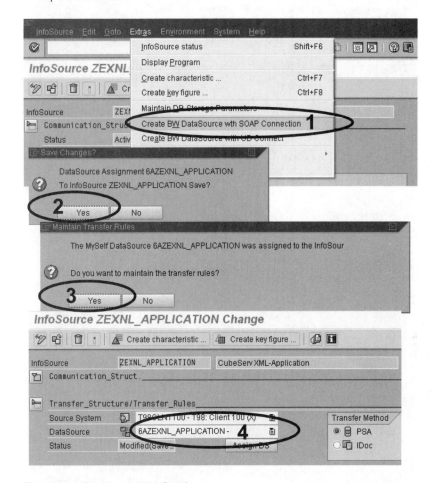

Figure 4.59 Creating an XML DataSource

While you see the XML DataSource on your screen, a function module is created in the background that will be used later to receive XML data that is sent to this DataSource. Its name contains the following elements: /BI0/QI<name of DataSource>_RFC. You can view this function module in BW by using Transaction code SE37, as shown in Figure 4.60.

RFC-capable function module

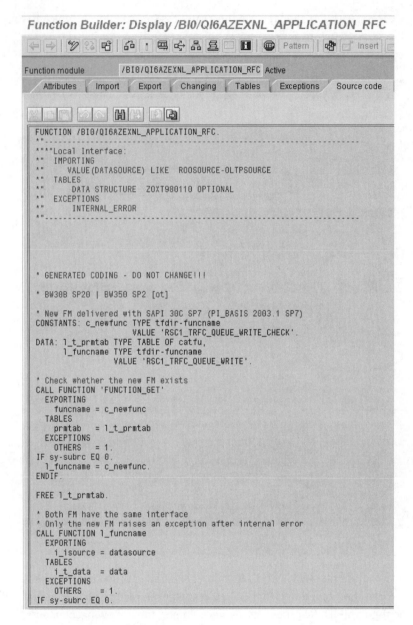

Figure 4.60 RFC-Capable Function Module

Initializing the Delta Procedure

▶ After the DataSources have been created and the update into the data targets has been established, an InfoPackage can be created in the myself system for the XML DataSource (see Figure 4.61, Step 1).

- To start this process, you use the **Initialize Delta Process** (without data transfer) option (Step 2).

- The delta queue is now initialized in SAP BW for the XML DataSource (Step 3) and data can be loaded.

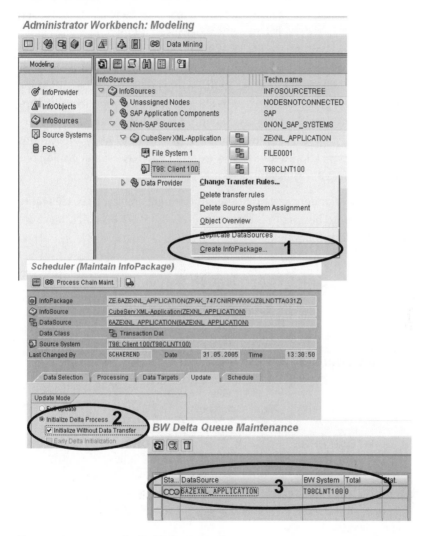

Figure 4.61 Preparing the BW Delta Queue

Because of the synchronous communication, the SOAP interface of the BW server can ensure a *guaranteed data delivery*. This means that the server returns a SOAP message to the client in either case (success or failure of the XML data transfer). The client then decides, whether a specific data package has to be resent.

Guaranteed delivery

4.8 Extraction via DB Connect

4.8.1 Architecture

Multi-connect When you start a BW application server, the SAP kernel opens a connection to the database on which the SAP system is running. This connection is referred to as a default connection because all Open SQL and native SQL statements automatically refer to this connection. If, however, in addition to the default connection, you want to create further connections to other (Database Management Systems (DBMS) of the same type or other types, you can do this with DB Connect by using the multi-connect function, a mySAP technology component. These database connections with DB Connect are independent of proprietary (Web) applications as a direct connection between the external database server to be connected and SAP BW is established.

DB Connect Architecture To get a better understanding of the DB Connect architecture, see Figure 4.62. In order to be able to use the functionality of DB Connect, there are some provisions that must be made.

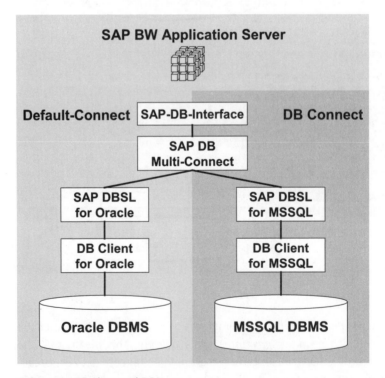

Figure 4.62 DB Client and DBSL

First you must install another database-specific DB client for the respec-   DB client
tive source DBMS on the SAP BW application server, provided that this
DBMS differs from the DBMS of the SAP system. This client can generally
be acquired via a software license from the database manufacturer.

You must install an SAP-specific Database Shared Library (DBSL) on the   DBSL
SAP BW application server. This DBSL can be purchased from SAP. The
database-dependent component of the SAP database interface is located
in its own library, which is dynamically linked to the SAP kernel. In addition to the DBSL mentioned, the library contains libraries for each respective database manufacturer, which are either statically or dynamically
linked to the database library.

Since SAP cannot provide a corresponding library for all database man-   Support of
agement systems available, the support is limited to the most important   selected
systems. These include Oracle, Microsoft SQL Server, Informix, and DB2.   databases

4.8.2 Schematic Data Flow

Before the required data can flow from the applications from the external
DBMS into SAP BW, some additional details about this data and the
metadata have to be exchanged.

With DB Connect, you can use the connection to the external system
supported by SAP as a source system for the SAP BW system, and you can
generate DataSources by using tables and database views from the database catalog of the database management system.

These DataSources are responsible for notifying SAP BW about the data
(see Figure 4.63). After the metadata has been transferred, the normal
staging process of SAP BW can begin.

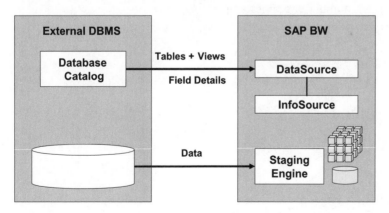

Figure 4.63 Schematic Data Exchange

4.8.3 Procedure for DB Connect

Source system creation
First, the database source system must be created in the Administrator Workbench (Transaction code RSA1). Here you set the connection data, which is required to identify the source database and for the authentication of this database.

DataSource generation
Next, you must generate the DataSource for the DB source system created by using Transaction code RSDBC. To do this, open the connection for the DB source system and then select the corresponding tables or database views whose metadata is to be transferred to SAP BW.

The DataSource consists of a maximum of 30 characters, four of which are reserved for the prefix 6DB_. The table or view names are added to the prefix. Therefore, you should keep in mind that the table names shouldn't contain more than 26 characters (capital letters, numbers, and underscores). For this reason, we recommend that you create views with corresponding shortened names and convert the original names with capital letters; otherwise, these tables and views will not be available for extraction.

The same holds true for the field names: The technical names are also created according to the ABAP dictionary and can only have a maximum of 16 characters (capital letters, numbers, and underscores). You must select the fields to be transferred before the DataSource is generated and stored under the application components hierarchy of the database source system (see Figure 4.64).

Loading data
In the next step, you can request data with an InfoPackage from the external database management system. A delta update for this type of data retrieval is only possible if you specify a selection criterion such as a document number or a timestamp.

Figure 4.64 Example of an Extraction with DB Connect

4.9   UDI—Universal Data Integration

Since concepts such as XML or Web services have become fashionable in the last few years, today Enterprise Application Integration (EAI) has become prominent. The goal here is to homogenize the various data

Enterprise application integration

sources of a heterogeneous system landscape and to enable data exchange.

Universal data integration

SAP BW 3.5 also takes the approach of combining data from heterogeneous sources into BW. In SAP NetWeaver, the keyword is *Universal Data Integration (UDI)*. Figure 4.65 gives you an overview of the architecture of UDI.

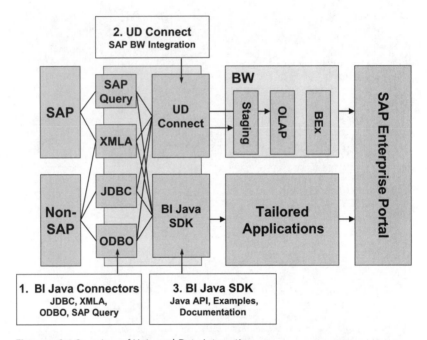

Figure 4.65 Overview of Universal Data Integration

BI Java connectors

The source systems are shown in the left area: SAP source systems and external source systems of other vendors. Access and extraction of this data is carried out via four connectors, which are provided by SAP BW 3.5: SAP Query, XML for analysis (XMLA), JDBC and ODBO. While BI JDBC Connector and BI SAP Query Connector are responsible for access to relational data sources, you can also access multidimensional data structures with BI ODBO Connector and BI XMLA Connector.

Based on industry standards such as JDBC or XML/A, the connectors transfer the data to two further components.

UD Connect

On the one hand, there is a component that was supplied with SAP BW 3.5: UD Connect enables the integration of data in the SAP BW staging process up to data provision in SAP Enterprise Portal.

On the other hand, the BI Java SDK enables the development of customized applications, sometimes with the intent of publishing the acquired
data in the SAP Enterprise Portal.

If you consider the entire architecture of the Universal Data Connector
more closely (see Figure 4.66), you will note that the Universal Data Connector and the four BI Java Connectors are all part of the J2EE Engine.

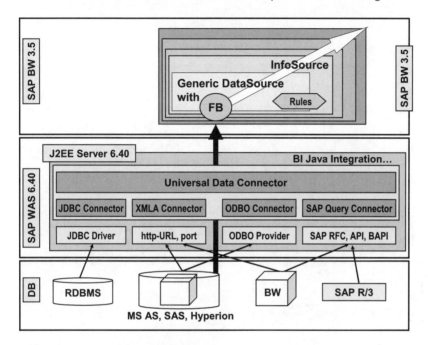

Figure 4.66 Universal Data Connector

The UDC layer consists of Java Beans for stateless session handling that
implement RFC capability. On the BW side, in turn, there is a wizard that
generates the function modules necessary for this new type of UDC Data-
Source. These ABAP modules transfer the relevant selection criteria to the
Java classes so that these Java connectors can access the data sources (see
Figure 4.67).

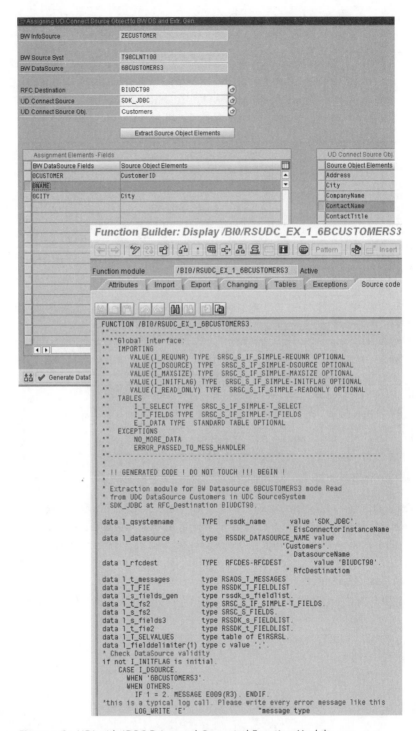

Figure 4.67 UDI with JDBC Driver and Generated Function Module

5   ETL Process: Master Data

Of what use are the most modern data warehousing systems, if they're based on master data for customers or material that is incomplete, outdated, or inconsistent? The quality of master data is critical to ensure the success of transactions and analytical processes in the company. Not only does the quality of master data substantially affect the efficiency of an organization; it also determines the quality of products and services.

5.1   General Overview

The essential objective of any normalization is to eliminate any redundancies and anomalies that occur when data is changed, for example, during insertions, or changes and deletions of data records. It is only by acquiring and storing master data that a relatively high degree of normalization—as is required for relational databases—is guaranteed in the SAP BW system. It is in this context that you must ensure that the acquired data is in a similarly normalized state when you store it.

Excursus

Normalization

The theory of normalization that was established by E. F. Codd[1] consists of nine rules. These rules are also referred to as the *first through ninth normal form*, the first three of them being the most important. In a step-by-step process, a database is converted into the status of the first through ninth normal form.

The first five normal forms, which are predominantly used, are defined as follows:

- **First normal form**
  In the first normal form, a relation exists if none of its attributes represents a subordinate relation and if all attributes contain only atomic values.

- **Second normal form**
  In the second normal form, a database must always be set at the status of the first normal form before it can be set into the second

---

1 See Codd, 1983.

normal form. In this context, all the attributes that are not part of the key must be functionally dependent on the key. If a key consists of several subkeys, the element that is dependent on only one subkey must be extracted.

▶ **Third normal form**
In addition to the specifications outlined for the second normal form, the rule for each key is that attributes that don't belong to the key are not transitively dependent on it. This means that all attributes depend only on the key attribute, and not on other attributes. A potential dependency between the attributes must be resolved.

▶ **Fourth normal form**
The fourth normal form deals with attribute groups that contain multiple dependencies to a superordinate key (*super key*). These multiple dependencies must be resolved into single dependencies (cf. the third normal form).

▶ **Fifth normal form**
If in the fourth normal form, you can create single dependencies without experiencing data loss, it may be necessary to resort to a second or third super key. You must repeat this step as often as needed so that only single dependencies of the attributes to one or more super keys remain.

Insufficient or incorrect master data acquisition

In addition, the effects of larger deficits in how consistent and up-to-date the master data is can be noticed very quickly:

▶ **Wrong decisions**
Caused by a lack of transparency and incomplete data basis

▶ **High administration costs**
Caused by multiple data entries, troubleshooting, and complaint processing

▶ **High IT costs**
Arise when data is distributed among many different types of systems

▶ **Long runtimes for business processes**
Occur because individual units are constantly awaiting data from others, or responsibilities have not been clearly defined

For these reasons, we will now describe the process of master data acquisition in a clear and detailed manner.

5.2 Master Data

In SAP BW, three different types of master data can be differentiated in InfoObjects.

1. **Texts**

   Texts

   Texts are used to describe a master record. In SAP Business Information Warehouse (SAP BW), up to three texts can be maintained for each master record. These texts can consist of the following: one short text, one medium text, and one long text. An example of a master data text is the name of the supplier that goes with the supplier number.

2. **Attributes**

   Attributes

   Master data attributes are fields that are used to provide a more detailed description of master data elements. These attributes are used to display additional information so results can be better understood. An attribute table can be used by several InfoCubes. This ensures a higher level of transparency for the user and a more comprehensive consistency. An example of a master data attribute is the country of the supplier that goes with the supplier number.

3. **Hierarchies**

   Hierarchies

   Hierarchies can be used in the analysis to describe alternative views of the data. A hierarchy consists of a quantity of nodes that have a parent-child relationship with one another. The structures can be defined in a version-specific as well as a time-dependent manner. An example of this is the cost center hierarchy.

You can find a detailed description of the types of master data and their usage options as well as numerous examples in Volume 1 of the SAP BW Library.[2]

5.3 The ETL Process

As we already described at the beginning of this book, the extraction, transformation, and loading (ETL) process is the process of regularly updating the SAP BW data. For this process, the data must first be extracted from the source systems, then checked for consistency—and if necessary adapted—and finally loaded into a data target (see Figure 5.1).

---

2 See Egger, Fiechter, Rohlf: *SAP BW Data Modeling*. SAP PRESS 2005.

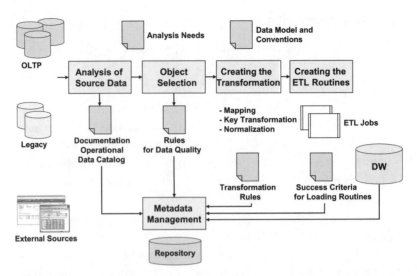

Figure 5.1 Schematic Diagram of the ETL Process

Phases of the ETL process

▶ **Extraction**
In this first step, you must select all the source data and then provide it for the transformation process that follows. In this phase, you generally see a high level of heterogeneity because all initial data is generated in different data processing systems.

▶ **Transformation**
Data transformation is the central task of the ETL process where the initial data must be adapted to the structure of the data target. Furthermore, the data quality should be analyzed and automatically increased.

▶ **Loading**
Once the data has been checked and made available, it is integrated into SAP BW. In this context, the work area where the data is located is called the *Persistent Staging Area (PSA)*. The process of loading data always includes a probable aggregation of the extracted and transformed data.

5.4 Data Targets

The process of transferring master data into the SAP Business Information Warehouse is referred to as *update into the data target*. This is a generic term for the physical objects that are relevant for modeling the data model and for loading the data. Data targets can be InfoObjects, Info-Cubes, or Operational Data Store (ODS) objects. You must distinguish between the following two data targets:

▶ **Pure data targets for which you cannot create or execute any queries**   InfoCubes may act as only a data source for another InfoCube. It is also possible that ODS objects and InfoObjects were not modeled for reporting purposes.

In margin: **Different data targets**

▶ **Data targets for which queries can be defined**
A characteristic can become a data target if it carries texts or attributes. You cannot load hierarchies by using update rules. In order to declare a characteristic as a data target, the InfoArea must be entered in the relevant field of the object properties.

Declaring Data Targets

By specifying an InfoArea, you can declare a characteristic as an InfoProvider (see Figure 5.2).

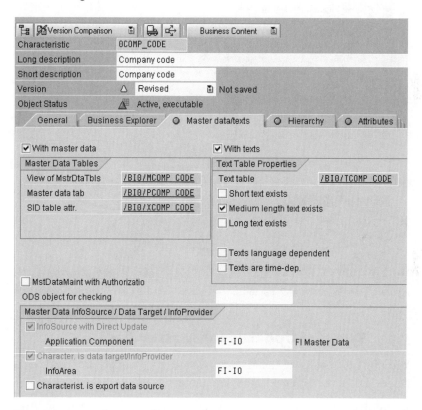

Figure 5.2 By Specifying an InfoArea, a Characteristic Is Declared as an InfoProvider.

Another option when declaring a data target is to call the Administrator Workbench via Transaction RSA10 and then to select the InfoArea to which you want to assign the InfoObject.

▶ Right-click on this InfoArea and select the **Insert Characteristic as Data Target** menu item (see Figure 5.3, Step 1).

▶ A popup prompts you to assign an InfoArea to an InfoObject (Step 2).

▶ After you have entered the object, confirm your entry so that the InfoObject is created as a data target and assigned to the InfoArea.

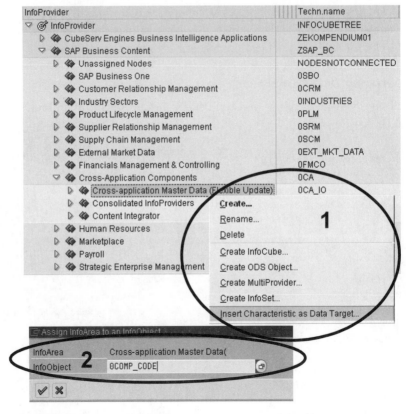

Figure 5.3 By Assigning a Characteristic to an InfoArea, the Characteristic Is Declared as an InfoProvider.

5.5 Types of Updates for Master Data

You must distinguish ETL processes with flexible update from ETL processes with direct update in the data target.

Flexible update   An InfoSource with flexible update means that you can update the data from its Communication Structure into any data target. Hierarchies, however, are exceptions to this type of update. For hierarchies, update rules are used. It is therefore possible to store data in master data and text tables as well as in ODS objects. In addition, by using an InfoSource, several data targets can be provided with data concurrently (see Figure 5.4).

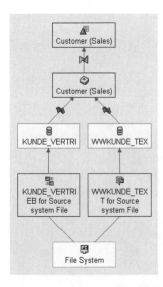

Figure 5.4 During a Flexible Update, the Extracted Data Is Written into the Data Target via a Separate InfoSource with Update Rules.

For data targets with direct update, only one data target can be populated by the data acquisition process (see Figure 5.5). This data target is always the data-carrying characteristic. Note that this type of update cannot provide ODS objects with master data.

Direct update

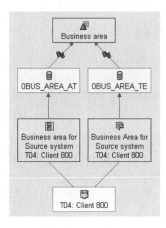

Figure 5.5 During a Direct Update, the Extracted Data Is Written Directly into the Data Target. The Characteristic Itself Represents the InfoSource.

Combined update You can also combine both update types (flexible and direct). For example, the attributes of an InfoProvider can be written flexibly into one or several data targets, whereas the texts for this characteristic are loaded by direct update (see Figure 5.6).

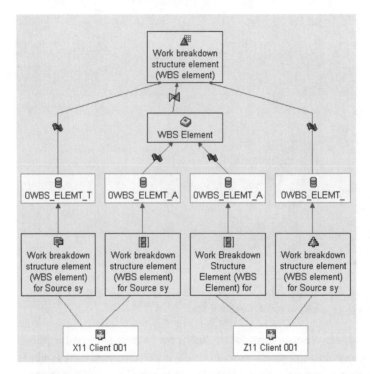

Figure 5.6 The Attributes of the "Work Breakdown Structure Element" Characteristic Are Updated Flexibly to the Data Target, Whereas Texts and Hierarchies Are Updated Directly into the Data Target.

5.6   ETL Process for Master Data

ETL Process up to the InfoSource In the following section, the ETL process will be described step-by-step. In this process, as shown in Figures 5.4 to 5.6, the levels of updating up to and including the Persistent Staging Area (PSA) are identical for both flexible and direct updates.

Therefore, we will now describe both of these types jointly up to that point. So that we can provide you with an overview of the process as well as position for you the exact level of updating that is being currently described, Figure 5.7 illustrates the ETL process.

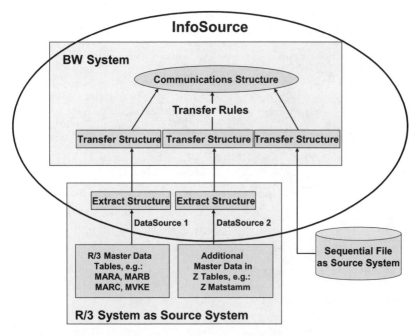

Figure 5.7 Overview of the ETL Process up to and Including the InfoArea

5.6.1 Extract Structure—DataSource/Transfer Structure

The transfer structure is the structure into which data from the SAP BW source system is transported. The structure represents a selection of the fields of an extract structure of the source system.

Definition

The transfer structure provides the SAP BW with all business process information available from the source system. An InfoSource in SAP BW requires at least one DataSource for data extraction. In an SAP source system, data for a DataSource that logically belongs together is provided in an extract structure.

Purpose

Source System: SAP System

In the SAP R/3 system, the extract structure is automatically generated from the DataSource. It describes the data structure of the relevant interface between the SAP R/3 and the SAP BW systems. An extract structure provides data from a DataSource of the source system. The content and the scope comprises the quantity of all fields that are provided by an extractor in the source system for the data loading process (see Figure 5.8). The extract structure is automatically generated in the data dictionary of the SAP R/3 system. Chapter 4, *Extractors: Overview of the Tech-*

SAP R/3 extract structures

niques, contains detailed descriptions and examples of the provision and enhancement of DataSources and the extract structures related to these.

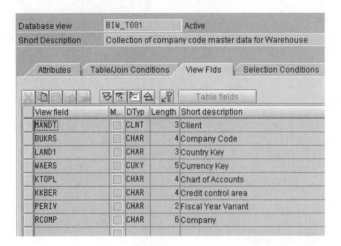

Figure 5.8 Extract Structure in the Form of a Database View

Replication of metadata Once the extract structure is available in the source system, the logical information of the data fields to be transferred such as quantity, type, and arrangement must be supplied to the SAP BW. This is done in SAP BW via a replication of the source system DataSources in SAP BW (see Figure 5.9).

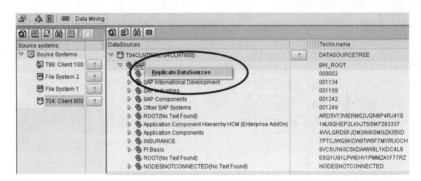

Figure 5.9 Replication of the Source System DataSources Transfers Metadata Information to the SAP BW

Assigning a DataSource to an InfoSource

If the information on a DataSource in the source system is available, this DataSource can be assigned to an InfoSource in SAP BW.

▶ To do this, call the Administrator Workbench using Transaction RSA12.

▶ Search for the InfoSource (that is, the InfoObject) to which you would like to assign the DataSource.

▶ Open the popup menu by right-clicking on the mouse and select **Assign DataSource** (see Figure 5.10, Step 1).

▶ Select your source system in the prompt that follows. For input help for this selection, press F4 (Step 2).

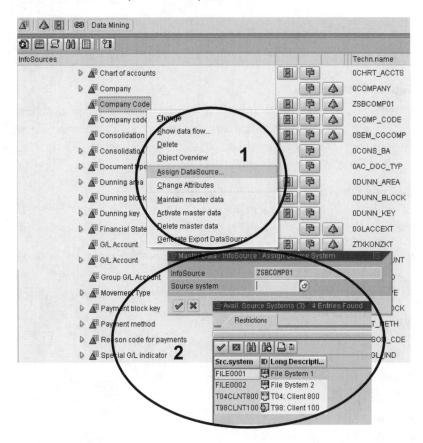

Figure 5.10 Assigning a Source System DataSource to an SAP BW InfoSource—Part 1

▶ Then, select the DataSources to be assigned (see Figure 5.11, Step 1) and confirm this selection (Step 2).

▶ The DataSources selected are then assigned to the SAP BW InfoSource.

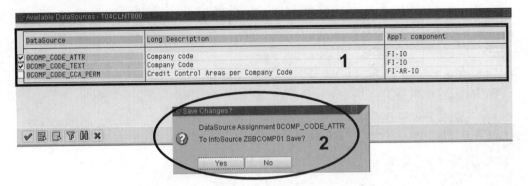

Figure 5.11 Assigning a Source System DataSource to an SAP BW InfoSource—Part 2

Source System File

When uploading flat files in SAP BW, you must manually define both the DataSource and the extract structure. In terms of logic, the structure of the sequential file corresponds to the DataSource since it describes all data fields available for extraction.

Defining the extract structure for CSV files

In order to define the extract structure for CSV files, you must carry out the following steps in the SAP BW system:

▶ Call **Administrator Workbench · Modeling · InfoSources** with Transaction code RSA12.

▶ Right-click on the required ETL process characteristic, and select **Assign DataSource** (see Figure 5.12, Step 1).

▶ Open the selection suggestions in the source system using the **F4** key (Step 2).

▶ Select the corresponding source system, in this case: PC_FILE – PC_FILE (Step 3).

▶ Confirm the assignment (Step 4).

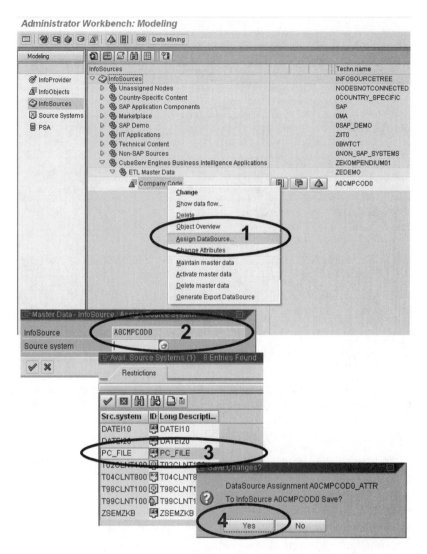

Figure 5.12 Assigning Sequential Files as a Source System

You are now in the **Transfer Structure/Transfer Rules** area of the characteristic, where by selecting the **DataSource/Transfer Structure** tab you can apply additional settings (see Figure 5.13). Here, you can define the structure of the DataSource according to the structure of the file.

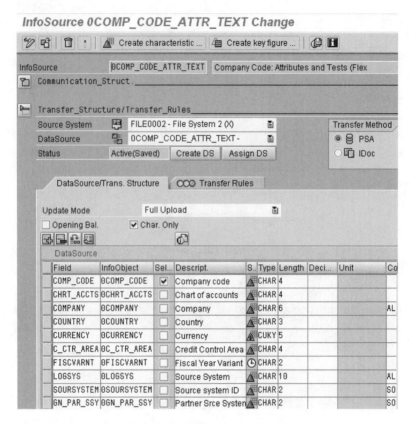

InfoSource 0COMP_CODE_ATTR_TEXT Change

| InfoSource | 0COMP_CODE_ATTR_TEXT | Company Code: Attributes and Tests (Flex |

🗂 Communication_Struct.

🚩 Transfer_Structure/Transfer_Rules

Source System	📇 FILE0002 - File System 2 (X)	Transfer Method
DataSource	📇 0COMP_CODE_ATTR_TEXT -	⦿ 🖴 PSA
Status	Active(Saved)	Create DS	Assign DS	○ 🖳 IDoc

| DataSource/Trans. Structure | ⚬⚬⚬ Transfer Rules |

Update Mode: Full Upload
☐ Opening Bal.   ☑ Char. Only

DataSource

Field	InfoObject	Sel...	Descript.	S..	Type	Length	Deci...	Unit	Co
COMP_CODE	0COMP_CODE	☑	Company code	🅰	CHAR	4			
CHRT_ACCTS	0CHRT_ACCTS	☐	Chart of accounts	🅰	CHAR	4			
COMPANY	0COMPANY	☐	Company	🅰	CHAR	6			AL
COUNTRY	0COUNTRY	☐	Country	🅰	CHAR	3			
CURRENCY	0CURRENCY	☐	Currency	🅰	CUKY	5			
C_CTR_AREA	0C_CTR_AREA	☐	Credit Control Area	🅰	CHAR	4			
FISCVARNT	0FISCVARNT	☐	Fiscal Year Variant	🕐	CHAR	2			
LOGSYS	0LOGSYS	☐	Source System	🅰	CHAR	10			AL
SOURSYSTEM	0SOURSYSTEM	☐	Source system ID	🅰	CHAR	2			SO
GN_PAR_SSY	0GN_PAR_SSY	☐	Partner Srce System	🅰	CHAR	2			SO

Figure 5.13 "DataSource/Transfer Structure" Tab

Administration options

The following individual administration options are available (see Figure 5.14).

▶ **Field** (Selection 1)
The name of a field within a table, a view, or a structure. You can freely define the field name at this point. The exact name appears later when assigning this field name in the transfer rules.

▶ **InfoObject** (Selection 2)
You can enter the InfoObject, which, by itself, corresponds to the source field and to which the data of the file field is to be transferred.

▶ **Selection** (Selection 3)
By selecting this field, you can specify that it is possible to select data directly from the source system for this field. Later, in the InfoPackage, a limited selection is possible for only those fields that have this specification.

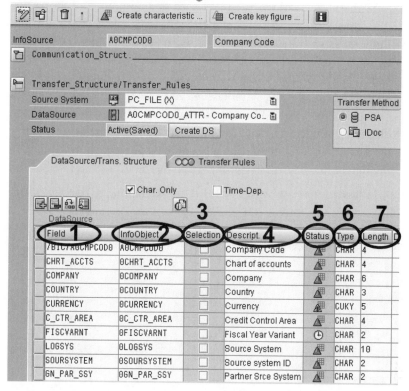

InfoSource A0CMPCOD0 Change

Field	InfoObject	Selection	Descript.	Status	Type	Length	D
/BIC/A0CMPCOD0	A0CMPCOD0	☐	Company Code	⚠	CHAR	4	
CHRT_ACCTS	0CHRT_ACCTS	☐	Chart of accounts	⚠	CHAR	4	
COMPANY	0COMPANY	☐	Company	⚠	CHAR	6	
COUNTRY	0COUNTRY	☐	Country	⚠	CHAR	3	
CURRENCY	0CURRENCY	☐	Currency	⚠	CUKY	5	
C_CTR_AREA	0C_CTR_AREA	☐	Credit Control Area	⚠	CHAR	4	
FISCVARNT	0FISCVARNT	☐	Fiscal Year Variant	🕐	CHAR	2	
LOGSYS	0LOGSYS	☐	Source System	⚠	CHAR	10	
SOURSYSTEM	0SOURSYSTEM	☐	Source system ID	⚠	CHAR	2	
GN_PAR_SSY	0GN_PAR_SSY	☐	Partner Srce System	⚠	CHAR	2	

Figure 5.14 Administration Options for the CSV DataSource

▶ **Description** (Selection 4)

You can specify that the field is freely described. The maximum number of characters is limited to 20. The name assigned here appears later during the assignment in the transfer rules and the name is identical.

▶ **Status** (Selection 5)

The status of the InfoObject (see selection 2) is displayed as an icon. It only displays if it is a characteristic, a time characteristic, a unit, or a key figure.

▶ **Type** (Selection 6)

The data type describes the data format in this interface. If this involves a field of a table or a structure or a data element that is used in an ABAP program, its format is automatically converted to the format required by the ABAP processor.

▶ **Length** (Selection 7)

Here the number of the valid positions of a field without formatting characters such as commas or periods is set. You should note that some data types have a fixed length. For example, the (client) data type CLNT always consists of three characters. If you enter a length for such a data type that is not permissable, it is automatically corrected by the system after the system issues you a warning. String data types (STRING, RAWSTRING) have an unrestricted length. However, in the dictionary you can specify a length (of at least 256 characters). This is used as a basis for optimization procedures when storing string fields in the database.

Other administration options By scrolling to the right, other fields in the **DataSource/Transfer Structure** tab become visible (see Figure 5.15):

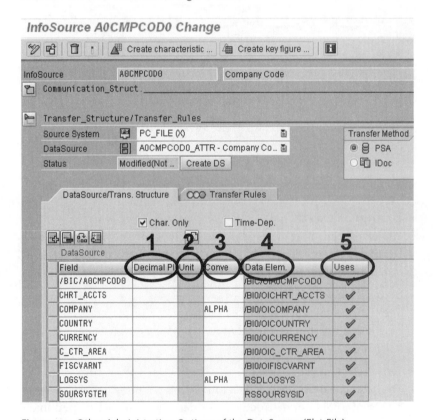

Figure 5.15 Other Administration Options of the DataSource (Flat File)

- **Decimal places** (see Figure 5.15, selection 1)
  Here you can set the number of permitted decimal places for a value. However, decimal places are useful only for the data types CURR, DEC, FLTP, and QUAN.

- **Unit** (selection 2)
  For key figures, the name of the relevant unit field is displayed here. A manual entry is not possible.

- **Conversion exit** (selection 3)
  Depending on the data type of the field, a conversion takes place when you transform the content of a dynpro field from the display format into the SAP-proprietary format (and vice versa), or when you output the content using the ABAP WRITE statement. If this standard conversion is inappropriate, you can specify a conversion routine in the underlying domain to be used instead. You identify a conversion routine with a name that consists of five characters and store it as a group of two function modules. The function modules have a precisely defined naming convention, for example, the conversion routine "xxxxx" is assigned to the following function modules:

  - **CONVERSION_EXIT_xxxxx_INPUT**
    The INPUT module converts from the display format into the proprietary format.

  - **CONVERSION_EXIT_xxxxx_INPUT**
    The OUTPUT module converts from the proprietary format into the display format.

  If a screen field references a domain with a conversion routine, the conversion routine is executed automatically for each entry on the screen or when displaying values on this screen field.

- **Data element** (selection 4)
  The underlying data element is displayed. A manual entry is not possible.

- **Uses** (Selection 5)
  Here you can see if an object is being used.

In addition to the administration options listed above, you can apply more settings for the DataSource on the **DataSource/Transfer Structure** tab (see Figure 5.16):

<aside>Further settings of the DataSource</aside>

▶ **Characters Only** (see Figure 5.16, Selection 1)

Here you can define that this structure only allows character fields. If this flag is checked, only characters (CHAR) or character-like data types (NUMC/UNIT/CUKY) can be set or permitted in the DataSource.

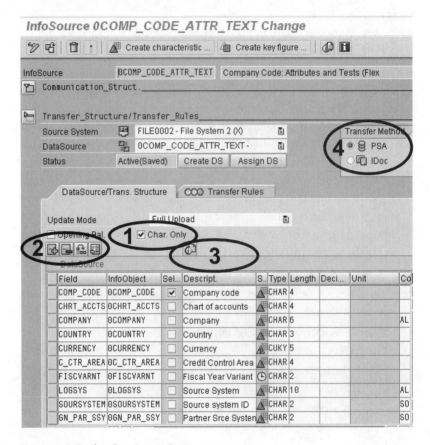

Figure 5.16 Further DataSource Settings

▶ **Buttons** (selection 2, from left to right)

- ▶ Insert new row

- ▶ Delete row

- ▶ Move to cursor position

- ▶ Position; other entry

▶ **Preview** (Selection 3)

By clicking on this button, you can display a preview of the data from the DataSource (see Figure 5.17 and Figure 5.18).

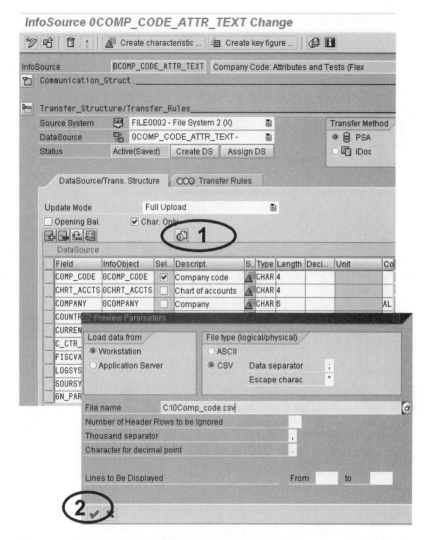

Figure 5.17 The File Is Selected for Display

Rec.no.	Company co	Chart of a	Company	Country	Currency	Credit Con	Fiscal Yea	Source Sys	Source sys
1	1000	1000	CUBE01	DE	EUR	1000	K4	SAPBW-350	1
2	2000	1000	CUBE02	CH	CHF	1000	K4	SAPBW-350	1
3	3000	1000	CUBE03	UK	EUR	1000	K4	SAPBW-350	1
4	4000	1000	CUBE04	FR	EUR	1000	K4	SAPBW-350	1

Figure 5.18 Preview of the Data from the DataSource

▶ Before you do this, however, it is imperative that you activate the
transfer structure (see Figure 5.19).

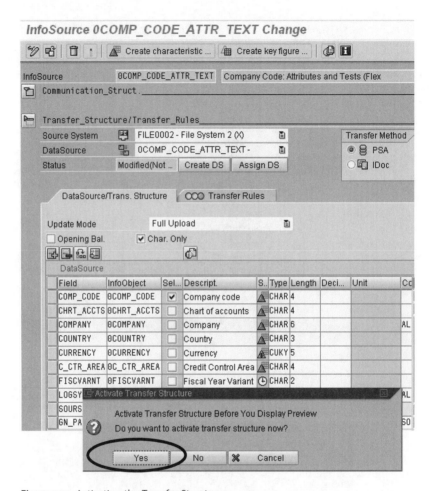

Figure 5.19 Activating the Transfer Structure

▶ **Transfer Method** (selection 4 in Figure 5.16)

▷ **PSA**

The data is directly sent from the source system to the SAP BW and where it is stored in the PSA (Persistent Staging Area). From there, you can manually or automatically update the data into the respective data targets. The transfer type for this process is Transactional Remote Function Call (TRFC).

▷ **IDoc**

The data is packed in IDocs by the source system and sent to SAP BW. In SAP BW, your data is saved persistently and intransparently in the IDoc storage. From there, the IDocs can be updated automatically or manually into the InfoCubes.

5.6.2 Communications Structure

Definition

The Communication Structure is the structure of the actual InfoSource. For master data acquisition, this means that the Communication Structure is identical to the structure of the InfoObject.

Consequently, the Communication Structure contains the InfoObject itself as well as its attributes and the objects required for compounding. The Communication Structure is always located in SAP BW, where, depending on its affiliation with the InfoSource, is always displayed with it (see Figure 5.20).

InfoSource 0COMP_CODE_ATTR_TEXT Change

Create characteristic ...   Create key figure ...

InfoSource	0COMP_CODE_ATTR_TEXT	Company Code: Attributes and Tests (Flex

Communication_Struct.

Status   Active

Transfer

Communication Structure

InfoObject	Descript.	S..	R...	Check object	Type	Length	Deci...	Unit	Field
0COMP_CODE	Company code			0COMP_C	CH...	4	0		COMP_
0CHRT_ACCTS	Chart of accounts			0CHRT_A	CH...	4	0		CHRT_
0COMPANY	Company			0COMPAN	CH...	6	0		COMPA
0COUNTRY	Country			0COUNTR	CH...	3	0		COUNT
0CURRENCY	Currency			0CURRENC	CU...	5	0		CURRE
0C_CTR_AREA	Credit Control Area			0C_CTR_	CH...	4	0		C_CTR
0FISCVARNT	Fiscal Year Variant			0FISCVAR	CH...	2	0		FISCV
0LOGSYS	Source System			0LOGSYS	CH...	10	0		LOGSY
0SOURSYSTEM	Source system ID			0SOURSY	CH...	2	0		SOURS
0GN_PAR_SSY	Partner Srce System			0GN_PAR	CH...	2	0		GN_PA
0TXTMD	Medium description				CH...	40	0		TXTMD

Figure 5.20 The Communication Structure Is Directly Linked with the InfoSource.

Purpose

From this structure, data is updated into the data targets. In this context, the system always accesses the actively saved version of the Communication Structure.

Maintaining the Communication Structure (Only with Flexible Updating)

By clicking on the **Transfer** button, you can open the transfer view.

▶ This enables you to adjust the Communication Structure to meet individual business requirements (see Figure 5.21).

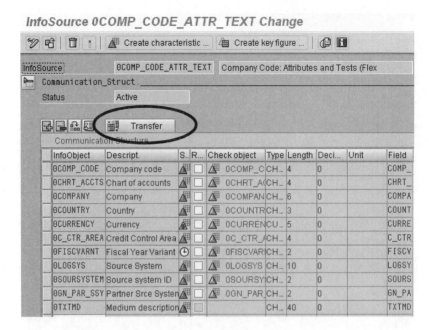

InfoSource 0COMP_CODE_ATTR_TEXT Change

InfoObject	Descript.	S..	R...	Check object	Type	Length	Deci...	Unit	Field
0COMP_CODE	Company code		☐	0COMP_C	CH..	4	0		COMP_
0CHRT_ACCTS	Chart of accounts		☐	0CHRT_A	CH..	4	0		CHRT_
0COMPANY	Company		☐	0COMPAN	CH..	6	0		COMPA
0COUNTRY	Country		☐	0COUNTR	CH..	3	0		COUNT
0CURRENCY	Currency		☐	0CURREN	CU..	5	0		CURRE
0C_CTR_AREA	Credit Control Area		☐	0C_CTR_A	CH..	4	0		C_CTR
0FISCVARNT	Fiscal Year Variant	⏲	☐	0FISCVAR	CH..	2	0		FISCV
0LOGSYS	Source System		☐	0LOGSYS	CH..	10	0		LOGSY
0SOURSYSTEM	Source system ID		☐	0SOURSY	CH..	2	0		SOURS
0GN_PAR_SSY	Partner Srce System		☐	0GN_PAR	CH..	2	0		GN_PA
0TXTMD	Medium description		☐		CH..	40	0		TXTMD

Figure 5.21 Clicking on the Transfer Button to Open the Transfer View

F4 help in selecting objects

▶ For maintenance of the Communication Structure, you can use templates on the right-hand side of the maintenance menu to limit the selection of the required InfoObjects. This leads to more clarity (see Figure 5.22).

▶ Once a suitable template has been selected, all the InfoObjects contained in this template are displayed on the right-hand side of the Communication Structure administration. Selecting a template is optional. If you don't select a template, all the InfoObjects currently available appear in SAP BW.

InfoSource 0COMP_CODE_ATTR_TEXT Change

InfoObject	Descript.	St	R...	Chec
0COMP_CODE	Company c...			
0CHRT_ACCTS	Chart of acc...			
0COMPANY	Company			
0COUNTRY	Country			
0CURRENCY	Currency			
0C_CTR_AREA	Credit Contr...			
0FISCVARNT	Fiscal Year ...			
0LOGSYS	Source Syst...			
0SOURSYSTEM	Source syst...			
0GN_PAR_SSY	Partner Src ...			
0TXTMD	Medium de...			

InfoObject	Field	S..	Type	Lengt
0CHRT_ACC..	CHRT_ACC..		CH..	4
0COMPANY	COMPANY		CH..	6
0COMP_CO..	COMP_CO..		CH..	4
0COUNTRY	COUNTRY		CH..	3
0CURRENCY	CURRENCY		CU..	5
0C_CTR_AR..	C_CTR_AR..		CH..	4
0FISCVARNT	FISCVARNT		CH..	2
0GN_PAR_S..	GN_PAR_S..		CH..	2
0LOGSYS	LOGSYS		CH..	10
0SOURSYST..	SOURSYST..		CH..	2
0TXTMD	TXTMD		CH..	40

InfoSource Template: InfoSources (3) 294 Entries Found

InfoSource	Long Description
0APO_LOCNO_ATTR	APO Location Attributes
0APO_LOCNO_TEXT	APO Location Text
0APO_PPDS_CDS_1	APO->BW: Due Delivery Schedules/Confirmations for Sales SAs
0APO_PROD_ATTR	APO Product Attributes
0APO_PROD_TEXT	APO Product Text
0APPR_REQU_ATTR	Appropriation Request - Master Data
0APPR_REQU_TEXT	Appropriation Request - Texts
0ASSET_ATTR_TEXT	Asset Subnumber (Flexible Update)
0BBP_BIDDER_ATTR	BP: EBP Bidder Data
0BBP_BPCOMPANY_ATTR	BP: Partner is (Purchasing) Company
0BBP_PARTNER_FLAG_CONTACT	BP: Partner Role "Contact Person"
0BBP_PARTNER_FLAG_LOCATION	BP: Partner Role "Location/Plant"
0BBP_PARTNER_FLAG_VENDOR	BP: Partner Role "Vendor"
0BBP_PLANT_ATTR	Business Partner Number Assgmt to R/3 Plant
0BBP_PRODUCT_ATTR	Product (BBP Attributes)
0BBP_PROD_ATTR	Product (EBP Attributes), only for EBP Release 3.5 or Lower
0BBP_PROD_TEXT	Product (Texts), only for EBP Release 3.5 or Lower
0BPARTNER_ATTR	BP: Master Record
0BPARTNER_TEXT	BP: Texts

294 Entries Found

Figure 5.22 The InfoObject Selection Can Be Limited by Selecting a Template in the Transfer View.

▶ To assign the existing Communication Structure to other objects, you must select these objects in the right pane of the administration screen and assign the structure using the arrow button in the template (see Figure 5.23).

Transfer using arrow keys

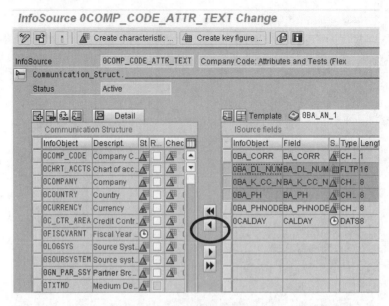

Figure 5.23 Individual Objects Are Transferred into the Communication Structure

▶ If you click on the double-arrow button, all the InfoObjects in the template are transferred (see Figure 5.24).

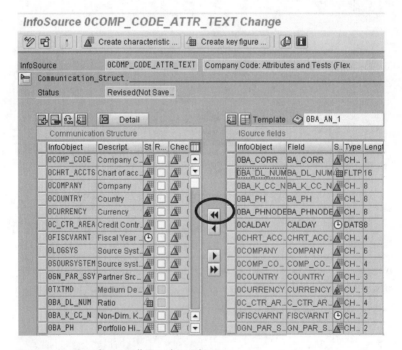

Figure 5.24 Transferring All Template Objects

▶ These functions are identical when removing InfoObjects from the Communication Structure (see Figures 5.23 and 5.24).

Limiting an exisiting Communication Structure is possible only if there is no master data in the data target. If master data has already been loaded, it must be deleted before limiting the Communication Structure. Because the deletion of master data can lead to considerable difficulties, for example, when used in InfoCubes, you must ensure that loading master and transaction data occurs only after the data model and the related structures have been approved by those responsible for the architecture.

Communication Structure with Direct Update

When master data is directly updated, no separate InfoSource is available. The separate InfoSource is based on the InfoObject structure, therefore, the resulting Communication Structure is impossible if not freely definable. For this reason, an individual maintenance is not possible. A **Transfer** button as in the case of the flexible update is not provided (see Figure 5.25).

Direct update

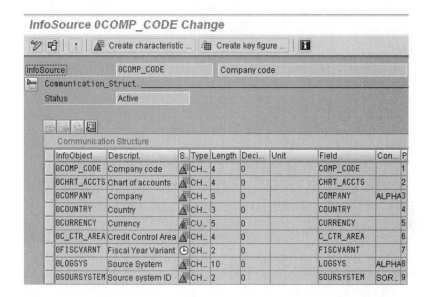

InfoSource 0COMP_CODE Change

Create characteristic ... | Create key figure ...

InfoSource: 0COMP_CODE — Company code
Communication_Struct.
Status: Active

Communication Structure

InfoObject	Descript.	S.	Type	Length	Deci...	Unit	Field	Con...	P
0COMP_CODE	Company code		CH...	4	0		COMP_CODE		1
0CHRT_ACCTS	Chart of accounts		CH...	4	0		CHRT_ACCTS		2
0COMPANY	Company		CH...	6	0		COMPANY	ALPHA	3
0COUNTRY	Country		CH...	3	0		COUNTRY		4
0CURRENCY	Currency		CU...	5	0		CURRENCY		5
0C_CTR_AREA	Credit Control Area		CH...	4	0		C_CTR_AREA		6
0FISCVARNT	Fiscal Year Variant		CH...	2	0		FISCVARNT		7
0LOGSYS	Source System		CH...	10	0		LOGSYS	ALPHA	8
0SOURSYSTEM	Source system ID		CH...	2	0		SOURSYSTEM	SOR...	9

Figure 5.25 The Communication Structure of an InfoObject with Direct Update

Referential Integrity (Flexible Update)

Also, referential integrity is only available with flexible updating of master data into a data target. In this case, you are allowed to define this check for specific or even for all characteristics by performing a selection in the Communication Structure (see Figure 5.26).

If the **Referential Integrity** flag is checked, this InfoObject is checked for referential integrity against the master data table or an ODS object. This function corresponds to a master data validation. During this process the value of every data record transferred in this field of the Communication Structure is checked for its validity. If a transferred value is not in the object being checked (master data or ODS), the data warehouse system analyzes an error situation and cancels the loading process.

InfoSource 0COMP_CODE_ATTR_TEXT Change

| | 🖅 | ↑ | | 🖋 Create characteristic … | 📇 Create key figure … | | 📋 🄷 |

InfoSource		0COMP_CODE_ATTR_TEXT	Company Code: Attributes and Tests (Flex
🗁 Communication_Struct.			
Status		Revised(Not Save…	

| 🔁 | ⬛ | 🔁 | 🔁 | 📇 Transfer |

Communication Structure

InfoObject	Descript.	S.	Referential Integrity	Check obj…	Type	Length	Deci…	Unit
0COMP_CODE	Company code	🔺	☐	🔺 0COMP	CH…	4	0	
0CHRT_ACCTS	Chart of accounts	🔺	☑	🔺 0CHRT	CH…	4	0	
0COMPANY	Company	🔺	☑	🔺 0COMP	CH…	6	0	
0COUNTRY	Country	🔺	☑	🔺 0COUN	CH…	3	0	
0CURRENCY	Currency	🔺	☐	🔺 0CURR	CU…	5	0	
0C_CTR_AREA	Credit Control Area	🔺	☐	🔺 0C_CTR	CH…	4	0	
0FISCVARNT	Fiscal Year Variant	🕐	☐	🔺 0FISCV	CH…	2	0	
0LOGSYS	Source System	🔺	☐	🔺 0LOGSY	CH…	10	0	
0SOURSYSTEM	Source system ID	🔺	☐	🔺 0SOUR	CH…	2	0	
0GN_PAR_SSY	Partner Srce System	🔺	☐	🔺 0GN_P	CH…	2	0	
0TXTMD	Medium description	🔺	☐		CH…	40	0	

Figure 5.26 Selecting the Required Objects in the Communication Structure

The setting as to which object (master data table or ODS object) should be checked against is done in the InfoObject itself. If an ODS object is stored to check the characteristic values of a characteristic, for the update and transfer rules, the valid values of the characteristic will not be provided by the master data of the characteristic but from the ODS object (see Figure 5.27).

A prerequisite for this ODS object is that it contains the characteristic itself and all fields from the compounding as key fields.

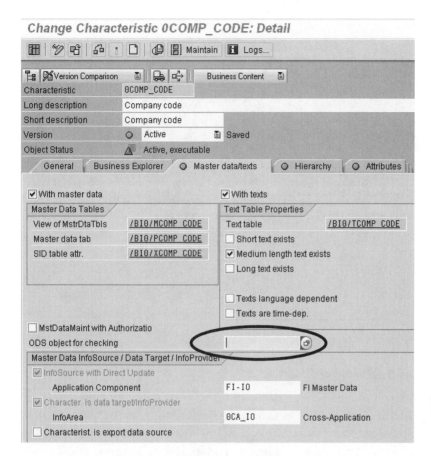

Change Characteristic 0COMP_CODE: Detail

| | | | | | | | Maintain | | Logs... |

	Version Comparison					Business Content	
Characteristic	0COMP_CODE
Long description	Company code
Short description	Company code
Version	○ Active		Saved
Object Status	⚠ Active, executable

General | Business Explorer | ○ Master data/texts | ○ Hierarchy | ○ Attributes

☑ With master data   ☑ With texts

Master Data Tables		Text Table Properties	
View of MstrDtaTbls	/BI0/MCOMP_CODE	Text table	/BI0/TCOMP_CODE
Master data tab	/BI0/PCOMP_CODE	☐ Short text exists	
SID table attr.	/BI0/XCOMP_CODE	☑ Medium length text exists	
		☐ Long text exists	

☐ Texts language dependent
☐ Texts are time-dep.

☐ MstDataMaint with Authorizatio

ODS object for checking   [   ] 🔘

Master Data InfoSource / Data Target / InfoProvider

☑ InfoSource with Direct Update
    Application Component   FI-IO   FI Master Data
☑ Character. is data target/InfoProvider
    InfoArea   0CA_IO   Cross-Application
☐ Characterist. is export data source

Figure 5.27 You Can Define on which Object the Referential Integrity Check Is to Be Performed on the InfoObject Itself.

Activating the Communication Structure

After all the required settings for communication during the transfer of master data have been maintained, you must activate the Communication Structure. After the successful maintenance, the structure is activated by clicking on the **Activate** button or by pressing the key combination **Alt + F3**. Only once this has been activated can the structure be used for the data transfer (see Figure 5.28).

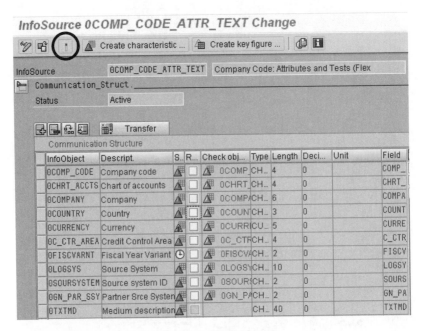

InfoObject	Descript.	S..	R...	Check obj...	Type	Length	Deci...	Unit	Field
0COMP_CODE	Company code			0COMP	CH..	4	0		COMP_
0CHRT_ACCTS	Chart of accounts			0CHRT	CH..	4	0		CHRT_
0COMPANY	Company			0COMP/	CH..	6	0		COMPA
0COUNTRY	Country			0COUN'	CH..	3	0		COUNT
0CURRENCY	Currency			0CURR	CU..	5	0		CURRE
0C_CTR_AREA	Credit Control Area			0C_CTR	CH..	4	0		C_CTR
0FISCVARNT	Fiscal Year Variant			0FISCV/	CH..	2	0		FISCV
0LOGSYS	Source System			0LOGSY	CH..	10	0		LOGSY
0SOURSYSTEM	Source system ID			0SOUR$	CH..	2	0		SOURS
0GN_PAR_SSY	Partner Srce System			0GN_P/	CH..	2	0		GN_PA
0TXTMD	Medium description				CH..	40	0		TXTMD

Figure 5.28 Activating the Communication Structure

5.6.3 Transfer Rules

Purpose After maintaining the transfer and Communication Structures, you can determine via transfer rules how the fields of the transfer structure are to be assigned to the InfoObjects of the Communication Structure. The assignment can be on a direct or 1:1 basis, or by using routines or constants. The maintenance options for the transfer rules are the same for both flexible and direct updating.

Maintaining Transfer Rules

To access the maintenance for the transfer rules, right-click on the source system of the master data to be updated. In the popup menu that appears, select **Change Transfer Rules...** (see Figure 5.29).

Another option is to open the **Transfer Structure/Transfer Rules** in the Communication Structure maintenance (see Figure 5.30).

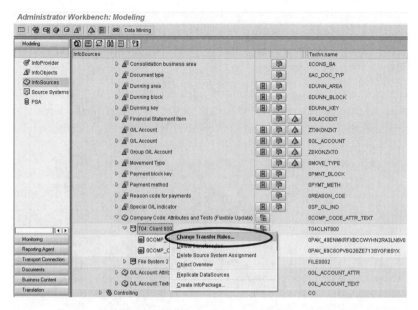

Figure 5.29 Accessing the Transfer Rules Maintenance Using the Context Menu

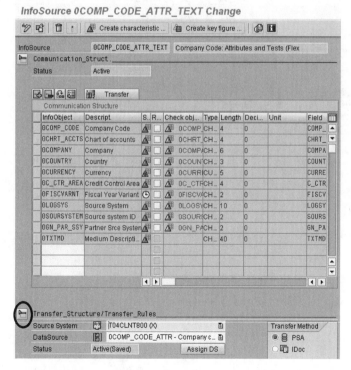

Figure 5.30 By Opening the "Transfer Structure/Transfer Rules" in the Communication Structure, You Can Also Access the Transfer Rules Maintenance.

InfoSource Maintaining the transfer rules corresponds to the mapping of data sources (DataSource plus transfer structure) and data targets (Communication Structure). In SAP BW, the total of all possible combinations of these settings is referred to as *InfoSource*.

Maintenance screen The screen to maintain the transfer rules is structured in two vertically separated areas. You can see the data target structure on the left-hand side and the data source structure on the right-hand side of the screen (see Figure 5.31).

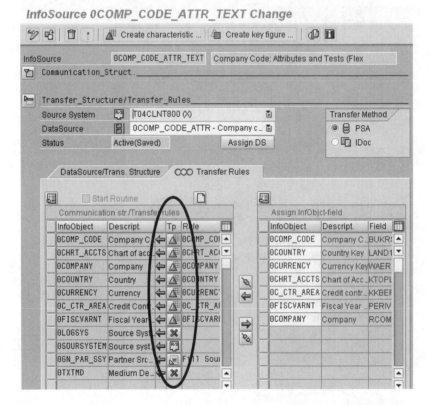

Figure 5.31 The Transfer Rules Are Also Optically Split as Data Source (Right) and Data Target (Left).

Selection Options for Transfer Rules

Data transfer In the following section, we will explain the various options for data transfer provided by SAP BW. The definition of which rule for the transfer is definitively used is performed by selecting the transfer type (see Figure 5.32).

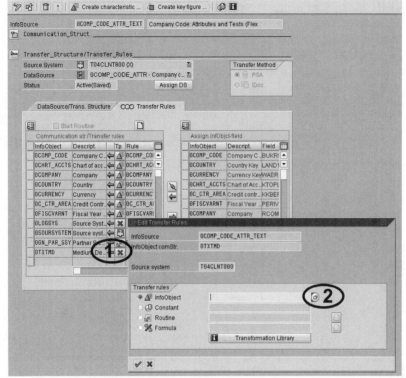

Figure 5.32 By Clicking on the "Type" Button in the Transfer Rules, You Can Determine Which Rule Will Be Used for This InfoObject.

The individual selection options are now described in detail:

▶ The **Field from transfer structure** transfer type enables you to assign an InfoObject of the data target to an InfoObject of the transfer structure. For this reason, we refer to it as a *1:1 assignment*.

▶ If you select the input help for the **Field from transfer structure** selection in the transfer rule selection menu, all fields of the transfer structure are listed and can be used by double-clicking on them (see Figure 5.33).

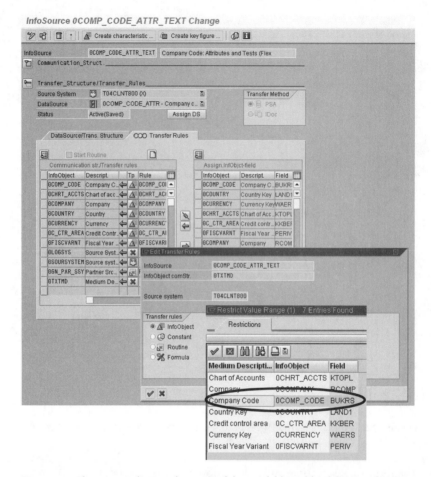

Figure 5.33 The Input Help Provides a List of the Available Fields of the Transfer Structure.

▶ Another and more convenient way for experienced users to perform this type of 1:1 assignment is to use the arrow keys or the automatic assignment. The automatic assignment is done by clicking on the corresponding button (see Figure 5.34, selection 1). All InfoObjects of the transfer and Communication Structures that have the same name are then mapped to one another. This function is comparable to the ABAP command MOVE CORRESPONDING FIELDS.

▶ To assign individual InfoObjects from the transfer and Communication Structures, you must first select the relevant InfoObjects and then click on the **Transfer** button (see Figure 5.34, selection 2).

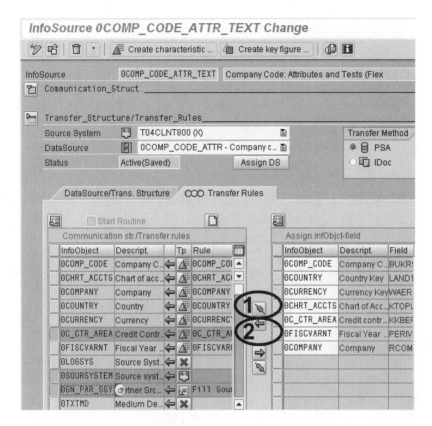

Figure 5.34 Assignment of InfoObjects by Selection and Arrow Key

▶ To counteract this function, you can delete an assignment that was previously selected in the transfer rules by clicking on the **Remove** button (see Figure 5.35, selection 1). In this context, you can also delete various transfer types here. **Deleting assignments**

▶ You can also delete the transfer rules assigned in these InfoSources by selecting the corresponding button (see Figure 5.35, selection 4).

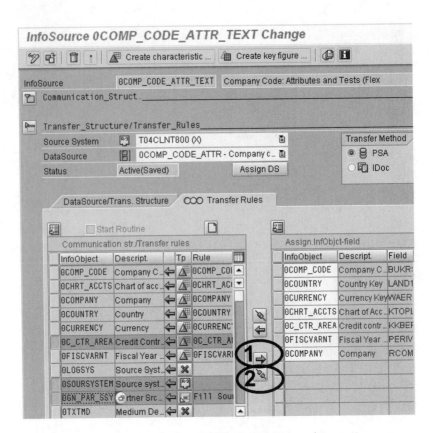

InfoSource 0COMP_CODE_ATTR_TEXT Change

Figure 5.35 Deleting InfoObject Transfer Rules by Selection and Arrow Key

Constant ▶ By defining a constant in the transfer rules, the Communication Structure is assigned a fixed value, which is the same for each data record transferred. This process ensures that the relevant field in the communication structure is not supplied with a value from the transfer structure; instead, it is supplied with the selected fixed value (see Figure 5.36).

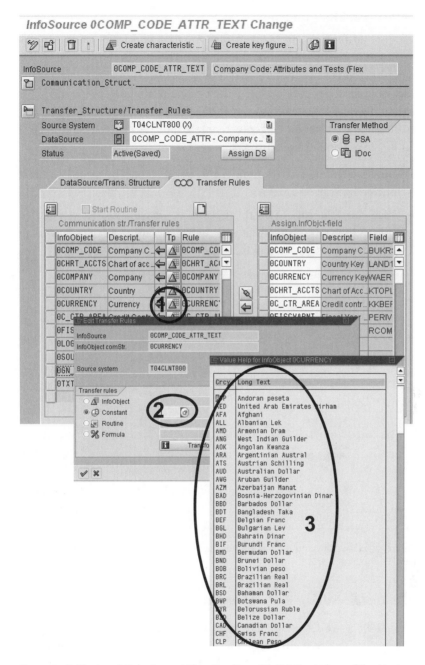

Figure 5.36 The Input Help Opens When You Press F4; Existing Values of the Master Data Are Suggested.

Creating a Start Routine

Via the transfer rules, SAP BW enables you to create a start routine that is executed at the beginning of the transfer. The biggest advantage of the differentiation between *start routines* and *routines* is that the start routine runs only once per data package; the routine itself, however, is called for each individual data record, which it then runs through. For example, you can use the start routine to generate internal tables that you can then use for key figure and characteristic routines..

▶ You can create a start routine in the transfer rules by using the **Start routine** button.

▶ Once you have clicked on this button, you have access to the source code of the start routine that you can modify using ABAP/4 according to meet your requirements (see Figure 5.37).

```
* Declaration of Datapackage
TYPES: TAB_TRANSTRU type table of TRANSFER_STRUCTURE.

* Global code used by conversion rules
*$*$ begin of global - insert your declaration only below this line   *-*

TABLES:   ---> Declararion of used Tables <---


DATA:    ---> Declararion of used Data <---

*$*$ end of global - insert your declaration only before this line    *-*

FORM STARTROUTINE
  USING    G_S_MINFO TYPE RSSM_S_MINFO
  CHANGING DATAPAK type TAB_TRANSTRU
           G_T_ERRORLOG TYPE rssm_t_errorlog_int
           ABORT LIKE SY-SUBRC. "set ABORT <> 0 to cancel datapackage
*$*$ begin of routine - insert your code only below this line        *-*
* DATA: l_s_datapak_line type TRANSFER_STRUCTURE,
*       l_s_errorlog TYPE rssm_s_errorlog_int.

    ----> Enter the code of the Routine <----

* abort <> 0 means skip whole data package !!!
  ABORT = 0.
*$*$ end of routine - insert your code only before this line         *-*
```

Figure 5.37 The Start Routine Can Be Adjusted to Your Personal Requirements Using ABAP/4 Program Code.

Example of Using a Start Routine

The ZSPECIALSIGNS table contains all the national special characters as well as the relevant permitted characters to be used for replacements. This table should be read into an internal table (i_TAB) to increase the efficiency of the read access. Then, all characters which are to be replaced (i_tab-zold) are sequentially written into a separate data field (i_specialsigns). The source code looks as follows:

```
TABLES: ZSPECIALSIGNS.
DATA:  begin of i_tab occurs 0.
include structure ZSPECIALSIGNS.
DATA: end of i_tab.
DATA: i_specialsigns(200) type c.
refresh i_tab.
select * from ZSPECIALSIGNS into table i_tab.
clear i_specialsigns.
Loop at i_tab.
concatenate i_tab-zold i_specialsigns into i_special-
signs.
endloop.
```

After you have created a start routine in the transfer rules, it is optically identified (see Figure 5.38, i.e., the Start Routine box is checked). Now the button to create a start routine is no longer available as there can be only one start routine per InfoSource.

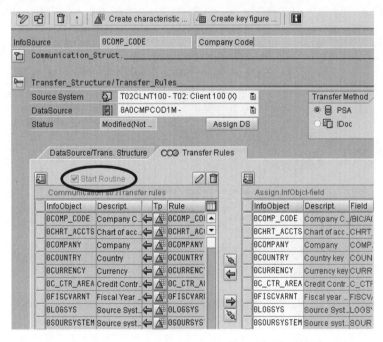

Figure 5.38 If a Start Routine Exists, This Is Made Visible Through the Selection.

Defining a Routine

Another modification option for master data while it is being transferred is a routine that is often based on a start routine. A routine enables you to define complex transfer rules for InfoSources. Routines are ABAP programs that consist of a predefined global *data declaration section* and an *ABAP form routine*. The form routine provides all functions of ABAP programming (see Figure 5.39).

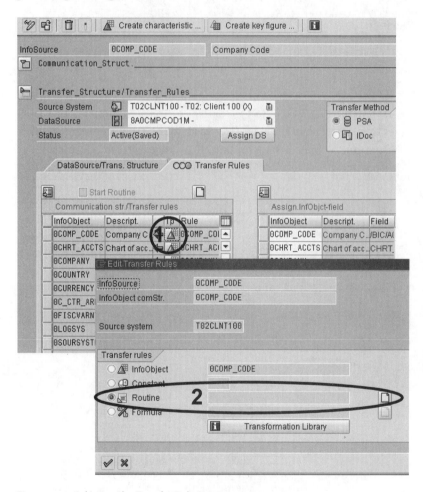

Figure 5.39 Selecting the Transfer Rule Routine

Before maintaining the routine, you must select all fields of the transfer structure that are to be addressed within the routine (see Figure 5.40).

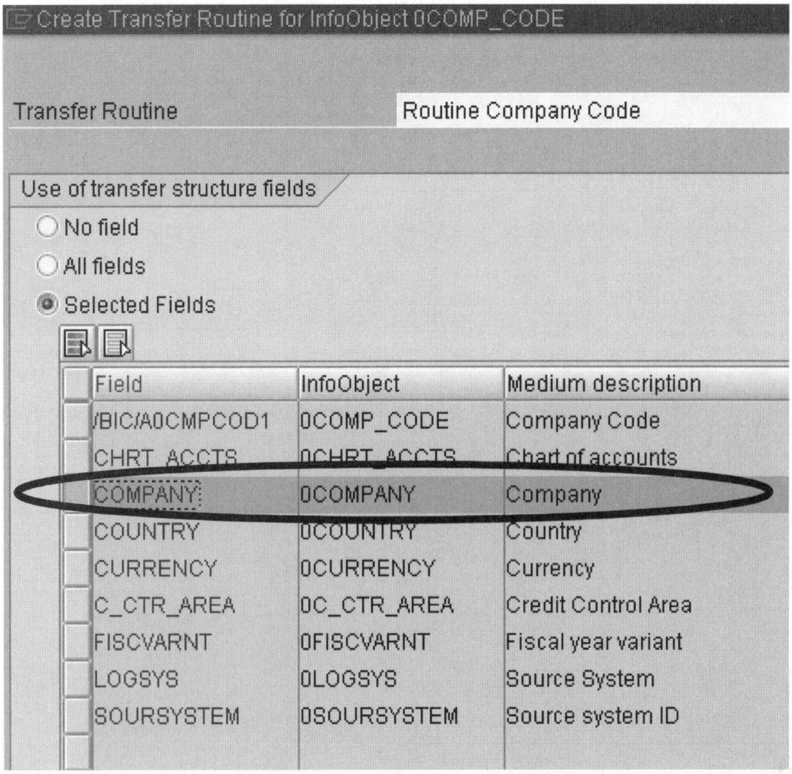

Transfer Routine	Routine Company Code

Use of transfer structure fields

○ No field
○ All fields
◉ Selected Fields

Field	InfoObject	Medium description
/BIC/A0CMPCOD1	0COMP_CODE	Company Code
CHRT_ACCTS	0CHRT_ACCTS	Chart of accounts
COMPANY	0COMPANY	Company
COUNTRY	0COUNTRY	Country
CURRENCY	0CURRENCY	Currency
C_CTR_AREA	0C_CTR_AREA	Credit Control Area
FISCVARNT	0FISCVARNT	Fiscal year variant
LOGSYS	0LOGSYS	Source System
SOURSYSTEM	0SOURSYSTEM	Source system ID

Figure 5.40 Selecting the Fields of the Transfer Structure

Example of Using a Routine

The internal table built up in the start routine as well as the internal populated field should be used to check and, if necessary, replace the values of a field of the transfer structure. This check takes place in the routine itself. If the check is positive you will access the form (SPECIALCHARACTERS) of a separate user exit (ZFUSERE0) where the replacement will be done (see Figure 5.41). The internal table I_TAB built in the start routine is passed on as well.

```
Edit Transfer Rules

🔍 🔁 🔀  Pattern    Pretty Printer  ℹ  ⑦ Routines Info.

🗙 🗐 🖺 🖉 🗐 🛗 🗐 🗐 🗐

*--------------------------------------------------------------------*
*       FORM COMPUTE_COMP_CODE
*--------------------------------------------------------------------*
* Compute value of InfoObject 0COMP_CODE
* in communication structure /BI0/MCOMP_CODE
*
* Technical properties:
*     field name      = COMP_CODE
*     data element    = /BI0/OICOMP_CODE
*     data type       = CHAR
*     length          = 000004
*     decimals        = 000000
*     ABAP type       = C
*     ABAP length     = 000004
*     reference field =
*--------------------------------------------------------------------*
* Parameters:
*   -->  RECORD_NO        Record number
*   -->  TRAN_STRUCTURE   Transfer structure
*   <--  RESULT           Return value of InfoObject
*   <->  G_T_ERRORLOG     Error log
*   <--  RETURNCODE       Return code (to skip one record)
*   <--  ABORT            Abort code (to skip whole data package)
*--------------------------------------------------------------------*
FORM COMPUTE_COMP_CODE
  USING    RECORD_NO LIKE SY-TABIX
           TRAN_STRUCTURE TYPE TRANSFER_STRUCTURE
           G_S_MINFO TYPE RSSM_S_MINFO
  CHANGING RESULT TYPE /BI0/OICOMP_CODE
           G_T_ERRORLOG TYPE rssm_t_errorlog_int
           RETURNCODE LIKE SY-SUBRC
           ABORT LIKE SY-SUBRC. "set ABORT <> 0 to cancel datapackage
*$*$ begin of routine - insert your code only below this line     *-*
* DATA: l_s_errorlog TYPE rssm_s_errorlog_int.

IF TRAN_STRUCTURE-/BIC/A0CMPCOD1 ca I_SONDERZEICHEN.
PERFORM SONDERZEICHEN(ZFUSERE0) tables I_TAB
USING TRAN_STRUCTURE-/BIC/A0CMPCOD1
  RESULT.

ELSE.
RESULT = TRAN_STRUCTURE-/BIC/A0CMPCOD1.
ENDIF.|


* returncode <> 0 means skip this record
  RETURNCODE = 0.
* abort <> 0 means skip whole data package !!!
  ABORT = 0.
*$*$ end of routine - insert your code only before this line      *-*
ENDFORM.
```

Figure 5.41 The Check Is Performed Using the Program Code in the Routine.

The actual replacement of prohibited characters takes place within a form of the separate user exit (see Figure 5.42). You can also maintain the source code of the user exit directly in the routine. However, this has one considerable disadvantage. If the **Routine** transfer position is inadvertently deleted, for example, by a hot package or by importing a new content version, the ABAP code, which can sometimes be very extensive, may be irretrievably lost.

```
*========================= Form SONDERZEICHEN =============================
* konvertion of disallowed signs into allowed signs
*

FORM SONDERZEICHEN tables I_TAB STRUCTURE ZSPECIALSIGNS
USING p_OLD
      p_NEW.
  set extended check off.
  loop at i_tab.
    WHILE p_old CA i_tab-zold.
      IF SY-SUBRC <> 0.
        EXIT.
      ENDIF.
      REPLACE i_tab-zold IN p_OLD WITH i_tab-znew.
    ENDWHILE.
    SY-SUBRC = 0.
  endloop.
  p_new = p_old.
  set extended check on.
ENDFORM.                       "SONDERZEICHEN

*========================= Form SONDERZEICHEN =============================
```

Figure 5.42 Replacing Prohibited Characters Is Carried Out in a Form of the Separate User Exit.

The method of navigating to a separate user exit, which is recommended by CubeServ, means that you only have to maintain a short code. The logic of a central maintenance and the applicability in different areas—a result of using a central maintenance—both speak for the latter variants.

Maintenance Options in the Routine

In the routine, the following maintenance options are provided by ABAP code:

Meaning of the individual codes

▶ **Global data declarations**
  Between ***$*$ begin of global** ... and ***$*$ end of global** ... you can define global data declarations, which are then available in all routines. This option can be used with provisional results in other routines, for example, or when recalling the same routine whereby you can use the same routine results of the first call again.

▶ **TRAN_STRUCTURE**
  In the TRAN_STRUCTURE variable, the content of the record to be converted is made available to the routine in the transfer structure format. In the editor, this structure contains only the fields that were previously marked as selected.

- ▶ **RECORD_NO**

  The RECORD_NO variable provides the number of the record that has just been processed.

- ▶ **RESULT**

  You must assign the RESULT variable to the result of the conversion.

- ▶ **RETURNCODE**

  The RETURNCODE variable lets you notify the conversion program about errors. RETURNCODE <> 0 means that there's an error in the calculation, that is, the current record is not transferred to the posting.

- ▶ **ABORT**

  You can notify the conversion program about errors using the ABORT variable. ABORT <> 0 indicates that a serious error occurred during processing, that is, the processing of the current data package is completely canceled.

Closing a Routine

- ▶ You can check the syntax of routines using the **Check** function (**CTRL+F2**).

- ▶ Then the routines can be transferred using the **Save** function.

- ▶ When you exit the editor, the routine maintenance closes.

- ▶ Then you must activate the transfer rules as data from the source system can be loaded only in an activated version.

The Formula Editor

The Formula Editor enables you to create formulas easily with the transformation library.

Structure | The structure of the Formula Editor can be broken down as follows:

- ▶ The formula is displayed in the upper part of the screen.

- ▶ In the middle of the lower half of the screen, you'll see the buttons to enter frequently used operators and functions and the buttons to enter character strings, figures, constants, and comments manually.

- ▶ To the right of this structure, you can see additional functions and operators. On the left-hand side are the available fields (table fields, InfoObjects, system fields, and so on, see Figure 5.43).

Operation | There are two edit modes available for using the Formula Editor: the *standard mode* and the *expert mode*. You can toggle between them at any time

using the corresponding button or via the main menu by selecting **Edit ·
Standard/Expert mode**. Both modes will now be described separately.

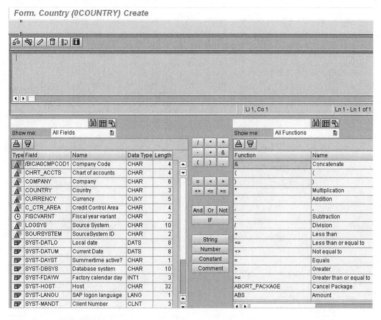

Figure 5.43 Overview of the Structure of the Formula Editor

The Standard Mode

Using the standard mode
▶ You can enter a formula in the standard mode for which you can select
  the formula elements in the lower part of the screen (see Figure 5.44).

▶ The operators on the buttons are added by single-clicking on them; if
  you double-click on them, the fields and functions in the inventory can
  be added at the end of the formula, or inserted at the point in the formula where you previously placed the cursor.

▶ You can call dialog windows using the buttons below the operators
  where the following fields can be inserted:

  ▶ **String**
    An alphanumeric constant in the form of a string of characters

  ▶ **Number**
    A numeric constant, that is, any number

▶ **Constant**

A constant of a particular type for which a corresponding input help is provided

▶ **Comment**

A comment that is not considered in formula calculation

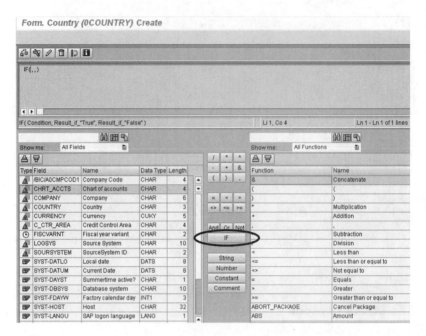

Figure 5.44 You Can Create a Formula by Selecting Formula Elements in the Lower Screen Section.

▶ You can select a field by double-clicking on it in the formula.

▶ You can also select a function by double-clicking on it. In the status line of the formula window, a syntax help appears.

▶ You will get more information on the functions by first selecting the required function and then pressing **F1** (see Figure 5.45). The fields are then only given a short description in the inventory and in the editor. Functions on the other hand are displayed with both a technical name and a short description.

▶ You can use the **Delete** and **Change** buttons to make changes to the formula. These functions can also be accessed via the context menu. A change or deletion of formula components is performed at this point without the request for confirmation.

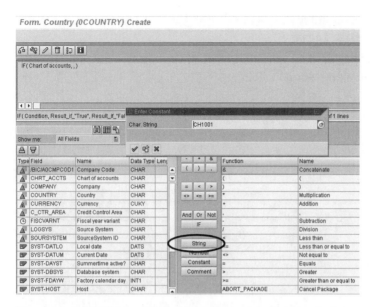

Figure 5.45 You Will See a Detailed Description of the Functionality by Selecting the Function and Pressing the F1 Help Button.

Checking Formulas: Syntax Check

▶ The syntax cannot be checked simultaneously but by using the **Check** button in the application toolbar. The field, the operator, or the function where the error appears is highlighted in color (see Figure 5.46).

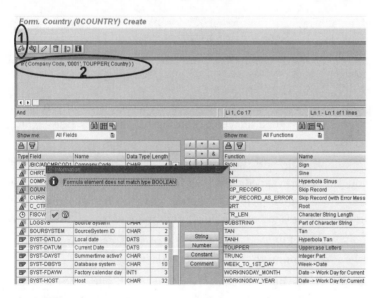

Figure 5.46 In Addition to the Error Message, the Field Containing the Error Is Highlighted in Color.

▶ When you exit the formula while it still contains syntax errors, a warning message appears.

▶ Depending on the application context, you can save the formula without exiting the Formula Editor.

Search and Sort Functions

▶ You can sort the entries in ascending or descending order by using the corresponding buttons (see Figure 5.47).

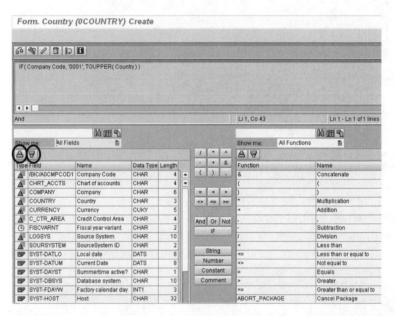

Figure 5.47 The Formula Editor Provides an Ascending or Descending Sort Function for Each Column.

▶ Using the drop-down list box above the inventory list, you can limit the number of entries displayed according to categories (see Figure 5.48).

▶ Using the input field and the two buttons above the drop-down list box, you can perform specific searches for entries. Enter the search criteria and select **Search**. All relevant entries will then be highlighted and the cursor will be placed on the next appropriate entry.

▶ If you select **Hit list** instead, you will see a cross-category display of all entries that correspond to the search criteria.

▶ You can search for parts of character strings both with and without wild cards (+ and *). The search will then take place in the technical names as well as in the short description (Figure 5.49).

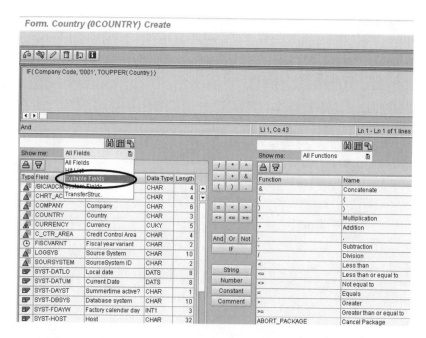

Figure 5.48 The Number of the Entries Can be Restricted by Category.

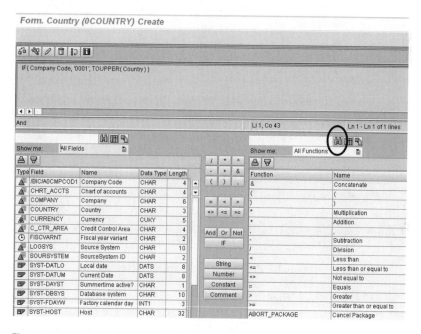

Figure 5.49 You Can Also Do a Specific Search for Keywords.

Expert Mode

Formula entry Most of the functions to enter a formula in the standard mode are also available in this mode. In addition, you can also enter the constants and comments directly in the formula (see Figure 5.50):

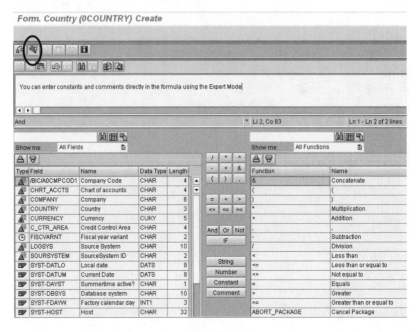

Figure 5.50 Formulas Can Be Manually Edited in the Expert Mode.

▶ In order to be able to differentiate them from field names, you must enter alphanumeric constants in single inverted commas ('constant') and enter comments in double inverted commas ("comment"). Numbers (numeric constants) are always displayed without a delimiter.

▶ You can also move fields and functions by dragging and dropping them to the required position. If a function is inserted, the required parentheses and inverted commas are also inserted simultaneously. The function parameters must then be entered in-between them. A syntax help also appears in the status line of the formula field that tells you which parameters with which meaning are required by the function.

Canceling changes Changes can also be canceled in the expert mode. When you do this, all text entries in the formula (excluding selections by single-click or double-click), or drag-and-drop actions within the Formula Editor, are considered as changes. The common text editing functions can also be selected using the buttons in the formula window. Fields in the inventory list and in the editor are displayed with a technical name and short description as is the case with the functions.

The syntax check is carried out in the standard mode by clicking on the **Check** button in the application toolbar. If an error occurs, its location is highlighted and the cursor is placed directly after the error location.

Syntax check

You can save formulas in their current state as a local file, or you can import existing local files into the Formula Editor. This enables you to reuse formula components that have already been defined and to save them if the Formula Editor is to be exited despite the formula being incomplete or incorrect (see Figure 5.51).

Editing and saving formulas

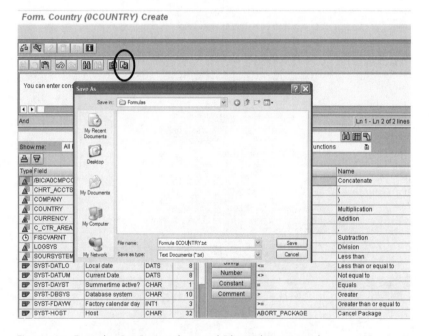

Figure 5.51 Formulas Can Be Saved as Local Files and Reimported

Frequently Used Transformations

Frequently used transformations can be found in the SAP transformation library. The list of functions that are provided provides you with a detailed overview and describes the functionality on the basis of examples. You can call the SAP transformation library using the **Help** button (see Figure 5.52).

SAP transformation library

Since we have described all the different modification options regarding transfer rules, we should add that you can use several or all of these options in the transfer rules at the same time (see Figure 5.53).

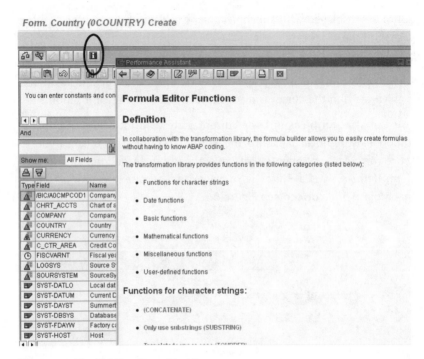

Figure 5.52 The SAP Transformation Library

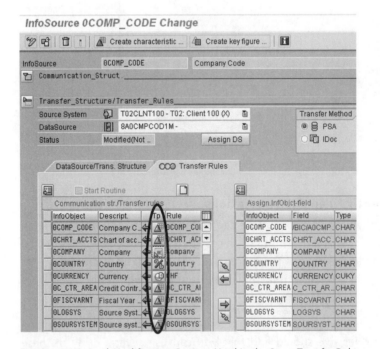

Figure 5.53 Several Modification Options Used in the Same Transfer Rules

Status of Transfer Rules

The status of the transfer rules is displayed with a green or yellow traffic Status display light. Because you don't have to transfer all fields from the transfer structure into the Communication Structure, you can activate the transfer rules with an assigned field. The status is designated by a yellow traffic light. A red traffic light indicates an error. In this case, the transfer rules cannot be activated.

After completing the maintenance of the transfer rules, the direct update of the master data has been set up. You can no longer interrupt the update just to modify the data.

As a last instrument to initiate data extraction and its update, you need the InfoPackage. We will describe this in more detail in the following sections.

5.6.4 Update Rules (Only Flexible Updating)

The update rules enable you to specify how the data from the Communication Structure of an InfoSource is updated to an InfoProvider. Thus, you can connect an InfoSource with an InfoProvider. A data target can be supplied by several InfoSources. In this case, separate update rules must be maintained for each of these InfoSources.

The InfoObjects of the Communication Structure that belongs to the Target InfoObjects InfoSource are referred to as source InfoObjects in the update; the InfoObjects of the InfoProvider, on the other hand, are referred to as target InfoObjects.

To access the overview of the InfoProviders and the corresponding update rules, you must call the menu item **Modeling/InfoProvider** in the Administrator Workbench or use Transaction code RSA11 (see Figure 5.54).

You can get into the change mode of the update rules for the data target Change mode either by double-clicking in this overview or by selecting the rule to be changed and then selecting the **Change** entry in the context menu (right mouse-click).

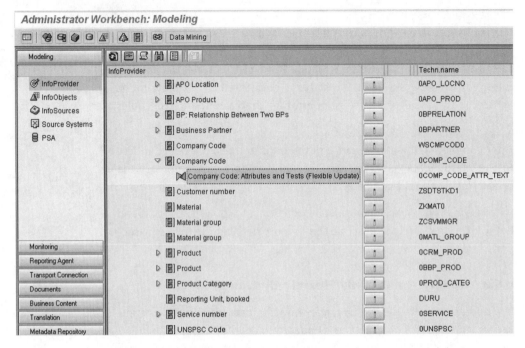

Figure 5.54 In the Menu Item "Modeling/InfoProvider," You Can Find the Data Targets with Their Existing Update Rules

The maintenance screen that appears is split into several sections (see Figure 5.55):

▶ Standard toolbar (selection 1)

▶ Additional standard toolbar (selection 2)

▶ Select between versions (selection 3)

▶ Last Changed By (selection 4)

▶ Create Start Routine (selection 5)

▶ Additional options: Details view and copy (selection 6)

▶ Mapping the update rules (selection 7)

We will now describe these sections individually in detail and show the individual entry points each time to execute a specific option.

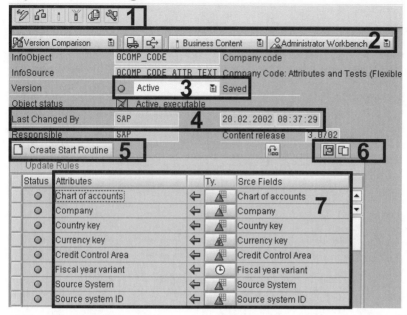

Update Rules change: Rules

InfoObject	0COMP_CODE	Company code
InfoSource	0COMP_CODE_ATTR_TEXT	Company Code: Attributes and Tests (Flexible
Version	○ Active **3** ▣ Saved	
Object status	☒ Active, executable	
Last Changed By	SAP **4**	20.02.2002 08:37:29
Responsible	SAP	Content release 3.0702

Update Rules

Status	Attributes	Ty.	Srce Fields
○	Chart of accounts	⇐ 🔺	Chart of accounts
○	Company	⇐ 🔺	Company
○	Country key	⇐ 🔺	Country key
○	Currency key	⇐ 🔺	Currency key
○	Credit Control Area	⇐ 🔺	Credit Control Area
○	Fiscal year variant	⇐ 🕐	Fiscal year variant
○	Source System	⇐ 🔺	Source System
○	Source system ID	⇐ 🔺	Source system ID

Figure 5.55 Options to Change the Update Rules for Master Data: Complete Overview

Standard Toolbar

Using the standard toolbar (see Figure 5.56) you can execute various functions by clicking on a button.

The individual buttons have the following meanings:

▶ **Display/Change** (see Figure 5.56, selection 1)
Use this button to switch between change and display modes. You can also switch using the key combination **Ctrl+F1**.

▶ **Check** (selection 2)
Use this button to check the update rules. If the check is carried out without errors, a corresponding message appears. If an error occurs during the check, another message notifies you. You can also use **Ctrl+F2** to run this check.

▶ **Activate** (selection 3)
Use this button to activate the update rules. An SAP BW system always works with the active version of the update rules. You can also use the key combination **Ctrl+F3** to enable activation.

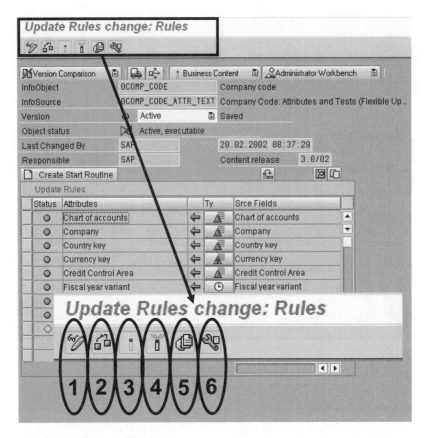

Figure 5.56 Standard Toolbar Buttons

▶ **Deactivation** (selection 4)
Use this button to deactivate the update rules. You can also use the key combination **Ctrl+F5** to disable activation.

▶ **Documentation** (selection 5)
Use this button to go to the update rules' documentation. Here, you can create definitions and other important documents for the update rules as well as maintain them (see Figure 5.57). Alternatively, you can use the **F5** key.

▶ **Display technical name** (see Figure 5.56, selection 6).
Use this button to display the technical names of the characteristics as well as their descriptions. You can also use the key combination **Ctrl+F9** (see Figure 5.58).

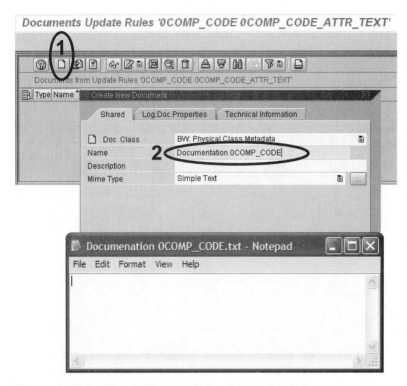

Figure 5.57 Maintaining the Documentation of the Update Rules

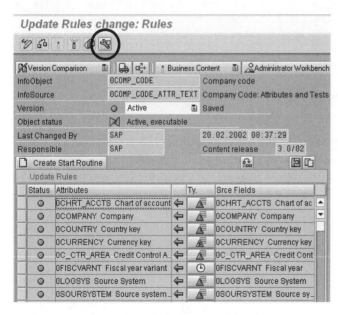

Figure 5.58 Displaying the Technical Names of the Characteristics

Additional Standard Toolbar

You can also use this menu bar to perform the following functions (see Figure 5.59):

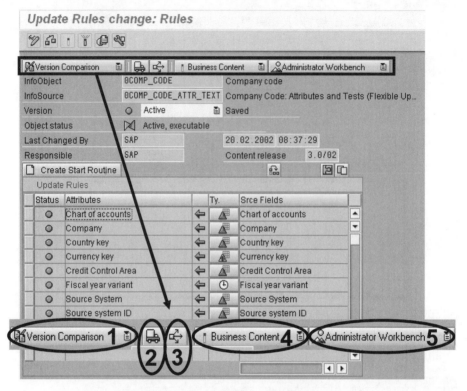

Figure 5.59 Additional Standard Toolbar Buttons

▶ **Version Comparison** (see Figure 5.59, selection 1)
This button enables you to compare several versions (see Figure 5.60).

▶ **Transport** (see Figure 5.59, selection 2)
This button allows you to write the created update rules into a transport request and thus enables you to transport these rules into another system (see Figure 5.61).

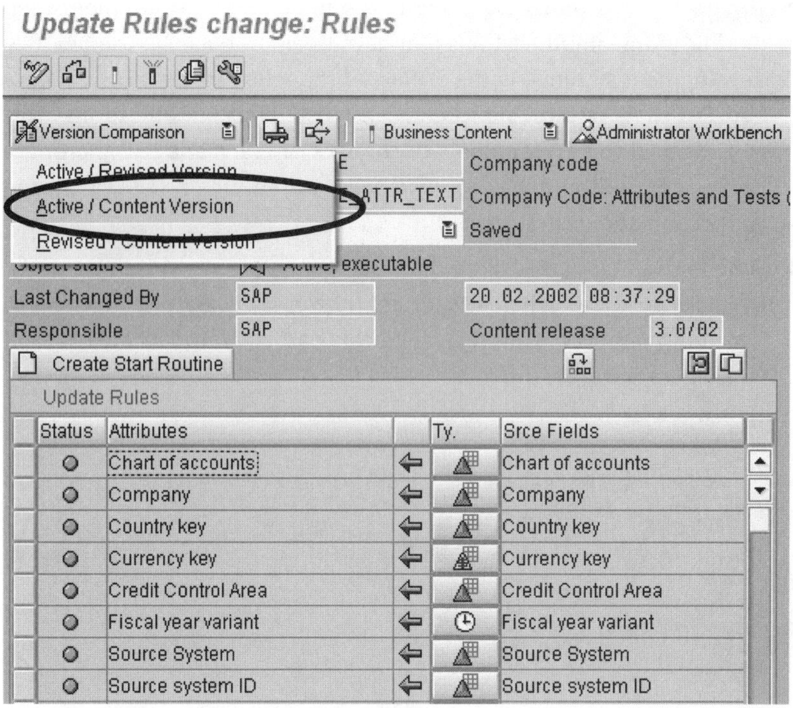

Update Rules change: Rules

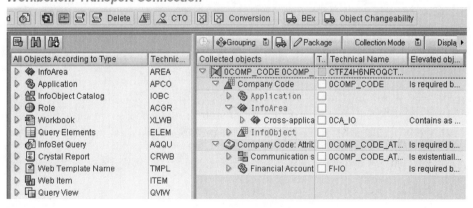

Figure 5.60 Selecting the Comparison Options

Workbench: Transport Connection

Figure 5.61 Writing the Update Rules into a Transport Request

▶ The goal of this transport request is to implement developments and modifications—modifications that have been produced in the SAP BW development system—in the SAP BW production system. The productive SAP BW system is protected against direct modifications. This ensures that no developments or changes can be made in the production system without having first been tested and accepted by the application administrators.

▶ **Where-Used List** (see Figure 5.59, selection 3)
By clicking on the **Where-Used List** button, a separate screen opens, which displays all the places where this particular update rule is used (see Figure 5.62).

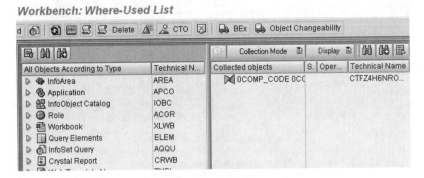

Figure 5.62 The Where-Used List of the Update Rule Selected

▶ **Business Content** (see Figure 5.59, selection 4)
This button allows you to move from the update rule to the Administrator Workbench in order to install parts of the Business Content provided by SAP (see Figure 5.63).

▶ **Administrator Workbench** (see Figure 5.59, selection 5)
This button allows you to move from the update rule directly to specific areas of the Administrator Workbench (see Figure 5.64).

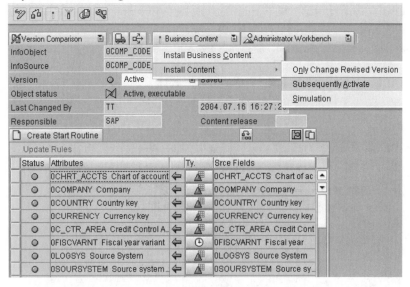

Figure 5.63 Business Content or Parts of it Can Be Activated from the Update Rule

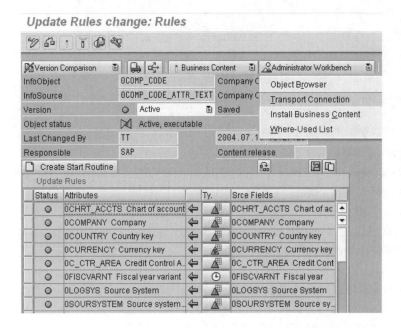

Figure 5.64 Navigating to Different Areas of the Administrator Workbench

Choosing Between Versions

One advantage to note is that because SAP BW objects are available in different versions (see Figure 5.65), update rules can be changed while an active executable version is always available.

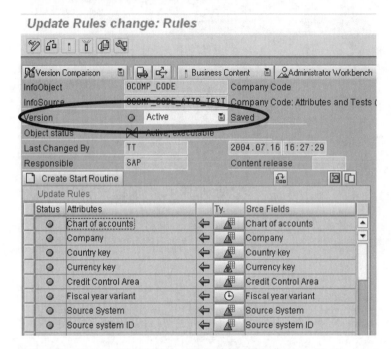

Figure 5.65 Changing Update Rules for Master Data: Selecting a Version

The following individual versions are available:

Version types ▶ **Edited/not saved**

This version exists only when update rules are being edited. The status shows that the changes have not yet been saved.

▶ **Revised/saved**

After saving an edited version without activating it, the version status changes to revised/saved.

▶ **Active**

When you activate a processed version, the status changes to "active." It is irrelevant whether or not the previous version was saved. Only this active version can be executed.

▶ **Delivered**

This version type refers to the version delivered by SAP with business content.

Last Changed By

This section shows you which user last changed the update rules. In addition, you can also see on which date and at which time this change was implemented (see Figure 5.66).

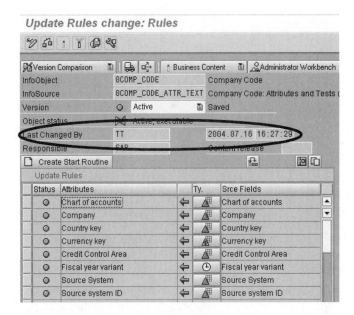

Figure 5.66 Changing Update Rules for Master Data: Last Changed By

Creating a Start Routine

SAP BW also allows you to create a start routine for the update rules, which is executed at the beginning of an update (see Figure 5.67). The start routine in the update rules area has a similar definition and functionality to the start routines that were previously described for the transfer rules.

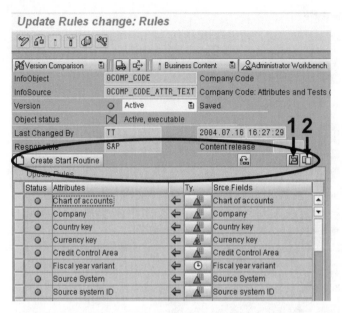

Figure 5.67 Changing Update Rules for Master Data: Create Start Routine

Additional Options

The buttons selected in Figure 5.67 provide additional administration options for update rules:

▶ **Details** (see Figure 5.67, selection 1)
This control button displays details of the individual characteristics to be transferred.

▶ **Copy** (selection 2)
This control button enables you to copy a selected object of the update rule.

Update Rules: Mapping

Similar to the transfer rules, you can also see a mapping in the lower half of the screen for the update rules where you can see the characteristics fields of the *data target* on the left-hand side and the characteristics fields of the *data source* (transfer rules) on the right-hand side. In-between these fields the type is identified which is used to update the data (see Figure 5.68, selection 1).

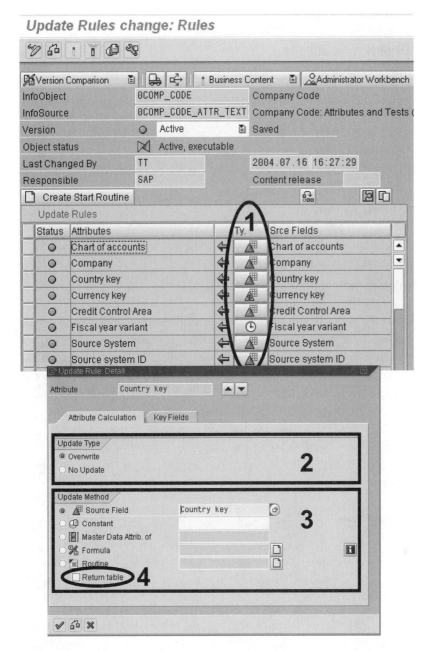

Figure 5.68 When Updating the Data Target, You Can Select Different Update Methods.

"Attribute Calculation" Tab

You can also select different options for these update rules in the **Attribute Calculation** tab:

▶ **Update Type** (see Figure 5.68, selection 2)
You must first determine whether the target structure data should be updated for this characteristic. This definitely makes sense, given not all characteristics of all attributes can be transferred to a data target from one specific data source. Example: Attributes 1, 2, and 5 are to be filled from data source A; however, attributes 3, 4, and 6 are to be filled from data source B.

▶ **Update Method** (selection 3)
Because most update methods are identical with those of the transfer rules, we won't repeat them here. Instead, we'll focus on the definition within the transfer rules.

▶ **Return table** (selection 4)
The update rules also provide a return table that you can use for routines. In general, routines in the update rules have only one return value. By selecting the **Return table** field, the corresponding key figure routine no longer has a return value (strored in RESULT); instead, it has a return table (which is stored in RESULT_TABLE). In this case, you can create any number of key figure values from a data record. Return table routines replace the RESULT parameter with the return table RESULT_TABLE. The return table has the same structure as the data target, but only the key figure or data field is filled for which the routine has been created, including its characteristics and key fields. Therefore, aggregate values can be distributed.

Excursus

InfoSource

The InfoSource provides the sales figures for the individual sales organizations. However, the sales figures for each employee need to be displayed. To display the sales figures, you must adhere to the following processing steps:

▶ Read the IDs of the sales organization employees from the master data table provided by the InfoSource.

▶ Divide the sales total by the number of employees who were read from the master data table.

▶ Create an entry in your return table for each employee.

▶ In addition, the parameter ICUBE_VALUES is available. The calculated characteristic values are stored here.

▶ The easiest way to fill the return table RESULT_TABLE is to copy the ICUBE_VALUES structure to the RESULT_TABLE table as often as necessary, fill only the corresponding key figure, and adjust the characteristic value.

"Key Fields" Tab

In the **Key Fields** tab, you can see the respective key field (or key fields) of the characteristic. This is always the characteristic itself. If the object is compounded with further characteristics, these characteristics are also key fields (see Figure 5.69).

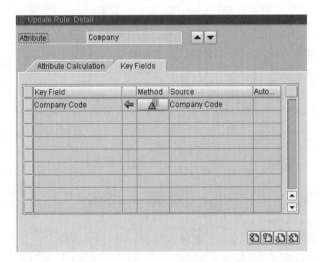

Figure 5.69 If a Characteristic Has not Been Compounded with Other Characteristics, the Characteristic Itself Is the Only Key Field for the Update.

Activating the Update Routine

▶ After the update routine has been customized to meet the requirements of the data model, you must save it. When you save the routine, the check function is automatically executed.

▶ After you save the routine, you must activate the update routine. Its status then changes from **Revised/saved** to **active**.

▶ Furthermore, the sign for the update routine changes from white (nonexecutable) to green (executable).

▶ After this activation has occurred, the data update to the data target has been established.

Now that the entire metadata structure for the data transfer and update has been set up, published, and activated, all prerequisites have been met for extracting data from a data target into SAP BW and for transferring and updating it in a data target.

5.6.5 InfoPackage

An InfoPackage enables you to determine conditions for selecting data requests from a source system. Furthermore, additional settings can be defined regarding the data target and data transfer. We will describe these options in the following sections.

Creating and Editing an InfoPackage

All editing of InfoPackages takes place in the Administrator Workbench.

▶ In the menu item **Modeling · InfoSources**, an InfoPackage is always assigned to exactly one source system. To create a new InfoPackage, select a source system for the desired InfoSource and click on the right mouse button.

▶ In the context menu that opens, select the menu item **Create Info-Package** (see Figure 5.70). Once you have created the InfoPackage, you can change it by double-clicking on it. You can now edit and change the InfoPackage.

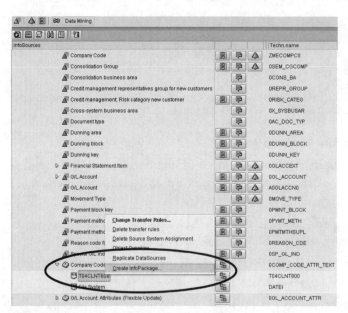

Figure 5.70 Creating a New InfoPackage

▶ After selecting this menu item, you are prompted by another popup window, which displays information such as the source system and InfoSource for the InfoPackage, to enter a name to identify the package.

▶ If the InfoSource is assigned to several DataSources, you must explicitly select one of these DataSources (see Figure 5.71). However, if an InfoSource is assigned to only one DataSource, the assignment is automatic and doesn't require you to select the specific DataSource.

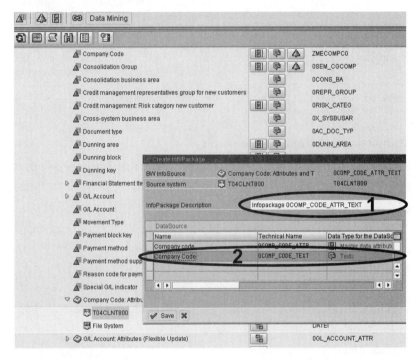

Figure 5.71 Assigning a Name to an InfoPackage and Selecting One DataSource That Will Be Used by This InfoPackage

▶ After you have confirmed the selected settings, the maintenance screen of the InfoPackage is displayed (see Figure 5.72).

Figure 5.72 Maintenance Screen: Upper Area—InfoPackage Information, Lower Area—Additional Settings

Maintenance Screen: Upper Area

In the upper area of the screen, the information that has been selected and saved up to now is displayed (see Figure 5.72):

▶ **InfoPackage**
The name that you have assigned to the InfoPackage and the technical name (in parenthesis) of the InfoPackage are displayed.

▶ **InfoSource**
The InfoSource for which the InfoPackage was created is displayed.

▶ **DataSource**
The DataSource used for extraction is displayed.

▶ **Data Class**
The type of the data to be transferred is displayed. This data can be both master data such as attributes, texts, or hierarchies, and transaction data.

▶ **Source System**
The source system from which the data is extracted is displayed.

▶ **Last Changed By/Date/Time**
The exact time of the last change and the last person who performed the change is displayed. However, an entry will only appear here once the newly created InfoPackage has been saved.

Maintenance Screen: Lower Area

In the lower area of the maintenance screen, there are four tabs available which you can use to make further settings (see Figure 5.72). These tabs are described in the following sections.

"Data Selection" Tab

You can define the selection values for the InfoPackage on the **Data Selection** tab. You can define selection limits for InfoObjects, which are mapped in the transfer structure, and for unmapped fields of the source system. The fields are displayed in the selection table in the column **Technical name in the source system**. In order to differentiate between InfoObjects and fields, fields are displayed in parentheses (for example, when displaying the initialization selection for source systems in the scheduler).

You can enter individual values or intervals directly in the **From Value** and, if necessary, in the **To Value** fields, or use a variable to limit your selection.

For a DataSource from an SAP source system, the DataSource determines which selection options are possible. All DataSources allow the selection of individual values (sign = 'I' and option = 'EQ') and intervals (sign = 'I' and option = 'BT'). You can enter additional selection options for a data request such as CP, NE, or LE via a routine or variable. These selection options must then be supported by the DataSource to enable a correct data request.

<aside>
DataSources from SAP-source systems
</aside>

When loading the data, the defined selections are checked to determine whether they are supported by the DataSource. If you have defined selections for the data request that are not supported by the DataSource, the data request results with an error.

When using the selection criteria, the data for an InfoObject or field is requested from the source system according to the selection limit. With regard to InfoObjects and fields for which no selection was defined, all available data is requested from the source system.

You can define several selections for an InfoObject or field by inserting duplicate lines. In the selection table, additional lines for making entries for this InfoObject or field are then inserted. If you select individual values or intervals and do not confirm this selection, you can select an additional variable selection type in the same line of the InfoObject or field. The system then automatically inserts another line in the selection table for this selection. Thus, your selections for an InfoObject or field will be clearly displayed.

Data from file systems and external systems You can also define selection criteria for data from files and external systems. In this case, only those records that correspond to the selection criteria will be loaded.

To set selections for a field in the Scheduler, first select the field in the **Selection** column of the transfer structure maintenance and save and activate the transfer structure.

By defining the selection criteria, you can also execute the **Automatic delete** and **Check data consistency functions of requests in InfoCube** for data from files and external systems.

Updating from an ODS object If you want to update data from an ODS object by full update to other data targets, you can define selection criteria for this planning:

► **Conversion exits**
When you enter the selections, the conversion exits displayed in the selection table are executed in the OLTP and the results are temporarily stored in the SAP BW. If the conversion for a selection has already been executed, it is available in SAP BW. If it is not available in SAP BW, it is executed in the OLTP. If the conversion cannot be executed in the OLTP because there is no system access available or the conversion exit is not functioning correctly in the OLTP, the conversion is carried out in SAP BW. If this is not possible, the **Conversion exit** field is ignored, that is, you must enter the selections in the internal format. In this case, entries in the external format cause errors in the load process. If you simply want to switch off the conversion exit, deselect the **Use conversion exit** field. Then, enter the selections in the internal format.

► **Archive selections**
If you reload the data from an archive file, select your archive file using the **Archive Selections** button. Note that initially you can only load archive data within SAP BW.

► If a field of a DataSource is assigned to the InfoObject OLANGU, the field will not be provided as a selection field in the Scheduler although it is available for selection. In this case, all languages of the language vector that is active in SAP BW are implicitly requested by the source system.

► If you load time-dependent data, the time interval is defined in the **Update** tab of the Scheduler. Therefore, the DATETO and DATEFROM fields and the fields that are assigned to the 0DATETO and 0DATEFROM InfoObjects are not available as selection fields in the **Data Selection** tab.

▶ In the selection criteria of the Scheduler, only uppercase letters are permitted. If you enter a value in lowercase letters and confirm this entry, the value is automatically converted into uppercase letters. You can only use lowercase letters if you make the selection using a routine.

"Processing" Tab

In the **Processing** tab, you can maintain settings for the processing of data that has been extracted and transferred from the source system.

Here you can activate a consistency check of the characteristic values. You do this by checking the corresponding flag (see Figure 5.73).

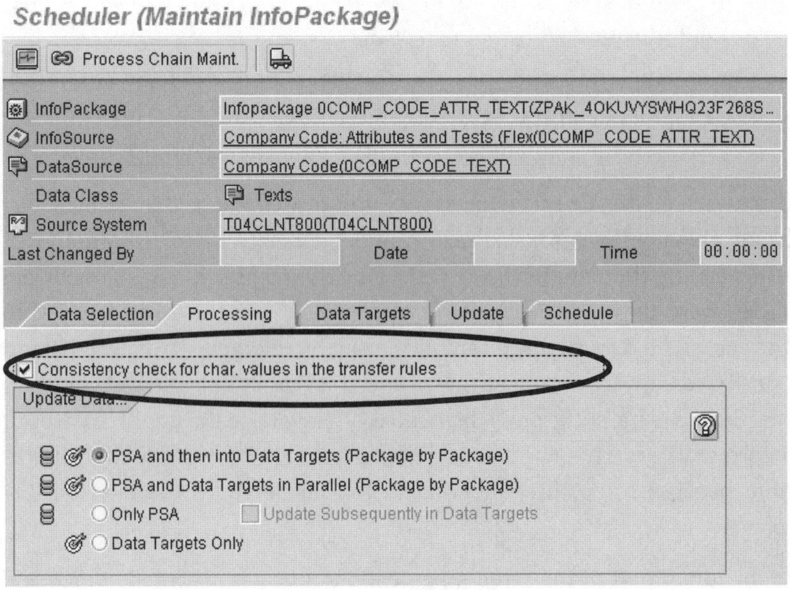

Checking the consistency of characteristics

Figure 5.73 Activating the Consistency Check for the Characteristic Values

When checking the consistency of the characteristic values, the characteristic values are examined for the use of lowercase letters, special characters, the plausibility of the date and time fields, the use of character values in fields of the NUMC data type, and the correct adherence to the ALPHA conversion routine.

► For InfoObjects of the character type, lowercase letters are not permitted as values. Only if the **Characteristic** is exclusively used as a display attribute can you control its permission through the **Lowercase** flag. If you have not selected this flag, the consistency check is performed. Special characters are also not allowed in the characteristic values, the reason being that special characters in the country-specific character sets can be stored at different positions in the ASCII table, and therefore be incorrectly displayed after having been transferred from the source system.

► Date and time fields values must be plausible. For example, for the 0CALMONTH characteristic (calendar year/month), the values 199913 or 121999 are not valid. Appropriate values for this characteristic are the values YYYYMM, where the year must be larger than 1000 and the month must be between 01 and 12 (Y = year, M = month).

► Fields of the NUMC data type can contain only figures.

► Correct adherence to the ALPHA conversion routine means that figures are provided with leading zeros.

► If lowercase letters and special characters are not explicitly permitted, this results in an error for data updates in the InfoCube or in the master data table of the InfoObject. The entire data package is not updated.

If you select the **Check consistency for the characteristic values** flag when planning an InfoPackage in the Scheduler, a check is carried out after reading the data from the PSA/IDoc during the update. If incorrect values exist, they are displayed in the monitor. Once the errors have been corrected, the data package can once again be updated. For new data and non-R/3 data, you should always check this flag during the test phase. If the data is of a sufficiently high quality (several data imports without incorrect values), the flag should be unchecked for the productive operation, because using this functionality further degrades the load performance.

Options for updating data in the InfoPackage In the lower part of the screen, a selection option is provided, which lets you define how the transferred data should be updated. A graphical overview of the update options in the InfoPackage is displayed in Figure 5.74.

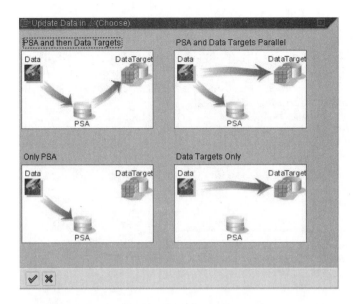

Figure 5.74 Update Options in the InfoPackage

Select the field **PSA and then into Data Targets (Package by Package)**, if you want to first update the data in the PSA table and then update the data in the data targets (see Figure 5.75). In this case, a process is started per data package in order to write the package into the PSA table. If the data has been successfully updated in the PSA table, the same process writes the data into the data targets. The data update takes place sequentially by package. The request processing, on the other hand, occurs at the same time as several processes are used simultaneously for the processing of several data packages.

In PSA and then directly in InfoCube or InfoObject

If you select this processing option and consequently the request processing occurs at the same time as loading, the global data is deleted, because a new process is used for each data package for all further processing.

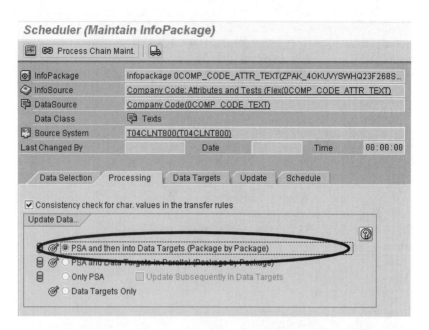

Figure 5.75 Options for Updating Data in the InfoPackage: PSA and Then InfoObject

In PSA and in
InfoCubes or
InfoObject

Select the field **PSA and Data Targets in Parallel (Package by Package)**, if you want to update the data into the PSA table and into the data targets at the same time (see Figure 5.76). Per data package, a process is started in which the data from this data package is written to the PSA table. If the data has successfully been updated in the PSA table, a second, parallel process is started as long as a sufficient number of dialog processes are still available. In this process, the transfer rules are applied for the data records of the package, the data is transferred to the Communication Structure, and then it is written into the data targets. The data update takes place in parallel package by package. The request processing takes place in parallel, too, as several parallel processes are used for several packages. If you select this processing option and the request processing occurs at the same time as loading, the global data is deleted because a new process is used for each data package for all further processing.

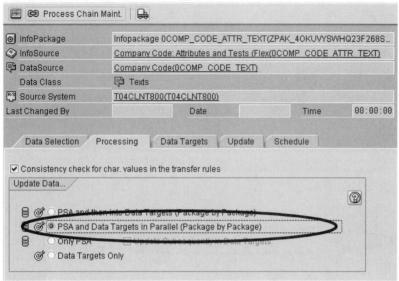

Scheduler (Maintain InfoPackage)

Figure 5.76 Options for Updating Data in the InfoPackage: PSA and InfoObject in Parallel

Select the field **Only PSA** if you want to update only the data into the PSA table, but do not want to update it automatically into the data targets (see Figure 5.77). In this case, a process is started per data package in order to write the package into the PSA table. If you then activate further processing and the data is updated into the data targets, a process is started for the request in order to write the data packages one after another into the data targets. The data update occurs sequentially by request. You can start the further processing manually in the PSA tree as soon as the data request is technically acceptable. You recognize this level of acceptability by the green overall status of the data request in the monitor. If you select this processing option and the request processing occurs sequentially during loading, global data remains available as long as the process by which the data is processed exists.

In PSA but not immediately in InfoCubes or the InfoObject

To activate this update option, check the field **Update Subsequently in Data Targets** (see Figure 5.77). If you check this flag, the data is updated into the data targets after it has been successfully loaded in the PSA. If you use the InfoPackage in a process chain, this setting is hidden in the Scheduler since it is represented in the process chain maintenance by its own process type and is therefore maintained there.

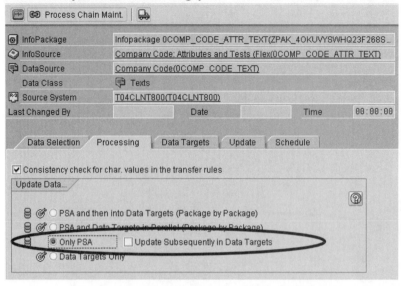

Figure 5.77 Options for Updating Data in the InfoPackage: Only PSA

Only InfoObject

Select the field **Data Targets Only** if you don't want to update the data into the PSA table; instead, you want to update it directly into the data targets (see Figure 5.78). If the update fails, data can be forwarded from the TRFC overview in the source system to SAP BW, depending on the error. Under certain circumstances, however, you may have to request it again. This method has advantages in terms of performance, but runs the risk of losing data. Therefore, we recommend this method only for loading from flat files or from data sources that are always available since the data is not saved in a persistent inbound storage in SAP BW.

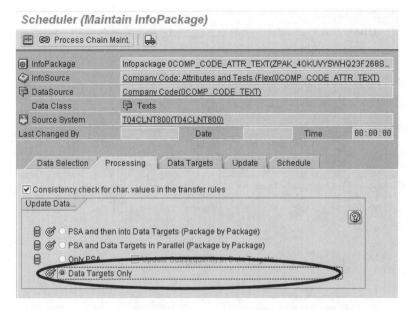

Figure 5.78 Options for Updating Data in the InfoPackage: Only InfoObject

"DataTargets" Tab

In the **Data Targets** tab, you can determine which master data or text table of an InfoObject the data of the data request is to be updated into (see Figure 5.79). You can also navigate from this tab to the update rules maintenance and the data target content maintenance screens.

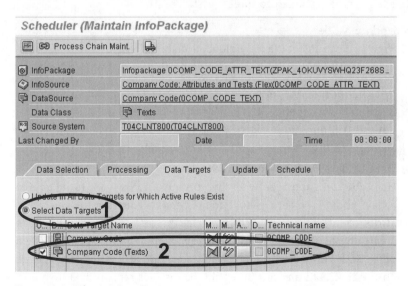

Figure 5.79 Selecting Data Targets

"Update" Tab

In the **Update** tab, you can manipulate the data update into the data target (see Figure 5.80).

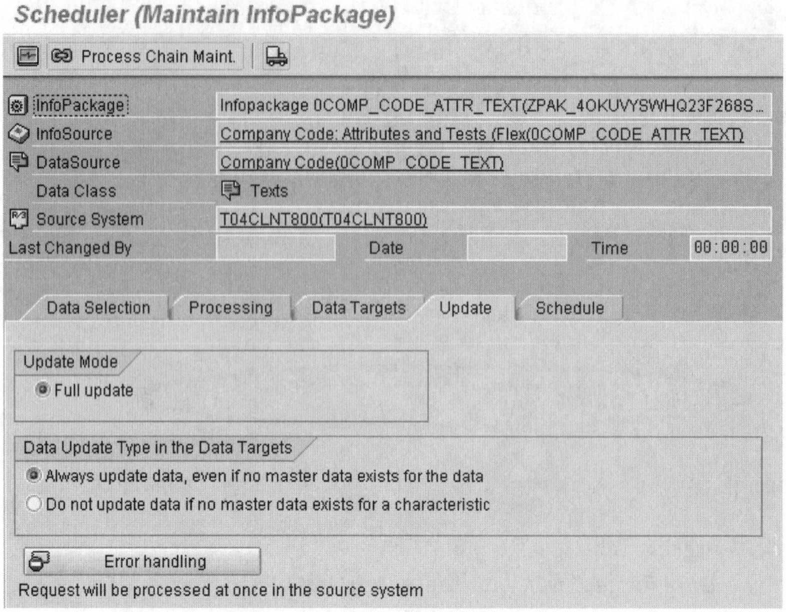

Scheduler (Maintain InfoPackage)

⊞ ⭫ Process Chain Maint.	⬚

⚙ InfoPackage	Infopackage 0COMP_CODE_ATTR_TEXT(ZPAK_4OKUVYSWHQ23F268S...
◈ InfoSource	Company Code: Attributes and Tests (Flex(0COMP_CODE_ATTR_TEXT)
▣ DataSource	Company Code(0COMP_CODE_TEXT)
Data Class	▣ Texts
▣ Source System	T04CLNT800(T04CLNT800)
Last Changed By	Date	Time	00:00:00

Data Selection	Processing	Data Targets	Update	Schedule

Update Mode
- ⦿ Full update

Data Update Type in the Data Targets
- ⦿ Always update data, even if no master data exists for the data
- ◯ Do not update data if no master data exists for a characteristic

⬚ Error handling

Request will be processed at once in the source system

Figure 5.80 Setting Options for the InfoPackage "Update" Tab

This tab can be divided into three parts:

▸ **Update Mode**
Here you can select if a full upload, a delta upload, or an initialization upload for a later delta upload should be started by the InfoPackage.

Whether or not you are provided with a selection option at this point is completely dependent on the nature of the DataSource. Further options will only be provided if the DataSource is delta-capable. The DataSource displayed in Figure 5.80 is not delta-capable.

Updating data ▸ **Data Update Type in the Data Targets**
Here you can choose between two options. If you want to be able to always update the data, even if no master data exists for the navigation attributes of the loaded records, select the first option. You can then create the master data from the loaded transaction data. The system pulls SIDs. You can also load the master data at a later stage. Please ensure that texts and attributes and hierarchies remain unknown during this process. We generally recommend that you do not set this flag

for productive systems and thus ensure a prior loading of relevant master data that you can also monitor. In our opinion, selecting this flag is only useful for test purposes.

The purpose of the second option is to achieve the exact opposite, that is, no data is updated in the data targets if no master data exists for a characteristic. This option is only active for ODS objects if the **BEx Reporting** flag is checked in the ODS maintenance. If you select this radio button, you must publish the master data of all relevant characteristics in SAP BW prior to loading the transaction data.

▶ **Error handling**
Here you can define how the system should respond in the event of errors (see Figure 5.81). In this context, you can determine the number of data records to be accepted when handling erroneous data records. If more errors occur, the load process is canceled; however, errors that have occurred up to that point can be displayed in the PSA. If you don't enter anything here, no erroneous data records will be accepted, and error handling will be switched off.

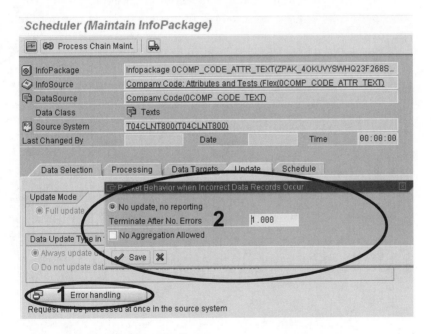

Figure 5.81 Options for Error Handling

If you set the **No Aggregation Allowed** flag, the request is assessed as containing an error when the number of records received in SAP BW does not correspond to the number of updated records, that is, if in

"No Aggregation Allowed"

transfer rules, update rules, or updates, records have been sorted, aggregated, or inserted. If the number of selected records does not correspond to the number of records received in SAP BW, this will be considered as containing an error, independently of this flag.

"Schedule" Tab

In the **Schedule** tab, you can choose when you want to load the selected data (see Figure 5.82). Basically, an immediate data load is differentiated from a loading of data at later point in time. This differentiation is also based on technical facts. For example, an immediate data load corresponds to a synchronous process that is executed in the dialog. A load at a later stage is executed asynchronously using a batch process.

If you check the **Start Data Load Immediately** radio button, and confirm this by clicking on the **Start** button (**F8**), a request IDoc is automatically sent to the source system to start the load process.

If, however, you decide on an asynchronous data load in the background, check the **Start Later in Background** radio button. A more detailed window opens, whereby you are prompted to define the start time for the data load.

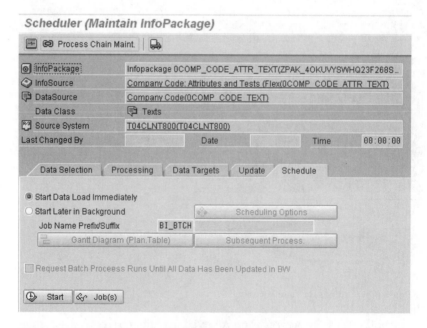

Figure 5.82 Immediate Data Load in the Dialog Process

Several options are provided here:

▶ **Immediate start**

The loading of the required data is started immediately. Unlike the load procedure previously described, here, a background process (batch) is used to perform the load process. The number of dialog processes that users need for their work in SAP BW is not reduced. A period interval can be defined for this start method. At the end of this interval, the load process is constantly repeated (see Figure 5.83).

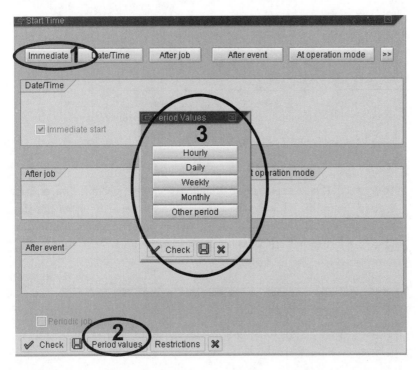

Figure 5.83 Immediate Data Loading in the Batch Process and Defining a Repetitive Period

▶ **Date/Time**

You can use this option to define at what time the load process is to be triggered. To do this, you must maintain the exact date and time. In addition, you can also define the latest possible time to execute this InfoPackage in the eventuality of system delays. If this time is exceeded, the scheduling is no longer executed (see Figure 5.84).

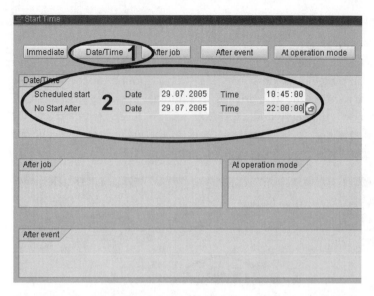

Figure 5.84 The InfoPackage Is Executed After an Exact Time Is Defined

▶ **After job**
  You can define a specific job that exists in the system. The data is loaded when this job is finished. You can also specify whether the status of the completed job is relevant. When you check this option, the load process is initiated only if the job referred to was successfully completed (see Figure 5.85).

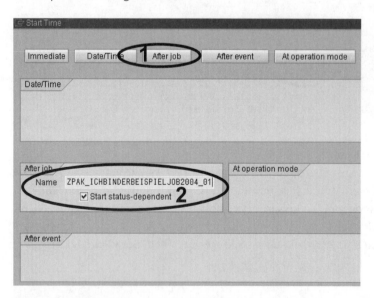

Figure 5.85 The InfoPackage Is Performed After a Specific Job

▶ **After event**

An event indicates that a predefined state has been achieved in the system. The background processing system receives events and then starts the background job or jobs that are linked with an event. If you use this option, you can determine after which event the loading of your data begins (see Figure 5.86).

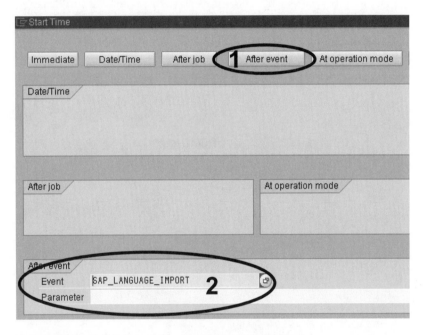

Figure 5.86 The InfoPackage Is Executed After a Specific Event

▶ **At operation mode**

The load process is started if a specific operation mode has been switched to in SAP BW. A menu (**F4**) is provided for selecting the corresponding operation mode (see Figure 5.87).

▶ **Additional options**

▷ A factory calendar is also provided as a further option. You can start the InfoPackage using the settings defined here (see Figure 5.88).

▷ Using the **Gantt Diagram (Plan.Table)** button, you can access a tool developed by SAP that displays your schedulings in a timeline (Figure 5.89).

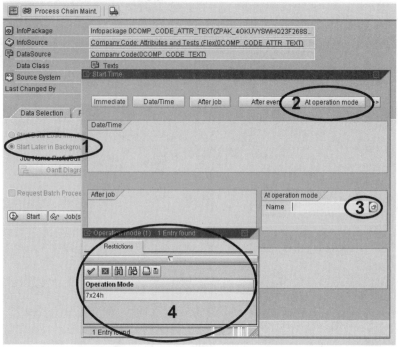

Figure 5.87 The InfoPackage Is Executed When You Switch to a Specific Operation Mode

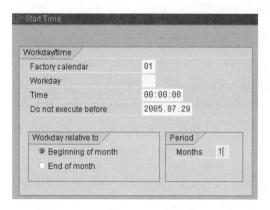

Figure 5.88 The Execution Is Carried Out According to the Factory Calendar Settings

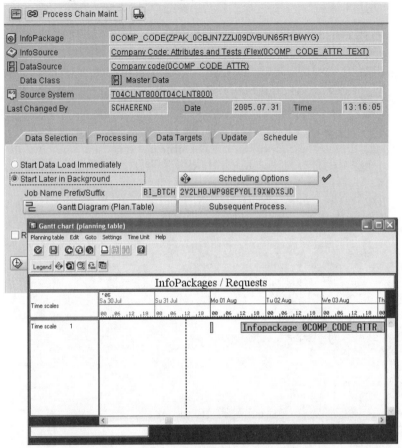

Scheduler (Maintain InfoPackage)

⚙ InfoPackage	0COMP_CODE(ZPAK_0CBJN7ZZIJ09DVBUN65R1BWYG)	
◇ InfoSource	Company Code: Attributes and Tests (Flex(0COMP_CODE_ATTR_TEXT)	
🔲 DataSource	Company code(0COMP_CODE_ATTR)	
Data Class	🔲 Master Data	
🔲 Source System	T04CLNT800(T04CLNT800)	
Last Changed By	SCHAEREND Date 2005.07.31 Time 13:16:05	

Data Selection | Processing | Data Targets | Update | Schedule

○ Start Data Load Immediately
◉ Start Later in Background   Scheduling Options
   Job Name Prefix/Suffix   BI_BTCH 2V2LH0JWP98EPY0LI9XWDXSJD
   Gantt Diagram (Plan.Table)   Subsequent Process.

Figure 5.89 The SAP Planning Table to Show Scheduled Load Processes

▶ Using the **Subsequent Processing** button, you can select methods that are always executed after the load process (see Figure 5.90).

Figure 5.90 Selecting Post-Processing Methods After the Load Process

Triggering Events

▶ When the data load process is completed, an event can be triggered.

▶ Depending on whether the load process was successful (green) or unsuccessful (red), different events can be triggered. At the same time, you can also define the execution of business add-ins.

▶ By clicking on the **Start** button, you can save the settings. Jobs that are generated by this action are then scheduled and activated.

▶ After triggering a load process using an InfoPackage, you can go to this load process by clicking on the **Monitor** button. There you have the option of analyzing the load process triggered by the InfoPackage and if necessary, correcting errors that might have occurred (see Figure 5.91).

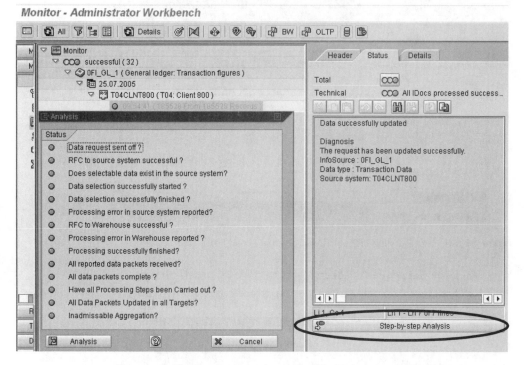

Figure 5.91 The Monitor Is the Central Tool for Monitoring and Analyzing Data Load Processes

5.6.6 Hierarchies

Until now, we have described the ETL process for master data in the form of attributes and texts. In this context, you have been provided with the option of direct or flexible updates.

In addition, you can also provide data to hierarchies using an ETL process. The advantage of hierarchies is that you can use them for analysis and get different views of the data. This type of transfer involves assigning a certain set of nodes that have a parent-child relationship with each other. An update of this assignment is only possible in the form of a direct update (see Figure 5.92).

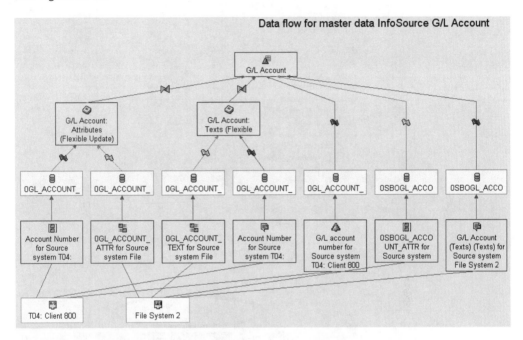

Figure 5.92 Texts and Attributes Can Be Flexible and Directly Updated. Hierarchies Can Only Be Directly Updated.

Implementing Master Data Acquisition via Hierarchies

We will now describe how you can implement master data acquisition in the SAP R/3 source system by setting up hierarchies.

▶ First, you must assign the corresponding hierarchy DataSource of the SAP R/3 system as a source to retrieve hierarchy data to the InfoSource of the SAP BW system. This assignment is identical to the process used for master data in the form of texts and attributes, which was described in Section 5.6.1 and is illustrated once more in Figure 5.93 and Figure 5.94.

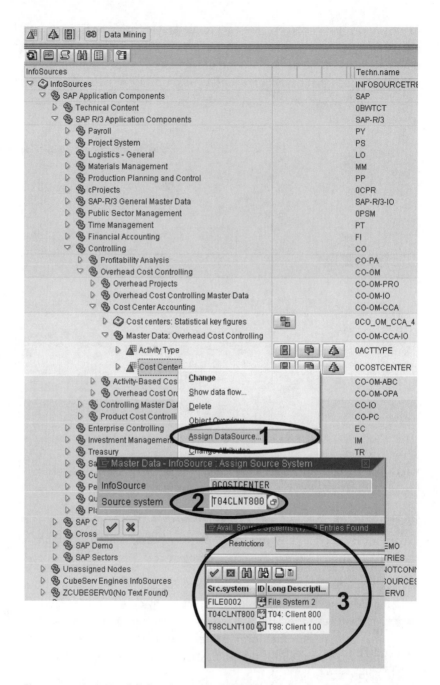

Figure 5.93 Assigning R/3 DataSources to SAP BW InfoSources—Part 1

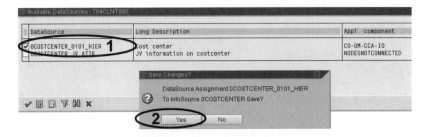

Figure 5.94 Assigning R/3 DataSources to SAP BW InfoSources—Part 2

▶ Once the assignment has been completed, the InfoSource of the data target will be displayed. In its **DataSource/Transfer Structure** tab, this InfoSource displays the fields provided by SAP R/3 that are used to map the hierarchy in the source system.

Setting up the InfoSource

▶ In the white administrable fields of the **InfoObject** column, you must enter those InfoObjects that you want to use to map the hierarchy in SAP BW (see Figure 5.95). There are no other adminstration options available.

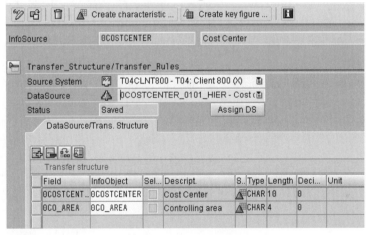

Figure 5.95 Administering a Hierarchy InfoSource

▶ After the InfoSource has been entered, you must save it (select **Save** from the context menu in Figure 5.96). You don't need to activate it as you did with regard to the attributes and texts areas.

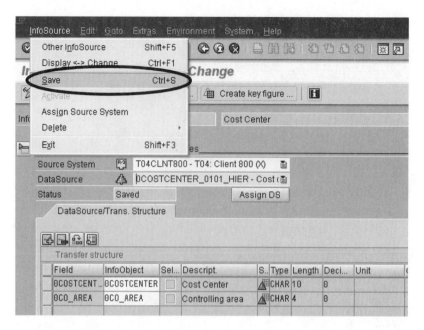

Figure 5.96 Saving a Hierarchy InfoSource

▶ After saving the InfoSource, you can create InfoPackages exactly in the same way as you did for master data in the form of texts and attributes, which you can use to load your hierarchies from the SAP R/3 system into SAP BW.

▶ InfoPackages used to load hierarchies are created in the exact same way as described in the process in Section 5.6.5. This method is once again illustrated in Figure 5.97.

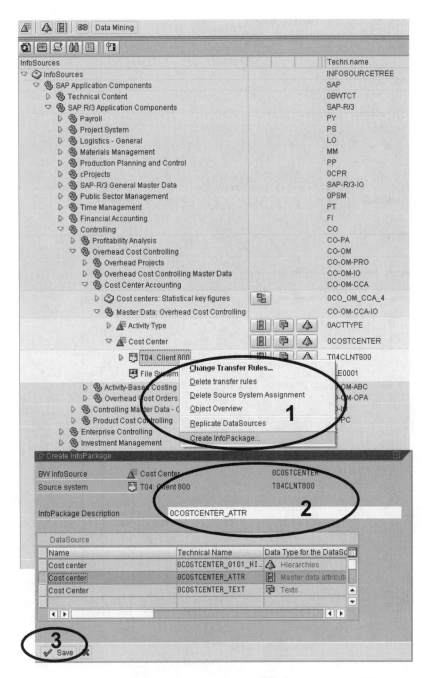

Figure 5.97 Creating an InfoPackage to Transfer Hierarchies

Setting Up an InfoPackage

After the InfoPackage has been created, four tabs are once again provided, which enable you to define additional settings for the ETL process (see Figure 5.98).

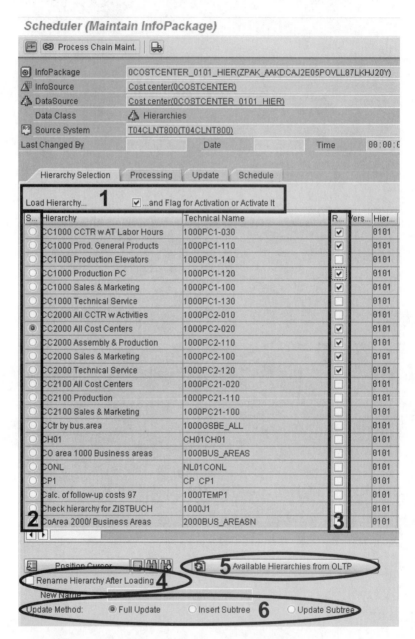

Figure 5.98 Creating an InfoPackage to Transfer Hierarchies

"Hierarchy Selection" Tab

In the **Hierarchy Selection** tab, you can define the following settings:

▶ **Load Hierarchy and Flag for Activation or Activate It** (see Figure 5.98, selection 1)
In order to automatically activate the hierarchy after a successful loading, select this field. The hierarchy cannot be activated if it is used in an aggregate. In that case, it will be marked for a later activation. The hierarchy is then automatically activated the next time the hierarchy attributes are changed.

A non-active hierarchy is not used in queries!

▶ **Selected** (selection 2)
Here you should select the hierarchy that you would like to load in SAP BW using the InfoPackage.

▶ **Relevant for BW** (selection 3)
Here you should select all hierarchies that you think are relevant for operating your SAP BW.

▶ **Rename Hierarchy After Loading** (selection 4)
Set this flag if you want to rename the loaded hierarchy in SAP BW. To do this, you must enter the new name that the hierarchy should have in SAP BW.

▶ **Available Hierarchies from OLTP** (selection 5)
By clicking on this button, the hierarchies from the source system are updated and displayed in the InfoPackage.

▶ **Update Method** (selection 6)
Select one of the three different options to store a loaded hierarchy in SAP BW:

  ▶ **Full Update**
  The hierarchy is stored under the selected technical name. A hierarchy that already exists in SAP BW will be overwritten in this case.

  ▶ **Insert Subtree**
  The hierarchy is inserted as a subtree without deleting nodes in the original hierarchy. If a hierarchy is inserted twice as a subtree, for example, it is available twice in the target hierarchy.

  ▶ **Update Subtree**
  The hierarchy is inserted as a subtree, however, all nodes in the target hierarchy that are located under the interface node will be

deleted. Contrary to inserting a subtree, the old subtree is replaced by the new one during a new upload.

"Processing" Tab

Now, you can choose the update type and specify a consistency check for the character values in the transfer rules (see Figure 5.99):

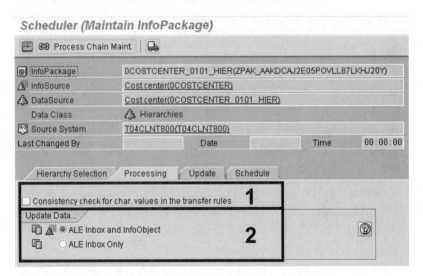

Figure 5.99 Administration Options for Processing Within an InfoPackage for Hierarchies

▶ **Consistency check for characteristic values** (see Figure 5.99, selection 1)
When performing consistency checks on characteristic values, the characteristic values are examined against the following criteria:

- ▶ Use of lowercase letters
- ▶ Use of special characters
- ▶ Plausibility of the date fields
- ▶ Plausibility of the time fields
- ▶ Use of letter values in fields of the data type NUMC
- ▶ Correct use of the conversion routine ALPHA

▶ **Update Data** (selection 2)
Here you can determine how the hierarchy data should be updated. The following two options are available to do this (see Figure 5.100):

- ▶ **ALE Inbox and InfoObject**
  If you select this field, the data is loaded via an IDoc into the ALE inbox of SAP BW and is immediately further updated in the master

data table of an InfoObject. This corresponds to the standard setting.

▶ **ALE Inbox Only**
If you select this field, the data is only loaded in the ALE inbox of SAP BW and not updated immediately into the data target.

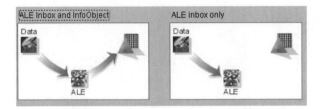

Figure 5.100 Visual Display of the Update Options

"Update" Tab
The update of a hierarchy always takes place via a full update. This means that you cannot generate a delta here. The tab provides the settings displayed in Figure 5.101:

▶ **Update Mode** (see Figure 5.101, selection 1)
When you select **Full update**, all data belonging to the InfoPackage and corresponding to the selection criteria defined in the Scheduler is loaded from the source system into SAP BW.

▶ **Error handling** (selection 2)
You can set error handling during the update using the **Error handling** button. Here you have the following options (selection 3):

▶ **No update, no reporting**
This flag is constantly checked. No update takes place when an error has occurred during the update. Consequently, no data is available for reporting.

▶ **Terminate After No. Errors**
Here you can specify after which number of errors the update is canceled.

▶ **No Aggregation Allowed**
If you check this flag, the request is deemed as containing an error, if the number of records received in SAP BW does not match the number of updated records (that is, in cases where records are sorted, aggregated, or inserted in the transfer rules, update rules, or update).

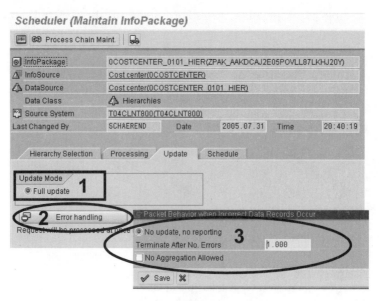

Figure 5.101 Update Options in the InfoPackage for Hierarchies

"Schedule" Tab

In the **Schedule** tab, you can choose at what time you want to load your hierarchy data (see Figure 5.102). Because all possible settings are identical to those settings described in Section 5.6.5, this reference alone should suffice.

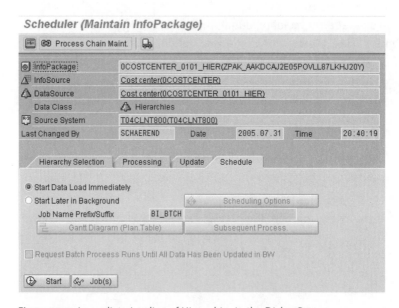

Figure 5.102 Immediate Loading of Hierarchies in the Dialog Process

6 ETL Process: Transaction Data

While master data serves as the foundation for all analytical applications, the main analysis generally relies on transaction data. The timely and accurate provision of transaction data is critical for the productive usability of business intelligence solutions. Chapter 6 introduces you to the basics of transaction data retrieval for the SAP Business Information Warehouse.

6.1 Exemplary Transaction Data Retrieval for Profitability Analysis

6.1.1 Delivering Interface Files for Profitability Analysis

Different units of our model company "CubeServ Engines" must supply the transaction data for profitability analysis through interface files, because they don't contain a productive SAP profitability analysis (CO-PA) or similar components that provide data for profitability analysis via interface files. To this extent, the extraction, transformation, and loading (ETL) process is reduced by the actual extraction in this case since the extraction is sometimes omitted if necessary (if the data for the interface file is to be manually entered), or created in the corresponding transaction systems through individual programming.

Delivery using a flat file

As is the case with master data retrieval, from the SAP BW viewpoint, the ETL process begins with the transfer structure and flows with the transfer rules in a communication structure that may be used with other source systems. Then, you can use the update rules for the various source systems.

Specific ETL-components for interface files

Creating Source System Files

Processing the interface files is performed using a dedicated source system, FILE0001. To do this, carry out the following steps:

▶ Call the **Source systems** view (Transaction RSA13) in the **Administrator Workbench**.

▶ Open the **Source Systems** in the upper hierarchy node by right-clicking on the context-sensitive menu and select **Create** (see Figure 6.1, Step 1).

▶ In the **Select Source System Type** popup, select the type **File System (Manual Metadata, Data Using File Interface)** and click on the **Enter** button (Steps 2 and 3).

▶ In the **Create Source System** popup, enter the logical system name and the name of the source system and confirm your entry by clicking on the **Enter** button (Steps 4 and 5).

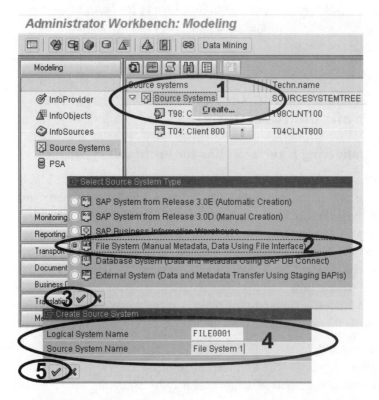

Figure 6.1 Creating the Source System File

The source system is then available for configuring the ETL process (see Figure 6.2).

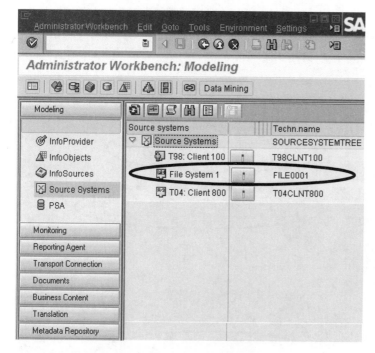

Figure 6.2 The Source System "File Interface 1"

Creating an Application Component

InfoSources that are not based on SAP Business Content InfoSources must be assigned their own application components according to the conceptional requirements of our model company. Therefore, these application components must be created.

▶ Creating customer-specific application components is carried out in the **InfoSources** view of the **Administrator Workbench** (Transaction RSA12).

▶ Open the context-sensitive menu by right-clicking on **InfoSources** in the upper hierarchy node and then select the **Create application component** (see Figure 6.3, Step 1).

▶ In the **Create Application Components** popup, enter the technical name as well as the description of the application component and confirm your entry by clicking on the **Enter** button (Steps 2 and 3).

▶ Then the new application component is available to be assigned to InfoSources or other (sub-) application components (Step 4).

▶ You can create other (downstream) application components by once again right-clicking on an application component to open the context-sensitive menu and selecting the **Create...** menu option (Step 5).

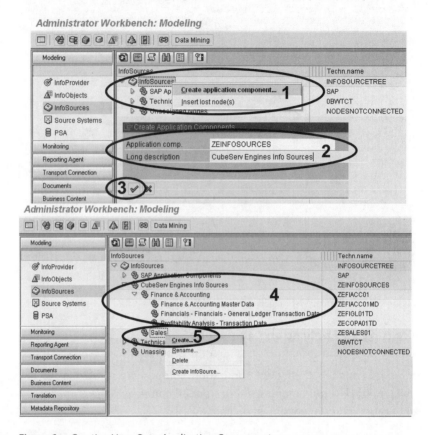

Figure 6.3 Creating Your Own Application Components

Defining Metadata for the Source System Type "File System"

As you can see from the description of the source system type **File System**, you must describe the metadata manually.

▶ You can do this in the **InfoSources** view of the **Administrator Workbench** (Transaction RSA12).

▶ To carry out the configuration of such a transfer structure, you can use an existing InfoSources. If such an InfoSource doesn't exist, you must create it.

Creating an InfoSource

▶ InfoSources are created in the **InfoSources** view of the **Administrator Workbench**. To create InfoSources, you must click on the application components for which you want to assign the InfoSource.

▶ Right-click to open the context-sensitive menu and select the **Create InfoSource...** menu option (see Figure 6.4, Steps 1 and 2).

▶ In the **Create InfoSource** popup, select the relevant InfoSource type. For transaction data, this is the **Flexible Update in any Data Target (Except Hierarchies)** type.

▶ For this type, enter the name of the InfoSource and the description and click on **Enter** (Steps 3 and 4).

▶ Subsequently, the InfoSource is available in the application components hierarchy of the Administrator Workbench (Step 5).

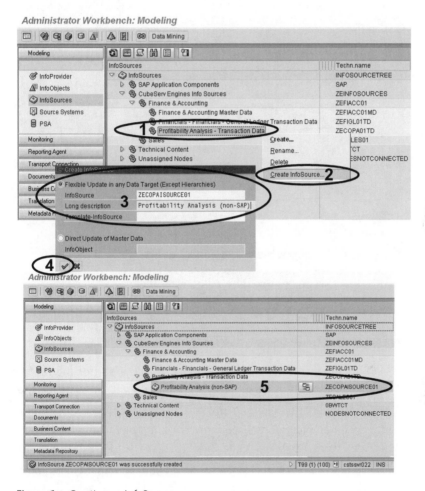

Figure 6.4 Creating an InfoSource

<cell>Assigning a
DataSource</cell>
▶ Then, select the InfoSource. Right-click to open the context-sensitive menu and select the **Assign DataSource...** menu option (see Figure 6.5, Steps 1 and 2).

▶ In the **Transaction Data-InfoSource**: **Assign Source System** popup, enter the name of the file source system, or select it using the drop-down menu and click on the **Enter** button (Steps 3 and 4).

▶ When prompted to save changes, click on **Yes** (Step 5).

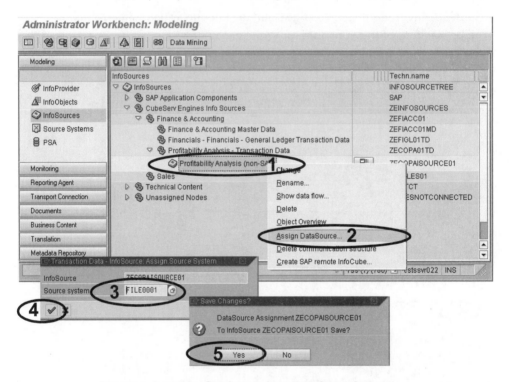

Figure 6.5 Assigning a DataSource: Assigning a Source System

<cell>Defining a transfer
structure</cell>
▶ The **InfoSource ... Change** screen opens. As required (for the model company in our example, see also Appendix B), you must define the transfer structure in that screen.

▶ Enter the InfoObjects in the sequence specified by the interface structure (see Figure 6.6, Steps 1 and 2).

▶ Because (according to our concept of the model company) each data delivery can contain only data of its own DataSource as well as the period to be delivered, you must check the **Selection** flag for the source system and the fiscal year/period (Steps 3 and 4, see Section *InfoPackage* below).

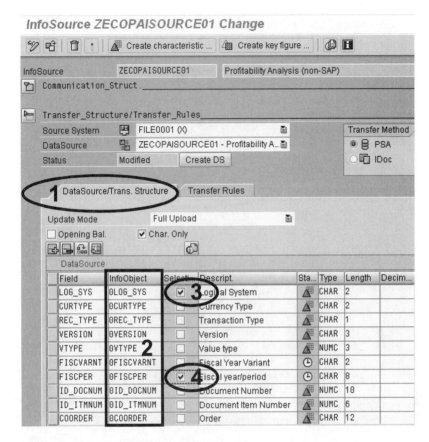

InfoSource ZECOPAISOURCE01 Change

InfoSource	ZECOPAISOURCE01	Profitability Analysis (non-SAP)		

Communication_Struct.

Transfer_Structure/Transfer_Rules

Source System	FILE0001 (X)		Transfer Method
DataSource	ZECOPAISOURCE01 - Profitability A...		● 🖥 PSA
Status	Modified	Create DS	○ 🖳 IDoc

1 DataSource/Trans. Structure   Transfer Rules

Update Mode	Full Upload
☐ Opening Bal.	☑ Char. Only

DataSource

Field	InfoObject	Select.	Descript.	Sta...	Type	Length	Decim...
LOG_SYS	0LOG_SYS	☑ **3**	Logical System		CHAR	2	
CURTYPE	0CURTYPE	☐	Currency Type		CHAR	2	
REC_TYPE	0REC_TYPE	☐	Transaction Type		CHAR	1	
VERSION	0VERSION	☐	Version		CHAR	3	
VTYPE	0VTYPE **2**	☐	Value type		NUMC	3	
FISCVARNT	0FISCVARNT	☐	Fiscal Year Variant		CHAR	2	
FISCPER	0FISCPER	☑ **4**	Fiscal year/period		CHAR	8	
ID_DOCNUM	0ID_DOCNUM	☐	Document Number		NUMC	10	
ID_ITMNUM	0ID_ITMNUM	☐	Document Item Number		NUMC	6	
COORDER	0COORDER	☐	Order		CHAR	12	

Figure 6.6 Defining a Transfer Structure

Defining Transfer Rules and Communication Structure

On the basis of the transfer structure, you can then create the transfer rules and the communication structure.

▶ Select the **Transfer Rules** tab (see Figure 6.7, Step 1).

▶ Click on the **Suggest Transfer Rules** button (Step 2).

▶ Confirm the information popup (Step 3).

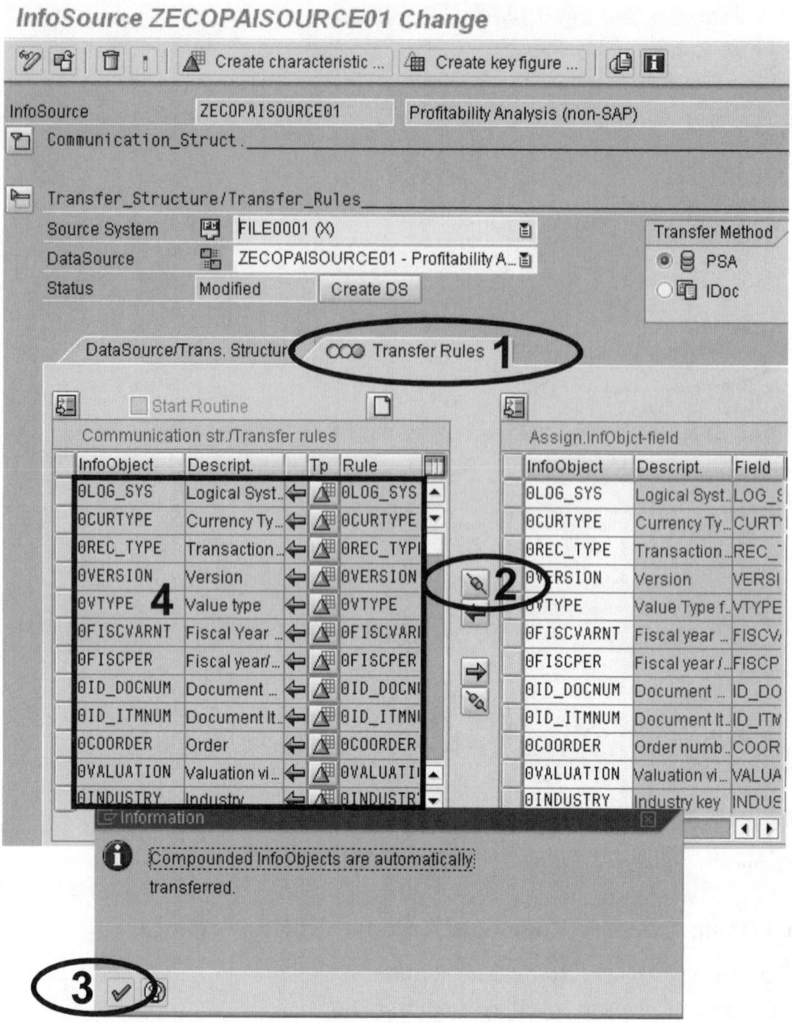

InfoSource ZECOPAISOURCE01 Change

Figure 6.7 Suggesting Transfer Rules

▶ The SAP BW system transfers all InfoObjects of the transfer structure into the transfer rules (see Figure 6.7, Step 4) and creates a communication structure (see Figure 6.8, Step 2).

▶ This can be displayed by clicking on the **Expand Communication structure** button (see Figure 6.8, Step 1).

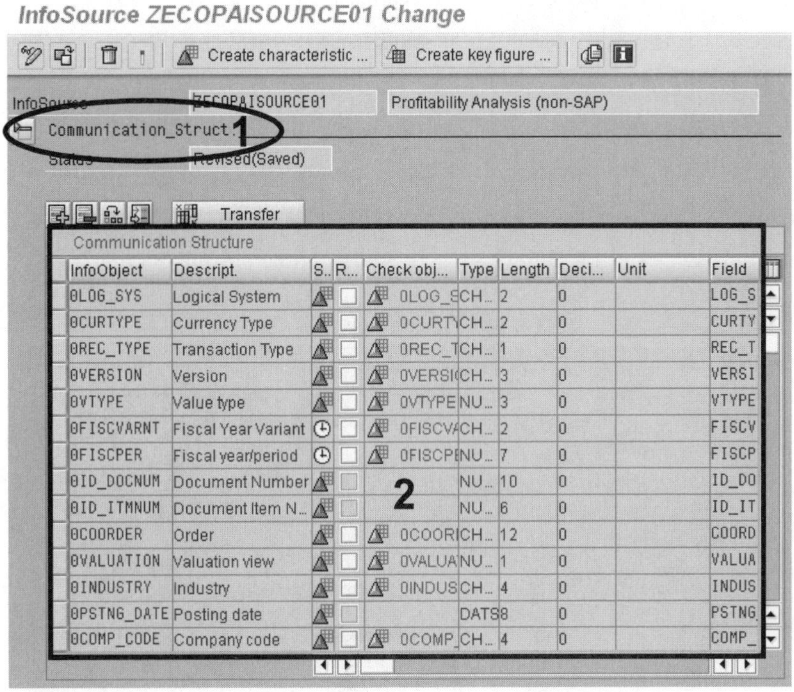

InfoSource ZECOPAISOURCE01 Change

Figure 6.8 The Suggested Communication Structure is Based on the Suggested Transfer Rules

Postprocessing the Communication Structure and Transfer Rules

The suggested communication structure does not completely correspond to the requirements in this case, because the data target to be assigned (the ODS object **Profitability Analysis** with the technical name ZECOPAO1 created in the first volume of the SAP BW Library)[1] contains different fields (see Figures 6.9 and 6.10) and also additional fields (see Figures 6.13 through 6.15).

On the one hand this was forced by SAP BW: The InfoObject **Source System** (0SOURSYSTEM) must not contained in transfer structures. Consequently, the InfoObject **Logical System** (0LOG_SYS) that references the InfoObject 0SOURSYSTEM was used as a transfer structure component.

Specific characteristic of the InfoObject 0SOURSYSTEM

On the other hand, the communication structure in the model company *CubeServ Engines* should already contain the final InfoObjects to ensure that the elements in the data targets are uniform. Therefore, you must

---

1 See Egger, Fiechter, Rohlf: *SAP BW Data Modeling*. SAP PRESS 2005.

replace the InfoObject **Logical System** (0LOG_SYS) in the communication structure with the InfoObject **Source System** (0SOURSYSTEM). You must adjust the transfer rules correspondingly.

Deleting a transfer rule

Before you can adjust the transfer rules, you must delete the transfer rule of the InfoObject 0LOG_SYS:

▶ Select the transfer rule for this InfoObject (see Figure 6.9, Steps 1 and 2).

▶ Then, click on the **Delete selected rules** button (Steps 3 and 4).

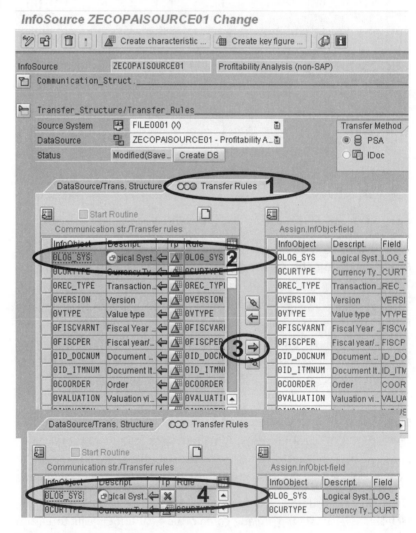

Figure 6.9 Deleting the Transfer Rules

Then you can change the communication structure:

Changing the communication structure

▶ Display the communication structure by clicking on the **Expand** button (see Figure 6.10, Step 1).

▶ Select the InfoObject **Logical System** (0LOG_SYS) to be deleted from the communication structure and click on the **Delete selected lines** button (Steps 2 and 3).

▶ Add the InfoObject 0SOURSYSTEM (Step 4—if this is not already contained in the communication structure due to compounding).

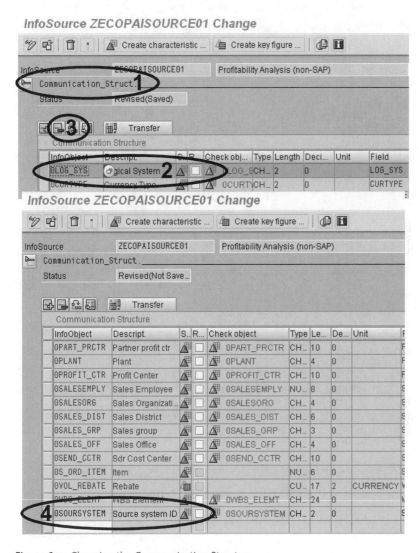

Figure 6.10 Changing the Communication Structure

In the next step, the transfer rule is set up:

▶ On the InfoObject to be set up, select the button for editing transfer rules in the **Transfer Rules** tab (see Figure 6.11, Steps 1 and 2).

▶ Then, select the field to be assigned from the transfer structure, or enter the technical name of the InfoObject and confirm the assignment by clicking on the **Enter** button (Steps 3 and 4).

▶ The transfer rule is now set up (Step 5).

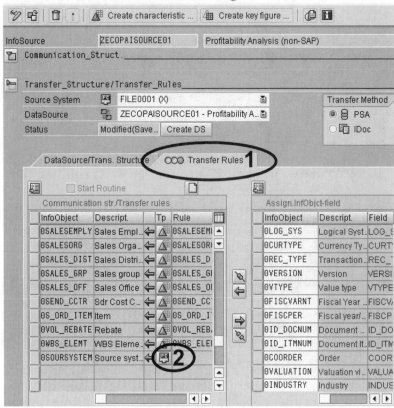

Figure 6.11a Transfer Rule for the InfoObject "Source System"—Part 1

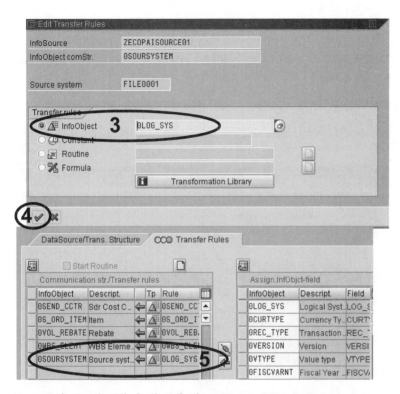

Figure 6.11b Transfer Rule for the InfoObject "Source System" — Part 2

Implementing the Local Characteristics "Version" and "Value Type"

In addition, the file interface for the identification of actual and plan data provides the InfoObjects **Version** (0VERSION) and **Value Type** (0VTYPE) that contain local characteristics of the source system. According to our concept of the model company (see Chapter 3, *Sample Scenario*), these characteristics must be converted to the InfoObject **Harmonized (reporting) version** ZEVERSION that is used throughout SAP BW at CubeServ Engines.

According to the conceptual considerations of the case study, the implementation should take place by using tables.

Derivation table

▶ To do this, you must create an InfoObject ZEVERSABL to derive the harmonized version from the characteristics **Source System**, **Version**, and **Value Type**.[2]

---

2 Compare the procedure implemented in Egger, Fiechter, Rohlf: *SAP BW Data Modeling*. SAP PRESS 2005, Section 5.5.

▶ In the master data maintenance for this InfoObject, you can enter the assignments of the harmonized version for the valid combinations of the characteristic attributes **Source System**, **Version**, and **Value Type** (see the sample data in Figure 6.12).

Figure 6.12 InfoObject for Deriving a Harmonized Version

Start routine ▶ To minimize the number of database accesses, you must ensure that the control data required to derive the harmonized version is read into the start routine of the InfoSource. You can create the start routine by clicking on the **Create Start Routine** button in the transfer rules (see Figure 6.13, Steps 1 and 2).

You must load the control data into an internal table so that the control table data is available when the provided data records are processed later on:

▶ To do this, in a global declaration section (after ***$*$ begin of global**) declare the table in the routine (see the following **TABLES:** ...) and a similarly structured internal table (see the following **DATA:** ...) (see Figure 6.13, Step 3).

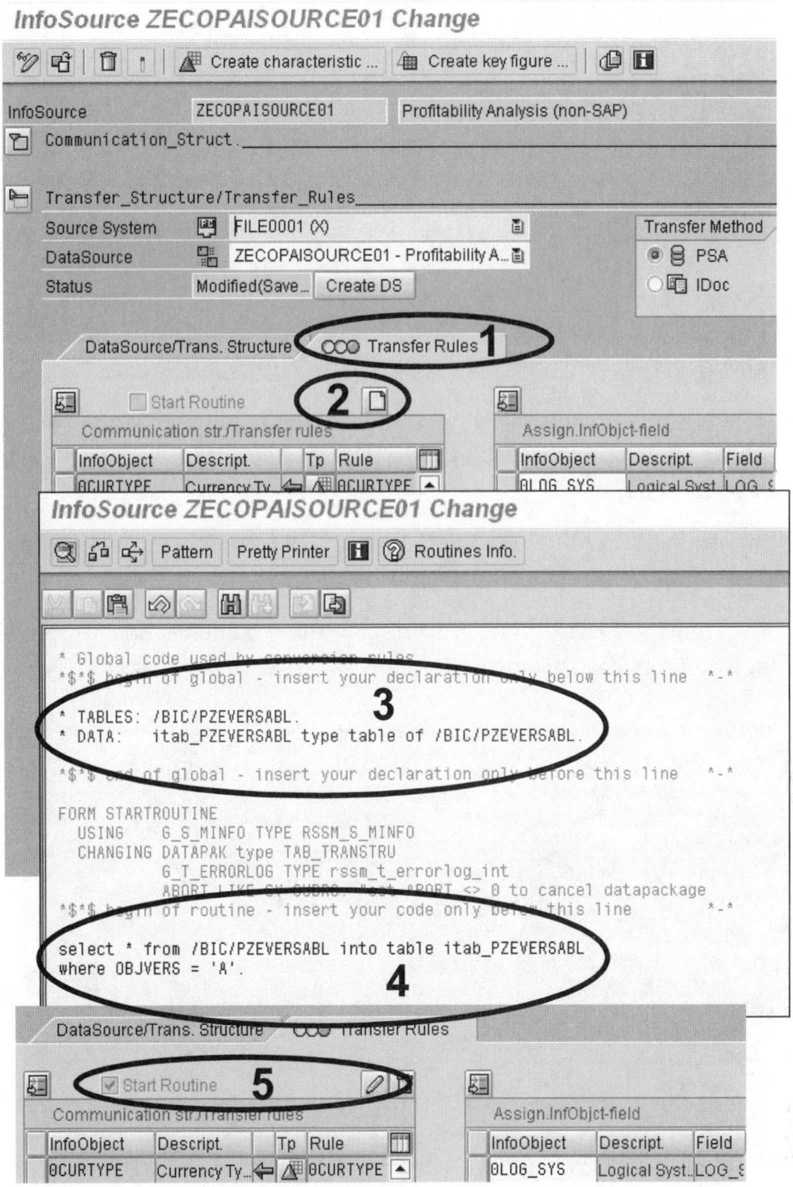

InfoSource ZECOPAISOURCE01 Change

Figure 6.13 Creating a Start Routine

▶ The control table data is read in the routine itself (after ***$*$ begin of routine**) by using a SELECT statement. Because you can use only active control table data, you must select **OBJVERS = 'A'** in the SELECT statement (Step 4):

Coding the start routine

```
* Global code used by conversion rules
*$*$ begin of global - insert your declaration only
below
TABLES: /BIC/PZEVERSABL.
DATA:   itab_PZEVERSABL type table of /BIC/PZEVERSABL.
*$*$ end of global - insert your declaration only before
FORM STARTROUTINE
...
*$*$ begin of routine - insert your code only below
select * from /BIC/PZEVERSABL into table itab_PZEVERSABL
where OBJVERS = 'A'.
```

▶ When you have completed the coding, save the routine. The existence of the start routine is displayed in the transfer rules (see Figure 6.13, Step 5).

Enhancing the communication structure Now you must add the InfoObject **Version (Reporting)** (ZEVERSION) to the communication structure:

▶ Click on the **Expand** button to display the communication structure and add the InfoObject (see Figure 6.14, Steps 1 and 2).

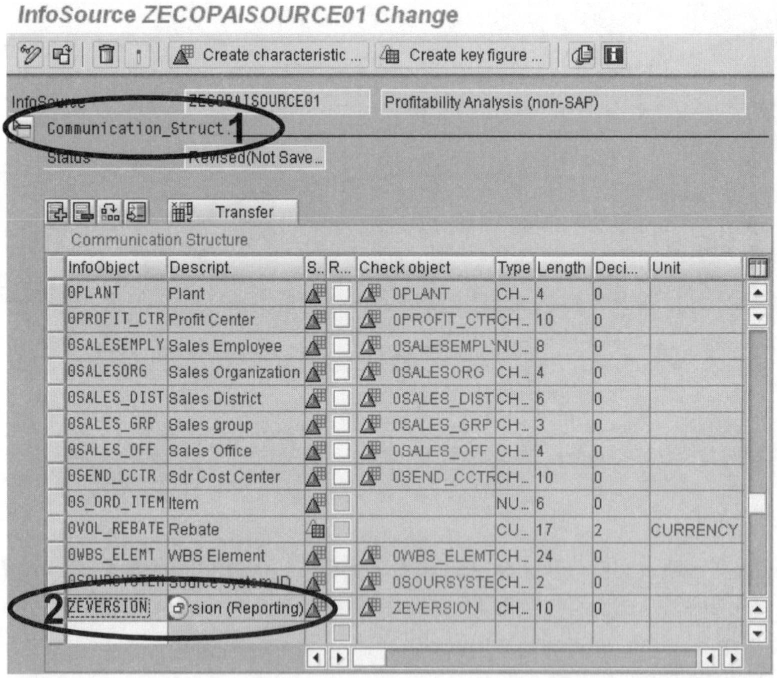

Figure 6.14 Enhancing the Communication Structure

Then you create the routine for the InfoObject **Version (Reporting)**
(ZVERSION):

▶ In the transfer rules, click on the button for setting up the transfer rule for the harmonized version (see Figure 6.15, Steps 1 and 2).

▶ In the **Edit Transfer Rules** dialog box, select the **Routine** type and click on the button to create the routine version (Steps 3 and 4).

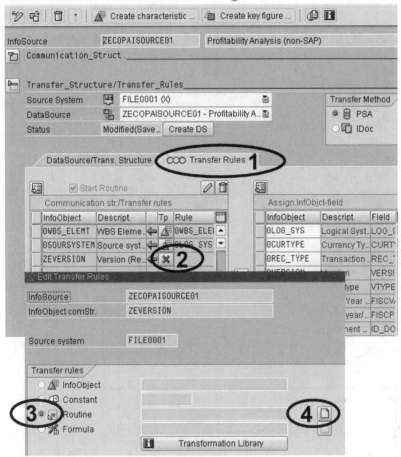

Figure 6.15 Transfer Rule, Type "Routine"

▶ In the **Create Transfer Routine for InfoObject...** dialog box, enter the description for the routine (see Figure 6.16, Step 1).

▶ Then, select the option **All fields** (Step 2) and confirm the entries by clicking on the **Enter** button (Step 3).

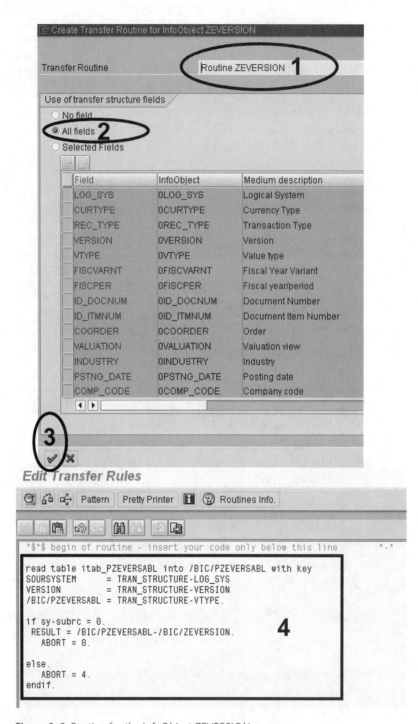

Figure 6.16 Routine for the InfoObject ZEVERSION

▶ In the routine code, access the internal table with the source data for the source system, version, and value type (see **READ...** below) and if this is successful, transfer the harmonized version that was found. So as not to make the example overly complex and possibly unreadable, we will not explore other optimization options here:

```
read table itab_PZEVERSABL into /BIC/PZEVERSABL with key
SOURSYSTEM      = TRAN_STRUCTURE-LOG_SYS
VERSION         = TRAN_STRUCTURE-VERSION
/BIC/ZEVERSABL  = TRAN_STRUCTURE-VTYPE.
if sy-subrc = 0.
  RESULT = /BIC/PZEVERSABL-/BIC/ZEVERSION.
    ABORT = 0.
else.
  ABORT = 4.
endif.
```

▶ If an error occurs, the entire processing is canceled (see Figure 6.16, Step 4).

▶ After saving the routine and clicking on the **Enter** button in the **Edit Transfer Rules** dialog box, the routine is available in the transfer rules (see Figure 6.17).

▶ Lastly, you must activate the transfer rules.

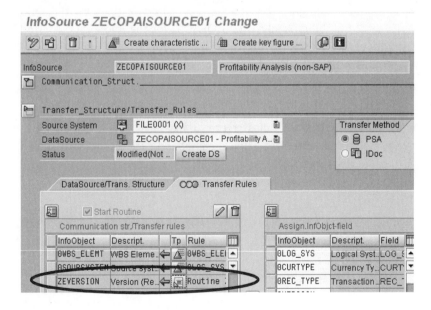

Figure 6.17 Routine in Transfer Rules

6.1.2 Updating the InfoSource "Profitability Analysis (Non-SAP) (ZECOPAISOURCE01)"

The data of the interface files is then provided for the subsequent ETL process via InfoSource **Profitability Analysis (non-SAP) (ZECOPAISOURCE01)**. According to the concept (see Chapter 3, *Sample Scenario*), the update should be carried out via an ODS object.

A precondition for the update in the ODS object is that the key fields are unique:

▶ Source system ID

▶ Currency type

▶ Record type

▶ Version

▶ Value type for reporting

▶ Fiscal year variant

▶ Fiscal year/period

▶ Document number

▶ Document item number

Creating Update Rules

▶ In order to configure the update, create update rules for the ODS object **Profitability Analysis** (ZECOPAO1) for the InfoSource referred to above in the **InfoProvider** view (Transaction RSA11) of the **SAP BW Administrator Workbench**.

▶ Right-click on the ODS object to activate the context-sensitive menu and select **Create Update Rules** (see Figure 6.18, Steps 1 and 2).

▶ In the dialog **Update Rules create: Start**, select the InfoSource as a data source (or enter its technical name) and click on the **Next screen** button (Steps 3 and 4).

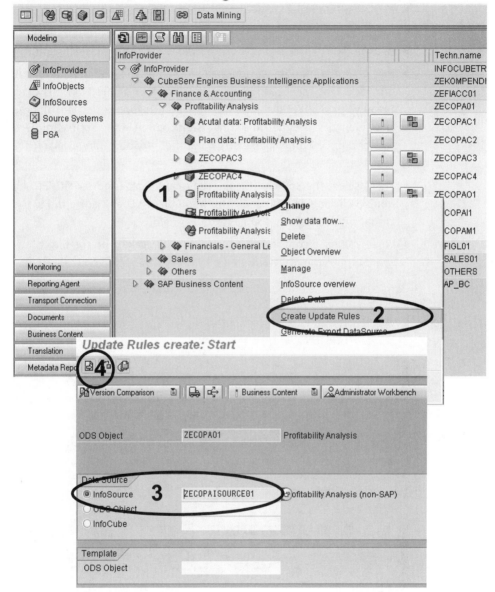

Figure 6.18 Creating Update Rules—Part 1

Editing Update Rules

▶ While update rules can be used for most of the InfoSource fields, there are no equivalents for the InfoObjects **Posting period** (0FISCPER3) and **Fiscal year** (0FISCYEAR) (see Figure 6.19, Step 1).

▶ To postprocess the update rules, click on the **No Update** button (Step 2).

▶ In the **Update Rule: Detail** popup, select the **Overwrite** update type in the **Data Field Calculation** tab (Steps 3 and 4).

▶ As an update method, select **Source Field** and activate the menu (Step 5).

▶ In the **Source InfoObject** popup, all InfoObjects of the InfoSource are provided that can be updated in the target InfoObject (in this case, **Fiscal year**). As SAP BW provides time conversion routines for all time characteristics (see the **Time conversion** column in the **Source InfoObject** popup), all time characteristics of the InfoSource are available for selection.

▶ Then, select the source InfoObject **Fiscal year/period** (0FISCPER) by double-clicking on it (Step 6). This InfoObject is then transferred to the **Update Rule: Detail** popup as a source field.

▶ Once you have confirmed your selection by clicking on the **Enter** button (Step 7), the update rules are set up for this InfoObject (Step 8).

Carry out the same process for the InfoObject **Posting period** (0FISCPER3).

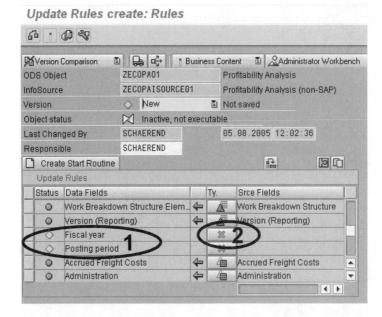

Figure 6.19a Creating Update Rules—Part 2

▶ Then, activate the update rules (see Figure 6.20).

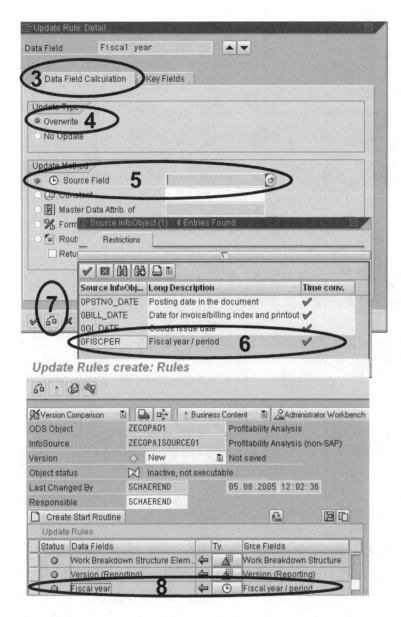

Figure 6.19b Creating Update Rules—Part 3

You can now update data from the assigned InfoSource into the data target.

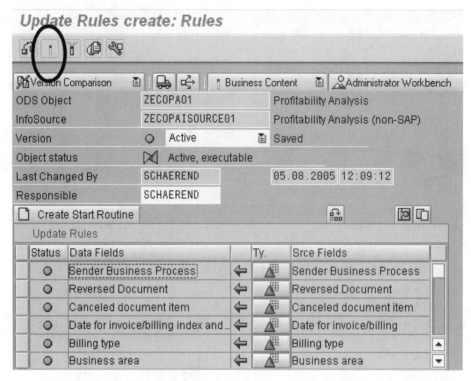

Figure 6.20 Activating the Update Rules

6.1.3 Update Requirements and Monitoring for the InfoSource "Profitability Analysis (Non-SAP) (ZECOPAISOURCE01)"

For the data retrieval process that has been previously established, an InfoPackage can now be set up to carry out the load process.

Setting up an InfoPackage

▶ To do this, go to the **InfoSources** view (Transaction RSA12) in the Administrator Workbench.

▶ Select the relevant source system for the corresponding InfoSource and right-click to activate the context-sensitive menu (see Figure 6.21, Steps 1 and 2).

▶ In the **Create InfoPackage** popup, assign the required InfoPackage name (Step 3) and click on the **Save** button (Step 4).

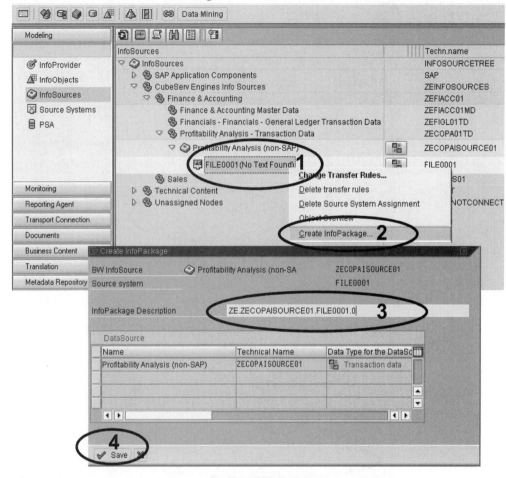

Figure 6.21 Setting Up an InfoPackage for a File Interface—Part 1

▶ Specify the selection in the dialog **Scheduler (Maintain InfoPackage)**, in the **Data Selection** tab (see Figure 6.22, Step 1) (in the example: source system **F1**, fiscal year/period **2004.001**, see Step 2).

Data selection

▶ In the **External data** tab (Step 3), you must enter the path and file name, the file type and other interface file-specific data (in the example: the number of header rows to be ignored) (Steps 4 to 6).

External data

▶ After entering the basic details, click on the **Start** button in the **Schedule** tab (Steps 7 and 8) to start the InfoPackage.

Schedule

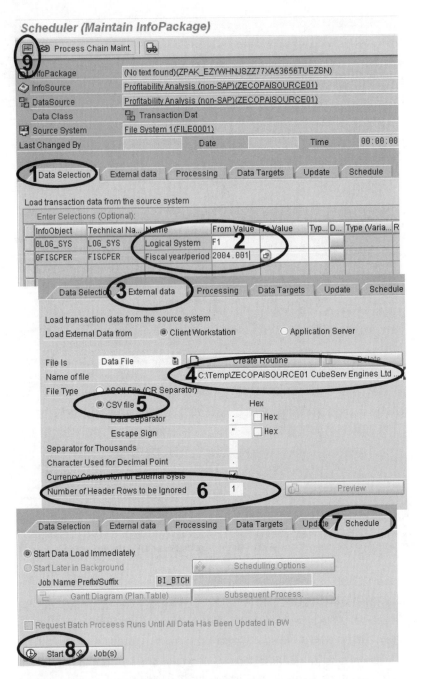

Figure 6.22 Setting Up an InfoPackage for a File Interface—Part 2

Other options to define an InfoPackage were already explained in Chapter 5, *ETL Process: Master Data.*

The Monitor

After processing the request, the message **Data has been requested** is displayed in the status bar. Then you can check the load process by calling the monitor (see Figure 6.22, Step 9).

In addition to the summary provided in the **Header** tab (see Figure 6.23), the **Status** tab contains more detailed information on the update success. In case of an error, tracing of the error source is supported there. In the **Details** tab, the individual steps of the update process are displayed.

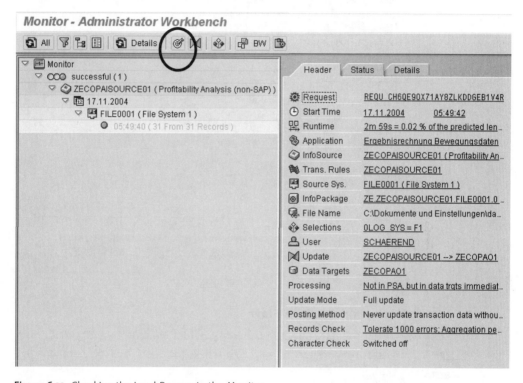

Figure 6.23 Checking the Load Process in the Monitor

▶ By clicking on the **Manage data targets** button (see Figure 6.23), you can monitor and manage the update process in the data targets.   **Administration**

▶ In the case of the present update in the ODS object **Profitability analysis** (ZECOPAO1), the data target content display in the automatically activated **Contents** tab provides the active data or the new data, depending on the settings of the ODS object, (see Figure 6.24, Steps 1 and 2).

▶ In the **Requests** tab (Step 3), you can monitor the availability of the individual requests for reporting, in addition to other activities.

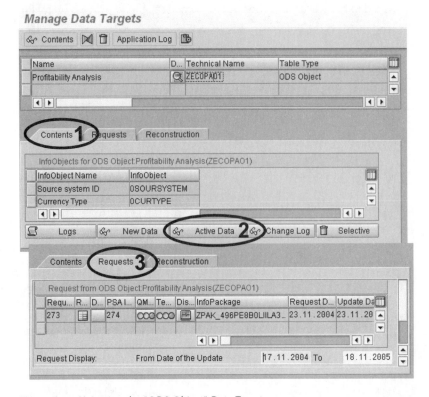

Figure 6.24 Managing the "ODS Object" Data Target

Displaying the Data Flow

▶ Select the data target in the **InfoProvider** view of the SAP BW **Administrator Workbench** and right-click to open the context-sensitive menu.

▶ If you select the **Show data flow** menu option (see Figure 6.25), a new frame opens that contains a graphical display of the data flow.

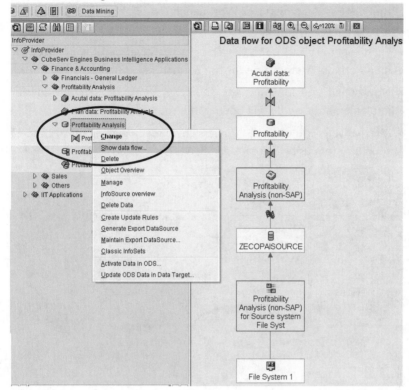

Figure 6.25 The Data Flow to the ODS Object "Profitability Analysis"

6.1.4 Extracting SAP R/3 Data for Profitability Analysis

Any units of our model company "CubeServ Engines" that contain a productive SAP profitability analysis (CO-PA) can use SAP functionality for both extraction and data transfer. This means that tools can be used to configure the DataSource and for the automated support of incremental updates (initial load and delta mechanism).

Creating the DataSource in SAP R/3

As the structures of SAP profitability analysis (CO-PA) are defined as customer-specific, for SAP R/3 CO-PA you must create a customer-specific and application-specific DataSource for each respective SAP R/3 source system.

You can implement the configuration in the following manner for SAP systems that are used as source systems:

▶ Select the corresponding SAP system in the **Source Systems** view of the SAP BW **Administrator Workbench** (Transaction RSA13) (see Figure 6.26, Step 1).

▶ Then, right-click to open the context-sensitive menu and select the menu option **Customizing for the Extractors...** (Step 2).

▶ Now when you log onto the source system, the SAP BW-specific implementation guide will open in the source system.

▶ Alternatively, you can call the menu by directly logging on to the SAP source system using Transaction SBIW.

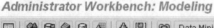

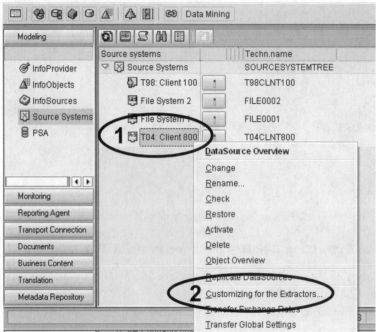

Figure 6.26 Calling the SAP BW-Specific Implementation Guide in the SAP Source System from the SAP BW Administrator Workbench

▶ In the Implementation Guide in the SAP source system, select the menu option **Create Transaction Data DataSource** under the menu item **Settings for Application-Specific DataSources (PI) · Profitability Analysis** (see Figure 6.27, Step 1).

Setting up the DataSource ▶ Specify the technical name of the DataSource (or transfer or complement the suggested generic name, see Figure 6.28, Step 1).

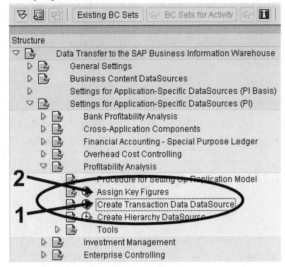

Figure 6.27 Call: Creating a Transaction Data DataSource for Profitability Analysis (CO-PA)

▶ Select the **Create** function (Step 2) and select the required operating concern (in this case **S_GO**, see Step 3).

▶ Then click on the **Execute** button (Step 4).

▶ Whether the setting Costing-based or Account-based profitability analysis is set depends on the CO-PA configuration. As you can see in the example shown, **Costing-based** profitability analysis is selected.

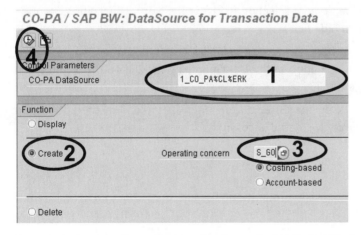

Figure 6.28 Creating a Transaction Data DataSource for SAP Profitability Analysis

▶ In the dialog **CO-PA/SAP BW: DataSource for Transaction Data**, enter a descriptive text for the DataSource (see Figure 6.29, Step 1).

▶ Any characteristics of the operating concern that are imperative for a correct extraction are already selected and locked. You can also select any **Characteristics from the segment level** that you want to extract. For the model company, all characteristics are selected since maximum granularity must be available in SAP BW reporting (Step 2).

▶ Now you can select the **Characteristics from the line items** and the **Value fields**. To achieve maximum granularity, you should also select all objects (see Figure 6.30, Steps 1 and 2).

▶ The calculated key figures from the calculating schema aren't required because that definition is extraneous for the CO-PA definition (see Figure 6.27, Selection 2, menu item **Assign Key Figures**).

▶ You can continue the configuration of the DataSource for profitability analysis by clicking on the **InfoCatalog** button (see Figure 6.30, Step 3).

▶ To ensure that the settings for SAP development systems can be transported into SAP production systems,[3] you must specify a customer-specific package in the **Create Object Directory Entry** popup, and click on the **Save** button (see Figure 6.31, Steps 1 and 2).

▶ The **Prompt for local Workbench request** popup opens and prompts you to select the corresponding workbench request (Step 3).

▶ Click on the **Enter** button (Step 4) to display the dialog **DataSource: Customer version Edit.** Here you can configure the CO-PA Data-Source, implement selection fields for the existing DataSource, and, if necessary, hide fields.

▶ This is not necessary in the current scenario, therefore, you can conclude the definition of the DataSource by clicking on the **Save** button (see Figure 6.32, Step 1).

▶ Then, click on the **Enter** button (Step 2) to confirm the notification **DataSource … created sucessfully**.

---

3 See also the SAP documentation on the transport system.

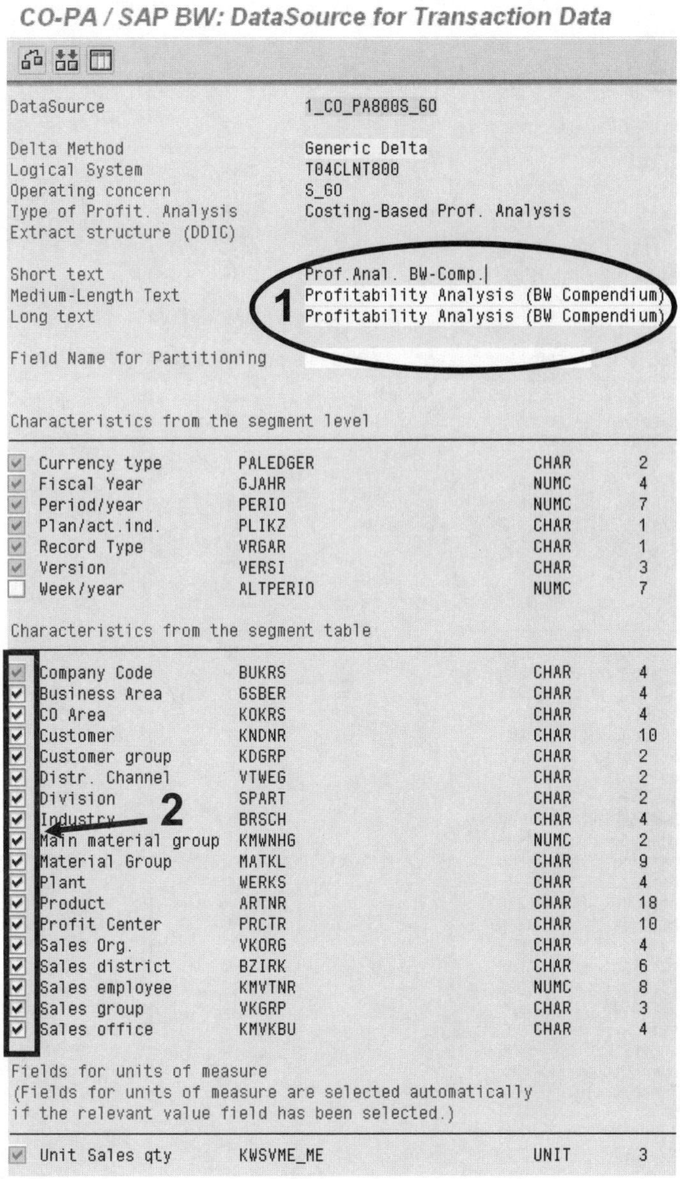

CO-PA / SAP BW: DataSource for Transaction Data

```
[icons]

DataSource                        1_CO_PA800S_GO

Delta Method                      Generic Delta
Logical System                    T04CLNT800
Operating concern                 S_GO
Type of Profit. Analysis          Costing-Based Prof. Analysis
Extract structure (DDIC)

Short text                        Prof.Anal. BW-Comp.|
Medium-Length Text                Profitability Analysis (BW Compendium)
Long text                         Profitability Analysis (BW Compendium)

Field Name for Partitioning


Characteristics from the segment level

☑  Currency type      PALEDGER              CHAR      2
☑  Fiscal Year        GJAHR                 NUMC      4
☑  Period/year        PERIO                 NUMC      7
☑  Plan/act.ind.      PLIKZ                 CHAR      1
☑  Record Type        VRGAR                 CHAR      1
☑  Version            VERSI                 CHAR      3
☐  Week/year          ALTPERIO              NUMC      7

Characteristics from the segment table

☑  Company Code       BUKRS                 CHAR      4
☑  Business Area      GSBER                 CHAR      4
☑  CO Area            KOKRS                 CHAR      4
☑  Customer           KNDNR                 CHAR     10
☑  Customer group     KDGRP                 CHAR      2
☑  Distr. Channel     VTWEG                 CHAR      2
☑  Division           SPART                 CHAR      2
☑  Industry           BRSCH                 CHAR      4
☑  Main material group KMWNHG               NUMC      2
☑  Material Group     MATKL                 CHAR      9
☑  Plant              WERKS                 CHAR      4
☑  Product            ARTNR                 CHAR     18
☑  Profit Center      PRCTR                 CHAR     10
☑  Sales Org.         VKORG                 CHAR      4
☑  Sales district     BZIRK                 CHAR      6
☑  Sales employee     KMVTNR                NUMC      8
☑  Sales group        VKGRP                 CHAR      3
☑  Sales office       KMVKBU                CHAR      4

Fields for units of measure
(Fields for units of measure are selected automatically
if the relevant value field has been selected.)

☑  Unit Sales qty     KWSVME_ME             UNIT      3
```

Figure 6.29 Setting Up the CO-PA DataSource—Part 1

CO-PA / SAP BW: DataSource for Transaction Data

🔲 🔲 🔲 **3**

Characteristics from the line items

☑	Record Currency	REC_WAERS	CUKY	5
☑	Billing Date	FADAT	DATS	8
☑	Billing Type	FKART	CHAR	4
☑	Canceled doc.	STO_BELNR	CHAR	10
☑	Canceled item	STO_POSNR	CHAR	6
☑	Cost Element	KSTAR	CHAR	10
☑	Cost Object	KSTRG	CHAR	12
☑	Document number	BELNR	CHAR	10
☑	Goods issue	WADAT	DATS	8
☑	Item number	POSNR	CHAR	6
☑	Order	RKAUFNR	CHAR	12
☑	Partner Pr.Ctr	PPRCTR	CHAR	10
☑	Posting date	BUDAT	DATS	8
☑	Ref.doc.number	RBELN	CHAR	10
☑	Reference item	RPOSN	CHAR	6
☑	Sales Order	KAUFN	CHAR	10
☑	Sales ord. item	KDPOS	NUMC	6
☑	Sender BProc	PRZNR	CHAR	12
☑	Sender cost ctr	SKOST	CHAR	10
☑	WBS Element	PSPNR	NUMC	8

1

Value fields

☑	Administration Costs	KWGOHD	CURR	15	REC_WAERS
☑	Anticipd ship. costs	KWKLFK	CURR	15	REC_WAERS
☑	Bonuses	KWBONI	CURR	15	REC_WAERS
☑	Cash discount	KWSKTO	CURR	15	REC_WAERS
☑	Customer Discount	KWKDRB	CURR	15	REC_WAERS
☑	Direct mat. costs	KWMAEK	CURR	15	REC_WAERS
☑	Fixed prod. costs	KWFKFX	CURR	15	REC_WAERS
☑	Gross sales	KWBRUM	CURR	15	REC_WAERS
☑	Marketing provision	KWMKDP	CURR	15	REC_WAERS
☑	Mat. overhead costs	KWMAGK	CURR	15	REC_WAERS
☑	Material discount	KWMARB	CURR	15	REC_WAERS
☑	Other overhead	KWSGEK	CURR	15	REC_WAERS
☑	Other variances	KWABSG	CURR	15	REC_WAERS
☑	Price variances	KWABPR	CURR	15	REC_WAERS
☑	Quantity discount	KWMGRB	CURR	15	REC_WAERS
☑	Quantity variances	KWABMG	CURR	15	REC_WAERS
☑	Research & Developmt	KWFOEN	CURR	15	REC_WAERS
☑	Sales commission	KWVKPV	CURR	15	REC_WAERS
☑	Sales costs	KWSOHD	CURR	15	REC_WAERS
☑	Sales quantity	KWSVME	QUAN	15	KWSVME_ME
☑	SalesSpecDirectCosts	KWVSEK	CURR	15	REC_WAERS
☑	Variable prod.costs	KWFKVA	CURR	15	REC_WAERS

2

Figure 6.30 Setting Up the CO-PA DataSource—Part 2

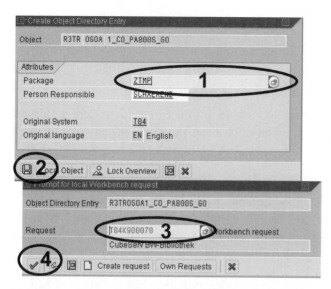

Figure 6.31 Request "Object Directory Entry" and "Transport Request"

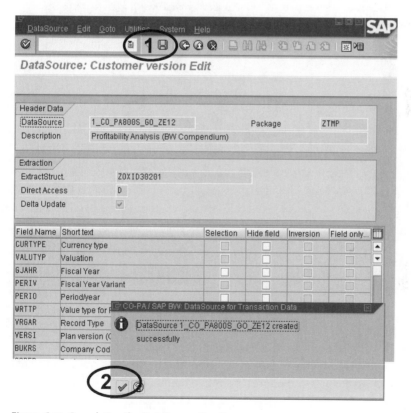

Figure 6.32 Completing the DataSource Creation

The DataSource for the extraction of data is now available in the SAP BW system. You can then return to SAP BW by clicking on the **Back** button (or the **F3** function key) several times.

Replicating the DataSource in SAP BW

The newly established DataSource in the SAP source system is still not known by SAP BW. For you to be able to use this DataSource, you must replicate the DataSources from the source system into SAP BW.

▶ You can do this in the **Source systems** view of the **Administrator Workbench** (Transaction RSA13).

▶ In the corresponding source system (here **system T04 client 800**) you can right-click to open the context-sensitive menu and then select the **DataSource Overview** menu option (see Figure 6.33).

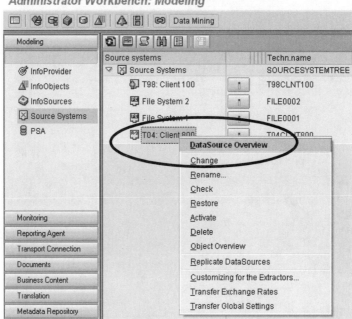

Figure 6.33 Calling the DataSource Overview

▶ In the DataSource overview open the application components and DataSource hierarchy up to the **Profitability Analysis** node and right-click to activate the context-sensitive menu.

▶ If you select the **Replicate DataSources** function, SAP BW starts the replication (see Figure 6.34, Step 1).

▶ Once this has been done, the message **Tree data refreshed: InfoSource tree** is displayed in the status bar.

▶ If you then expand the application component **Profitability Analysis**, the reconfigured and replicated transaction data DataSource is displayed (Step 2).

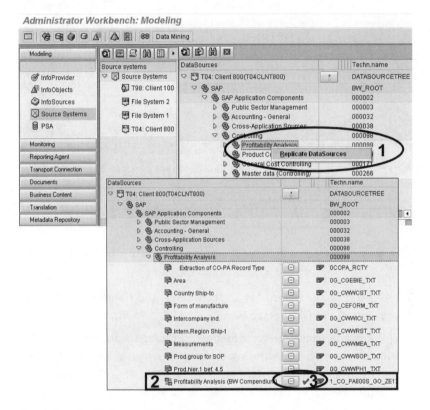

Figure 6.34 Replicating and Displaying DataSources

Creating the InfoSource with Transfer Rules

The newly created SAP DataSource must also be assigned to an Info-Source in SAP BW. You can use the SAP BW standard functionality to create a new InfoSource.

▶ In the **Source systems** view of the SAP BW **Administrator Workbench** (Transaction *RSA13*), click on the button "-" next to a DataSource that has not yet been assigned to an InfoSource in order to execute the function **Assign InfoSource** (see Figure 6.34, Step 3).

▶ The **InfoSource for DataSource** popup opens. There, SAP BW recommends that you choose an InfoSource with the same name as the

DataSource. You can accept this suggestion by clicking on the **Confirm** button (see Figure 6.35, Step 1).

▶ Confirm the query in the **Save changes?** popup by clicking on the **Yes** button (Step 2).

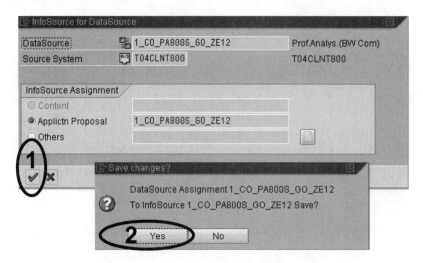

Figure 6.35 Assigning the CO-PA DataSource to an InfoSource to be Generated by the System

Suggesting and maintaining transfer rules

▶ The SAP BW system creates an InfoSource and transfers the transfer structure of the DataSource into it.

▶ In the maintenance screen **InfoSource...Change**, you can then maintain the transfer rules on this basis. To do this, select the **Suggest Transfer Rules** button (see Figure 6.36, Step 1). This transfers 1:1 transfer rules for all the source fields to be assigned.

▶ Then, check the suggested transfer rules and complement or correct them correspondingly.

▶ For the model company, source system compounding of attributes of the generated InfoSource[4] produces the **Source System** (0SOURSYS-TEM) InfoObject. The DataSource, however, does not provide any corresponding field so that no transfer rule can be suggested for this InfoObject of the InfoSource (see Figure 6.36, Step 2).

Start routine

▶ To ensure accurate master data, this InfoSource field must not remain initial. Therefore, a routine-supported determination of the source system ID is performed.

---

4 See Egger, Fiechter, Rohlf: *SAP BW Data Modeling*. SAP PRESS 2005.

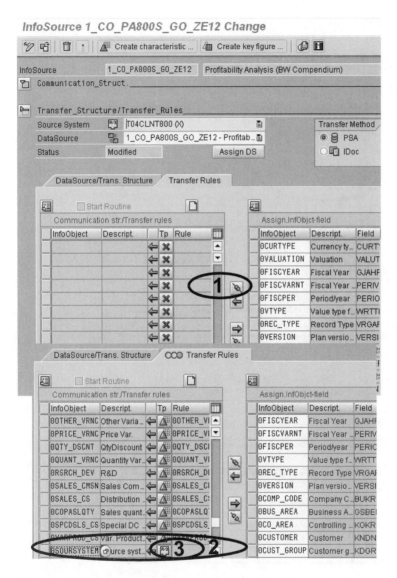

Figure 6.36 Displaying and Checking Transfer Rules Suggestions

► To do this, you must define a start routine that uses the logical system (LOGSYS) available in the transfer rules to derive the source system ID (SOURSYSID) (Steps 2 to 4) from Table RSSOURSYSTEM (see Figure 6.37, Step 1).

In the same start routine, the requirements for deriving the harmonized (reporting) version (InfoObject ZEVERSION), used throughout SAP BW at CubeServ Engines, from the local characteristics of the InfoObjects **Ver-**

sion (0VERSION) and **Value type** (0VTYPE) are created in the same way as are the settings for the transfer rules for the file interface—by providing the derivation information in an internal table (Step 5).[5]

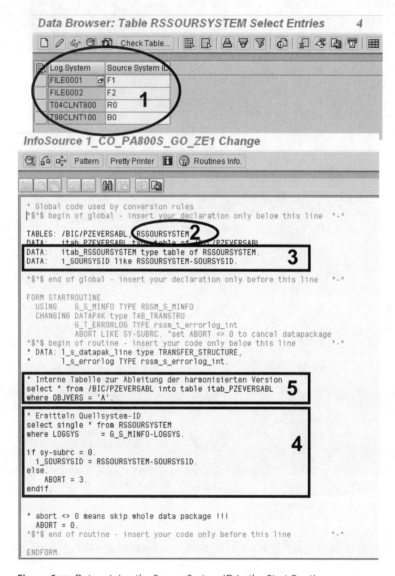

Figure 6.37 Determining the Source System ID in the Start Routine

---

5   See the previous section on defining transfer rules and communication structures.

▶ The start routine can be coded as follows:

```
*$*$ begin of global -
 insert your declaration only below
TABLES: /BIC/PZEVERSABL, RSSOURSYSTEM.
DATA:   itab_PZEVERSABL type table of /BIC/PZEVERSABL.
DATA:   itab_RSSOURSYSTEM type table of RSSOURSYSTEM.
DATA:   i_SOURSYSID like RSSOURSYSTEM-SOURSYSID.
*$*$ end of global - insert your declaration only before
FORM STARTROUTINE
   USING    G_S_MINFO TYPE RSSM_S_MINFO
 . . .
*$*$ begin of routine - insert your code only below
 . . .
* Internal table to derive the harmonized version
select * from /BIC/PZEVERSABL into table itab_PZEVERSABL
where OBJVERS = 'A'.

* Determine source system ID
select single * from RSSOURSYSTEM
where LOGSYS = G_S_MINFO-LOGSYS.

if sy-subrc = 0.
  i_SOURSYSID = RSSOURSYSTEM-SOURSYSID.
  ABORT = 0.
else.
  ABORT = 3.
endif.
*$*$ end of routine - insert your code only before
```

▶ With regard to the routine to derive the harmonized version, you can carry out a process similar to the one that you used for the transfer rules for the file interface settings.[6] Only the parameterization of the source system ID occurs dynamically.

Deriving the harmonized version

▶ In the transfer rules (see Figure 6.38, Step 1) you can create the routines for the source system (0SOURSYSTEM) and the harmonized version (ZEVERSION) by clicking on the **Type** button (Steps 2 and 3).

---

6 See the previous section on defining transfer rules and communication structures.

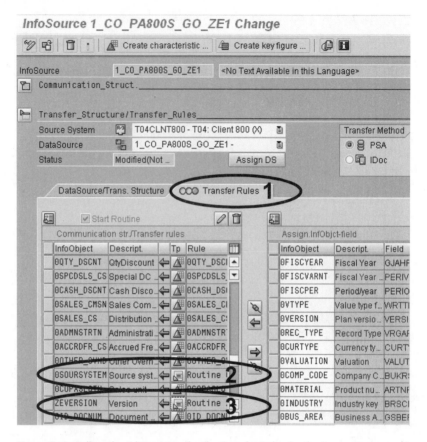

Figure 6.38 Calling the Editing View for the Transfer Rules for the Source System and Harmonized Version

▶ In the **Edit Transfer Rules** and **Change Transfer Routine for InfoObject...** popups, you must first select the routine creation (see Figure 6.39, Steps 1 and 2).

▶ Next, select the routine name and the option **All fields** (Steps 3 to 5).

▶ In the dialog screen used to code the routine, enter the routine that has been modified with the dynamic source system parameterization (see Figure 6.40, Step 1).

▶ After saving the routine (Step 2) and returning to the **Edit Transfer Rules** popup, you must confirm the definition (see Figure 6.39, Step 6).

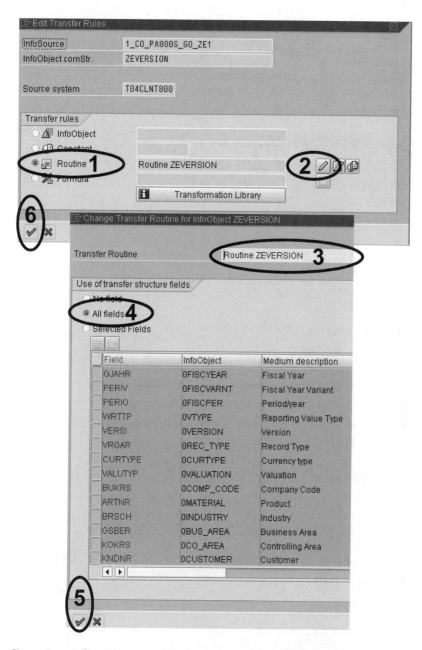

Figure 6.39 Calling Routine Creation for the Harmonized Version

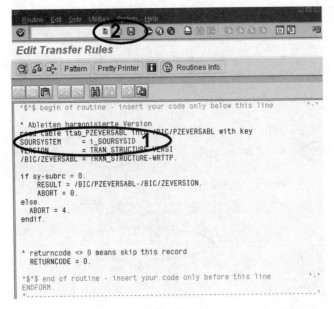

Figure 6.40 Routine with Dynamically Determined Source System ID

Coding the routine:

```
*$*$ begin of routine - insert your code only below
* Derive harmonized version
read table itab_PZEVERSABL into /BIC/PZEVERSABL with key
SOURSYSTEM     = i_SOURSYSID
VERSION        = TRAN_STRUCTURE-VERSI
/BIC/ZEVERSABL = TRAN_STRUCTURE-WRTTP.

if sy-subrc = 0.
    RESULT = /BIC/PZEVERSABL-/BIC/ZEVERSION.
    ABORT = 0.
else.
  ABORT = 4.
endif.
```

In the routine for the source system ID, the routine consists only of the assignment of the value determined in the start routine.

```
*$*$ begin of routine - insert your code only below
    RESULT = i_SOURSYSID.
```

6.1.5 Updating the InfoSource "Profitability Analysis (1_CO_PA800S_GO_ZE1)"

After activating the transfer rules, the InfoSource needed to create the update rules is available in the consolidated ODS object. To create the update rules, proceed in the same way that you did when creating the update of the InfoSource of the file interface.

Creating Update Rules

Only the InfoObject **Posting Period** (0FISCPER3) is not automatically updated from the SAP R/3 CO-PA-based InfoSource.

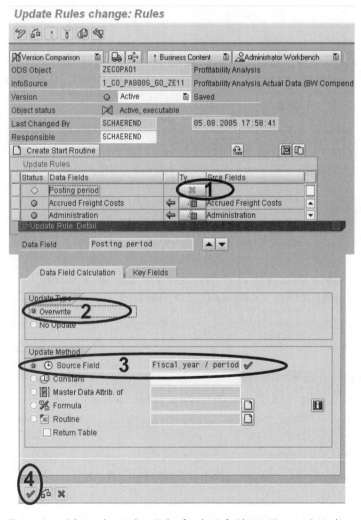

Figure 6.41 Editing the Update Rules for the InfoObject "Posting Period"

▶ To update this InfoOject, click on the **Type** button after calling the update rule creation view for the data field **Posting period** (see Figure 6.41, Step 1).

▶ In the **Update Rule: Detail** popup, select the update type **Overwrite** and then select the **Source Field Fiscal year/period** as update method and transfer the update rule using the **Confirm** button (Steps 2 to 4).

▶ Upon activation, the SAP R/3 CO-PA-based InfoSource (1_CO_PA800S_GO_ZE1) is also updated in the ODS object (see Figure 6.42).

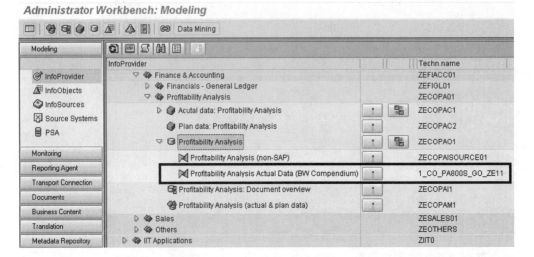

Figure 6.42 Updating the SAP R/3 CO-PA-Based InfoSource in the ODS Object "Profitability Analysis"

6.1.6 Update Request and Monitor for the InfoSource "Profitability Analysis (1_CO_PA800S_GO_ZE1)"

To carry out the load process, you can now set up an InfoPackage for the data retrieval process that was previously set up.

Setting up an InfoPackage

▶ Start the SAP BW **Administrator Workbench** and go to the **Info-Sources** view (Transaction RSA12), where you must right-click to activate the context-sensitive menu on the SAP source system that is assigned to the InfoSource (see Figure 6.43, Step 1).

▶ In the context menu, select **Create InfoPackage** (Step 2).

▶ In the **Create InfoPackage** popup that opens, enter an InfoPackage name and save this entry (Steps 3 and 4).

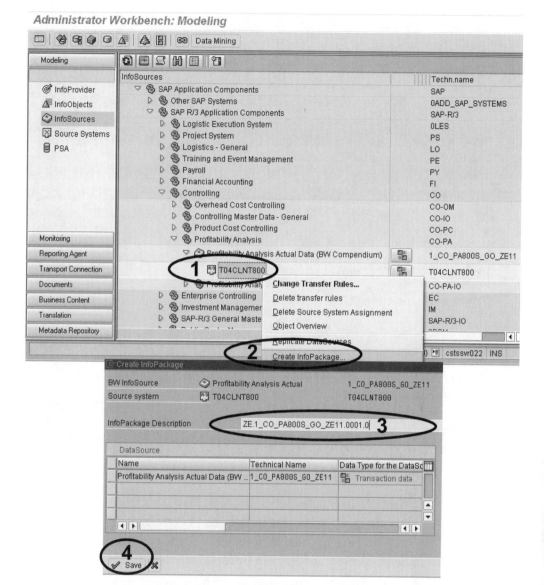

Administrator Workbench: Modeling

Figure 6.43 Calling the InfoPackage Creation

▶ In the **Update** tab, select the **Update Mode** option **Initialize Delta Process** (see Figure 6.44, Steps 1 and 2).

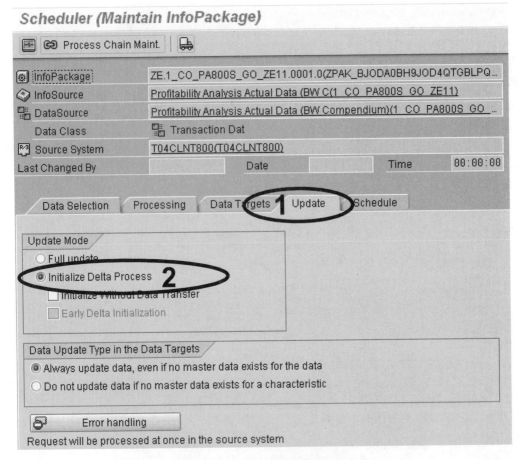

Figure 6.44 Update Mode "Initialize Delta Process"

▶ After a successful initialization, a new option is available when creating InfoPackages: In the **Update** tab, you can always transfer any data that has not been updated from the source system into SAP BW by selecting the update mode **Delta Update** (see Figure 6.45, Steps 1 and 2).

▶ By selecting the data target in the **InfoProvider** view of the SAP BW **Administrator Workbench** and right-clicking, you can open the context-sensitive menu.

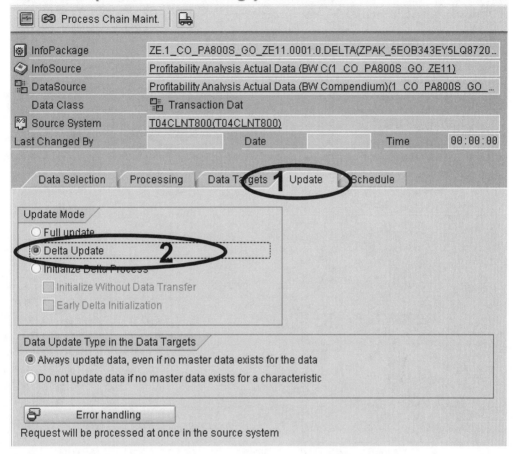

Figure 6.45 Update Mode: Delta Update

▶ If you select the entry **Display Data flow** (see Figure 6.46), a new frame opens in which the graphical display of the data flow shows the parallel updating of interface data and SAP data in the ODS object **Profitability Analysis** (ZECOPAO1).

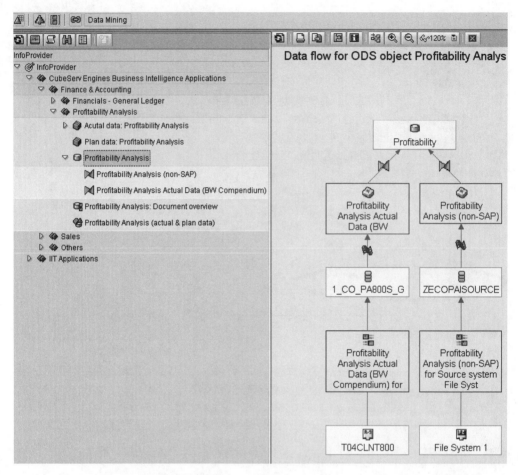

Figure 6.46 Data Flow with Parallel Update of Interface Data and SAP Data in the ODS Object "Profitability Analysis (ZECOPAO1)"

6.1.7 Connecting other Data Sources for Profitability Analysis via UD Connect

For the remaining units of our model company, "CubeServ Engines," you can extract the data for profitability analysis directly from the source databases. Use **UD Connect** to extract the data. The **Sales** table of the SQL Server database contains the required data (see the table overview of the SQL Server database as well as design and content of the **Sales** table in Figure 6.47).

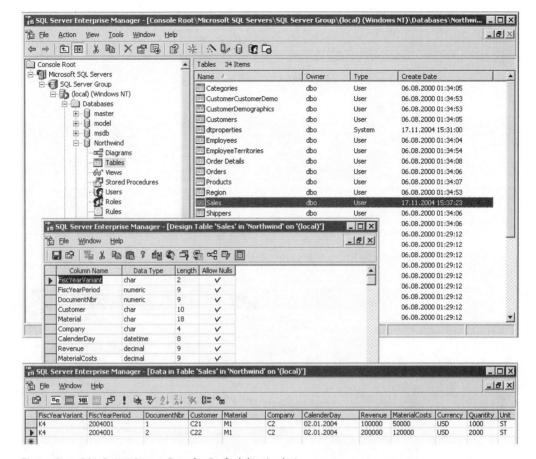

Figure 6.47 SQL Server Source Data for Profitability Analysis

Creating a UD Connect DataSource

You can implement data retrieval via UD Connect in the **InfoSources** view of the SAP BW **Administrator Workbench**.

▶ There, right-click on the relevant InfoSource to activate the context-sensitive menu and select the **Change** menu option (see Figure 6.48).

▶ In the **InfoSource ... Change** dialog, open the pull-down menu **Extras** and select the **Create BW DataSource with UD Connect** menu option (see Figure 6.49, Steps 1 and 2).

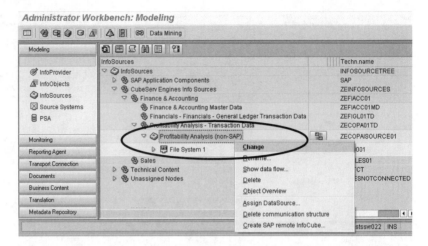

Figure 6.48 To Create Data Retrieval via UD Connect: Call InfoSource Change

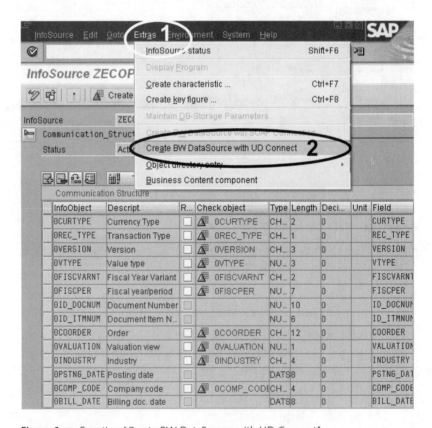

Figure 6.49 Function "Create BW DataSource with UD Connect"

Setting up a UD Connect DataSource

▶ In the popup **Assigning UD Connect Source Object to BW DS and Extr. Gen.,** select the **RFC Destination** to be connected, the **UD Connect Source** and the **UD Connect Source Object** (see Figure 6.50, Steps 1 to 3).

▶ The fields of the source are then displayed in the list **UD Connect Source Object**, **Source Object Elements**. The InfoObjects of the Info-Source are displayed in the list **Assignment Elements-Fields**, BW **DataSource Fields**.

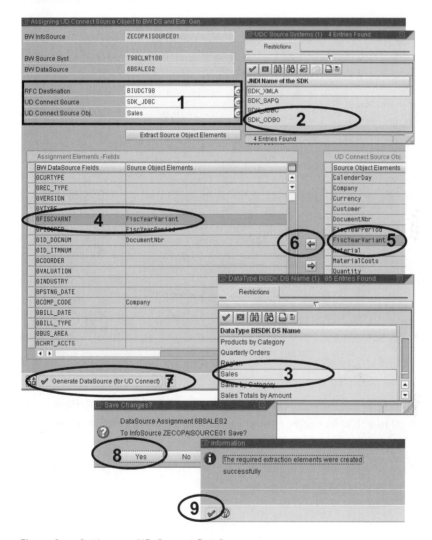

Figure 6.50 Setting up a UD Connect DataSource

- In the list **Assignment Elements · Fields**, select an InfoObject that is to be assigned a source field (Figure 6.50, Step 4).

- Then, select a field to be assigned to an InfoObject in the **Source Object Elements** list where you must highlight the respective line (Step 5).

- Complete the assignment by clicking on the **Assign** button (Step 6).

- After you have assigned all fields, click on the **Generate DataSource (for UD Connect)** button and confirm the query and information pop-ups (Steps 7 to 9).

- When you return to the **InfoSources view** of the **Administrator Work-bench** of SAP BW, after the UD Connect DataSource has been assigned, the SAP BW source system is itself displayed as a connected source system (see Figure 6.51).

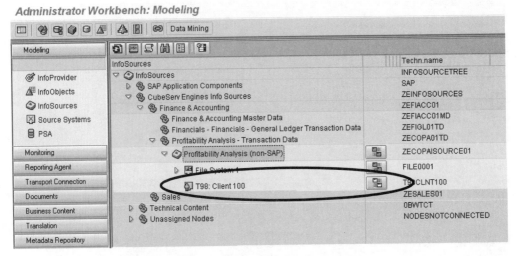

Figure 6.51 Display of SAP BW as a Source System Due to the Assignment of the UD Connect DataSource

Transfer rules   For the connected UD Connect DataSource, the transfer rules are to be created and activated similar to the procedure for file interfaces and SAP R/3.

InfoPackage   You can use a process similar to the one used to create an InfoPackage for other source systems (for example, SAP R/3) when you want to create a data request.

6.1.8 Updating the Data of the ODS Object in the InfoCube "Actual Data: Profitability Analysis (ZECOPAC1)"

According to our concept, the ODS object **Profitability Analysis** serves as a data warehouse layer and transfers the consolidated data to the Info-Cubes of the application.

Generating an Export DataSource

The first part of this transfer involves the Export DataSource on the ODS object **Profitability Analysis**.

▶ It is generated in the **InfoProvider view** of the **Administrator Work-bench** of SAP BW by right-clicking on the ODS object to display the context-sensitive menu and then selecting the **Generate Export Data-Source** menu option (see Figure 6.52, Steps 1 and 2).

▶ Confirm the popup that notifies you that the Export DataSource has been successfully generated (Step 3).

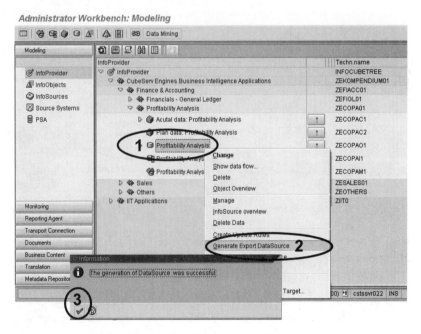

Figure 6.52 Generating an Export DataSource for the Transfer of Data of the ODS Object

Creating Update Rules

Once you have generated the Export DataSource, the generated Data-Source, an assigned InfoSource and 1:1 transfer rules are available in SAP BW. Since the InfoCube **Actual Data: Profitability Analysis** (ZECOPAC1) contains the same InfoObject as the ODS object **Profitability Analysis** (ZECOPAO1) the automatically generated rules for 1:1 transfer can be used. The easiest way to create an update is to use these objects.

▶ To create an update, right-click to activate the context-sensitive menu for the InfoCube to be updated in the **InfoProvider** view of the **Administrator Workbench** of SAP BW (see Figure 6.53, Step 1).

▶ Select the **Create Update Rules** menu option (Step 2) to open the dialog **Update Rules create: Start** (see Figure 6.54).

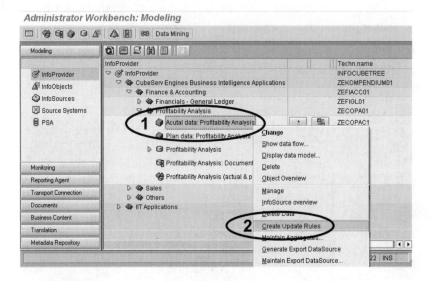

Figure 6.53 Update Rules for InfoCube ZECOPAC1

▶ After entering the source ODS object (see Figure 6.54, Step 1) and clicking on the **Next screen** button (Step 2), the dialog **Update Rules create: Rules** is displayed (see Figure 6.55).

▶ As all key figures of the data target (that is, the InfoCube) are also contained in the source object (that is, ODS object), all the key figures will be populated in the dialog **Update Rules create: Rules** (see Figure 6.55, Step 1).

Update Rules create: Start

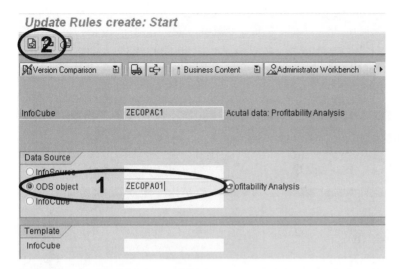

Figure 6.54 Update Rules Create: Start

Update Rules create: Rules

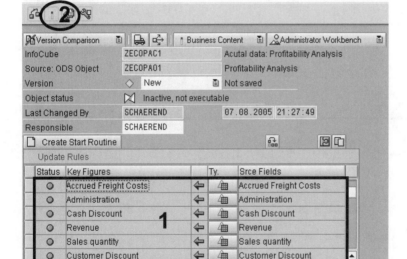

Figure 6.55 Updating All Key Figures and Activating Update Rules

▶ The same holds true for the characteristics and time characteristics of the InfoCube **Actual Data: Profitability Analysis** (ZECOPAC1). All of these characteristics are also available in the source ODS object and are suggested as 1:1 updates.

▶ The **Update Rule: Detail** dialog appears when you double-click on a key figure. In the **Key Figure Calculation** tab, the update type **Addition** is suggested with identical source and target key figures, as well as identical currency keys and units (for amounts and quantities) for cumulative key figures (see Figure 6.56, Steps 1 and 2).

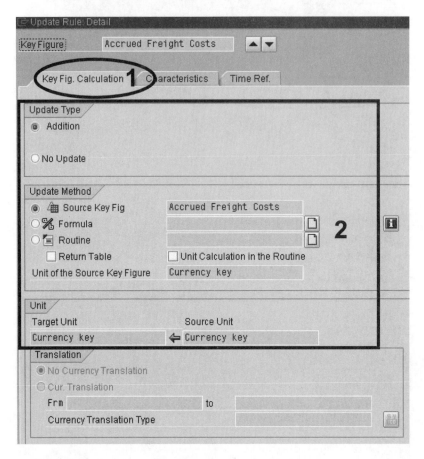

Figure 6.56 Update Rule: Key Figure Calculation

▶ In the **Characteristics** and **Time Reference** tabs (see Figure 6.57, Steps 1 and 3), the source and target characteristics are also identical (Steps 2 and 4).

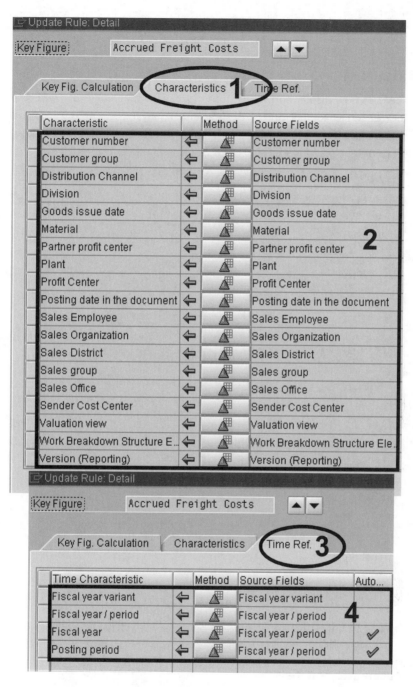

Figure 6.57 Update Rule: Characteristic and Time Reference per Key Figure

▶ Once you have activated the update rules (see Figure 6.55, Step 2), these are also available for data retrieval.

Data Flow

The data flow display shows the consolidation of the data of the different sources via the ODS object **Profitability Analysis** (ZECOPAO1) and a direct update in the InfoCube **Actual Data: Profitability Analysis** (ZECOPAC1) (see Figure 6.58).

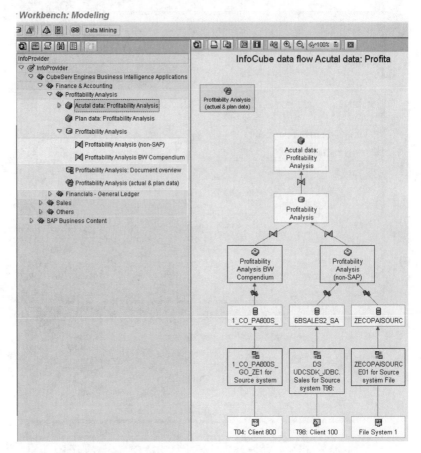

Figure 6.58 Data Flow from the Different Data Sources via ODS Object to the Info-Cube "Actual Data: Profitability Analysis"

Automatic Update

Starting the administration of the ODS object

If the automatic update of the different request packages (that is, the InfoPackages for the file interface, UD Connect, and SAP R/3) is to be performed via the ODS object into the InfoCube, this can be established in the administration for the ODS object.

▶ To do this, go to the **InfoProvider** view of the SAP BW **Administrator Workbench**, right-click on the ODS object to open the context-sensitive menu, and select the **Manage** menu option (Figure 6.59, Steps 1 and 2).

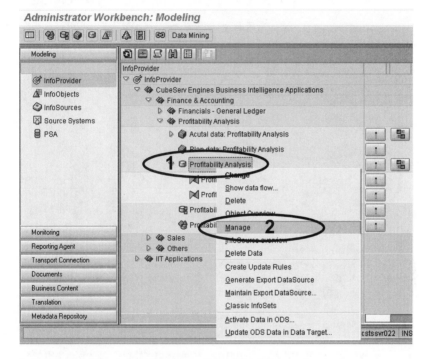

Figure 6.59 Calling the Administration of the ODS Object to Set the Request Processing

▶ In the **Manage Data Targets** dialog, click on the pull-down menu **Environment** and select the **Automatic Request Processing** function (see Figure 6.60, Steps 1 and 2).

▶ The **Maintenance of the automatisms** dialog opens.

▶ In this dialog, activate the options **Set quality status to 'OK,' Activate ODS object data** and **Update data targets from ODS object** (Step 3). This last option ensures that the data updated in the ODS object is directly updated in the downstream data targets (in this case, InfoCube **Actual Data: Profitability Analysis**).

▶ Complete the configuration by clicking on the **Save** button (Step 4).

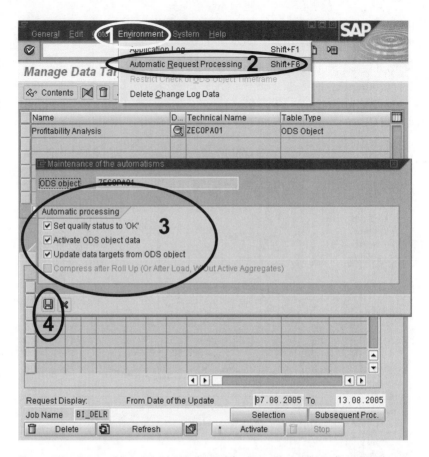

Figure 6.60 Setting the Automatic Update of the Data Targets from the ODS Object

Implementing the update in the ODS object and InfoCube	▶ After executing an InfoPackage that writes into the ODS object **Profitability Analysis** (ZECOPA01) (see also Sections 6.1.3, 6.1.6, or 6.1.7), the automatic update into the InfoCube **Actual Data: Profitability Analysis** (ZECOPAC1) follows.
Monitoring additional updates	▶ In the display of a monitor entry for a request that writes into the ODS object **Profitability Analysis** (ZECOPAO1) (see also Figure 6.22 and Figure 6.1), you can monitor the status of the additional update into the downstream data targets that follow the ODS object by selecting and activating the **Detail** tab (see Figure 6.61, Steps 1 and 2).

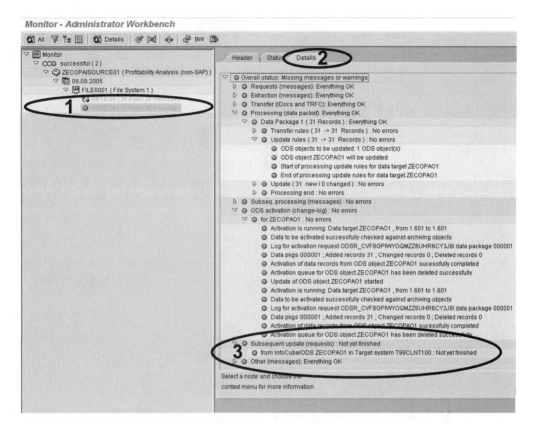

Monitor - Administrator Workbench

Figure 6.61 Information on the Status of the Follow-Up Update in the Monitor

6.2 Exemplary Transaction Data Retrieval for Sales Order Stocks

6.2.1 Specific Characteristics of the Data Retrieval for Sales Order Stocks

Profitability analysis can serve as a data source for sales order stock analysis when the collection of invoicing and incoming sales order data in profitability analysis tables has been configured. If this collection does not occur, the logistics extractors for incoming sales orders and invoices must be linked directly. In this volume of the SAP BW Library, profitability analysis is used. The data of the ODS object **Profitability Analysis** (ZECOPAO1) is used as a data source for the InfoCube **Sales Order Stock** (ZEKDABC1).

Profitability analysis or logistics extractors

Key figures	When using profitability analysis data, different key figures are transferred to the Export DataSource of the ODS object **Profitability Analysis** (ZECOPAO1). In the InfoCube **Sales Order Stock** (ZEKDABC1), the net value of the incoming sales order must be updated as a stock-increasing value while the net sales value must be updated as a stock-decreasing value. Consequently, you must calculate the net value as a gross value reduced by the decreases in sales orders or revenue. In addition, the stock changes are processed via the key figure **Amount** (ZEBETRAG, see Figure 6.62), which is why the stock-increasing value of the incoming sales order is positive and the stock-decreasing value of net sales is negative. This ensures a correct balancing. Because the data source provides both key figures as positive, you must balance and adjust the algebraic signs when updating.
Stock key figure	To update the stock key figure itself, no settings are necessary in the update since these are located in the settings in the InfoObject **Stock Value** (ZEBESTAND).[7]

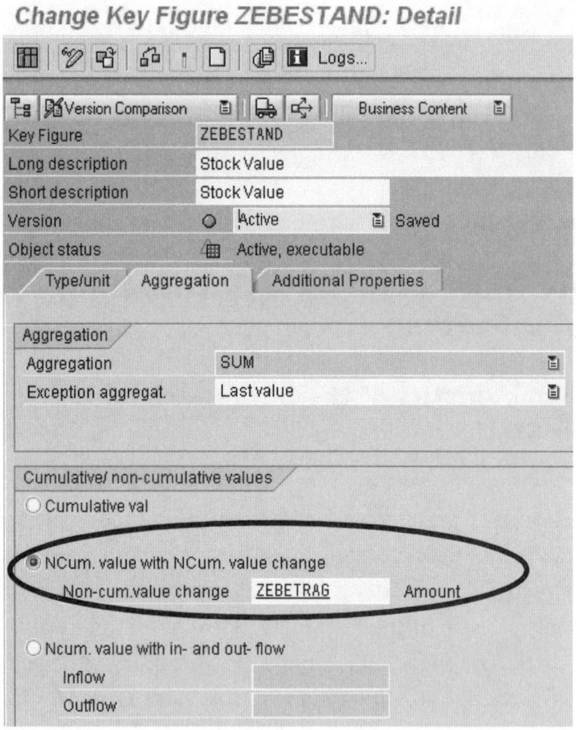

Figure 6.62 Updating the Stock Key Figure via a Stock-Changing Key Figure

---

7 See also Egger, Fiechter, Rohlf: *SAP BW Data Modeling*. SAP PRESS 2005.

When using profitability analysis data, different record types are trans- **Record types**
ferred to the Export DataSource of the ODS object **Profitability Analysis**
(ZECOPAO1). However, you only have to transfer the record types
Incoming Sales Orders and Invoices to the stock InfoCube. Just as the
generated export DataSource of the ODS object **Profitability Analysis**
(ZECOPAO1) must be generated with the InfoSource of the same name—
for all updates of data targets from the ODS object in question—to
ensure the consistency of the data targets, so, too, must all irrelevant
record types be eliminated from the update.

6.2.2 Implementing the Update of Sales Order Stocks

The generated export DataSource of the ODS object **Profitability Analy-**   **Data source**
sis (ZECOPAO1) functions as a data source, for which you must create   **Export**
the update in the InfoCube **Sales Order Stock** (ZEKDABC1).   **DataSource**

Creating Update Rules

▶ To create this update, go to the **InfoProvider** view in the SAP BW
Administrator Workbench and right-click on the InfoCube to be
updated so as to activate the context-sensitive menu. This process is
similar to the one used for the update of the InfoCube **Actual Data:**
Profitability Analysis (ZECOPAC1, see Figures 6.53, 6.59, and 6.54).

▶ After you have selected the **Create Update Rules** menu option, the
dialog **Update Rules create: Start** opens.

▶ When you have entered the source ODS object and clicked on the
Next screen button, the information popup opens because of the key
figure constellation described in Section 6.2.1. This popup window
shows that the key figures were set to 'no update'.

▶ To confirm this, click on the **Next** button (see Figure 6.63, Step 1).

▶ Then, the dialog **Update Rules create: Rules** opens. The only key figure that can be updated in this dialog, namely, (ZEBETRAG) **Amount**, is
set to 'no update' (Step 2).

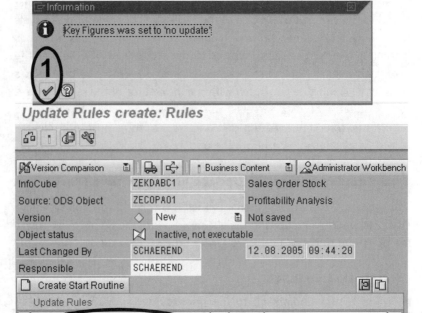

Figure 6.63 Creating Update Rules for the InfoCube "Sales Order Stock"

Creating a Routine in the Update Rules

▶ By double-clicking on the key figure, you can open the **Update Rule: Detail** dialog.

▶ There select the update type **Addition** in the **Key Figure Calculation** tab (see Figure 6.64, Steps 1 and 2).

▶ Select **Routine** as the update method and click on the **Create Routine** button (Steps 3 and 4).

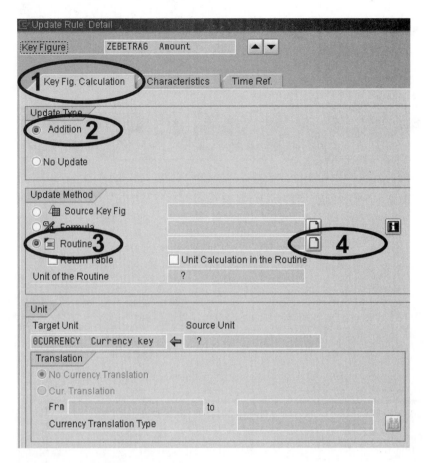

Figure 6.64 Updating the Key Figure

▶ In the **Update … Create routine** dialog, enter a name and click on the **Editor** button (see Figure 6.65, Steps 1 and 2).

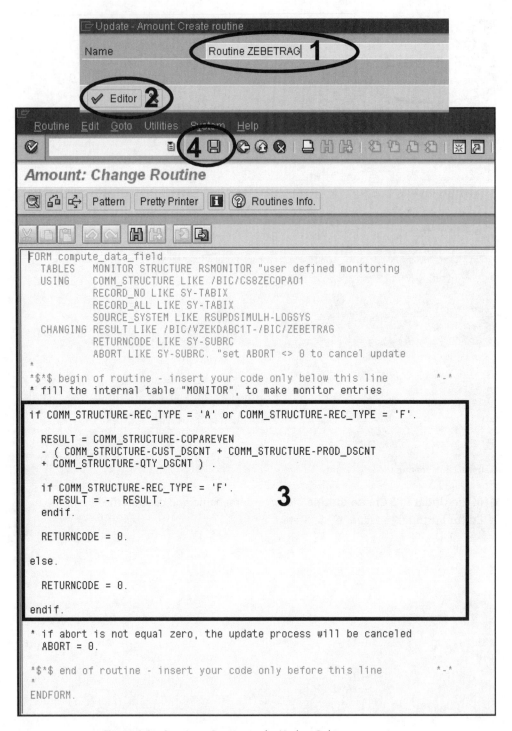

Figure 6.65 Creating a Routine in the Update Rules

▶ This opens the dialog screen **... Create routine** (see Figure 6.65, Step 3), where you can enter the code for the routine:

```
if COMM_STRUCTURE-REC_TYPE = 'A' or COMM_STRUCTURE-REC_
TYPE = 'F'.

  RESULT = COMM_STRUCTURE-COPAREVEN
  - ( COMM_STRUCTURE-CUST_DSCNT + COMM_STRUCTURE-PROD_
DSCNT
  + COMM_STRUCTURE-QTY_DSCNT ) .

  if COMM_STRUCTURE-REC_TYPE = 'F'.
    RESULT = - RESULT.
  endif.

  RETURNCODE = 0.

else.

  RETURNCODE = 0.

endif.
```

Defining the Unit of the Routine

▶ If you click on the **Save** button (see Figure 6.65, Step 4), the screen closes and the **Update Rule: Detail** dialog is displayed again where you can select the **Unit of the Routine** (see Figure 6.66, Step 1).

▶ As all characteristics and time characteristics of the target InfoCube are already contained in the source ODS object, no further settings are necessary in the **Characteristics** and **Time Reference** tabs.

▶ You can complete the update rule creation for the key figure **Amount** by clicking on the **Enter** button (see Figure 6.66, Step 2).

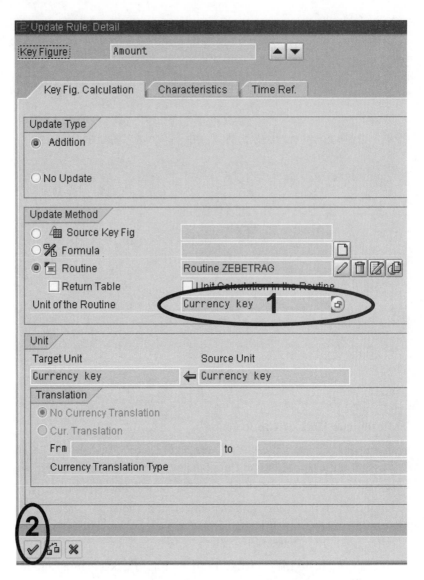

Figure 6.66 Update Rule, Detail: Defining the Unit of the Routine

▶ In the **Update Rules create: Rules** dialog, complete the configuration
with the **Activate** button (see Figure 6.67).

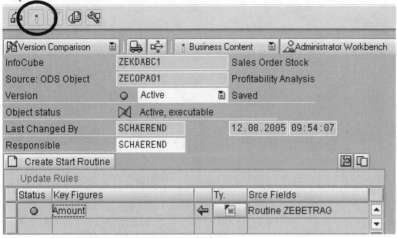

Update Rules create: Rules

Version Comparison				Business Content		Administrator Workbench
InfoCube	ZEKDABC1			Sales Order Stock		
Source: ODS Object	ZECOPAO1			Profitability Analysis		
Version	○ Active			Saved		
Object status	⋈ Active, executable					
Last Changed By	SCHAEREND			12.08.2005 09:54:07		
Responsible	SCHAEREND					

Create Start Routine		

Update Rules

	Status	Key Figures		Ty.	Srce Fields	
	○	Amount	⇐	≣	Routine ZEBETRAG	▲
						▼

Figure 6.67 Activating the Update Rules for the InfoCube "Sales Order Stock"

6.2.3 Updating the Sales Order Stocks

After creating the update rules for the InfoCube **Sales Order Stock** — Data flow
(ZEKDABC1), you can update the data from the various source systems
via the ODS object **Profitability Analysis** (ZECOPAO1) into both the Info-
Cube **Actual Data: Profitability Analysis** (ZECOPAC1) and the InfoCube
Sales Order Stock (see data flow in Figure 6.68).

When updating the data in the InfoCube, opening stocks and stock
changes are updated. Based on this information, SAP BW determines the
stocks (see Volume 1 of the SAP BW Library[8] and Figure 6.69).

---

8 Egger, Fiechter, Rohlf: *SAP BW Data Modeling*. SAP PRESS 2005.

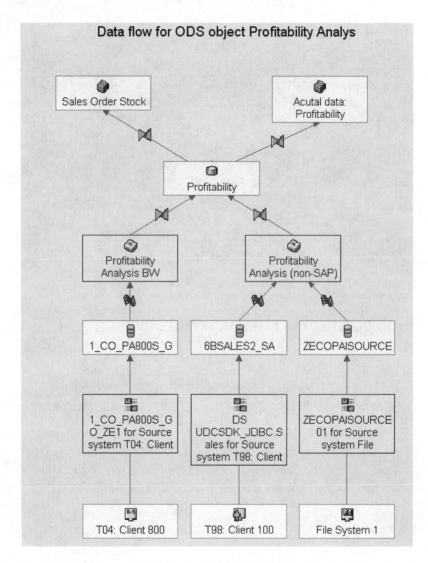

Figure 6.68 Data Flow in the InfoCube "Sales Order Stock for the ODS Object Profitability Analysis"

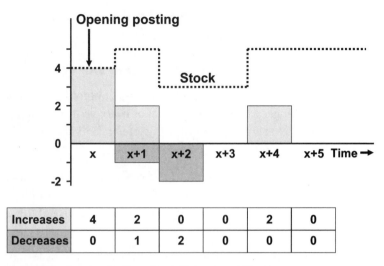

Increases	4	2	0	0	2	0
Decreases	0	1	2	0	0	0

Figure 6.69 Opening Postings, Stock Changes, and Stocks

Queries for stock analysis are possible, based on the posted stock changes and the determined stocks (see Volume 3 of the SAP BW Library[9] and Figure 6.70)

Stock reporting

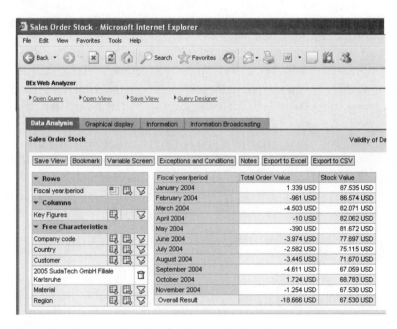

Figure 6.70 Query on the InfoCube "Sales Order Stock"

---

9 Egger et al.: *SAP BW Reporting and Analysis*. SAP PRESS 2006.

6.3 Exemplary Transaction Data Retrieval for Financial Reporting

6.3.1 Extracting General Ledger Data from SAP R/3

Using SAP Business Content-Extractors

SAP OLTP systems such as SAP R/3 provide Business Content for the data retrieval of general ledger transaction figures. For example, these extraction tools are installed as *plug-ins* in SAP R/3 systems, and are available for use after activation during the ETL process for SAP BW.

Wherever these SAP standard extraction tools provide at least the basic required data, we recommend that you use these SAP Business Content components. In the following section, we'll demonstrate the use of these ETL components.

Extractor enhancement

If the SAP Business Content extractors do not provide all the necessary data, they can be enhanced.[10]

Extractor enhancement

SAP Business Content also provides a range of extractors for the general ledger from where you can select the most suitable extractors to meet your requirements.

General ledger: Transaction figures using delta extraction

To meet the requirements of our model company—for representing financial reporting including balance sheet and profitability accounting (profit and loss accounting)—an extractor is necessary to provide the general ledger transaction figures for financial accounting. Since plug-in Release 2003.1, SAP has provided the extractor **General Ledger: Transaction Figures using Delta Extraction** (OFI_GL_6). This DataSource replaces the extractor **General Ledger: Transaction Figures** (OFI_GL_1), which has been available for quite some time and is not delta-capable.[11] The Data-Source to be selected extracts data from the totals record table **G/L Account Master Record Transaction Figures** (GLT0) (see Table 6.1).

---

10 The enhancement of extractors is not addressed in this volume.
11 See also SAP OSS Note 619454: "FI Extraction Figures/Credit Management. Extractors for BW Content 3.20."

Field in the extract structure	Description of the field	Table of origin
KTOPL	Chart of accounts	T001
SAKNR	Number of the G/L account	GLT0
BUKRS	Company code	GLT0
GSBER	Business area	GLT0
WRTTP	Value type for reporting	GLT0
VERSN	Version	GLT0
FISCPER	Fiscal year/period	GLT0
FISCVAR	Fiscal year variant	T001
CURTYPE	Currency type	GLT0
CURRENCY	Currency key	GLT0
UMSOL	Currency key for the debit postings	GLT0
UMHAB	Currency key for the credit postings	GLT0
KUMSL	Cumulative balance	GLT0
UPDMOD	Update mode	GLT0
SHKZG	Debit/credit indicator	GLT0

Table 6.1 Fields of the Extract Structure

6.3.2 Activating the SAP Business Content DataSource

Prior to the initial use of an SAP Business Content DataSource, you must activate it in the SAP OLTP system after installing the plug-ins. To activate it, open the SAP BW-specific implementation guide in the SAP OLTP system.

SAP BW-specific implementation guide in SAP R/3

You can do this in two different ways: either by directly logging onto the SAP R/3 system and calling Transaction **SBIW in IMG of OLTP** (SBIW), or via the **Source systems** view (Transaction RSA13) in the **Administrator Workbench** of SAP BW.

Transferring the Application Hierarchy

▶ In the implementation guide, open the structure **Business Content DataSources** and, if necessary, transfer the application component hierarchy by executing the function with the same name in the implementation guide (see Figure 6.71, Step 1).

▶ When prompted to confirm the transfer, click on **Yes** (Step 2).

▶ The status message **The application component hierarchy has been transfered from the Content** is displayed.

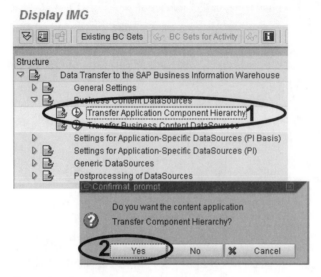

Figure 6.71 Providing the SAP R/3 Application Component Hierarchy for Transfer

Activating and Transferring the SAP Business Content DataSource

Once the application component hierarchy has been activated and is available for replication in SAP BW, the required DataSource can be provided.

▶ The provision of the DataSource is started similarly to the provision of the application component hierarchy, namely, by executing the function **Transfer Business Content DataSources** in the IMG (see Figure 6.72, Step 1).

▶ Then, the screen **Installation of DataSource from Business Content** displays the DataSources according to the application components assigned to them in an overview tree.

▶ To open the application component hierarchy to the required Data-Source that you want to transfer into the active version, position the cursor on the node that contains the respective DataSource, and click on the **Select subtree** button (see Figure 6.72, Steps 2 and 3).

▶ Click on the **Transfer DataSources** button (Step 4).

▶ Confirm all confirmation requests that might appear.

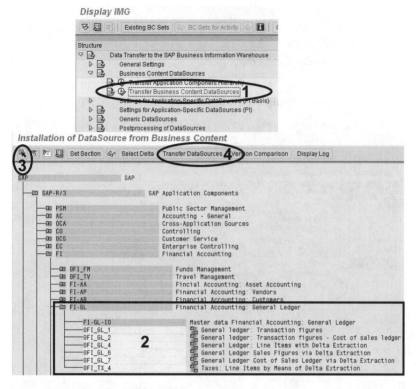

Figure 6.72 Providing DataSources for the Transfer

6.3.3 Implementing the ETL Process by Using SAP Business Content DataSources, InfoSources, and Transfer and Update Rules

Transferring an SAP Business Content DataSource into SAP BW

▶ To transfer the SAP Business Content DataSource into SAP BW, start the **Administrator Workbench** and go to the **Source systems** view.

▶ Right-click to activate the context-sensitive menu and select the **Data-Source Overview** menu option (see Figure 6.73, Step 1).

▶ Alternatively, you can also select the menu option **Replicate Data-Sources** to transfer *all* DataSources of the SAP R/3 source system.

Note that the entire transfer can take a considerable amount of time. Therefore, we recommend that you use a selective transfer process. The entire transfer should be carried out only for initial transfers.

▶ If you have not selected the entire replication of the DataSource, open and scroll through the application component hierarchy until you reach the nodes that you want (here **Financial Accounting: General Ledger**) in the DataSource overview.

▶ Select this node and right-click to open the context-menu and activate the menu option **Replicate DataSources** (see Figure 6.73, Step 2).

▶ After completing the replication, the DataSources are available in SAP BW under the selected node (Step 3).

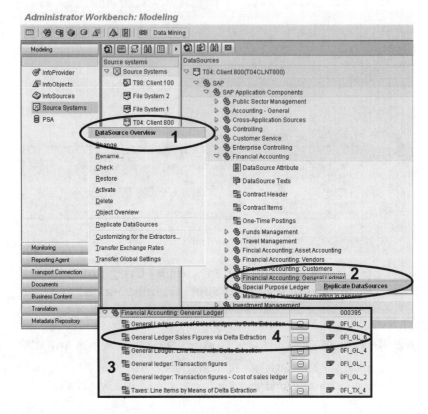

Figure 6.73 Replicating SAP Business Content DataSource

Assigning the SAP Business Content InfoSource in SAP BW

▶ By clicking on the button "-" (see Figure 6.73, Step 4), you can start the assignment of the DataSource to an InfoSource.

▶ The **InfoSource for DataSource** popup then provides you with a suggested Business Content InfoSource for the Business Content DataSources with corresponding Business Content ETL components in SAP BW.

▶ Confirm this suggestion by clicking on the button of the same name (see Figure 6.74, Step 1).

▶ SAP BW automatically collects all required SAP Business Content components (for example, communication rules, transfer rules, and transfer structure) and opens the SAP Business Content transfer.

▶ Click on the **Confirm** button (Step 2).

▶ After a successful activation, the activation status is displayed in the corresponding frame (Step 3).

▶ After activation, you can exit the **Business Content** view of the Administrator Workbench by selecting **Finish** (function key **F3**).

▶ This action automatically returns you to the **Source systems** view in the SAP BW **Administrator Workbench**. The processed DataSource is now identified as assigned by the symbol "**+**".

▶ If you go to the **InfoSources** view of the SAP BW **Administrator Workbench**, you can see the activated Business Content InfoSource with the assigned SAP R/3 source system (see Figure 6.75).

▶ Upon completing the activation, you can transfer data from the SAP R/3 source system to the assigned InfoSource in SAP BW.

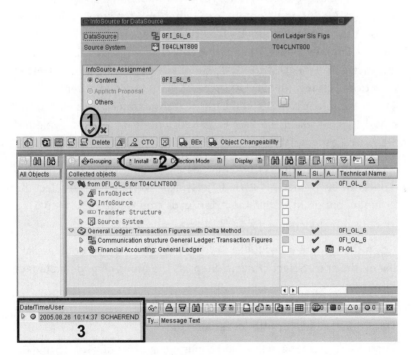

Figure 6.74 Assigning the SAP Business Content InfoSource and Activating the Necessary SAP Business Content Components

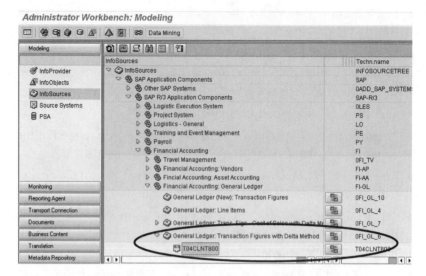

Figure 6.75 SAP Business Content InfoSource and the Assigned Source System

Activating SAP Business Content Update Rules in SAP BW

SAP Business
Content update
rules To receive the maximum benefit from SAP Business Content, we recommend that you activate the Business Content InfoSource update in a corresponding SAP Business Content data target, and transfer it as a suggestion for the customer-specific data target. Because the ODS object
CubeServ Engines General Ledger: Transaction Figures (ZEFIGLO1) is
really an enhancement of the SAP Business Content ODS object **FIGL:
Transaction Figures** (0FIGL_O06), the SAP Business Content update
rules—of the InfoSource **General Ledger: Transaction Figures with Delta
Method** (0FI_GL_6) in the SAP Business Content ODS object referred
to—are ideal as templates.

▶ To activate SAP Business Content update rules, change to the **Business
Content** view of the SAP BW **Administrator Workbench** and select the
grouping option **In Data Flow Afterwards** (see Figure 6.76, Step 1).

▶ Then, select the **Object Types** view (Step 2).

▶ Open the **Update Rules** folder and start the selection by double-clicking on the entry **Select Objects** (Step 3). The **Input help for Metadata**
popup opens.

▶ Click on the column heading **Long Description** (Step 4) to open the
Determine values for filter criteria popup.

▶ Enter ***0FIGL_O06*** as a filter and confirm this selection (Steps 5 and 6).

► Select the required update rule in the filtered view of the **Input help for Metadata** popup (Steps 7 and 8).

► Lastly, activate the update rules by clicking on the **Install** button (Step 9).

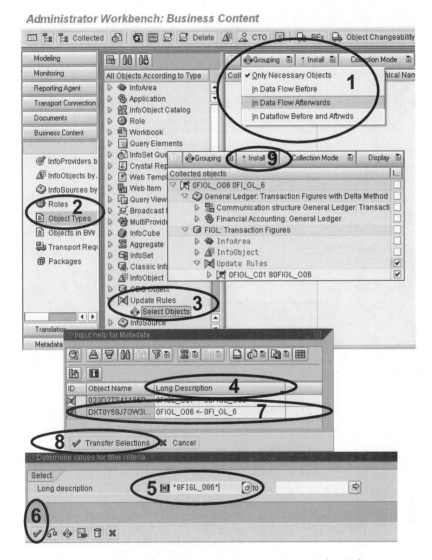

Figure 6.76 Transferring and Activating SAP Business Content Update Rules

Using SAP Business Content Update Rules as Templates

By using SAP Business Content update rules as templates, you can create the update rules for the data transfer from the Business Content InfoSource in the customer-specific ODS object.

▶ To do this, call the SAP BW **Administrator Workbench** and go to the **InfoProvider** view.

▶ Right-click on the ODS object **CubeServ Engines General Ledger: Transaction Figures** (ZEFIGLO1) to open the context menu and select the **Create Update Rules** menu option (see Figure 6.77, Steps 1 and 2).

▶ In the **Update Rules create: Start** dialog, enter the Business Content InfoSource and the ODS object that is to be used as a template for the update rules (Steps 3 and 4).

▶ By clicking on the **Next screen** button (Step 5), you enter the **Update Rules create: Rules** dialog.

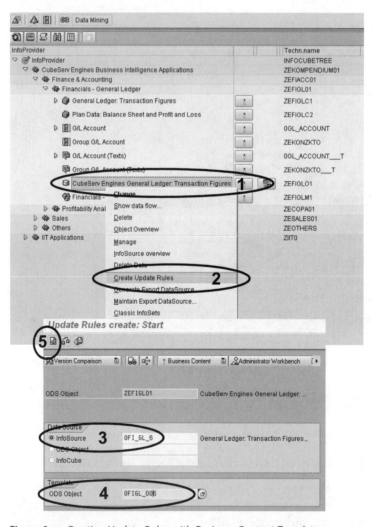

Figure 6.77 Creating Update Rules with Business Content Template

▶ Although you can use the suggested rules, you must supplement them because the InfoSource doesn't transfer all InfoObjects required for the customer-specific ODS object. In this example, you must supplement the update rules for the InfoObjects **Version (Reporting)** (ZEVERSION) and **Source system-ID** (0SOURSYSTEM). In the **Update Rules create: Rules** dialog, you can see the missing update for the InfoObject **Version (Reporting)** (see Figure 6.78, Step 1).

▶ By double-clicking on an InfoObject (in our example 0CURRENCY), you can see in the **Update Rule: Detail** dialog that the InfoObject **Source System** (0SOURSYSTEM) is also not being updated (steps 2 and 3).

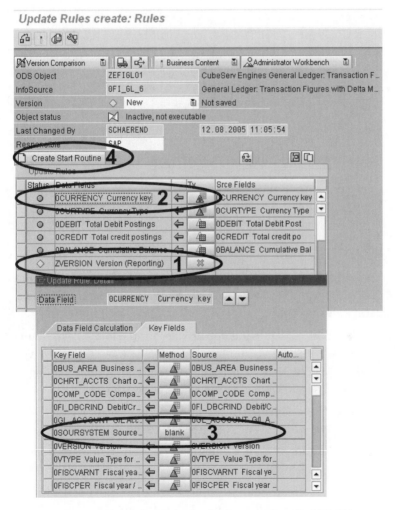

Figure 6.78 Incomplete Update Rules for the Customer-Specific ODS Object

Completing Update Rules

Start routine in the update rules

In the Start routine of the update rules, you can determine the source system that is to provide the data by using a similar process as the one already described to ascertain the source system ID in the transfer rules.

▶ Click on the **Create Start Routine** button in the **Update Rules create: Rules** dialog (see Figure 6.78, Step 4).

▶ As for the start routine in the transfer rules, enter the ABAP/4 code in the **Create Start Routine** dialog to populate the derivation table for the harmonized version and to determine the source system ID (see Figure 6.79, Step 1):

Coding the start routine

```
*$*$ begin of routine - insert your code only below this
*Internal table to derive the harmonized version*
select from /BIC/PZEVERSABL into table itab_PZEVERSABL
where OBJVERS = 'A'.
*Determine source system ID
select single* from RSSOURSYSTEM
where LOGSYS = G_S_MINFO-LOGSYS.

if sy-subrc = 0.
  i_SOURSYSID = RSSOURSYSTEM-SOURSYSID.
  ABORT = 0.
else.
  ABORT = 3.
endif.
*$*$ end of routine - insert your code only before this
```

▶ After entering the ABAP/4 code, click on the **Save** button (see Figure 6.79, Step 2) which will automatically return you to the **Update Rules create: Rules** dialog.

▶ Now, you must configure the update rules for the InfoObjects **Source System** (0SOURSYSTEM) and the derivation of the harmonized **Version** (ZEVERSION). Call the harmonized version by double-clicking on the **Version (Reporting)** entry (see Figure 6.78, Step 1).

Derivation of version (reporting)

▶ In the **Data Field Calculation** tab of the **Update Rule: Detail** dialog, select the **Overwrite** update type (see Figure 6.80, Steps 1 and 2).

▶ Select the **Routine** update method and click on the **Create Routine** button (Steps 3 and 4).

▶ The **Update ... Create routine** popup opens. Enter the desired name and then click on the **Editor** button (Steps 5 and 6).

```
FORM startup
  TABLES   MONITOR STRUCTURE RSMONITOR "user defined monitoring
           MONITOR_RECNO STRUCTURE RSMONITORS " monitoring with record n
           DATA_PACKAGE STRUCTURE DATA_PACKAGE
  USING    RECORD_ALL LIKE SY-TABIX
           SOURCE_SYSTEM LIKE RSUPDSIMULH-LOGSYS
  CHANGING ABORT LIKE SY-SUBRC. "set ABORT <> 0 to cancel update
*
*$*$ begin of routine - insert your code only below this line      *-*
* Interne Tabelle zur Ableitung der harmonisierten Version
select * from /BIC/PZEVERSABL into table itab_PZEVERSABL
where OBJVERS = 'A'.

* Ermitteln Quellsystem-ID
select single * from RSSOURSYSTEM
where LOGSYS = SOURCE_SYSTEM.

if sy-subrc = 0.
  i_SOURSYSID = RSSOURSYSTEM-SOURSYSID.
  ABORT = 0.
else.
  ABORT = 3.
endif.
*$*$ end of routine - insert your code only before this line       *-*
*
ENDFORM.
```

Figure 6.79 Creating the Start Routine

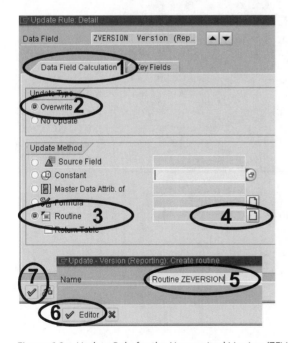

Figure 6.80 Update Rule for the Harmonized Version (ZEVERSION)

► Then, enter the program code in the **... Create Routine** dialog (see Figure 6.81, Step 1):

```
*$*$ begin of routine - insert your code only below
* Derive harmonized version
read table itab_PZEVERSABL into /BIC/PZEVERSABL with key
SOURSYSTEM      = i_SOURSYSID
VERSION         = TRAN_STRUCTURE-VERSI
/BIC/ZEVERSABL = TRAN_STRUCTURE-WRTTP.

if sy-subrc = 0.
    RESULT = /BIC/PZEVERSABL-/BIC/ZEVERSION.
    ABORT = 0.
else.
  ABORT = 4.
endif.
*$*$ end of routine - insert your code only before this
```

► Conclude your entry by clicking on the **Save** button (see Figure 6.81, Step 2).

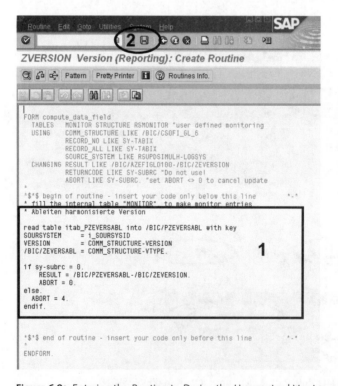

Figure 6.81 Entering the Routine to Derive the Harmonized Version

▶ After saving the routine, the **Update Rule: Detail** dialog is displayed automatically. Go to the **Key Fields** tab and click on the **blank** button next to the **Source System ID** entry (0SOURSYSTEM) (see Figure 6.82, Steps 1 and 2).

Updating the key field "source system"

▶ The **Change Source** dialog opens. Select **Routine** as the source and click on the **Create routine** button (Steps 3 and 4).

▶ In the **Update ...: Create routine** popup, enter the name of the routine and click on the **Editor** button (Steps 5 and 6).

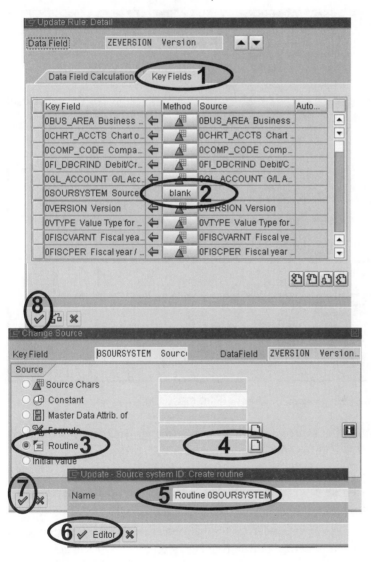

Figure 6.82 Creating Update Rules for the Key Field "Source System ID (0SOURSYSTEM)"

▶ The dialog ... **Create Routine** opens again. Assign the source system ID that was determined in the Start routine (see Figure 6.83, Step 1):

```
*$*$ begin of routine - insert your code only below this
RESULT = i_SOURSYSID.
. . .
*$*$ end of routine - insert your code only before this
```

▶ Save the routine (see Figure 6.83, Step 2).

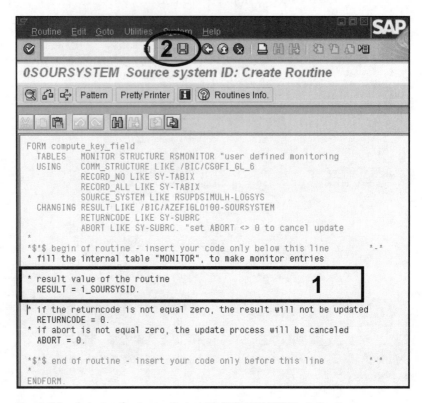

Figure 6.83 Assigning the Source System ID (0SOURSYSTEM) via Routine

▶ Confirm the source assignment in the **Change Source** dialog by clicking on the **Enter** button (see Figure 6.82, Step 7).

▶ Transfer the routine for this characteristic to all the key figures for this update rule by clicking on the **Yes** button in the **Create Characteristic Routine** popup (see Figure 6.84).

Activating update rules
▶ Transfer the update rules for the harmonized version (ZEVERSION) by clicking on the **Enter** button (see Figure 6.82, Step 8) and activate the update rules.

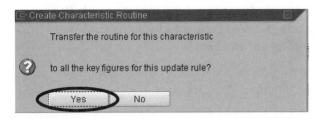

Figure 6.84 Transferring the Routine into All Key Figures of the Update Rule

▶ After activation, you can update the data of the DataSource **General Ledger: Transaction Figures with Delta Method** (0FI_GL_6) via the InfoSource of the same name and update rules (0FI_GL_6), including the table-controlled source system determination and the derivation of the harmonized version in the ODS object **CubeServ Engines General Ledger: Transaction Figures** (ZEFIGLO1) (see Figure 6.85, Steps 1 and 2).

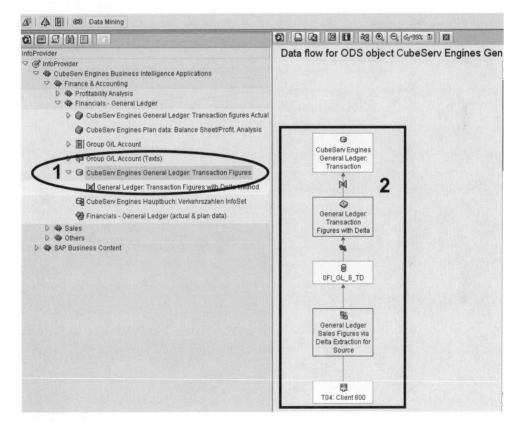

Figure 6.85 Rules and Data Flow for "General Ledger: Transaction Figures with Delta Method"

6.3.4 Updating the Data of the ODS Object with the General Ledger Transaction Figures in the Corresponding InfoCube

InfoCube for financial reporting

Financial reporting should be carried out in an OLAP-conformant manner based on an efficient InfoCube. For this reason, the general ledger transaction figures must be transferred from the ODS object to an InfoCube.

Creating Update Rules

▶ Start the **SAP BW Administrator Workbench** and go to the **InfoProvider** view.

▶ Right-click on the existing InfoCube to open the context-sensitive menu and select the **Create Update Rules** menu option (see Figure 6.86, Steps 1 and 2).

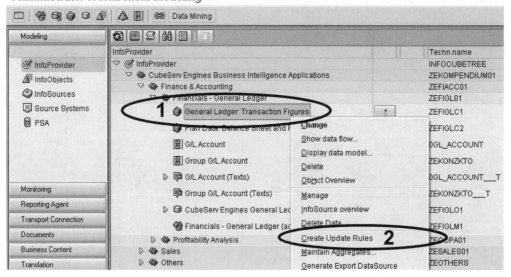

Figure 6.86 Rules for the InfoCube "CubeServ Engines General Ledger: Transaction Figures (ZEFIGLCI)"

▶ In the dialog **Update Rules create: Start**, select **ODS object** as the data source and enter the name of the relevant ODS object **ZEFIGLO1** (see Figure 6.87, Step 1).

▶ Then click on the **Next screen** button (Step 2).

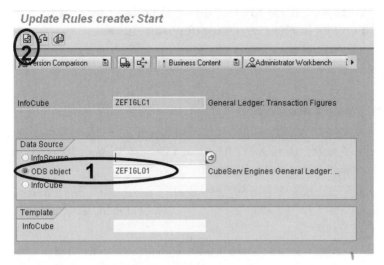

Figure 6.87 Update Rules create: Start

▶ Since all InfoObjects of the InfoCube already exist in the source ODS object, you can accept the suggested transfer rules and activate these directly (see Figure 6.88).

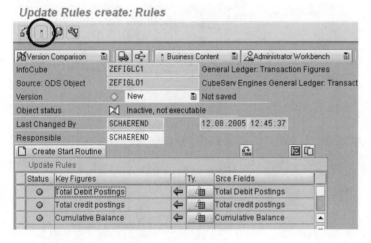

Figure 6.88 Activating the Suggested Update Rules

This ensures that the data of the DataSource **General Ledger: Transaction Figures** is automatically transferred to the InfoCube that forms the basis for OLAP reporting.

6.3.5 Data Retrieval for the General Ledger Transaction Figures in the Corresponding InfoCube

After you have configured the ETL process, you can configure a data request.

Creating an InfoPackage

▶ Launch the SAP BW **Administrator Workbench**, go to the **InfoSources** view, and select the relevant InfoSource **General Ledger: Transaction Figures with Delta Method** (0FI_GL_6).

▶ In the application hierarchy that opens, select the corresponding source system (in the example of our model company **T04CLNT800**, see Figure 6.89, Step 1).

▶ Right-click to open the context-sensitive menu and select **Create Info-Package** (Step 2).

▶ In the **Create InfoPackage** popup, enter the InfoPackage name and click on the **Save** button (Steps 3 and 4).

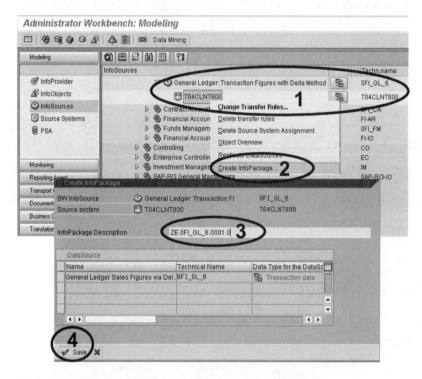

Figure 6.89 InfoPackage for the General Ledger Transaction Figures

▶ Because the DataSource supports delta updates, you must select the update mode **Initialize Delta Process** in the **Update** tab of the Info-Package (see Figure 6.90, Steps 1 and 2).

▶ For future delta updates, you can create an additional InfoPackage with the **Delta Update** setting in the same tab.

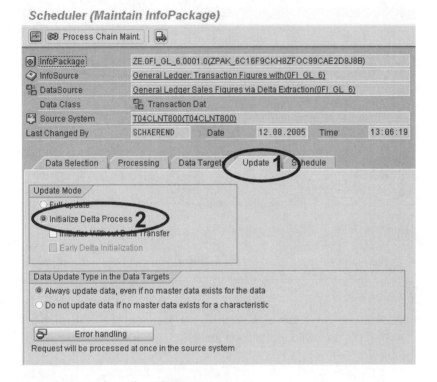

Figure 6.90 Initializing the Delta Process

Retrieving Data

▶ Then you can start the data retrieval by clicking on the **Start** button in the **Schedule** tab (see Figure 6.91, Steps 1 and 2).

▶ You can monitor the execution by clicking on the **Monitor** button (Step 3).

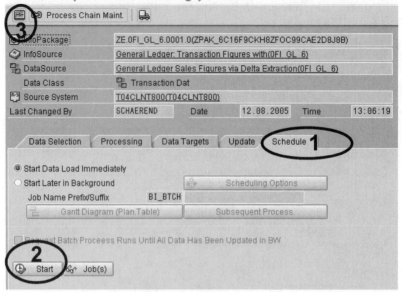

Figure 6.91 Scheduling the Data Retrieval

▶ In the Administrator Workbench monitor, you can conduct a sophisticated analysis of the ETL process by clicking on the **Details** button (see Figure 6.92).

▶ After successfully completing the data load process, the monitor entries are displayed in the color green.

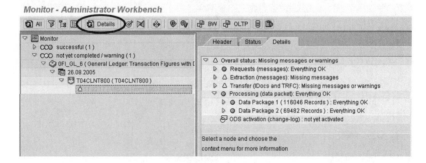

Figure 6.92 Monitoring the ETL Process

▶ If the settings of the ODS object are set to **Activate ODS object data** and **Update data targets from ODS object**, the data targets following the ODS object are updated without further manual intervention (see Figure 6.93).

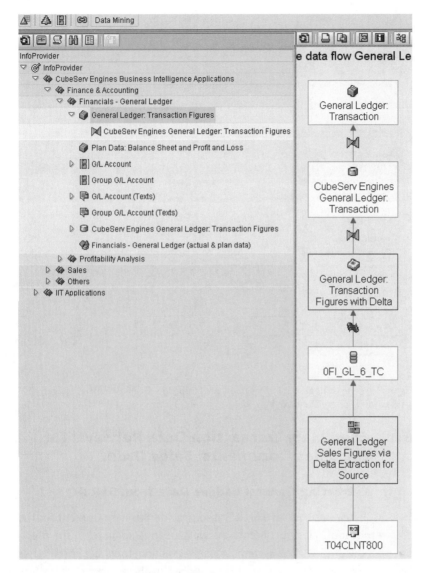

Figure 6.93 Updating the General Ledger Transaction Figures from the SAP R/3 Data-Source via InfoSource and ODS Object in the InfoCube

After successfully updating the data in the ODS object, the parameters mentioned above will start an InfoPackage called **Init Package for updating ODS ZEFIGLO1** for the InfoSource **CubeServe Engines General Ledger: Transaction Figures** (8ZEFIGLO1). This InfoPackage has been automatically created while the export DataSource was generated, and it updates the data in the target InfoCube (see Figure 6.94).

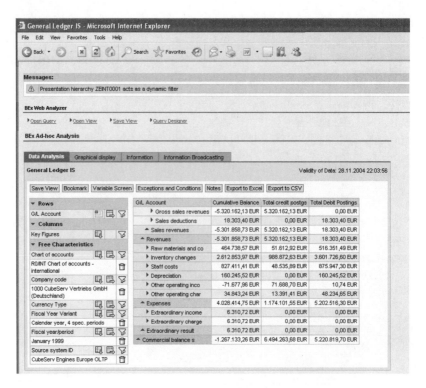

Figure 6.94 Reporting on the InfoCube Data "CubeServ Engines General Ledger: Transaction Figures (ZEFIGLC1)"

6.4 Exemplary Transaction Data Retrieval for the Sales Documents: Sales Order

6.4.1 Extracting General Ledger Data from SAP R/3

SAP Business Content extractors at the document level

SAP OLTP systems such as SAP R/3 also provide Business Content for the data retrieval of sales documents. As was already explained in the previous section, in SAP R/3 systems these extraction tools are installed as *Plug-Ins (PI)* and once activated can be used in the ETL process for SAP BW. In cases where these standard SAP extraction tools provide at least the most important parts of the required data, we recommend that you use these SAP Business Content components for the documents as well.

As we described in our sample scenario (see Chapter 3), data from the SAP module *Sales & Distribution (Sales, SD)* is required for the management level and for operative reporting. In the following section, we'll demonstrate how to use these ETL components. We'll use extractors for the sales documents or sales orders in this case as examples.

6.4.2 Configuring the SAP Business Content DataSource for the Sales Document Header

In order to use the logistics extractors, which have been available since SAP BW 2.0, to extract document data and the update methods, which have been available since PI 2003.1 for the extractors, it is necessary to make the required settings in the SAP OLTP system. To do this, you can either start the **Customize Extractors** function on the corresponding SAP OLTP source system in the **Source systems** view of the SAP BW **Administrator Workbench**, or logon directly to the SAP OLTP system and start the SAP BW-specific implementation guide (Transaction SBIW).

In the SAP BW-specific implementation guide, use the menu path **Settings for Application-Specific DataSources (PI) · Logistics · Managing Extract Structures** (see Figure 6.95).

Starting the Logistics extract structure Customizing Cockpit

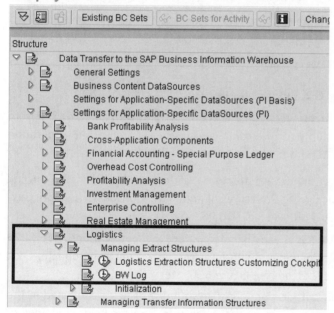

Figure 6.95 Calling the Logistics Extract Structures Customizing Cockpit

In the logistics extract structures Customizing Cockpit, you can maintain extract structures and DataSource settings, activate the update, set the update mode, and, if necessary, carry out the job control for the update mode. After selecting the function in the IMG, the **LO Data Extraction: Customizing Cockpit** is displayed (see Figure 6.96). For the different

LO Data extraction: Customizing Cockpit

logistics document components (here **SD Sales BW Document Header**, that is, sales order header), SAP provides extractors.

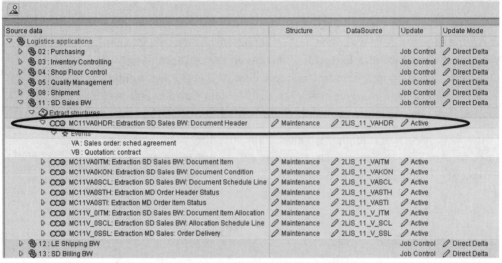

LO Data Extraction: Customizing Cockpit

Source data	Structure	DataSource	Update	Update Mode
▽ 🏵 Logistics applications				
▷ 🏵 02 : Purchasing			Job Control	✎ Direct Delta
▷ 🏵 03 : Inventory Controlling			Job Control	✎ Direct Delta
▷ 🏵 04 : Shop Floor Control			Job Control	✎ Direct Delta
▷ 🏵 05 : Quality Management			Job Control	✎ Direct Delta
▷ 🏵 08 : Shipment			Job Control	✎ Direct Delta
▽ 🏵 11 : SD Sales BW			Job Control	✎ Direct Delta
▽ 🔾 Extract structures				
▽ ⚙ MC11VA0HDR: Extraction SD Sales BW: Document Header	✎ Maintenance	✎ 2LIS_11_VAHDR	✎ Active	
▽ 🌟 Events				
VA : Sales order: sched.agreement				
VB : Quotation: contract				
▷ ⚙ MC11VA0ITM: Extraction SD Sales BW: Document Item	✎ Maintenance	✎ 2LIS_11_VAITM	✎ Active	
▷ ⚙ MC11VA0KON: Extraction SD Sales BW: Document Condition	✎ Maintenance	✎ 2LIS_11_VAKON	✎ Active	
▷ ⚙ MC11VA0SCL: Extraction SD Sales BW: Document Schedule Line	✎ Maintenance	✎ 2LIS_11_VASCL	✎ Active	
▷ ⚙ MC11VA0STH: Extraction MD Order Header Status	✎ Maintenance	✎ 2LIS_11_VASTH	✎ Active	
▷ ⚙ MC11VA0STI: Extraction MD Order Item Status	✎ Maintenance	✎ 2LIS_11_VASTI	✎ Active	
▷ ⚙ MC11V_0ITM: Extraction SD Sales BW: Document Item Allocation	✎ Maintenance	✎ 2LIS_11_V_ITM	✎ Active	
▷ ⚙ MC11V_0SCL: Extraction SD Sales BW: Allocation Schedule Line	✎ Maintenance	✎ 2LIS_11_V_SCL	✎ Active	
▷ ⚙ MC11V_0SSL: Extraction MD Sales: Order Delivery	✎ Maintenance	✎ 2LIS_11_V_SSL	✎ Active	
▷ 🏵 12 : LE Shipping BW			Job Control	✎ Direct Delta
▷ 🏵 13 : SD Billing BW			Job Control	✎ Direct Delta

Figure 6.96 LO Data Extraction: Customizing Cockpit

Maintaining the Extract Structure

The extract structures contain a selection of fields configured by SAP from a communication structure connected to the respective SAP application (for example, SD) from which the required fields can be selected.

▶ You can start the extract structure maintenance by clicking on the link **Maintenance** in the **Structure** column of the **LO Data Extraction: Customizing Cockpit** (see Figure 6.96, Step 1).

▶ If the update has already been activated, the **Notifications MCEX 029** popup will provide you with information regarding the update. Click on the **Enter** button (see Figure 6.97, Step 1).

Integrating fields in the extract structure ▶ A **Selection criteria** popup displays the list of fields contained in the extract structure (field list, left-hand side) and the fields contained in the extract structure which have not yet been used (field list, right-hand side).

▶ By clicking on the line where you want to add fields select the fields which are to be transferred (Step 2).

▶ Then click on the **Transfer selection** button (Step 3). Then the field is transfered in the extract structure (Step 4).

▶ Confirm your entries by clicking on the **Enter** button in the **Selection criteria** popup and **Yes** in the **Entry Confirmation** popup (Steps 5 and 6).

▶ Then you must enter the details for the SAP transport system. The maintenance of the extract structure is completed once you confirm the final **Notifications MCEX 027** popup by clicking on **Enter**. You may have to carry out steps according to the instructions in the last popup.

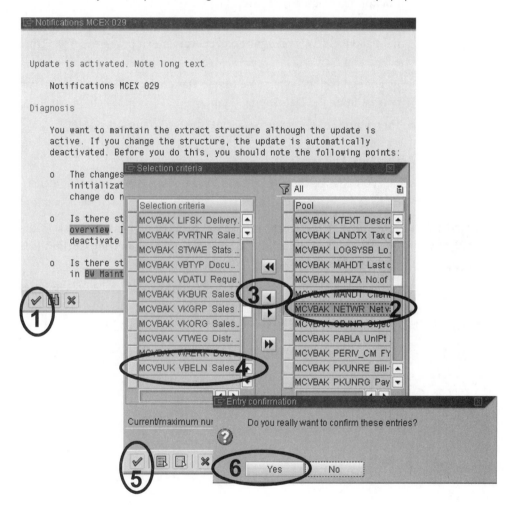

Figure 6.97 Maintaining the Extract Structure

Maintaining the DataSource

After making the changes, you must postprocess the DataSource correspondingly.

▶ You can start the DataSource by clicking on the link 2LIS_11_VAHDR in the **DataSource** column of the **LO Data Extraction: Customizing Cockpit** (see Figure 6.96, Step 1).

▶ In the dialog **DataSource: Customer version edit**, deactivate the **Hide field** and **Field only recognized in customer exit** properties (see Figure 6.98, Step 1).

▶ By generating the DataSource (menu **DataSource · Generate**), you can finish editing the DataSource (Step 2).

▶ Then you must enter the details for the SAP transport system.

Activating the Update

When you change the ETL settings, the update is automatically deactivated.

▶ You can start the reactivation by clicking on the **Inactive** link in the **Update** column in the **LO Data Extraction: Customizing Cockpit** (see Figure 6.99, Step 1).

▶ Confirm the **Notifications MCEX 146** popup by clicking on the **Enter** button (Step 2). The update is then activated.

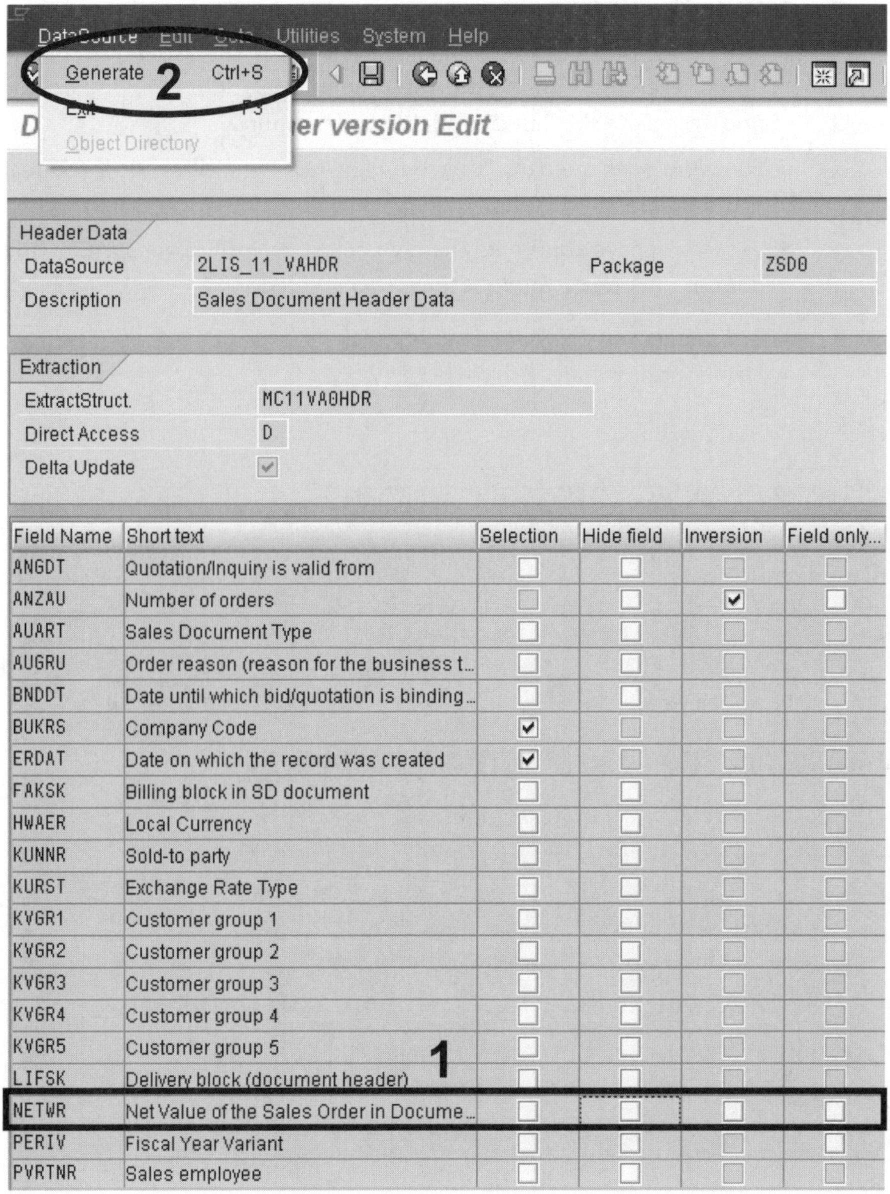

Figure 6.98 Maintaining the DataSource

Setting the Update Mode

▶ To set the update mode, click on the link in the **Update Mode** column (in our example: **Direct Delta**, see Figure 6.99, Step 3) and select the update type in the **Select Update Mode** popup.

▶ For our model company "CubeServ Engines," we will select the **Direct Delta** update mode (Step 4).[12]

▶ When you have confirmed the entry and the **Notifications MCEX 162** popup, the update mode setting is completed.

After reorganizing, sales documents which have already been updated are available for data transfer into SAP BW.

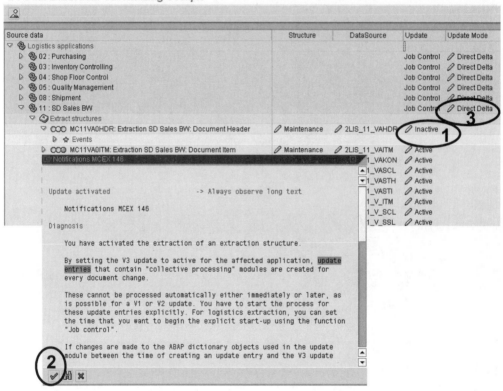

Figure 6.99a Setting the Update Mode—Part 1

---

12 See also OSS Note 505700: "New Update Methods from PI 2002.1 onwards."

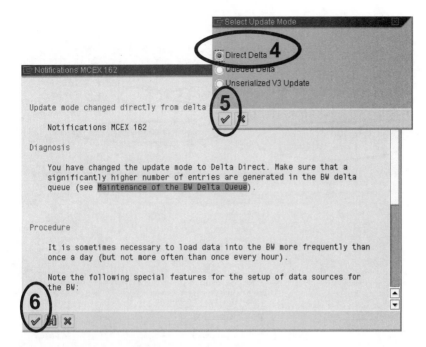

Figure 6.99b Setting the Update Mode—Part 2

6.4.3 Setting the ETL Process for the Sales Document Header

Replicating the DataSource for the Sales Document Header

The customer-specific DataSource must be replicated before it is used in the SAP BW system.

▶ To do this, go to the **Source systems** view of the SAP BW **Administrator Workbench**.

▶ Right-click on the SAP OLTP source system to open the context-sensitive menu and select the **DataSource Overview** menu option (see Figure 6.100, Step 1).

▶ Then position the DataSource overview on the DataSource **Sales Document Header Data** (2LIS_11_VAHDR), right-click to open the context-sensitive menu, and select **Replicate DataSources** (Steps 2 and 3).

▶ After a successful replication, the modified DataSource field list is available (display with **Object overview** function, Step 4).

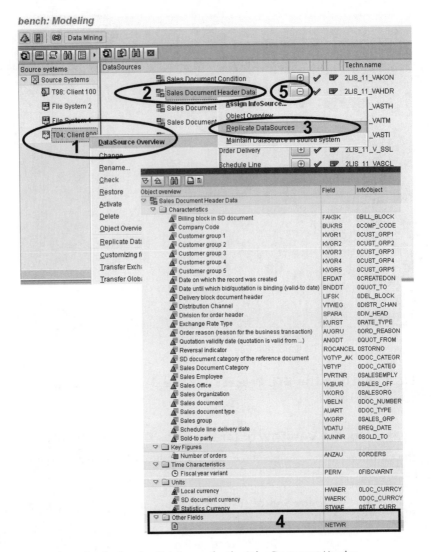

Figure 6.100 Replicating the DataSource for the Sales Document Header

Activating SAP Business Content and Setting Up the InfoSource

▶ By clicking on the "-" button, which shows that this DataSource hasn't yet been assigned to an InfoSource, start the ETL process setup in SAP BW (see Figure 6.100, Step 5).

▶ The **InfoSource for DataSource** popup opens. To accept the suggested value **Content**, click on the **Enter** button (see Figure 6.101, Steps 1 and 2).

▶ This automatically brings you to the **Administrator Workbench: Business Content** view. Click on the **Install** button (Step 3).

▶ After activating the Business Content, the activation log is displayed in the lower part of the dialog (Step 4).

▶ If the activation was successful, you can click on the **Finish** button (**shift** key and **F3** function key) to return to the **Source systems** view of the **SAP BW Administrator Workbench**. There the DataSource usage is indicated by the "+" symbol.

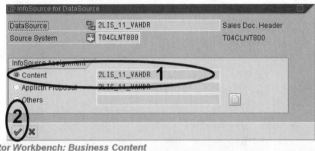

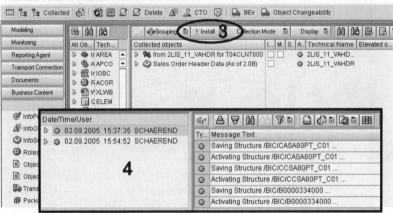

Figure 6.101 Assigning an InfoSource and Activating Business Content

Post-processing InfoSources

The activated Business Content contains all components that are necessary for the transfer of the SAP extract structure template. Customer-specific enhancements are not included. Therefore, the entire InfoSource, that is, the transfer structure, the transfer rules, and the communication structure must be post-processed accordingly.

▶ To do this, go to the **InfoSources** view of the **SAP BW Administrator Workbench**, right-click to activate the context-sensitive menu, and select **Change Transfer Rules...** (see Figure 6.102).

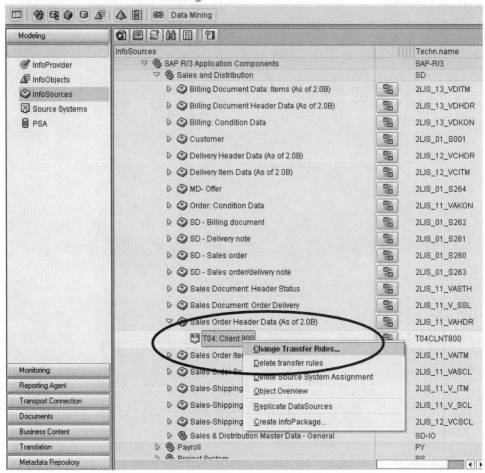

Figure 6.102 Changing SAP Business Content Transfer Rules

Post-processing the transfer structure ▶ To post-process the transfer structure, go to the **DataSource/Transfer Structure** tab (see Figure 6.103, Step 1).

▶ Select the additional fields to be transfered to the InfoSource (these fields are those that have been included recently into the DataSource in the source system, in this case, NETWR), and click on the **Transfer selected InfoObjects** button (Steps 2 and 3).

▶ Then, the additional fields are also available in the transfer structure.

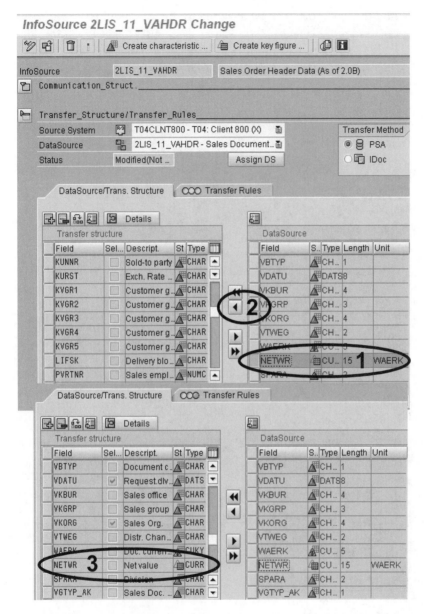

InfoSource 2LIS_11_VAHDR Change

InfoSource   2LIS_11_VAHDR   Sales Order Header Data (As of 2.0B)

Communication_Struct.

Transfer_Structure/Transfer_Rules

Source System	T04CLNT800 - T04: Client 800 (X)
DataSource	2LIS_11_VAHDR - Sales Document...
Status	Modified(Not ...

Assign DS

Transfer Method
- ● PSA
- ○ IDoc

DataSource/Trans. Structure | ○○○ **Transfer Rules**

Details

Transfer structure

Field	Sel...	Descript.	St	Type
KUNNR	☐	Sold-to party	⚠	CHAR
KURST	☐	Exch. Rate ...	⚠	CHAR
KVGR1	☐	Customer g...	⚠	CHAR
KVGR2	☐	Customer g...	⚠	CHAR
KVGR3	☐	Customer g...	⚠	CHAR
KVGR4	☐	Customer g...	⚠	CHAR
KVGR5	☐	Customer g...	⚠	CHAR
LIFSK	☐	Delivery blo ...	⚠	CHAR
PVRTNR	☐	Sales empl ...	⚠	NUMC

DataSource

Field	S..	Type	Length	Unit
VBTYP		CH...	1	
VDATU		DATS	8	
VKBUR		CH...	4	
VKGRP		CH...	3	
VKORG		CH...	4	
VTWEG		CH...	2	
WAERK		CU...	5	
NETWR		CU...	15	WAERK
SPARA		CH...	2	

DataSource/Trans. Structure | ○○○ **Transfer Rules**

Details

Transfer structure

Field	Sel...	Descript.	St	Type
VBTYP	☐	Document c..	⚠	CHAR
VDATU	☑	Request.dlv..	⚠	DATS
VKBUR	☐	Sales office	⚠	CHAR
VKGRP	☐	Sales group	⚠	CHAR
VKORG	☑	Sales Org.	⚠	CHAR
VTWEG	☐	Distr. Chan..	⚠	CHAR
WAERK	☐	Doc. curren..		CUKY
NETWR	☐	Net value		CURR
SPARA	☐	Division	⚠	CHAR
VGTYP_AK	☐	Sales Doc.	⚠	CHAR

DataSource

Field	S..	Type	Length	Unit
VBTYP		CH...	1	
VDATU		DATS	8	
VKBUR		CH...	4	
VKGRP		CH...	3	
VKORG		CH...	4	
VTWEG		CH...	2	
WAERK		CU...	5	
NETWR		CU...	15	WAERK
SPARA		CH...	2	
VGTYP_AK		CH...	1	

Figure 6.103 Changing the Transfer Structure

▶ The newly included fields in the transfer structure must also be transferred into the communication structure. Furthermore, the origin of the data, that is, the source system ID, must be added in the transfer rules. You do this by expanding the communication structure—clicking on the button of the same name (see Figure 6.104, Step 1).

Post-processing the communication structure

▶ Add the new objects to be included to the list. In our example, these objects are the characteristic **Source system ID** (0SOURSYSTEM) and the key figure **Net value of the order in document currency** (0NET_VAL_HD) (Step 2), and confirm this by clicking on the **Enter** button.

▶ Close the communication structure by clicking on the **Collapse** button (Step 3).

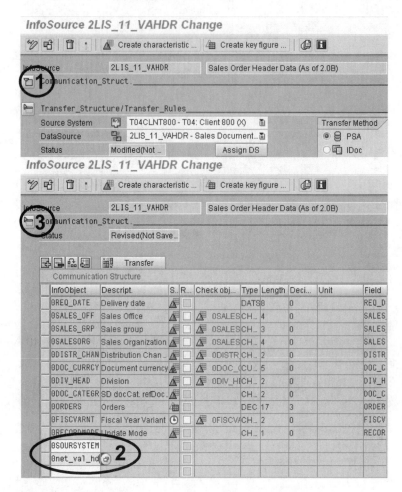

Figure 6.104 Changing the Communication Structure

Post-processing transfer rules

▶ The newly included fields in the transfer structure must also be transfered to the transfer rules. To do this, go to the **Transfer Rules** tab (see Figure 6.105, Step 1).

▶ In the **Communication structure/Transfer rules** list, select the key figure **Net value of the order in document currency** (0NET_VAL_HD) and in the **Assign InfoObject-field** list, select the row **Net value of the order in document currency** (NETWR) (Steps 2 and 3).

▶ Define the transfer as a 1:1 transfer for this field by clicking on the **Transfer in transfer rules** button (Step 4).

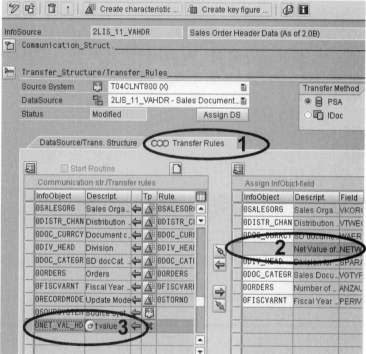

Figure 6.105 Post-Processing Transfer Rules

Creating the Start Routine

The source system ID (0SOURSYSTEM) is to be updated using a method similar to that described in Section 6.1.4 for the extraction of SAP R/3 data for profitability analysis via start routine and transfer via routine.

▶ To do this, enter the start routine to determine the source system ID (0SOURSYSTEM) as described above and save it (see Figure 6.106, Steps 1 and 2).

```
*$*$ begin of global - insert your declaration only below
TABLES: RSSOURSYSTEM.
DATA:   itab_RSSOURSYSTEM type table of RSSOURSYSTEM.
DATA:   i_SOURSYSID like RSSOURSYSTEM-SOURSYSID.
```

```
*$*$ end of global - insert your declaration only before

FORM STARTROUTINE
  USING    G_S_MINFO TYPE RSSM_S_MINFO
. . .
* Determine source system ID
select single * from RSSOURSYSTEM
where LOGSYS = G_S_MINFO-LOGSYS.

if sy-subrc = 0.
  i_SOURSYSID = RSSOURSYSTEM-SOURSYSID.
  ABORT = 0.
else.
  ABORT = 3.
endif.
*$*$ end of routine - insert your code only before
```

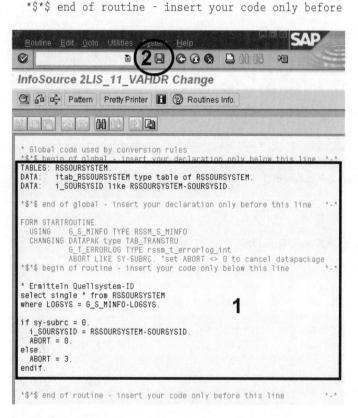

Figure 6.106 Start Routine to Determine the Source System ID

▶ Then, create a routine for the source system ID to transfer the determined value, as described in the process above (see Figure 6.107):

Transfer rule routine

```
*$*$ begin of routine - insert your code only below
. . .
   RESULT = i_SOURSYSID.
. . .
*$*$ end of routine - insert your code only before
```

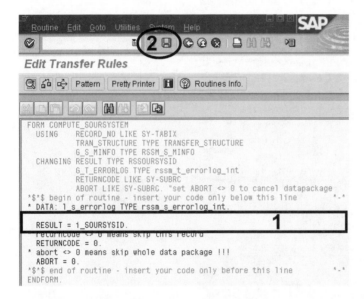

Figure 6.107 Routine to Transfer the Source System ID

▶ Transfer this rule by clicking on the corresponding button and then activate the transfer rules.

Creating an Update Rule

The edited InfoSource is to be updated in the document ODS object **Sales Document Header Data** (ZEVAHDO1).

▶ To do this, go to the **InfoProvider** view of the **Administrator Workbench**, right-click on the ODS object to activate the context-sensitive menu, and select the **Create Update Rules** menu option (see Figure 6.108, Steps 1 and 2).

▶ In the dialog **Update Rules create: Start**, select the processed InfoSource 2LIS_11_VAHDR and click on the **Next screen** button (Steps 3 and 4).

▶ Confirm the **Information** popup by clicking on the **Next** button (Step 5).

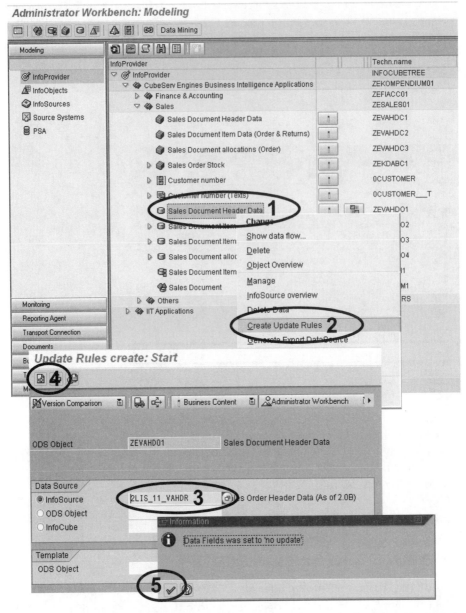

Figure 6.108 Creating Update Rules for the ODS Object "Sales Document Header Data (ZEVAHDO1)"

▶ From this InfoSource, only the fields provided by the DataSource or those that have been added in the communication structure are updated (see Figure 6.109, Step 1).

▶ Then activate the update rules (Step 2).

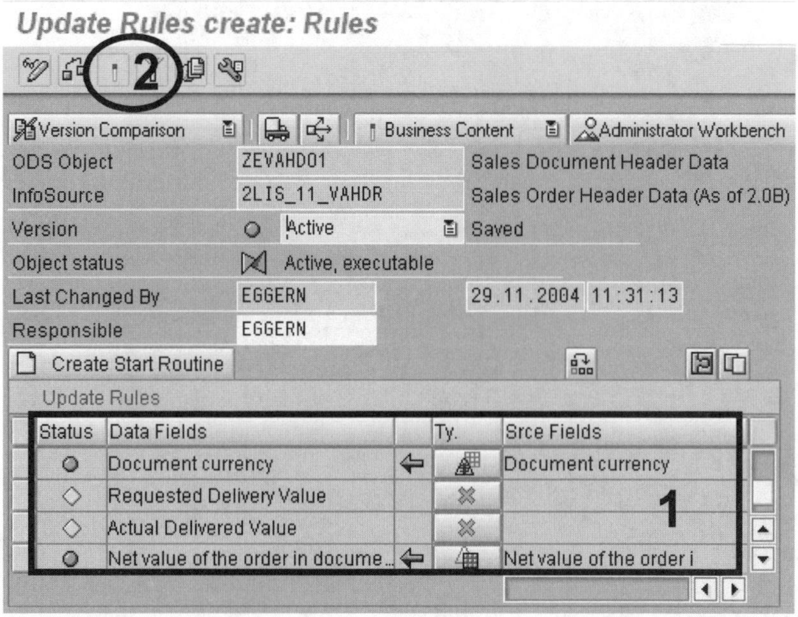

Update Rules create: Rules

%/ ⌐⊙ 1 **②** ⌐⊙ ⌐

| 🔍Version Comparison | 🖹 | 📠 | 📤 | ⏐ Business Content | 🖹 | 🧑Administrator Workbench |

ODS Object	ZEVAHD01	Sales Document Header Data
InfoSource	2LIS_11_VAHDR	Sales Order Header Data (As of 2.0B)
Version	⊙ Active 🖹 Saved
Object status	⊠ Active, executable
Last Changed By	EGGERN	29.11.2004 11:31:13
Responsible	EGGERN

🗋 Create Start Routine   🔢   🖺🗗

Update Rules

Status	Data Fields		Ty.	Srce Fields
⊙	Document currency	⇐	🔨	Document currency
◇	Requested Delivery Value		✖	
◇	Actual Delivered Value		✖	**1**
⊙	Net value of the order in docume..	⇐	🔳	Net value of the order i

◀ ▶

Figure 6.109 Activating Update Rules for the ODS Object "Sales Document Header Data (ZEVAHDO1)"

Creating Update Rules for the InfoCube "Sales Document Header Data (ZEVAHDO1)"

Similar to the process for updating the InfoCube in Section 6.3.4 (see Figure 6.86 and Figure 6.87), you can now create the update rules for the InfoCube **Sales Document Header Data (ZEVAHDC1)**.

▶ Go to the **InfoProvider** view in the **Administrator Workbench**. Open the context-sensitive menu on the InfoCube and select the menu option **Create Update Rules**.

▶ In the dialog **Update Rules create: Start**, enter the ODS object **Sales Document Header Data (ZEVAHDO1)** as the data source and click on the **Next screen** button.

▶ In the popup that opens, confirm the information that not all key figures are updated by clicking on the **Enter** button (see Figure 6.110, Step 1).

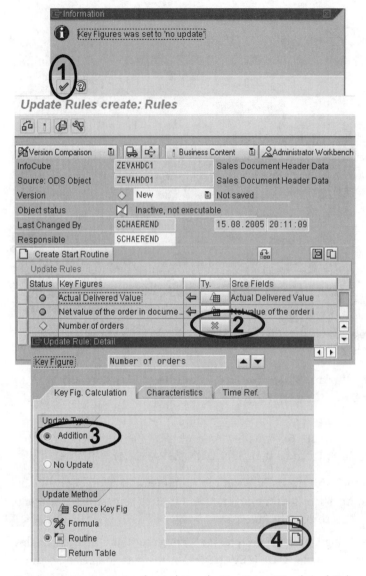

Figure 6.110 No Suggestion for Updating the Key Figure "Number of Orders (0ORDERS)"

SAP Business
Content routines
for key figures

▶ In this case, you can find the logic for the non-updated key figures in the Business Content by opening the update rules of the InfoCube **Service Level: Orders (0SD_C13)**.

▶ There you will note that this key figure is updated in SAP Business Content by using a routine (see Figure 6.111, Step 1).

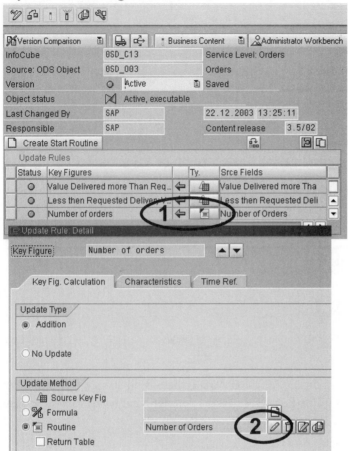

Update Rules change: Rules

Figure 6.111 Updating the Key Figure "Number of Orders (0ORDERS)" in SAP Business Content by Using a Routine

▶ By double-clicking on the **Routine** button, the dialog **Update Rule: Detail** opens.

▶ By clicking on the **Change Routine** button (see Figure 6.111, Step 2) the dialog **Number of orders: Change Routine** displays the code (see Figure 6.112).

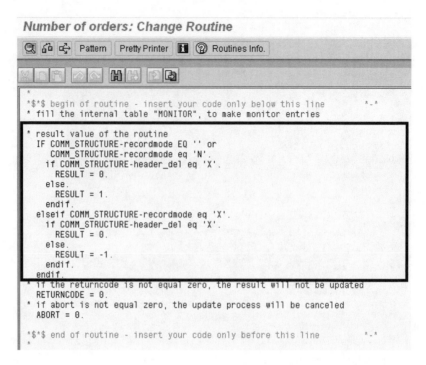

Figure 6.112 Routine to Update "Number of Orders (0ORDERS)" in SAP Business Content

▶ Depending on the RECORDMODE, there is no change to the number of orders (value RESULT = 0) if the counter is set (value RESULT = 1) or if there is a cancellation (value RESULT = –1):

```
IF COMM_STRUCTURE-recordmode EQ '' or
   COMM_STRUCTURE-recordmode eq 'N'.
  if COMM_STRUCTURE-header_del eq 'X'.
    RESULT = 0.
  else.
    RESULT = 1.
  endif.
elseif COMM_STRUCTURE-recordmode eq 'X'.
  if COMM_STRUCTURE-header_del eq 'X'.
    RESULT = 0.
  else.
    RESULT = -1.
  endif.
endif.
```

► You can transfer this routine into your update rules by using Cut & Paste (see below).

► You must also consider the rules to update the characteristics and time characteristics. The update of the time characteristics is transferred from the source characteristic **Date on which the record was created** (0CREATEDON) into the update of your own InfoCubes (see Figure 6.113).

Updating the characteristics

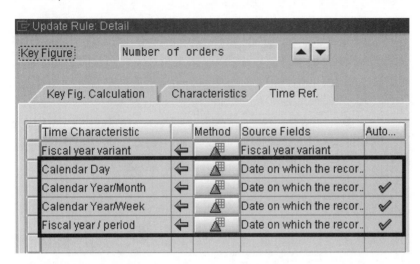

Figure 6.113 Updating the Time Characteristics in SAP Business Content

► To configure the update for your own InfoCubes, select the **Type** button which is set to **No update** (see Figure 6.110, Step 2).

Manual transfer

► In the **Update Rule: Detail** dialog, select the update type **Addition** (see Figure 6.110, Step 3).

► Then you can click on the **Create Routine** button (see Figure 6.110, Step 4).

► In the **Update ... Create routine** popup, enter a name and click on the **Editor** button (see Figure 6.114, Steps 1 and 2).

► Transfer the code into the routine between the comments

```
*$*$ begin of routine - insert your code only below
```

and

```
*$*$ end of routine - insert your code only before
```

and save the routine (see Figure 6.114, Steps 3 and 4).

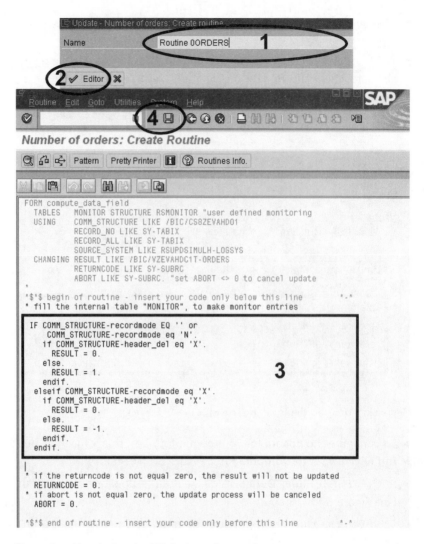

```
Update - Number of orders: Create routine

Name                    Routine 0ORDERS     1

  2  ✓ Editor  ✗

Routine  Edit  Goto  Utilities  System  Help

⊘          4  💾  🔙🔛⊗  💾🔍🔊  💳💳💳💳  ⬜

Number of orders: Create Routine

🔍 🔐 🖨  Pattern   Pretty Printer  ⓘ  ⓘ  Routines Info.

FORM compute_data_field
   TABLES    MONITOR STRUCTURE RSMONITOR "user defined monitoring
   USING     COMM_STRUCTURE LIKE /BIC/CS8ZEVAHDO1
             RECORD_NO LIKE SY-TABIX
             RECORD_ALL LIKE SY-TABIX
             SOURCE_SYSTEM LIKE RSUPDSIMULH-LOGSYS
   CHANGING RESULT LIKE /BIC/VZEVAHDC1T-ORDERS
             RETURNCODE LIKE SY-SUBRC
             ABORT LIKE SY-SUBRC. "set ABORT <> 0 to cancel update
*
*$*$ begin of routine - insert your code only below this line    *-*
* fill the internal table "MONITOR", to make monitor entries

IF COMM_STRUCTURE-recordmode EQ '' or
   COMM_STRUCTURE-recordmode eq 'N'.
 if COMM_STRUCTURE-header_del eq 'X'.
   RESULT = 0.
 else.
   RESULT = 1.                          3
 endif.
elseif COMM_STRUCTURE-recordmode eq 'X'.
 if COMM_STRUCTURE-header_del eq 'X'.
   RESULT = 0.
 else.
   RESULT = -1.
 endif.
endif.

* if the returncode is not equal zero, the result will not be updated
  RETURNCODE = 0.
* if abort is not equal zero, the update process will be canceled
  ABORT = 0.

*$*$ end of routine - insert your code only before this line     *-*
```

Figure 6.114 Transferring the SAP Business Content Routine

▶ When you return to the **Update Rule: Detail** dialog the name of the routine will be displayed in the **Key Figure Calculation** tab (see Figure 6.115).

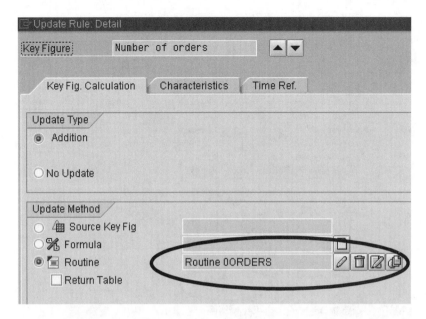

Figure 6.115 After Creating the Routine 0ORDERS

▶ Click on the **Time Reference** tab (see Figure 6.116, Step 1).

▶ Edit the update for all time characteristics with the exception of the **Fiscal year variant** (0FISCVARNT) characteristic, by clicking on the **Method** button. For the time characteristic **Weekday** (0WEEKDAY1), for instance, it has the value **blank** (Step 2).

▶ In the **Change Source** popup, select the source field **Source Chars** and click on the menu (Steps 3 and 4).

▶ The **Source InfoObject** popup opens. Here, you can select the entry **0CREATEDON** by double-clicking on it (Step 5).

▶ This means the selection is transferred to the **Change Source** popup and displayed as a source characteristic (see Figure 6.117, Step 1).

▶ Transfer the setting by selecting the corresponding button (Step 2).

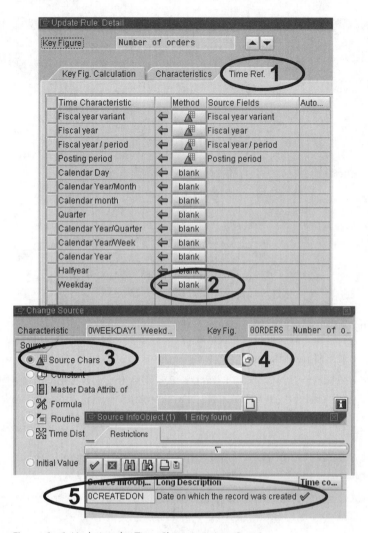

Figure 6.116 Updating the Time Characteristics—Part 1

▶ Continue to transfer these settings in all key figure rules by clicking on the **Yes** button in the **Copy Source Characteristic** popup (Step 3).

▶ After you have made these settings for all time characteristics, click on the **Enter** button (Steps 4 and 5).

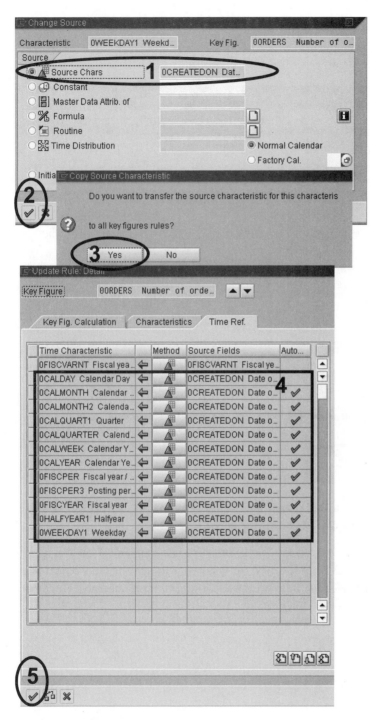

Figure 6.117 Updating the Time Characteristics—Part 2

▶ The update rule in the **Update Rules change: Rules** overview screen is displayed (see Figure 6.118, Step 1).

▶ These update rules can then be activated (Step 2).

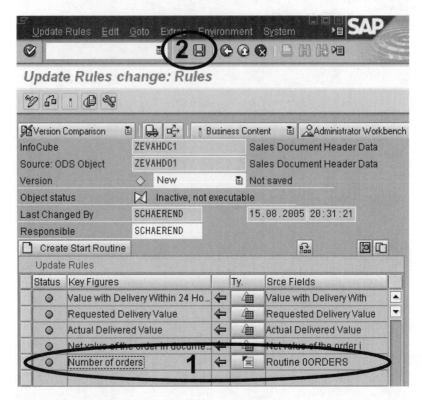

Figure 6.118 Activating the Update Rules

6.4.4 Data Retrieval for Sales Document Header Data in the Corresponding InfoCube

After the ETL process has been configured (see Figure 6.119), the update can take place from the SAP OLTP system through the ODS object **Sales Document Header Data** (ZEVAHDO1) in the InfoCube **Sales Document Header Data** (ZEVAHDC1).

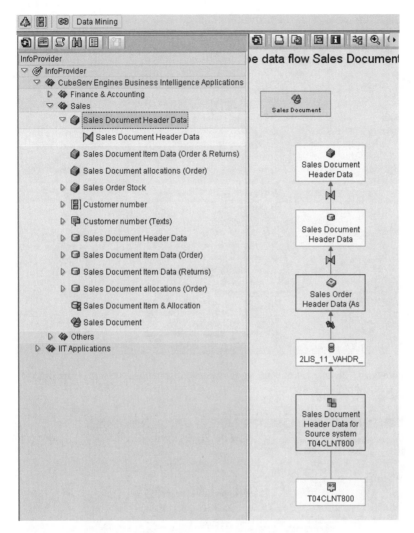

Figure 6.119 Data Flow for the Sales Document Header Data

Creating the InfoPackage

▶ For the corresponding SAP R/3 source system, InfoSources **Sales Order Header Data** (2LIS_11_VAHDR), create an InfoPackage by opening the context-sensitive menu in the **SAP BW Administrator Workbench InfoSources** view by right-clicking in the source system under the InfoSource and selecting the menu option **Create InfoPackage...** (see Figure 6.120, Steps 1 and 2).

▶ Enter an **InfoPackage Description** and click on the **Save** button (see Figure 6.121, Steps 1 and 2).

Configuring the InfoPackage

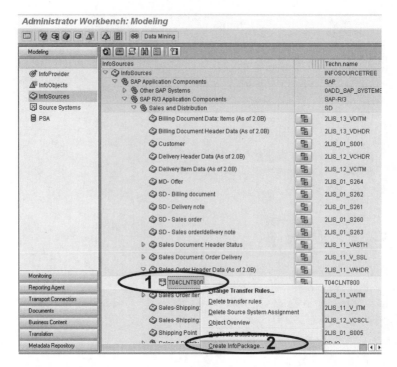

Figure 6.120 Creating an InfoPackage for the InfoSource "Sales Order Header Data (2LIS_11_VAHDR)"

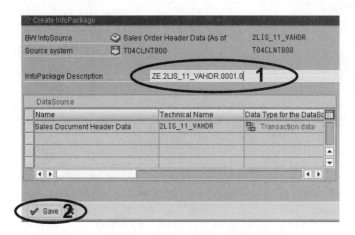

Figure 6.121a Configuring the InfoPackage for the DataSource "Sales Order Header Data (2LIS_11_VAHDR)"—Part 1

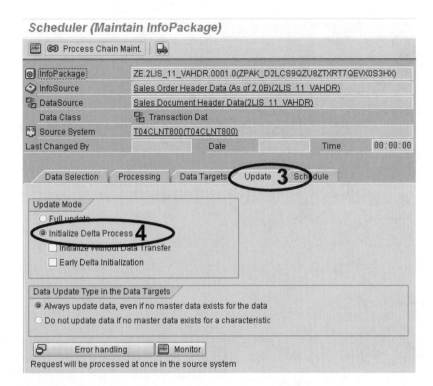

Figure 6.121b Configuring the InfoPackage for the DataSource "Sales Order Header Data (2LIS_11_VAHDR)"—Part 2

▶ In the **Update** tab, select the update mode **Initialize Delta Process** (Steps 3 and 4).

▶ Start the update using the **Start** button in the **Schedule** tab (see Figure 6.122, Steps 1 and 2).

▶ To monitor the update process, you can click on the corresponding button in the scheduler (Step 3).

▶ The update is carried out via PSA in the ODS object **Sales Document Header Data** (ZEVAHDO1) and from there directly to the InfoCube **Sales Document Header Data** (ZEVAHDC1) (see monitor in Figure 6.123).

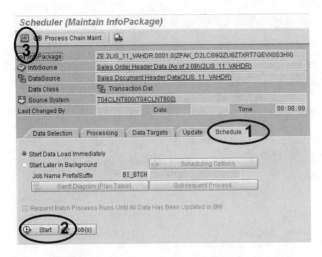

Figure 6.122 Starting the Data Load and Calling the Monitor

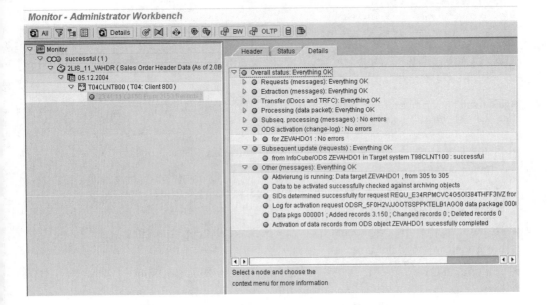

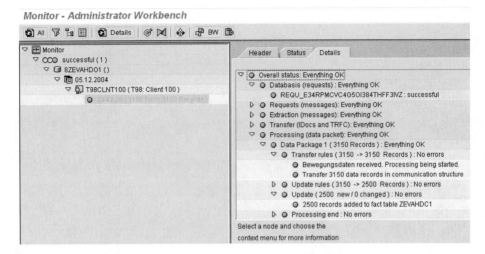

Figure 6.123 Monitoring the Update via ODS Object in the InfoCube "Sales Document Header Data (ZEVAHDC1)"

▶ The updated data is then available for reporting (see Figure 6.124).

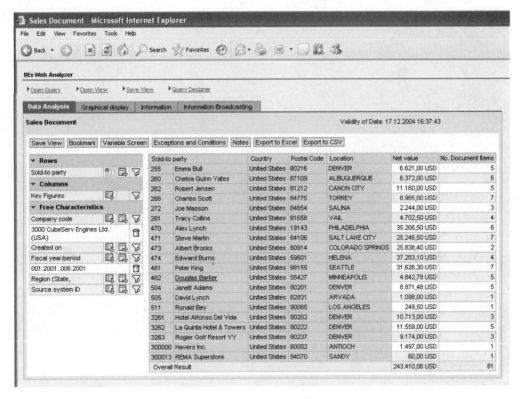

Figure 6.124 Document Reporting for Customer Order Data

7   SAP Business Content

This chapter describes SAP Business Content—the preconfigured solution that SAP delivers with SAP BW. In particular, this chapter illustrates the solution's strengths and weaknesses, and recommends ways in which you can leverage Business Content for data acquisition purposes.

The SAP Business Content comprises a wide range of predefined analytical solutions that are part of the SAP BW package.

SAP Business Content is a preconfigured set of role and task-related information models based on consistent metadata in SAP Business Intelligence. Business Content provides selected roles within a company with the information they need to carry out their tasks.[1]

Definition of SAP Business Content

These predefined solutions greatly help to reduce the time and effort required to set up and implement SAP BW, because they contain all the required components, from extraction (the ETL process) to the data model to reports. This essentially makes it possible to implement an application such as Profit Center Reporting relatively easily and quickly. However, as we will demonstrate in this chapter, you should not accept the provided solutions unquestioningly—even with all their benefits—because they frequently fail to adequately meet the specific requirements of the real-world company.

This chapter focuses solely on Business Content for the ETL process. Please refer to other volumes of the SAP BW Library for information regarding data modeling and reporting.

SAP BC for the ETL process

While Business Content is often not used or only partly used for elements of the data model and reporting, the DataSources should be used as essential components for extraction on the source system (mostly SAP R/3) in as far as possible, because the functionality supplied is complex and can be developed only with considerable effort.

---

1 SAP AG, online documentation SAP BW, http://help.sap.com/saphelp_hw04/help-data/en/37/5fb13cd0500255e10000000a114084/frameset.htm

7.1 Elements of SAP Business Content

Business Content for the extraction, transformation, and loading processes (ETL) consists of the following elements:

- ▶ DataSources
- ▶ InfoSources
- ▶ Transfer rules between the DataSource and the InfoSource
- ▶ Update rules between the InfoSource and the data target

Covering the entire ETL process Using these components, the entire process between the data source and the data target in SAP BW (InfoCube, ODS or InfoObject) can be defined. Figure 7.1 illustrates a sample process.

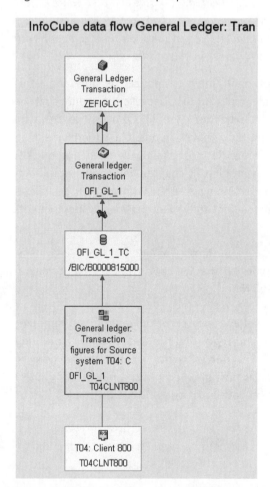

Figure 7.1 Elements of the ETL Process

The Business Content also contains the following objects to control the load process:

Controlling the load process

- ▶ InfoPackages
- ▶ Process chains
- ▶ InfoPackageGroups

> InfoPackageGroups have been replaced by process chains since SAP BW Release 3.0, but are still supplied with Business Content. We will not consider them further in the following discussion.

As parts of the supplied Business Content are not located in SAP BW but in the SAP R/3 source system, in addition to the SAP BW release, you must consider the particular release status of the plug-in in SAP R/3. The following description is based on Plug-in Release 2004_1_470.

Note the SAP R/3 plug-in release

In addition to the extraction from the SAP R/3 system, which is still important in your daily work, ETL processes are also supplied for other SAP data sources—including SAP Advanced Planning Optimizer (APO) and mySAP Customer Relationship Management (CRM)—and for non-SAP systems like Oracle Financials or Dun & Bradstreet.

7.2 Fundamental Problems of SAP Business Content

At this point, we should mention that in our opinion SAP has done an outstanding job in a number of areas.

> Our descriptions are based on a great deal of individual experiences from projects that differed in various respects such as the company size, the industry, or the management style. The weaknesses discussed in the following section pose no problem for certain configurations, and therefore, might have little if any effect on your project.

7.2.1 Delta Capability

> Basically any ETL process can be made delta-capable. However, for reasons of cost-utility-based considerations, delta handling should be carried out as closely as possible to the data source.

Pushed delta   From the perspective of SAP Business Information Warehouse, *Pushed Delta* (FI, LO) is the optimal procedure. In this process, the SAP R/3 application writes data records into the delta queue without any participation of SAP BW, either as a single update (V1) or as a collection run (V3). When starting the InfoPackage in SAP BW, only the data records from the SAP R/3 delta queue are read and transferred into SAP BW.

Pulled delta   In the *Pulled delta* (CO-PA, LIS) procedure, an extraction program is called after starting the BW InfoPackage in R/3, which extracts the data records directly from the application tables of R/3. This process places a greater load on the source system than pushed delta.

If the extraction program in the source system is not delta-capable, the delta can be generated in SAP BW via an Operational Data Store (ODS) object. Here, data is sent with key fields from the source system to the ODS. In cases where changes to the data fields occur in the same key fields, a *Deltarecord* (Changelog) that can then be transferred to an Info-Cube is created. You can optimize this process by excluding such data records in the InfoPackage that are no longer subject to any relevant changes. Use the number range or document date as selection criteria.

Delta-capable extractors   Business Content provides a great portfolio of delta-capable extractors in the area of transaction data. However, it is still important to clarify whether the delta determined by the extractor is reasonable from a business point of view, and therefore, based on the underlying business process, and whether the extractor recognizes all relevant changes as delta. For example, in the project management area, it used to be very difficult to check connections between the network and the project for changes and to deliver a delta to the SAP Business Information Warehouse.

In the master data area, many extractors are delta-capable. Technically, this is largely done via ALE change pointers, which, until recently, were used to coordinate master data across several SAP R/3 systems.

Non-delta capable extractors   Non-delta-capable extractors generally cause considerable time lapses when loading data. Through clever staging, these disadvantages can be reduced; however, it is critical that user departments are told exactly how up to date the loaded data is in the SAP Business Information Warehouse.

7.2.2 Non-Optimal Routines

> Avoid including logic in the update and transfer rules. Instead, you should call function modules or subprograms that contain the actual business logic and can be used more than once. Then, implementing changes is limited to one or a few routines and does not involve the entire staging scenario.

Another point for criticism is the hard coding of key terms in update or transfer rules This quickly leads to a very imprecise system. Storing the derivation rules in tables can ensure transparency here.

Hard coding

For performance-critical data acquisition processes, you should increasingly use start routines. You can employ this method to implement or enrich the data in the internal tables before processing rules for the InfoObjects. In particular, for master data enrichment or cleansing, the benefits far outweigh the costs of the internal tables and start routines, which are relatively low.

7.2.3 Key Figure Presentation

In the financials area, the presentation of key figures is of particular importance. Here it is essential that you know whether an amount is to be interpreted as a positive value with a characteristic (debit/credit), or if the amount per se is already provided as a positive or negative figure and the additionally provided flag is to be used only for information or control. This problem carries through to reporting, where each value can also be displayed with an inverted algebraic sign.

7.2.4 Performance

If the extract structures of the Business Content are used to their full extent, this can very quickly lead to performance problems due to the large quantity of data. Specifically in the area of material master data, where, for instance, the SAP R/3 tables MARA or MARC contain between 100 and 200 fields and the Business Content extract structures are correspondingly wide, it is beneficial to limit the number of transferred fields. By hiding fields in the DataSource, you can reduce the data volume for the transfer between SAP R/3 and SAP BW significantly (see Figure 7.2).

Avoiding performance problems

DataSource: Business content version Display

Header Data			
DataSource	0MATERIAL_ATTR	Package	
Description	Material Number		

Extraction	
ExtractStruct.	BIW_MARA_S
Direct Access	D
Delta Update	☑

Field Name	Short text	Selection	Hide field	Inversion	Field only...
LAEDA	Date of Last Change	☐	☐	☐	☐
LAENG	Length	☐	☐	☐	☐
LIQDT	Deletion date	☐	☐	☐	☐
LVORM	Flag Material for Deletion at Client Level	☐	☐	☐	☐
MAGRV	Material Group: Packaging Materials	☐	☐	☐	☐
MATKL	Material Group	☐	☐	☐	☐
MATNR	Material Number	☑	☐	☐	☐
MBRSH	Industry Sector	☐	☐	☐	☐
MEABM	Unit of dimension for length/width/height	☐	☐	☐	☐
MEINS	Base Unit of Measure	☐	☐	☐	☐
MFRNR	Manufacturer number	☐	☐	☐	☐
MFRPN	Manufacturer part number	☐	☐	☐	☐
MHDHB	Total shelf life	☐	☐	☐	☐
MHDLP	Storage percentage	☐	☐	☐	☐
MHDRZ	Minimum remaining shelf life	☐	☐	☐	☐
MLGUT	Empties Bill of Material	☐	☐	☐	☐
MPROF	Mfr part profile	☐	☐	☐	☐
MSTAE	Cross-Plant Material Status	☐	☐	☐	☐
MSTAV	Cross-distribution-chain material status	☐	☐	☐	☐
MSTDE	Date from which the cross-plant materia...	☐	☐	☐	☐

Figure 7.2 Hiding Fields in the DataSource

Selecting the delta process

As already discussed above, the choice of delta process has a considerable influence on the performance. Therefore, it is imperative that you know whether a serialization of the data records is required. If this is not necessary, through parallel updating of data packages, you can use the full capacity of the application server or of several application servers, if you use a logon group (see also Figure 7.3).

 This process requires certain technical settings on the side of the BW basis; otherwise, all dialog processes are allocated, which could lead to a crash of the entire SAP BW system.

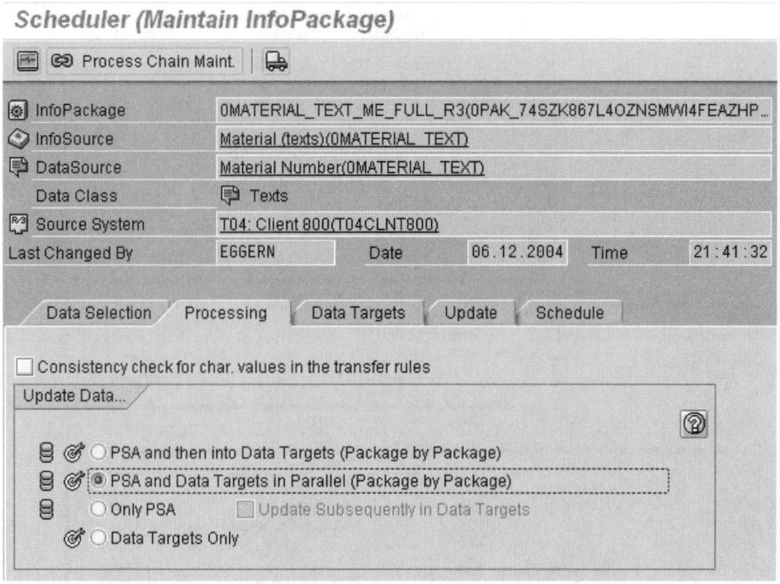

Figure 7.3 Parallelization of the Data Packages

7.3 SAP Business Content for Master and Transaction Data

SAP Business Content can basically be divided into master and transaction data (even if this differentiation constrains the data warehouse approach).

7.3.1 SAP Business Content for Master Data

SAP Business Content for master data provides an enormous amount of ETL components and contains the InfoObjects that carry the master data and the relevant extractors, InfoSources, transfer rules, and existing update rules.

A "downside" is that the field selection for the extract structures in SAP Business Content is not always apparent. For example, if you look at the extract structure for the general ledger account attributes (DataSource 0ACCOUNT_ATTR), as shown in Figure 7.4, you will note that G/L account group, Company ID of Trading Partner, and the Functional Area are missing.

Downside

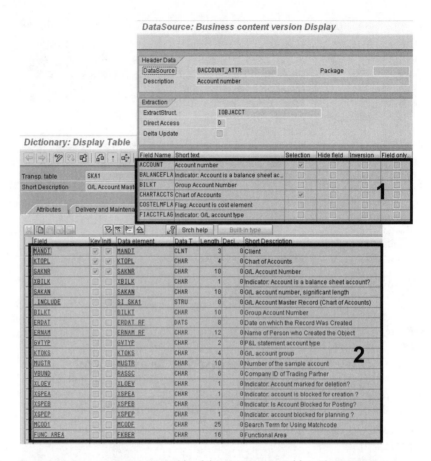

Figure 7.4 Comparing SAP R/3 Fields of the Master Data Table with SAP Business Content Extractor 0ACCOUNT_ATTR

Note that part of SAP Business Content, which deals with master data, can basically be used.

7.3.2 SAP Business Content for Transaction Data

SAP Business Content for transaction data also provides an enormous amount of ETL components and contains extractors, InfoSources, transfer rules, and update rules.

Different qualities In addition to the problem of the field selection referred to in Section 7.3.1, there are greater differentiations in terms of the quality of ETL components for transaction data (see also Section 7.4.5).

With regard to transaction data, you should also try to use SAP Business Content as much as possible even though the requirements for enhancements and corrections are often considerably higher. In certain circumstances, it can be very useful to create a customer-specific (generic) extractor.

7.4 SAP Business Content in Selected Areas of Use

In Version 3.5, SAP Business Information Warehouse provides ETL solutions primarily for the following areas (see also Figure 7.5):

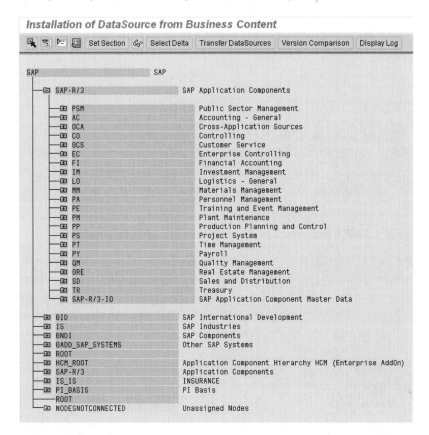

Figure 7.5 Business Content Installed in SAP R/3 Due to the Plug-In

▶ Financials (FI)

▶ Human Resources Management (HR)

▶ Customer Relationship Management (CRM)

▶ Supplier Relationship Management (SRM)

▶ Supply Chain Management (SCM)

- Product Lifecycle Management (PLM)
- Business Content for various industry solutions (IS)

7.4.1 SAP Business Content for Financials

Due to the numerous accounting principles, the FI area (FI-GL, FI-AP, FI-AR, FI-AA) is largely standardized and therefore very well covered by Business Content.

Performance by presummarization Depending on the requirements from the line items or the totals tables, the extractors read the data in each case directly from the SAP R/3 tables. Due to the presummarization in SAP R/3, the entire staging in BW is very efficient.

In the line-items area, larger quantities of data must be processed, which never approximate the size of CO line items or logistics documents.

> In our experience, Business Content for extracting FI data from R/3 can be adopted without any restriction. It just needs to be further enhanced. You can expect the biggest effort to be in the query creation in reporting. However, this topic is not part of this volume.

7.4.2 SAP Business Content for Profitability Analysis

The profitability analysis in SAP CO (in short CO-PA) is in itself already a kind of data warehouse in SAP R/3. For this reason, no business logic must be implemented during extraction. The entire customizing of the key figures and characteristics occurs in SAP R/3 and must be copied only to the Business Information Warehouse.

> SAP's strategy still ensures that the data collection in CO-PA won't be eliminated. But, in the future, all reporting is supposed to take place in BW only.

In addition to 19 predefined profitability segments, CO-PA provides a maximum of 50 additional, self-defined profitability segments (*characteristics*). The contribution margin scheme is mapped via the various value fields (*key figures*). Figure 7.6 shows the creation screen for a CO-PA DataSource.

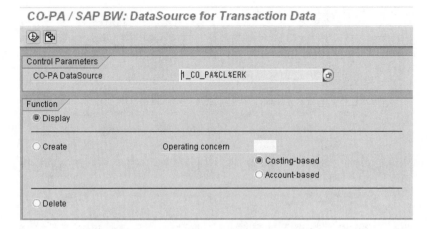

CO-PA / SAP BW: DataSource for Transaction Data

Control Parameters
CO-PA DataSource   1_CO_PA%CL%ERK

Function
⦿ Display

○ Create   Operating concern
⦿ Costing-based
○ Account-based

○ Delete

Figure 7.6 Creating the DataSource for CO-PA

Creating the DataSource for CO-PA is easy. Conversely, the load process can be difficult: The CO-PA extraction program for BW uses the same replication method as does the update program for CO-PA summarization levels. Consequently, there is a time lag of approximately 30 minutes to update the data into SAP BW (*Safety Delta*), that is, the data which is loaded into BW is at least half-an-hour old.

7.4.3 SAP Business Content for Logistics

Using Business Content in the logistics area (LO extraction) requires a very good knowledge of the processes in the SAP R/3 system. In particular, you must understand the events that lead to a BW-relevant data record (see Figure 7.7).

All events that are not provided in Business Content require the creation of a particular extractor and are therefore not a component of Business Content. LIS extraction is also not a part of Business Content as it is based on customer-specific settings in the R/3 system.

Elements outside of SAP Business Content

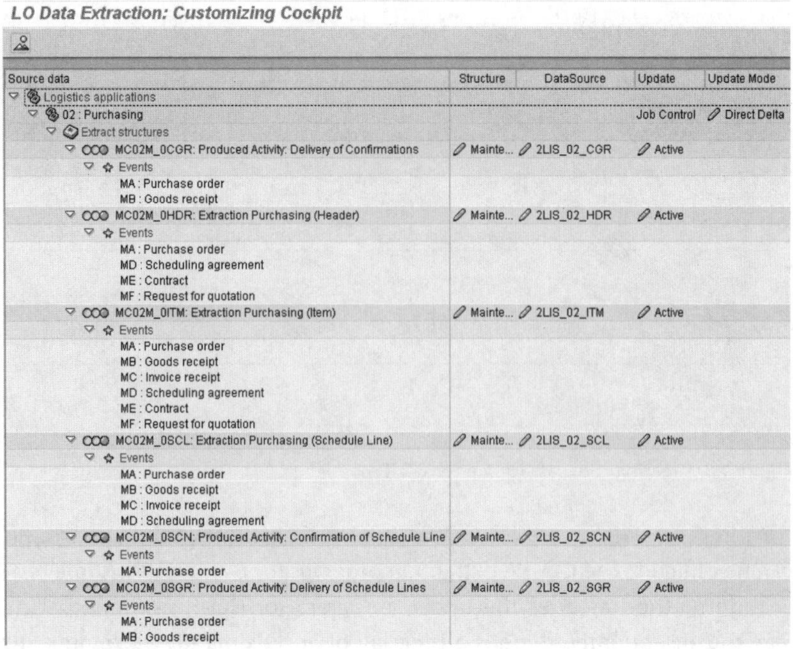

Figure 7.7 BW-Relevant Events in the Purchasing Area

Initialization of the dataset

Another special feature in the area of logistics data extraction from SAP R/3 is the initialization of the dataset. When the reconstruction tables are initialized, an initial dataset is provided that can then be "collected" by SAP BW. According to the settings for the ETL process, the data is collected after the initialization as a delta update or as a new full update. A full update in BW is carried out through the reconstruction tables (see Figures 7.8 and 7.9). A delta update is carried out via the delta queue, which consists of several tables.

The logistics reconstruction tables are cluster tables and cannot be displayed in the dialog.

Repository Info System: Tables Find (6 Hits)

Table Name	Short text
MC02M_0CGRSETUP	BW-Rebuild for MC02M_0CGR Storage
MC02M_0HDRSETUP	Storage BW Setup for MC02M_0HDR
MC02M_0ITMSETUP	Storage BW Setup for MC02M_0ITM
MC02M_0SCLSETUP	Storage BW Setup for MC02M_0SCL
MC02M_0SCNSETUP	BW-Rebuild for MC02M_0SCN Storage
MC02M_0SGRSETUP	BW-Rebuild for MC02M_0SGR Storage

Figure 7.8 Reconstruction Tables in the Purchasing Area

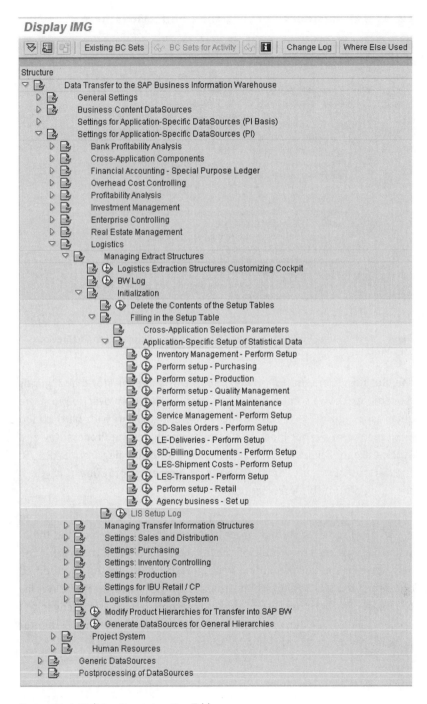

Display IMG

| | | | Existing BC Sets | BC Sets for Activity | ℹ | Change Log | Where Else Used |

Structure

▽ 🗋 Data Transfer to the SAP Business Information Warehouse
   ▷ 🗋 General Settings
   ▷ 🗋 Business Content DataSources
   ▷ Settings for Application-Specific DataSources (PI Basis)
   ▽ 🗋 Settings for Application-Specific DataSources (PI)
      ▷ 🗋 Bank Profitability Analysis
      ▷ 🗋 Cross-Application Components
      ▷ 🗋 Financial Accounting - Special Purpose Ledger
      ▷ 🗋 Overhead Cost Controlling
      ▷ 🗋 Profitability Analysis
      ▷ 🗋 Investment Management
      ▷ 🗋 Enterprise Controlling
      ▷ 🗋 Real Estate Management
      ▽ 🗋 Logistics
         ▽ 🗋 Managing Extract Structures
            🗋 ⊕ Logistics Extraction Structures Customizing Cockpit
            🗋 ⊕ BW Log
           ▽ 🗋 Initialization
              🗋 ⊕ Delete the Contents of the Setup Tables
              ▽ 🗋 Filling in the Setup Table
                  🗋 Cross-Application Selection Parameters
                ▽ 🗋 Application-Specific Setup of Statistical Data
                    🗋 ⊕ Inventory Management - Perform Setup
                    🗋 ⊕ Perform setup - Purchasing
                    🗋 ⊕ Perform setup - Production
                    🗋 ⊕ Perform setup - Quality Management
                    🗋 ⊕ Perform setup - Plant Maintenance
                    🗋 ⊕ Service Management - Perform Setup
                    🗋 ⊕ SD-Sales Orders - Perform Setup
                    🗋 ⊕ LE-Deliveries - Perform Setup
                    🗋 ⊕ SD-Billing Documents - Perform Setup
                    🗋 ⊕ LES-Shipment Costs - Perform Setup
                    🗋 ⊕ LES-Transport - Perform Setup
                    🗋 ⊕ Perform setup - Retail
                    🗋 ⊕ Agency business - Set up
              🗋 ⊕ LIS Setup Log
         ▷ 🗋 Managing Transfer Information Structures
         ▷ 🗋 Settings: Sales and Distribution
         ▷ 🗋 Settings: Purchasing
         ▷ 🗋 Settings: Inventory Controlling
         ▷ 🗋 Settings: Production
         ▷ 🗋 Settings for IBU Retail / CP
         ▷ 🗋 Logistics Information System
         🗋 ⊕ Modify Product Hierarchies for Transfer into SAP BW
         🗋 ⊕ Generate DataSources for General Hierarchies
     ▷ 🗋 Project System
     ▷ 🗋 Human Resources
   ▷ 🗋 Generic DataSources
   ▷ 🗋 Postprocessing of DataSources

Figure 7.9 Initializing Reconstruction Tables

7.4.4 SAP Business Content for Goods Movements

Figure 7.10 shows the result of the activation of a new Business Content version in the goods movements area.

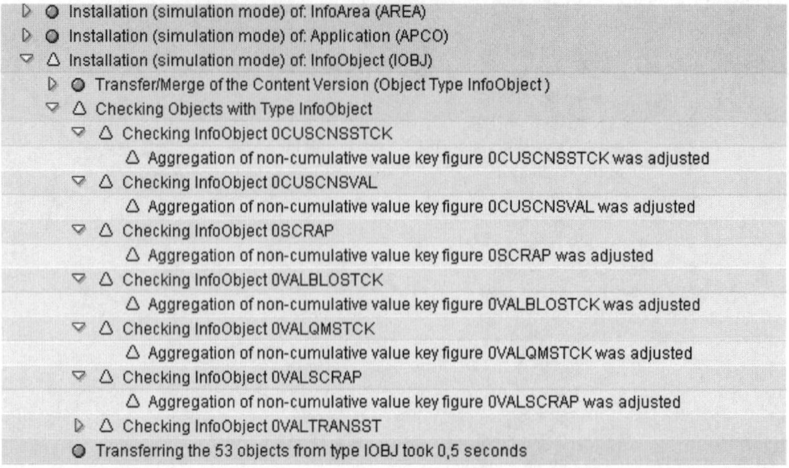

Figure 7.10 shows the result listing:

- ▷ ◉ Installation (simulation mode) of: InfoArea (AREA)
- ▷ ◉ Installation (simulation mode) of: Application (APCO)
- ▽ △ Installation (simulation mode) of: InfoObject (IOBJ)
  - ▷ ◉ Transfer/Merge of the Content Version (Object Type InfoObject)
  - ▽ △ Checking Objects with Type InfoObject
    - ▽ △ Checking InfoObject 0CUSCNSSTCK
      - △ Aggregation of non-cumulative value key figure 0CUSCNSSTCK was adjusted
    - ▽ △ Checking InfoObject 0CUSCNSVAL
      - △ Aggregation of non-cumulative value key figure 0CUSCNSVAL was adjusted
    - ▽ △ Checking InfoObject 0SCRAP
      - △ Aggregation of non-cumulative value key figure 0SCRAP was adjusted
    - ▽ △ Checking InfoObject 0VALBLOSTCK
      - △ Aggregation of non-cumulative value key figure 0VALBLOSTCK was adjusted
    - ▽ △ Checking InfoObject 0VALQMSTCK
      - △ Aggregation of non-cumulative value key figure 0VALQMSTCK was adjusted
    - ▽ △ Checking InfoObject 0VALSCRAP
      - △ Aggregation of non-cumulative value key figure 0VALSCRAP was adjusted
    - ▷ △ Checking InfoObject 0VALTRANSST
  - ◉ Transferring the 53 objects from type IOBJ took 0,5 seconds

Figure 7.10 Activating Business Content Causes Changes Compared to the Previous Version

The Business Content for the extraction of material stock and goods movements shows some weaknesses that we will now describe in more detail (see Figure 7.11). The Business Content solution with hard-coded implementations is not ideal. The extractor provides the **Process Key** and **Stock Category** fields as well as the **Stock Relevant** flag from SAP R/3. The various key figures of the **Goods Movements** InfoCube (0IC_C03) are derived from this information.

You must always conduct a thorough analysis of the transaction data in the SAP R/3 source system in order to receive the correct stock and transaction key figures. The result of this analysis becomes the basis for the derivation of the corresponding key figures in SAP BW. An unmodified transfer of the Business Content provides correct values in SAP BW only by chance. Furthermore, the coding of the implementation directly in the update rules is questionable. In this case, maintaining the implementations is very difficult and prone to errors.

```
*$*$ begin of routine - insert your code only below this line       *-*
* fill the internal table "MONITOR", to make monitor entries
* only goods receipt is considered
  IF ( COMM_STRUCTURE-processkey EQ '000'   "Other Receipts
    OR COMM_STRUCTURE-processkey EQ '001'   "Goods Receipt / Vendor
    OR COMM_STRUCTURE-processkey EQ '004'   "Material Transfer / Receipt
    OR COMM_STRUCTURE-processkey EQ '005'   "Stock Adjustment InvD
    OR COMM_STRUCTURE-processkey EQ '006'   "Stock Adjustment Other
    OR COMM_STRUCTURE-processkey EQ '010' ) "Receipt from Stock Transfer
  AND COMM_STRUCTURE-bwapplnm EQ 'MM'
* only movements which are relevant for stock control
  AND COMM_STRUCTURE-stockrelev EQ '1'
  AND COMM_STRUCTURE-cppvlc <> 0
* see OSS note 630254
  AND ( COMM_STRUCTURE-stockcat IS INITIAL OR
        ( COMM_STRUCTURE-stockcat CA 'EQ' AND
          COMM_STRUCTURE-indspecstk CA 'AM' ) ).
* result value of the routine
  RESULT = COMM_STRUCTURE-cppvlc.
*  if the returncode is zero, the result will be updated
  RETURNCODE = 0.
  ELSE.
*  if the returncode is not equal zero, the result will not be updated
  RETURNCODE = 4.
  ENDIF.
* if abort is not equal zero, the update process will be canceled
  ABORT = 0.
*$*$ end of routine - insert your code only before this line        *-*
```

Figure 7.11 Business Content Update Rule for "Receipt Value of Valued Stock"

A possible alternative is the use of an implementation table that provides a cause-effect relationship at a glance. The option of using key fields means that the multiple derivation of identical values becomes impossible.

Using function modules and subprograms provides further possibilities to centralize program functions, which simplifies their maintenance. Then, the update rule contains only the call for a subprogram with the corresponding parameters (**Call Function** or **Perform**).

By using an account model instead of the key figure model used here, you are provided with a starting point to improve the performance. We address both methods in a separate chapter in a later volume of this series of books.

7.4.5 SAP Business Content for Human Resources

In SAP Business Content for HR, more work is required in order to achieve a satisfactory data acquisition process and data modeling process.

You should note that the type of extraction can provide a methodical problem. The transaction data extractor for employee data (0HR_PA_0) only provides calendar year/month and employee data instead of providing complete data (see Figure 7.12).

Methodical problem

During the update all key figures are implemented in the InfoCube **Head-count and Personnel Actions** (0PA_C01) using hard-coded routines as described above (see also Figure 7.13).

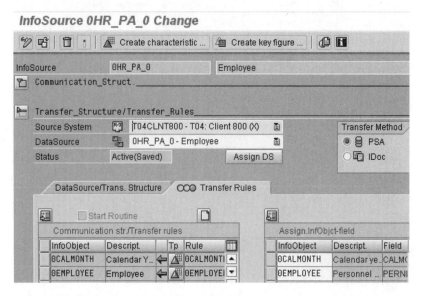

Figure 7.12 Extractor for Employee Data (0HR_PA_0)

Problem areas

This contains several problem areas: On the one hand, incorrect or not up-to-date master data (for example, if the data wasn't successfully loaded) will produce subsequent errors. On the other hand, this method causes a decrease in performance in the ETL process.

When determining the characteristic combinations of key figures, the performance problem is even more dramatic. In addition to routines, which contain the aforementioned problems, a multiple derivation of data takes place that also increases the runtime problem considerably (see Figure 7.14).

In addition, because the key figure types don't use the options of SAP BW, incorrect analyses or a quantity structure that is too large in the Info-Providers results. Thus, the key figure **Number of employees** (0HDCNT_LAST), which is a stock key figure in the logic, is not mapped as such (see Figure 7.15, Steps 1 and 2).

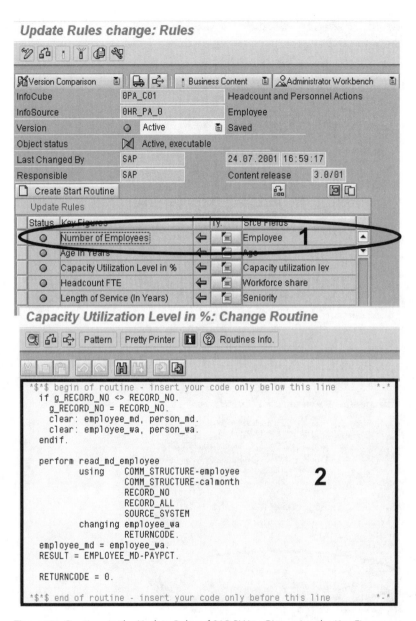

Figure 7.13 Routines in the Update Rules of SAP BW to Determine the Key Figures

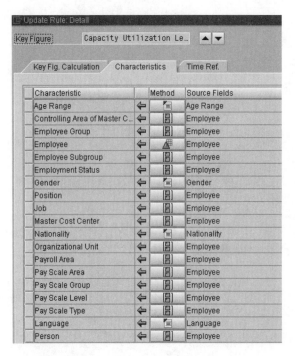

Figure 7.14 Derivation from Master Data

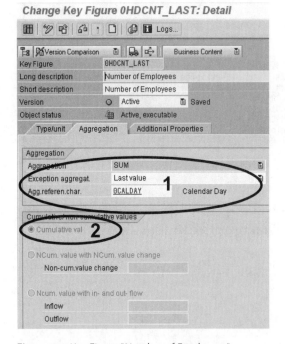

Figure 7.15 Key Figure "Number of Employees"

7.5 Conclusion

As this chapter has shown, the area of data extraction in SAP R/3 can draw on the extractors of SAP Business Content.

Note also that the comments in Chapter 7 of the first volume of the SAP BW Library also apply to the data extraction of Business Content:[2] Don't use the SAP Business Content without reflection. Without adapting it to the actual requirements of your company, it can result in additional project costs and a general dissatisfaction with SAP BW.

▶ In particular, in the area of logistics (SD, MM, PP), the form of the business processes in SAP R/3 is critical for the implementation of the corresponding data acquisition processes in SAP BW.

▶ The finance and controlling area is more strongly standardized in business practice (for example, due to IAS norms) than the area of activity output processes (logistics). Correspondingly, the use of Business Content is possible in the former without any problem.

▶ In the Human Resources area, according to our experience, large parts of the SAP Business Content must be replaced by customized ETL components.

▶ As soon as industry-specific or country-specific factors play a crucial role for analysis, the difficulty in adjusting the data extraction increases.

In large companies, efficient data loading is critical. Users want to see data as quickly as possible. To meet these requirements, you may want to deviate, at least in part, from the Business Content or even enhance it. In such a situation, you can also use tools from third-party providers (for example, Data Stage from Ascential).

But, due to the continued further development of SAP Business Information Warehouse and Business Content, this practice is becoming increasingly less necessary.

---

2 Egger, Fiechter, Rohlf: *SAP BW Data Modeling*. SAP PRESS 2005. Chapter 7, *SAP Business Content*.

A   Abbreviations

ABAP	Advanced Business Application Programming
ADK	Archiving Development Kit
ALE	Application Link Enabling
API	Application Programming Interface
ASCII	American Standard Code for Information Interchange
AWB	Administrator Workbench
BAPI	Business Application Programming Interface
BCT	Business Content
BEx	Business Explorer
BW	Business Information Warehouse
CSV	Comma-Separated Value
DDIC	Data Dictionary
DIM ID	Dimension Identification
DWH	Data Warehouse
ETL	Extraction, Transformation, and Loading
IDoc	Intermediate Document
LUW	Logical Unit of Work
ODBO	OLE DB (Object Linking and Embedding Database) for OLAP
ODS	Operational Data Store
OLAP	Online Analytical Processing
OLTP	Online Transaction Processing
RFC	Remote Function Call
RRI	Report-to-Report Interface
SAPI	Service API
SID	Surrogate Identification
SOAP	Simple Object Access Protocol
SQL	Structured Query Language
TCT	Technical Content
TRFC	Transactional RFC
WAD	Web Application Designer
WAS	Web Application Server
XML	Extensible Markup Language

B   InfoSources

In this appendix, we introduce you to the documentation of the ZECOPAISOURCE01 InfoSource used throughout this book, which was generated using the *CubeServ BW Documentation Tool*.[1]

B.1   InfoSource ZECOPAISOURCE01

B.1.1   Transfer Structures

Source system T98CLNT100   DataSource 6BSALES1

Pos	InfoObject	Description	Data type	Length	Decim	Conv-Exit	Data element
1	0COMP_CODE	Company Code	CHAR	4	0		
2	0COPAREVEN	Revenue	DEC	9	2		
3	0COPASLQTU	Sales QU	UNIT	3	0		
4	0COPASLQTY	Sales Quantity	DEC	9	3		
5	0CURRENCY	Currency	CUKY	5	0		
6	0CUSTOMER	Customer	CHAR	10	0		
7	0FISCPER	Fiscal Year/Period	NUMC	7	0		
8	0FISCVARNT	Fiscal Year Variant	CHAR	2	0		
9	0ID_DOCNUM	Document Number	NUMC	10	0		
10	0MATERIAL	Material	CHAR	18	0		
11	0VARPROD_CS	Var. Prod. Costs	DEC	9	2		

---

[1] The *CubeServ BW Documentation Tool* is the first professional documentation tool for SAP Business Information Warehouse. It enables you to create a documentation online "at the push of a button" from the SAP BW system. Due to various navigation options this documentation can be used as an online documentation and also be printed out. For further informationen, please visit *www.cubeserv.com*.

Source system FILE0001 DataSource ZECOPAISOURCE01

Pos	InfoObject	Description	Data type	Length	Decim	Conv-Exit	Data element
1	0LOG_SYS	Logical System	CHAR	2	0		/BI0/OILOG_SYS
2	0CURTYPE	Currency Type	CHAR	2	0		/BI0/OICURTYPE
3	0REC_TYPE	Record Type	CHAR	1	0		/BI0/OIREC_TYPE
4	0VERSION	Version	CHAR	3	0	ALPHA	/BI0/OIVERSION
5	0VTYPE	Value Type	NUMC	3	0		/BI0/OIVTYPE
6	0FISCVARNT	Fiscal Year Variant	CHAR	2	0		/BI0/OIFISCVARNT
7	0FISCPER	Fiscal Year/Period	CHAR	8	0	PERI7	/BI0/OIFISCPER
8	0ID_DOCNUM	Document Number	NUMC	10	0		/BI0/OIID_DOCNUM
9	0ID_ITMNUM	Document Item Number	NUMC	6	0		/BI0/OIID_ITMNUM
10	0COORDER	Order	CHAR	12	0	ALPHA	/BI0/OICOORDER
11	0VALUATION	Valuation View	NUMC	1	0		/BI0/OIVALUATION
12	0INDUSTRY	Industry	CHAR	4	0		/BI0/OIINDUSTRY
13	0PSTNG_DATE	Posting Date	CHAR	8	0		/BI0/OIPSTNG_DATE
14	0COMP_CODE	Company Code	CHAR	4	0		/BI0/OICOMP_CODE
15	0BILL_DATE	Billing Date	CHAR	8	0		/BI0/OIBILL_DATE
16	0BILL_TYPE	Billing Type	CHAR	4	0		/BI0/OIBILL_TYPE
17	0BUS_AREA	Business Area	CHAR	4	0		/BI0/OIBUS_AREA
18	0CHRT_ACCTS	Chart of Accounts	CHAR	4	0		/BI0/OICHRT_ACCTS
19	0COSTELMNT	Cost Element	CHAR	10	0	ALPHA	/BI0/OICOSTELMNT
20	0CO_AREA	Controlling Area	CHAR	4	0		/BI0/OICO_AREA
21	0COSTOBJ	Cost Object	CHAR	12	0		/BI0/OICOSTOBJ
22	0SALES_DIST	Sales District	CHAR	6	0		/BI0/OISALES_DIST
23	0CUST_GROUP	Customer Group	CHAR	2	0		/BI0/OICUST_GROUP
24	0CUSTOMER	Customer	CHAR	10	0	ALPHA	/BI0/OICUSTOMER
25	0MATERIAL	Material	CHAR	18	0	MATN1	/BI0/OIMATERIAL
26	0PART_PRCTR	Partner Profit Center	CHAR	10	0	ALPHA	/BI0/OIPART_PRCTR
27	0ME_REFITEM	CO-PA Ref. Item	CHAR	6	0	ALPHA	/BI0/OIME_REFITEM

Pos	InfoObject	Description	Data type	Length	Decim	Conv-Exit	Data element
28	0PROFIT_CTR	Profit Center	CHAR	10	0	ALPHA	/BI0/OIPROFIT_CTR
29	0WBS_ELEMT	WBS Element	CHAR	24	0	WBSEL	/BI0/OIWBS_ELEMT
30	0ME_REFDOC	CO-PA Ref. Doc. No.	CHAR	10	0	ALPHA	/BI0/OIME_REFDOC
31	0SEND_CCTR	Sending Cost Center	CHAR	10	0	ALPHA	/BI0/OISEND_CCTR
32	0BA_PRZNR	Sender Bus. Process	CHAR	12	0	ALPHA	/BI0/OIBA_PRZNR
33	0DIVISION	Division	CHAR	2	0		/BI0/OIDIVISION
34	0DOC_NUMBER	Sales Document	CHAR	10	0	ALPHA	/BI0/OIDOC_NUMBER
35	0S_ORD_ITEM	Item	NUMC	6	0		/BI0/OIS_ORD_ITEM
36	0SALES_OFF	Sales Office	CHAR	4	0		/BI0/OISALES_OFF
37	0SALESORG	Sales Organization	CHAR	4	0		/BI0/OISALESORG
38	0SALES_GRP	Sales Group	CHAR	3	0		/BI0/OISALES_GRP
39	0SALESEMPLY	Sales Employee	NUMC	8	0		/BI0/OISALESEMPLY
40	0DISTR_CHAN	Distribution Channel	CHAR	2	0		/BI0/OIDISTR_CHAN
41	0GI_DATE	Goods Issue	CHAR	8	0		/BI0/OIGI_DATE
42	0MATL_GROUP	Material Group	CHAR	9	0		/BI0/OIMATL_GROUP
43	0MAINMATGRP	Main Material Group	NUMC	2	0		/BI0/OIMAINMATGRP
44	0PLANT	Plant	CHAR	4	0		/BI0/OIPLANT
45	0BA_STO_PNR	Canceled Document Item	CHAR	6	0	ALPHA	/BI0/OIBA_STO_PNR
46	0BA_STO_BNR	Canceled Document	CHAR	10	0	ALPHA	/BI0/OIBA_STO_BNR
47	0COPASLQTY	Sales Quantity	CHAR	17	3		/BI0/OICOPASLQTY
48	0VOL_REBATE	Volume Rebate	CHAR	17	2		/BI0/OIVOL_REBATE
49	0COPAREVEN	Revenue	CHAR	17	2		/BI0/OICOPAREVEN
50	0FIXPROD_CS	Fixed Prod. Costs	CHAR	17	2		/BI0/OIFIXPROD_CS
51	0RSRCH_DEV	R&D	CHAR	17	2		/BI0/OIRSRCH_DEV
52	0ACCRDFR_CS	Accrued Freight Costs	CHAR	17	2		/BI0/OIACCRDFR_CS
53	0CUST_DSCNT	Customer Discount	CHAR	17	2		/BI0/OICUST_DSCNT
54	0MARKETING	Marketing	CHAR	17	2		/BI0/OIMARKETING
55	0DIRMAT_CS	Direct Material Costs	CHAR	17	2		/BI0/OIDIRMAT_CS

Pos	InfoObject	Description	Data type	Length	Decim	Conv-Exit	Data element
56	0MATOVHD	Material Overhead Costs	CHAR	17	2		/BI0/OIMATOVHD
57	0PROD_DSCNT	Product Discount	CHAR	17	2		/BI0/OIPROD_DSCNT
58	0QUANT_VRNC	Quantity Variances	CHAR	17	2		/BI0/OIQUANT_VRNC
59	0QTY_DSCNT	Quantity Discount	CHAR	17	2		/BI0/OIQTY_DSCNT
60	0PRICE_VRNC	Price Variance	CHAR	17	2		/BI0/OIPRICE_VRNC
61	0CASH_DSCNT	Cash Discount	CHAR	17	2		/BI0/OICASH_DSCNT
62	0SPCDSLS_CS	Special Direct Costs of Sales	CHAR	17	2		/BI0/OISPCDSLS_CS
63	0OTHER_VRNC	Other Variances	CHAR	17	2		/BI0/OIOTHER_VRNC
64	0OTHER_OVHD	Other Overhead Costs	CHAR	17	2		/BI0/OIOTHER_OVHD
65	0VARPROD_CS	Var. Prod. Costs	CHAR	17	2		/BI0/OIVARPROD_CS
66	0SALES_CMSN	Sales Commission	CHAR	17	2		/BI0/OISALES_CMSN
67	0SALES_CS	Sales Costs	CHAR	17	2		/BI0/OISALES_CS
68	0ADMNSTRTN	Administration	CHAR	17	2		/BI0/OIADMNSTRTN
69	0COPASLQTU	Sales QU	UNIT	3	0	CUNIT	/BI0/OICOPASLQTU
70	0CURRENCY	Currency	CUKY	5	0		/BI0/OICURRENCY

B.1.2　Communication Structure

Pos	InfoObject	Description	Type	Length	Field	Conver-Exit
1	0CURTYPE	Currency Type	CHAR	2	CURTYPE	
2	0REC_TYPE	Record Type	CHAR	1	REC_TYPE	
3	0VERSION	Version	CHAR	3	VERSION	ALPHA
4	0VTYPE	Value Type	NUMC	3	VTYPE	
5	0FISCVARNT	Fiscal Year Variant	CHAR	2	FISCVARNT	
6	0FISCPER	Fiscal Year/Period	NUMC	7	FISCPER	PERI7
7	0ID_DOCNUM	Document Number	NUMC	10	ID_DOCNUM	
8	0ID_ITMNUM	Document Item Number	NUMC	6	ID_ITMNUM	
9	0COORDER	Order	CHAR	12	COORDER	ALPHA

Pos	InfoObject	Description	Type	Length	Field	Conver-Exit
10	0VALUATION	Valuation View	NUMC	1	VALUATION	
11	0INDUSTRY	Industry	CHAR	4	INDUSTRY	
12	0PSTNG_DATE	Posting Date	DATS	8	PSTNG_DATE	
13	0COMP_CODE	Company Code	CHAR	4	COMP_CODE	
14	0BILL_DATE	Billing Date	DATS	8	BILL_DATE	
15	0BILL_TYPE	Billing Type	CHAR	4	BILL_TYPE	
16	0BUS_AREA	Business Area	CHAR	4	BUS_AREA	
17	0CHRT_ACCTS	Chart of Accounts	CHAR	4	CHRT_ACCTS	
18	0COSTELMNT	Cost Element	CHAR	10	COSTELMNT	ALPHA
19	0CO_AREA	Controlling Area	CHAR	4	CO_AREA	
20	0COSTOBJ	Cost Object	CHAR	12	COSTOBJ	
21	0SALES_DIST	Sales District	CHAR	6	SALES_DIST	
22	0CUST_GROUP	Customer Group	CHAR	2	CUST_GROUP	
23	0CUSTOMER	Customer	CHAR	10	CUSTOMER	ALPHA
24	0MATERIAL	Material	CHAR	18	MATERIAL	MATN1
25	0PART_PRCTR	Partner Profit Center	CHAR	10	PART_PRCTR	ALPHA
26	0ME_REFITEM	CO-PA Ref. Item	CHAR	6	ME_REFITEM	ALPHA
27	0PROFIT_CTR	Profit Center	CHAR	10	PROFIT_CTR	ALPHA
28	0WBS_ELEMT	WBS Element	CHAR	24	WBS_ELEMT	WBSEL
29	0ME_REFDOC	CO-PA Ref. Doc. No.	CHAR	10	ME_REFDOC	ALPHA
30	0SEND_CCTR	Sending Cost Center	CHAR	10	SEND_CCTR	ALPHA
31	0BA_PRZNR	Sender Bus. Process	CHAR	12	BA_PRZNR	ALPHA
32	0DIVISION	Division	CHAR	2	DIVISION	
33	0DOC_NUMBER	Sales Document	CHAR	10	DOC_NUMBER	ALPHA
34	0S_ORD_ITEM	Item	NUMC	6	S_ORD_ITEM	
35	0SALES_OFF	Sales Office	CHAR	4	SALES_OFF	
36	0SALESORG	Sales Organization	CHAR	4	SALESORG	
37	0SALES_GRP	Sales Group	CHAR	3	SALES_GRP	
38	0SALESEMPLY	Sales Employee	NUMC	8	SALESEMPLY	
39	0DISTR_CHAN	Distribution Channel	CHAR	2	DISTR_CHAN	

Pos	InfoObject	Description	Type	Length	Field	Conver-Exit
40	0GI_DATE	Goods Issue	DATS	8	GI_DATE	
41	0MATL_GROUP	Material Group	CHAR	9	MATL_GROUP	
42	0MAINMATGRP	Main Material Group	NUMC	2	MAINMATGRP	
43	0PLANT	Plant	CHAR	4	PLANT	
44	0BA_STO_PNR	Canceled Document Item	CHAR	6	BA_STO_PNR	ALPHA
45	0BA_STO_BNR	Canceled Document	CHAR	10	BA_STO_BNR	ALPHA
46	0COPASLQTY	Sales Quantity	QUAN	9	COPASLQTY	
47	0VOL_REBATE	Volume Rebate	CURR	9	VOL_REBATE	
48	0COPAREVEN	Revenue	CURR	9	COPAREVEN	
49	0FIXPROD_CS	Fixed Prod. Costs	CURR	9	FIXPROD_CS	
50	0RSRCH_DEV	R&D	CURR	9	RSRCH_DEV	
51	0ACCRDFR_CS	Accrued Freight Costs	CURR	9	ACCRDFR_CS	
52	0CUST_DSCNT	Customer Discount	CURR	9	CUST_DSCNT	
53	0MARKETING	Marketing	CURR	9	MARKETING	
54	0DIRMAT_CS	Direct Material Costs	CURR	9	DIRMAT_CS	
55	0MATOVHD	Material Overhead Costs	CURR	9	MATOVHD	
56	0PROD_DSCNT	Product Discount	CURR	9	PROD_DSCNT	
57	0QUANT_VRNC	Quantity Variances	CURR	9	QUANT_VRNC	
58	0QTY_DSCNT	Quantity Discount	CURR	9	QTY_DSCNT	
59	0PRICE_VRNC	Price Variance	CURR	9	PRICE_VRNC	
60	0CASH_DSCNT	Cash Discount	CURR	9	CASH_DSCNT	
61	0SPCDSLS_CS	Special Direct Costs of Sales	CURR	9	SPCDSLS_CS	
62	0OTHER_VRNC	Other Variances	CURR	9	OTHER_VRNC	
63	0OTHER_OVHD	Other Overhead Costs	CURR	9	OTHER_OVHD	
64	0VARPROD_CS	Var. Prod. Costs	CURR	9	VARPROD_CS	
65	0SALES_CMSN	Sales Commission	CURR	9	SALES_CMSN	
66	0SALES_CS	Sales Costs	CURR	9	SALES_CS	
67	0ADMNSTRTN	Administration	CURR	9	ADMNSTRTN	

Pos	InfoObject	Description	Type	Length	Field	Conver-Exit
68	0COPASLQTU	Sales QU	UNIT	3	COPASLQTU	CUNIT
69	0CURRENCY	Currency	CUKY	5	CURRENCY	
70	0SOURSYSTEM	Source System ID	CHAR	2	SOURSYSTEM	SORSY
71	ZEVERSION	Version	CHAR	10	/BIC/ZEVERSION	

B.1.3   Transfer Rules

Source system FILE0001   ZECOPAISOURCE01

InfoObject	Description	Rule	Fixed	Conversion Routine	Conver-sion
0ACCRDFR_CS	0ACCRDFR_CS	0ACCRDFR_CS			
0ADMNSTRTN	0ADMNSTRTN	0ADMNSTRTN			
0BA_PRZNR	0BA_PRZNR	0BA_PRZNR			
0BA_STO_BNR	0BA_STO_BNR	0BA_STO_BNR			
0BA_STO_PNR	0BA_STO_PNR	0BA_STO_PNR			
0BILL_DATE	0BILL_DATE	0BILL_DATE			
0BILL_TYPE	0BILL_TYPE	0BILL_TYPE			
0BUS_AREA	0BUS_AREA	0BUS_AREA			
0CASH_DSCNT	0CASH_DSCNT	0CASH_DSCNT			
0CHRT_ACCTS	0CHRT_ACCTS	0CHRT_ACCTS			
0COMP_CODE	0COMP_CODE	0COMP_CODE			
0COORDER	0COORDER	0COORDER			
0COPAREVEN	0COPAREVEN	0COPAREVEN			
0COPASLQTU	0COPASLQTU	0COPASLQTU			
0COPASLQTY	0COPASLQTY	0COPASLQTY			
0COSTELMNT	0COSTELMNT	0COSTELMNT			
0COSTOBJ	0COSTOBJ	0COSTOBJ			
0CO_AREA	0CO_AREA	0CO_AREA			
0CURRENCY	0CURRENCY	0CURRENCY			
0CURTYPE	0CURTYPE	0CURTYPE			
0CUSTOMER	0CUSTOMER	0CUSTOMER			

InfoObject	Description	Rule	Fixed	Conversion Routine	Conversion
0CUST_DSCNT	0CUST_DSCNT	0CUST_DSCNT			
0CUST_GROUP	0CUST_GROUP	0CUST_GROUP			
0DIRMAT_CS	0DIRMAT_CS	0DIRMAT_CS			
0DISTR_CHAN	0DISTR_CHAN	0DISTR_CHAN			
0DIVISION	0DIVISION	0DIVISION			
0DOC_NUMBER	0DOC_NUMBER	0DOC_NUMBER			
0FISCPER	0FISCPER	0FISCPER			
0FISCVARNT	0FISCVARNT	0FISCVARNT			
0FIXPROD_CS	0FIXPROD_CS	0FIXPROD_CS			
0GI_DATE	0GI_DATE	0GI_DATE			
0ID_DOCNUM	0ID_DOCNUM	0ID_DOCNUM			
0ID_ITMNUM	0ID_ITMNUM	0ID_ITMNUM			
0INDUSTRY	0INDUSTRY	0INDUSTRY			
0MAINMATGRP	0MAINMATGRP	0MAINMATGRP			
0MARKETING	0MARKETING	0MARKETING			
0MATERIAL	0MATERIAL	0MATERIAL			
0MATL_GROUP	0MATL_GROUP	0MATL_GROUP			
0MATOVHD	0MATOVHD	0MATOVHD			
0ME_REFDOC	0ME_REFDOC	0ME_REFDOC			
0ME_REFITEM	0ME_REFITEM	0ME_REFITEM			
0OTHER_OVHD	0OTHER_OVHD	0OTHER_OVHD			
0OTHER_VRNC	0OTHER_VRNC	0OTHER_VRNC			
0PART_PRCTR	0PART_PRCTR	0PART_PRCTR			
0PLANT	0PLANT	0PLANT			
0PRICE_VRNC	0PRICE_VRNC	0PRICE_VRNC			
0PROD_DSCNT	0PROD_DSCNT	0PROD_DSCNT			
0PROFIT_CTR	0PROFIT_CTR	0PROFIT_CTR			
0PSTNG_DATE	0PSTNG_DATE	0PSTNG_DATE			
0QTY_DSCNT	0QTY_DSCNT	0QTY_DSCNT			

InfoObject	Description	Rule	Fixed	Conversion Routine	Conversion
0QUANT_VRNC	0QUANT_VRNC	0QUANT_VRNC			
0REC_TYPE	0REC_TYPE	0REC_TYPE			
0RSRCH_DEV	0RSRCH_DEV	0RSRCH_DEV			
0SALESEMPLY	0SALESEMPLY	0SALESEMPLY			
0SALESORG	0SALESORG	0SALESORG			
0SALES_CMSN	0SALES_CMSN	0SALES_CMSN			
0SALES_CS	0SALES_CS	0SALES_CS			
0SALES_DIST	0SALES_DIST	0SALES_DIST			
0SALES_GRP	0SALES_GRP	0SALES_GRP			
0SALES_OFF	0SALES_OFF	0SALES_OFF			
0SEND_CCTR	0SEND_CCTR	0SEND_CCTR			
0SOURSYSTEM	0SOURSYSTEM	0LOG_SYS			
0SPCDSLS_CS	0SPCDSLS_CS	0SPCDSLS_CS			
0S_ORD_ITEM	0S_ORD_ITEM	0S_ORD_ITEM			
0VALUATION	0VALUATION	0VALUATION			
0VARPROD_CS	0VARPROD_CS	0VARPROD_CS			
0VERSION	0VERSION	0VERSION			
0VOL_REBATE	0VOL_REBATE	0VOL_REBATE			
0VTYPE	0VTYPE	0VTYPE			
0WBS_ELEMT	0WBS_ELEMT	0WBS_ELEMT			
ZEVERSION	ZEVERSION			Routine for ZEVERSION	

Source system T98CLNT100   6BSALES1

InfoObject	Description	Rule	Fixed	Conversion Routine	Conversion
0COMP_CODE	0COMP_CODE	0COMP_CODE			
0COPAREVEN	0COPAREVEN	0COPAREVEN			
0COPASLQTU	0COPASLQTU	0COPASLQTU			
0COPASLQTY	0COPASLQTY	0COPASLQTY			

InfoObject	Description	Rule	Fixed	Conversion Routine	Conversion
0CURRENCY	0CURRENCY	0CURRENCY			
0CURTYPE	0CURTYPE		B0		
0CUSTOMER	0CUSTOMER	0CUSTOMER			
0FISCPER	0FISCPER	0FISCPER			
0FISCVARNT	0FISCVARNT	0FISCVARNT			
0ID_DOCNUM	0ID_DOCNUM	0ID_DOCNUM			
0MATERIAL	0MATERIAL	0MATERIAL			
0REC_TYPE	0REC_TYPE		F		
0SOURSYSTEM	0SOURSYSTEM		F1		
0VARPROD_CS	0VARPROD_CS	0VARPROD_CS			
0VERSION	0VERSION		000		
0VTYPE	0VTYPE		010		
ZEVERSION	ZEVERSION		100		

Transfer Rules: Routines

Source system T98CLNT100   DataSource 6BSALES1
Start routine

Line No.	ABAP code
1	* Global code used by conversion rules
2	*$*$ begin of global - insert your declaration only below this line *-*
3	
4	TABLES: /BIC/PZEVERSABL.
5	DATA: itab_PZEVERSABL type table of /BIC/PZEVERSABL.
6	
7	*$*$ end of global - insert your declaration only before this line *-*
8	
9	select * from /BIC/PZEVERSABL into table itab_PZEVERSABL
10	where OBJVERS = 'A'.
11	

Line No.	ABAP code
12	* abort <> 0 means skip whole data package !!!
13	ABORT = 0.
14	

InfoObject ZEVERSION Routine
Routine for ZEVERSION

Line No.	ABAP code
1	
2	read table itab_PZEVERSABL into /BIC/PZEVERSABL with key
3	SOURSYSTEM = TRAN_STRUCTURE-LOG_SYS
4	VERSION = TRAN_STRUCTURE-VERSION
5	/BIC/ZEVERSABL = TRAN_STRUCTURE-VTYPE.
6	
7	if sy-subrc = 0.
8	RESULT = /BIC/PZEVERSABL-/BIC/ZEVERSION.
9	ABORT = 0.
10	else.
11	ABORT = 4.
12	endif.
13	
14	* returncode <> 0 means skip this record
15	RETURNCODE = 0.
16	
17	

C   ODS Objects

In this appendix, we will introduce you to the documentation of the ZECOPAO1 ODS object that is used throughout this book and was generated using the *CubeServ BW Documentation Tool*.[1]

C.1   ODS Object ZECOPAO1

InfoArea ZECOPA01 Profitability Analysis

InfoProvider ZECOPAO1 Profitability Analysis

ODS Object	ZECOPAO1
Description	Profitability analysis
Last Changed by	SCHAEREND
Last Change	11/15/2004/08:28:50
BEx Reporting	No
Type of ODS object	Standard
Unique Data Records	No
Check Table for InfoObject	
Set Quality Status to OK Automatically	Yes
Activate Data of the ODS Object Automatically	Yes
Update Data Targets from ODS Object Automatically	Yes

Key Fields

Text	InfoObject	Data Type	Length
Source System ID	0SOURSYSTEM	CHAR	2
Currency Type	0CURTYPE	CHAR	2
Record Type	0REC_TYPE	CHAR	1

---

1 The *CubeServ BW Documentation Tool* is the first professional documentation tool for SAP Business Information Warehouse. It enables you to create a documentation online "at the push of a button" from the SAP BW system. Due to various navigation options this documentation can be used as an online documentation and also be printed out. For further informationen, please visit *www.cubeserv.com*.

Text	InfoObject	Data Type	Length
Version	0VERSION	CHAR	3
Value Type for Reporting	0VTYPE	NUMC	3
Fiscal Year Variant	0FISCVARNT	CHAR	2
Fiscal Year/Period	0FISCPER	NUMC	7
Document Number	0ID_DOCNUM	NUMC	10
Document Item Number	0ID_ITMNUM	NUMC	6

Characteristics

Text	InfoObject	Data Type	Length
Company Code	0COMP_CODE	CHAR	4
Plant	0PLANT	CHAR	4
Sales Organization	0SALESORG	CHAR	4
Material	0MATERIAL	CHAR	18
Customer Number	0CUSTOMER	CHAR	10
Profit Center	0PROFIT_CTR	CHAR	10
Partner Profit Center	0PART_PRCTR	CHAR	10
Sending Cost Center	0SEND_CCTR	CHAR	10
Work Breakdown Structure Element (WBS Element)	0WBS_ELEMT	CHAR	24
Cost Element	0COSTELMNT	CHAR	10
Sender Business Process	0BA_PRZNR	CHAR	12
Canceled Document	0BA_STO_BNR	CHAR	10
Canceled Document Item	0BA_STO_PNR	CHAR	6
Date for Billing/Invoice Index and Printing	0BILL_DATE	DATS	8
Billing Type	0BILL_TYPE	CHAR	4
Business Area	0BUS_AREA	CHAR	4
Chart of Accounts	0CHRT_ACCTS	CHAR	4
Order Number	0COORDER	CHAR	12
Cost Object	0COSTOBJ	CHAR	12
Controlling Area	0CO_AREA	CHAR	4

Text	InfoObject	Data Type	Length
Customer Group	0CUST_GROUP	CHAR	2
Distribution Channel	0DISTR_CHAN	CHAR	2
Division	0DIVISION	CHAR	2
Sales Document	0DOC_NUMBER	CHAR	10
Sales Document Item	0S_ORD_ITEM	NUMC	6
Goods Issue Date	0GI_DATE	DATS	8
Industry Key	0INDUSTRY	CHAR	4
Main Material Group	0MAINMATGRP	NUMC	2
Material Group	0MATL_GROUP	CHAR	9
Reference Document Number of the Individual Item on the Profit and Loss Statement	0ME_REFDOC	CHAR	10
Item Number of the Reference Document (Profit and Loss Statement)	0ME_REFITEM	CHAR	6
Posting Date on the Document	0PSTNG_DATE	DATS	8
Sales Employee	0SALESEMPLY	NUMC	8
Sales District	0SALES_DIST	CHAR	6
Sales Group	0SALES_GRP	CHAR	3
Sales Office	0SALES_OFF	CHAR	4
Valuation View	0VALUATION	NUMC	1
Version (Reporting)	ZEVERSION	CHAR	10
Fiscal Year	0FISCYEAR	NUMC	4
Posting Period	0FISCPER3	NUMC	3
Currency Key	0CURRENCY	CUKY	5
Sales Unit	0COPASLQTU	UNIT	3

Key Figures

Text	InfoObject	Data Type	Length
Accrued Freight Costs	0ACCRDFR_CS	CURR	9
Administration	0ADMNSTRTN	CURR	9
Cash Discount	0CASH_DSCNT	CURR	9

Text	InfoObject	Data Type	Length
Revenue	0COPAREVEN	CURR	9
Sales Quantity	0COPASLQTY	QUAN	9
Customer Discount	0CUST_DSCNT	CURR	9
Direct Material Costs	0DIRMAT_CS	CURR	9
Fixed Production Costs	0FIXPROD_CS	CURR	9
Marketing	0MARKETING	CURR	9
Material Overhead Costs	0MATOVHD	CURR	9
Other Overhead Costs	0OTHER_OVHD	CURR	9
Other Variances	0OTHER_VRNC	CURR	9
Price Variances	0PRICE_VRNC	CURR	9
Material Discount	0PROD_DSCNT	CURR	9
Quantity Discount	0QTY_DSCNT	CURR	9
Quantity Variances	0QUANT_VRNC	CURR	9
Research and Development	0RSRCH_DEV	CURR	9
Sales Commission	0SALES_CMSN	CURR	9
Cost of Sales	0SALES_CS	CURR	9
Special Costs of Sales	0SPCDSLS_CS	CURR	9
Variable Production Costs	0VARPROD_CS	CURR	9
Volume Rebate	0VOL_REBATE	CURR	9

D   InfoCubes

In this appendix, we will introduce you to the documentation of the ZECOPAC1 and ZEKDABC1 InfoCubes that are used throughout this book and were generated using the *CubeServ BW Documentation Tool*.[1]

D.1   InfoCube ZECOPAC1

InfoArea ZECOPA01

Dimension Key Figures   **LineItem:**

InfoObject	Description	Navigation attributes	Description
0ACCRDFR_CS	Accrued Freight Costs		
0ADMNSTRTN	Administration		
0CASH_DSCNT	Cash Discount		
0COPAREVEN	Revenue		
0COPASLQTY	Sales Quantity		
0CUST_DSCNT	Customer Discount		
0DIRMAT_CS	Direct Material Costs		
0FIXPROD_CS	Fixed Production Costs		
0MARKETING	Marketing		
0MATOVHD	Material Overhead Costs		
0OTHER_OVHD	Other Overhead Costs		
0OTHER_VRNC	Other Variances		
0PRICE_VRNC	Price Variances		
0PROD_DSCNT	Material Discount		
0QTY_DSCNT	Quantity Discount		
0QUANT_VRNC	Quantity Variances		

---

1 The *CubeServ BW Documentation Tool* is the first professional documentation tool for SAP Business Information Warehouse. It enables you to create a documentation online "at the push of a button" from the SAP BW system. Due to various navigation options this documentation can be used as an online documentation and also be printed out. For further informationen, please visit *www.cubeserv.com*.

InfoObject	Description	Navigation attributes	Description
0RSRCH_DEV	Research and Development		
0SALES_CMSN	Sales Commission		
0SALES_CS	Cost of Sales		
0SPCDSLS_CS	Special Costs of Sales		
0VARPROD_CS	Variable Production Costs		
0VOL_REBATE	Volume Rebate		

Dimension ZECOPAC11 Organization   LineItem:

InfoObject	Description	Navigation attributes	Description
0BUS_AREA	Business Area		
0CHRT_ACCTS	Chart of Accounts		
0COMP_CODE	Company Code		
0CO_AREA	Controlling Area		
0PLANT	Plant		
0SOURSYSTEM	Source System ID		

Dimension ZECOPAC12 Sales Area   LineItem:

InfoObject	Description	Navigation attributes	Description
0DISTR_CHAN	Distribution Channel		
0DIVISION	Division		
0SALESEMPLY	Sales Employee		
0SALESORG	Sales Organization		
0SALES_GRP	Sales Group		
0SALES_OFF	Sales Office		

Dimension ZECOPAC13 Data Type

LineItem:

InfoObject	Description	Navigation attributes	Description
0VERSION	Version		
0VTYPE	Value Type for Reporting		
ZEVERSION	Version (Reporting)		

Dimension ZECOPAC14 Document Information

LineItem:

InfoObject	Description	Navigation attributes	Description
0BILL_TYPE	Billing Type		
0CURTYPE	Currency Type		
0REC_TYPE	Record Type		
0VALUATION	Valuation View		

Dimension ZECOPAC15 Customer

LineItem:

InfoObject	Description	Navigation attributes	Description
0CUSTOMER	Customer Number		
0CUSTOMER	Customer Number	0ACCNT_GRP	Account Group
0CUSTOMER	Customer Number	0COUNTRY	Country
0CUSTOMER	Customer Number	0INDUSTRY	Industry
0CUSTOMER	Customer Number	0REGION	Region
0CUST_GROUP	Customer Group		
0SALES_DIST	Sales District		

Dimension ZECOPAC16 Material

LineItem: X

InfoObject	Description	Navigation attributes	Description
0MATERIAL	Material		

InfoObject	Description	Navigation attributes	Description
0MATERIAL	Material	0MATL_GROUP	Material Group
0MATERIAL	Material	0PROD_HIER	Product Hierarchy

Dimension ZECOPAC17 Profit Center   LineItem: X

InfoObject	Description	Navigation attributes	Description
0PROFIT_CTR	Profit Center		

Dimension ZECOPAC18 Partner Profit Center   LineItem: X

InfoObject	Description	Navigation attributes	Description
0PART_PRCTR	Partner Profit Center		

Dimension ZECOPAC19 Sending Cost Center   LineItem: X

InfoObject	Description	Navigation attributes	Description
0SEND_CCTR	Sending Cost Center		

Dimension ZECOPAC1A Work Breakdown Structure Element   LineItem: X

InfoObject	Description	Navigation attributes	Description
0WBS_ELEMT	Work Breakdown Structure Element (WBS Element)		

Dimension ZECOPAC1B Cost Element   LineItem: X

InfoObject	Description	Navigation attributes	Description
0COSTELMNT	Cost Element		

Dimension ZECOPAC1C Order Number   LineItem: X

InfoObject	Description	Navigation attributes	Description
0COORDER	Order Number		

Dimension ZECOPAC1D Other   LineItem:

InfoObject	Description	Navigation attributes	Description
0BA_PRZNR	Sender Business Process		
0BILL_DATE	Date for Billing/Invoice Index and Printing		
0COSTOBJ	Cost Object		
0GI_DATE	Goods Issue Date		
0PSTNG_DATE	Posting Date on the Document		

Dimension ZECOPAC1P Data Package   LineItem:

InfoObject	Description	Navigation attributes	Description
0CHNGID	Change ID		
0RECORDTP	Record Type		
0REQUID	Request ID		

Dimension ZECOPAC1T Time   LineItem:

InfoObject	Description	Navigation attributes	Description
0FISCPER	Fiscal Year/Period		
0FISCPER3	Posting Period		
0FISCVARNT	Fiscal Year Variant		
0FISCYEAR	Fiscal Year		

Dimension ZECOPAC1U Unit   LineItem:

InfoObject	Description	Navigation attributes	Description
0COPASLQTU	Sales Unit		
0CURRENCY	Currency Key		

D.2   InfoCube ZEKDABC1

InfoArea ZESALES01

Dimension Key Figures   LineItem:

InfoObject	Description	Navigation attributes	Description
ZEBESTAND	Inventory Value		
ZEBETRAG	Amount		

Dimension ZEKDABC11 Organization   LineItem:

InfoObject	Description	Navigation attributes	Description
0COMP_CODE	Company Code		
0PLANT	Plant		
0SOURSYSTEM	Source System ID		

Dimension ZEKDABC12 Sales Organization   LineItem: X

InfoObject	Description	Navigation attributes	Description
0SALESORG	Sales Organization		

Dimension ZEKDABC13 Distribution Channel   LineItem: X

InfoObject	Description	Navigation attributes	Description
0DISTR_CHAN	Distribution Channel		

Dimension ZEKDABC14 Division   LineItem: X

InfoObject	Description	Navigation attributes	Description
0DIVISION	Division		

Dimension ZEKDABC15 Data Type   LineItem:

InfoObject	Description	Navigation attributes	Description
0VERSION	Version		
0VTYPE	Value Type for Reporting		
ZEVERSION	Version (Reporting)		

Dimension ZEKDABC16 Currency Type/Valuation View   LineItem:

InfoObject	Description	Navigation attributes	Description
0CURTYPE	Currency Type		
0VALUATION	Valuation View		

Dimension ZEKDABC17 Billing Type   LineItem: X

InfoObject	Description	Navigation attributes	Description
0BILL_TYPE	Billing Type		

Dimension ZEKDABC18 Sales Employee   LineItem: X

InfoObject	Description	Navigation attributes	Description
0SALESEMPLY	Sales Employee		

Dimension ZEKDABC19 Sales Group/Sales Office LineItem:

InfoObject	Description	Navigation attributes	Description
0SALES_GRP	Sales Group		
0SALES_OFF	Sales Office		

Dimension ZEKDABC1A Customer LineItem: X

InfoObject	Description	Navigation attributes	Description
0CUSTOMER	Customer Number		
0CUSTOMER	Customer Number	0COUNTRY	Country
0CUSTOMER	Customer Number	0INDUSTRY	Industry
0CUSTOMER	Customer Number	0REGION	Region
0CUSTOMER	Customer Number	0ACCNT_GRP	Account Group

Dimension ZEKDABC1B Customer Group LineItem: X

InfoObject	Description	Navigation attributes	Description
0CUST_GROUP	Customer Group		

Dimension ZEKDABC1C Sales District LineItem: X

InfoObject	Description	Navigation attributes	Description
0SALES_DIST	Sales District		

Dimension ZEKDABC1D Material LineItem: X

InfoObject	Description	Navigation attributes	Description
0SALES_DIST	Sales District		
InfoObject	Description	Navigation attributes	Description
0SALES_DIST	Sales District		

Dimension ZEKDABC1P Data Package

LineItem:

InfoObject	Description	Navigation attributes	Description
0CHNGID	Change ID		
0RECORDTP	Record Type		
0REQUID	Request ID		

Dimension ZEKDABC1T Time

LineItem:

InfoObject	Description	Navigation attributes	Description
0FISCPER	Fiscal Year/Period		
0FISCPER3	Posting Period		
0FISCVARNT	Fiscal Year Variant		
0FISCYEAR	Fiscal Year		

Dimension ZEKDABC1U Unit

LineItem:

InfoObject	Description	Navigation attributes	Description
0CURRENCY	Currency Key		

E   Update Rules

In this appendix, we will introduce you to the documentation of the ZECOPAISOURCE01 and 8ZECOPAO1 update rules that are used throughout this book and were generated using the *CubeServ BW Documentation Tool*.[1]

E.1   ZECOPAISOURCE01 Update Rules in ODS Object ZECOPAO1

E.1.1   InfoSource ZECOPAISOURCE01

Key Figure	Identification	Update rule	Type	Source fields
0RECORDMODE	Record Mode	NOP		
0COMP_CODE	Company Code	MOV		0COMP_CODE

Characteristics/ Time variant	Identification	Update rule	Type	Source fields
0CURTYPE	Currency Type			0CURTYPE
0ID_DOCNUM	Document Number			0ID_DOCNUM
0ID_ITMNUM	Document Item Number			0ID_ITMNUM
0REC_TYPE	Record Type			0REC_TYPE
0SOURSYSTEM	Source System ID			0SOURSYSTEM
0VERSION	Version			0VERSION
0VTYPE	Value Type			0VTYPE

---

1 The *CubeServ BW Documentation Tool* is the first professional documentation tool for SAP Business Information Warehouse. It enables you to create a documentation online "at the push of a button" from the SAP BW system. Due to various navigation options this documentation can be used as an online documentation and also be printed out. For further informationen, please visit *www.cubeserv.com*.

Characteristics/ Time variant	Identification	Update rule	Type	Source fields
0FISCVARNT				0FISCVARNT
0FISCPER	Fiscal Year/Period			0FISCPER

Key Figure	Identification	Update rule	Type	Source fields
0PLANT	Plant	MOV		0PLANT

Characteristics/ Time variant	Identification	Update rule	Type	Source fields
0CURTYPE	Currency Type			0CURTYPE
0ID_DOCNUM	Document Number			0ID_DOCNUM
0ID_ITMNUM	Document Item Number			0ID_ITMNUM
0REC_TYPE	Record Type			0REC_TYPE
0SOURSYSTEM	Source System ID			0SOURSYSTEM
0VERSION	Version			0VERSION
0VTYPE	Value Type			0VTYPE
0FISCVARNT	Fiscal Year Variant			0FISCVARNT
0FISCPER	Fiscal Year/Period			0FISCPER

Key Figure	Identification	Update rule	Type	Source fields
0SALESORG	Sales Organization	MOV		0SALESORG

Characteristics/ Time variant	Identification	Update rule	Type	Source fields
0CURTYPE	Currency Type			0CURTYPE
0ID_DOCNUM	Document Number			0ID_DOCNUM

Characteristics/ Time variant	Identification	Update rule	Type	Source fields
0ID_ITMNUM	Document Item Number			0ID_ITMNUM
0REC_TYPE	Record Type			0REC_TYPE
0SOURSYSTEM	Source System ID			0SOURSYSTEM
0VERSION	Version			0VERSION
0VTYPE	Value Type			0VTYPE
0FISCVARNT	Fiscal Year Variant			0FISCVARNT
0FISCPER	Fiscal Year/Period			0FISCPER

Key Figure	Identification	Update rule	Type	Source fields
0MATERIAL	Material	MOV		0MATERIAL

Characteristics/ Time variant	Identification	Update rule	Type	Source fields
0CURTYPE	Currency Type			0CURTYPE
0ID_DOCNUM	Document Number			0ID_DOCNUM
0ID_ITMNUM	Document Item Number			0ID_ITMNUM
0REC_TYPE	Record Type			0REC_TYPE
0SOURSYSTEM	Source System ID			0SOURSYSTEM
0VERSION	Version			0VERSION
0VTYPE	Value Type			0VTYPE
0FISCVARNT	Fiscal Year Variant			0FISCVARNT
0FISCPER	Fiscal Year/Period			0FISCPER

Key Figure	Identification	Update rule	Type	Source fields
0CUSTOMER	Customer	MOV		0CUSTOMER

Characteristics/ Time variant	Identification	Update rule	Type	Source fields
0CURTYPE	Currency Type			0CURTYPE
0ID_DOCNUM	Document Number			0ID_DOCNUM
0ID_ITMNUM	Document Item Number			0ID_ITMNUM
0REC_TYPE	Record Type			0REC_TYPE
0SOURSYSTEM	Source System ID			0SOURSYSTEM
0VERSION	Version			0VERSION
0VTYPE	Value Type			0VTYPE
0FISCVARNT	Fiscal Year Variant			0FISCVARNT
0FISCPER	Fiscal Year/Period			0FISCPER

Key Figure	Identification	Update rule	Type	Source fields
0PROFIT_CTR	Profit Center	MOV		0PROFIT_CTR

Characteristics/ Time variant	Identification	Update rule	Type	Source fields
0CURTYPE	Currency Type			0CURTYPE
0ID_DOCNUM	Document Number			0ID_DOCNUM
0ID_ITMNUM	Document Item Number			0ID_ITMNUM
0REC_TYPE	Record Type			0REC_TYPE
0SOURSYSTEM	Source System ID			0SOURSYSTEM

Characteristics/ Time variant	Identification	Update rule	Type	Source fields
0VERSION	Version			0VERSION
0VTYPE	Value Type			0VTYPE
0FISCVARNT	Fiscal Year Variant			0FISCVARNT
0FISCPER	Fiscal Year/Period			0FISCPER

Key Figure	Identification	Update rule	Type	Source fields
0PART_PRCTR	Partner Profit Center	MOV		0PART_PRCTR

Characteristics/ Time variant	Identification	Update rule	Type	Source fields
0CURTYPE	Currency Type			0CURTYPE
0ID_DOCNUM	Document Number			0ID_DOCNUM
0ID_ITMNUM	Document Item Number			0ID_ITMNUM
0REC_TYPE	Record Type			0REC_TYPE
0SOURSYSTEM	Source System ID			0SOURSYSTEM
0VERSION	Version			0VERSION
0VTYPE	Value Type			0VTYPE
0FISCVARNT	Fiscal Year Variant			0FISCVARNT
0FISCPER	Fiscal Year/Period			0FISCPER

Key Figure	Identification	Update rule	Type	Source fields
0SEND_CCTR	Sending Cost Center	MOV		0SEND_CCTR

Characteristics/Time variant	Identification	Update rule	Type	Source fields
0CURTYPE	Currency Type			0CURTYPE
0ID_DOCNUM	Document Number			0ID_DOCNUM
0ID_ITMNUM	Document Item Number			0ID_ITMNUM
0REC_TYPE	Record Type			0REC_TYPE
0SOURSYSTEM	Source System ID			0SOURSYSTEM
0VERSION	Version			0VERSION
0VTYPE	Value Type			0VTYPE
0FISCVARNT	Fiscal Year Variant			0FISCVARNT
0FISCPER	Fiscal Year/Period			0FISCPER

Key Figure	Identification	Update rule	Type	Source fields
0WBS_ELEMT	WBS Element	MOV		0WBS_ELEMT

Characteristics/Time variant	Identification	Update rule	Type	Source fields
0CURTYPE	Currency Type			0CURTYPE
0ID_DOCNUM	Document Number			0ID_DOCNUM
0ID_ITMNUM	Document Item Number			0ID_ITMNUM
0REC_TYPE	Record Type			0REC_TYPE
0SOURSYSTEM	Source System ID			0SOURSYSTEM
0VERSION	Version			0VERSION
0VTYPE	Value Type			0VTYPE

Characteristics/ Time variant	Identification	Update rule	Type	Source fields
0FISCVARNT	Fiscal Year Variant			0FISCVARNT
0FISCPER	Fiscal Year/Period			0FISCPER

Key Figure	Identification	Update rule	Type	Source fields
0COSTELMNT	Cost Element	MOV		0COSTELMNT

Characteristics/ Time variant	Identification	Update rule	Type	Source fields
0CURTYPE	Currency Type			0CURTYPE
0ID_DOCNUM	Document Number			0ID_DOCNUM
0ID_ITMNUM	Document Item Number			0ID_ITMNUM
0REC_TYPE	Record Type			0REC_TYPE
0SOURSYSTEM	Source System ID			0SOURSYSTEM
0VERSION	Version			0VERSION
0VTYPE	Value Type			0VTYPE
0FISCVARNT	Fiscal Year Variant			0FISCVARNT
0FISCPER	Fiscal Year/Period			0FISCPER

Key Figure	Identification	Update rule	Type	Source fields
0BA_PRZNR	Sender Bus. Process	MOV		0BA_PRZNR

Characteristics/ Time variant	Identification	Update rule	Type	Source fields
0CURTYPE	Currency Type			0CURTYPE
0ID_DOCNUM	Document Number			0ID_DOCNUM

Characteristics/ Time variant	Identification	Update rule	Type	Source fields
0ID_ITMNUM	Document Item Number			0ID_ITMNUM
0REC_TYPE	Record Type			0REC_TYPE
0SOURSYSTEM	Source System ID			0SOURSYSTEM
0VERSION	Version			0VERSION
0VTYPE	Value Type			0VTYPE
0FISCVARNT	Fiscal Year Variant			0FISCVARNT
0FISCPER	Fiscal Year/Period			0FISCPER

Key Figure	Identification	Update rule	Type	Source fields
0BA_STO_BNR	Cancelled Document	MOV		0BA_STO_BNR

Characteristics/ Time variant	Identification	Update rule	Type	Source fields
0CURTYPE	Currency Type			0CURTYPE
0ID_DOCNUM	Document Number			0ID_DOCNUM
0ID_ITMNUM	Document Item Number			0ID_ITMNUM
0REC_TYPE	Record Type			0REC_TYPE
0SOURSYSTEM	Source System ID			0SOURSYSTEM
0VERSION	Version			0VERSION
0VTYPE	Value Type			0VTYPE
0FISCVARNT	Fiscal Year Variant			0FISCVARNT
0FISCPER	Fiscal Year/Period			0FISCPER

Key Figure	Identification	Update rule	Type	Source fields
0BA_STO_PNR	Cancelled Document Item	MOV		0BA_STO_PNR

Characteristics/ Time variant	Identification	Update rule	Type	Source fields
0CURTYPE	Currency Type			0CURTYPE
0ID_DOCNUM	Document Number			0ID_DOCNUM
0ID_ITMNUM	Document Item Number			0ID_ITMNUM
0REC_TYPE	Record Type			0REC_TYPE
0SOURSYSTEM	Source System ID			0SOURSYSTEM
0VERSION	Version			0VERSION
0VTYPE	Value Type			0VTYPE
0FISCVARNT	Fiscal Year Variant			0FISCVARNT
0FISCPER	Fiscal Year/Period			0FISCPER

Key Figure	Identification	Update rule	Type	Source fields
0BILL_DATE	Billing date	MOV		0BILL_DATE

Characteristics/ Time variant	Identification	Update rule	Type	Source fields
0CURTYPE	Currency Type			0CURTYPE
0ID_DOCNUM	Document Number			0ID_DOCNUM
0ID_ITMNUM	Document Item Number			0ID_ITMNUM
0REC_TYPE	Record Type			0REC_TYPE
0SOURSYSTEM	Source System ID			0SOURSYSTEM

Characteristics/ Time variant	Identification	Update rule	Type	Source fields
0VERSION	Version			0VERSION
0VTYPE	Value Type			0VTYPE
0FISCVARNT	Fiscal Year Variant			0FISCVARNT
0FISCPER	Fiscal Year/Period			0FISCPER

Key Figure	Identification	Update rule	Type	Source fields
0BILL_TYPE	Billing Type	MOV		0BILL_TYPE

Characteristics/ Time variant	Identification	Update rule	Type	Source fields
0CURTYPE	Currency Type			0CURTYPE
0ID_DOCNUM	Document Number			0ID_DOCNUM
0ID_ITMNUM	Document Item Number			0ID_ITMNUM
0REC_TYPE	Record Type			0REC_TYPE
0SOURSYSTEM	Source System ID			0SOURSYSTEM
0VERSION	Version			0VERSION
0VTYPE	Value Type			0VTYPE
0FISCVARNT	Fiscal Year Variant			0FISCVARNT
0FISCPER	Fiscal Year/Period			0FISCPER

Key Figure	Identification	Update rule	Type	Source fields
0BUS_AREA	Business area	MOV		0BUS_AREA

Characteristics/ Time variant	Identification	Update rule	Type	Source fields
0CURTYPE	Currency Type			0CURTYPE
0ID_DOCNUM	Document Number			0ID_DOCNUM
0ID_ITMNUM	Document Item Number			0ID_ITMNUM
0REC_TYPE	Record Type			0REC_TYPE
0SOURSYSTEM	Source System ID			0SOURSYSTEM
0VERSION	Version			0VERSION
0VTYPE	Value Type			0VTYPE
0FISCVARNT	Fiscal Year Variant			0FISCVARNT
0FISCPER	Fiscal Year/Period			0FISCPER

Key Figure	Identification	Update rule	Type	Source fields
0CHRT_ACCTS	Chart of Accounts	MOV		0CHRT_ACCTS

Characteristics/ Time variant	Identification	Update rule	Type	Source fields
0CURTYPE	Currency Type			0CURTYPE
0ID_DOCNUM	Document Number			0ID_DOCNUM
0ID_ITMNUM	Document Item Number			0ID_ITMNUM
0REC_TYPE	Record Type			0REC_TYPE
0SOURSYSTEM	Source System ID			0SOURSYSTEM
0VERSION	Version			0VERSION
0VTYPE	Value Type			0VTYPE

Characteristics/ Time variant	Identification	Update rule	Type	Source fields
0FISCVARNT	Fiscal Year Variant			0FISCVARNT
0FISCPER	Fiscal Year/Period			0FISCPER

Key Figure	Identification	Update rule	Type	Source fields
0COORDER	Order	MOV		0COORDER

Characteristics/ Time variant	Identification	Update rule	Type	Source fields
0CURTYPE	Currency Type			0CURTYPE
0ID_DOCNUM	Document Number			0ID_DOCNUM
0ID_ITMNUM	Document Item Number			0ID_ITMNUM
0REC_TYPE	Record Type			0REC_TYPE
0SOURSYSTEM	Source System ID			0SOURSYSTEM
0VERSION	Version			0VERSION
0VTYPE	Value Type			0VTYPE
0FISCVARNT	Fiscal Year Variant			0FISCVARNT
0FISCPER	Fiscal Year/Period			0FISCPER

Key Figure	Identification	Update rule	Type	Source fields
0COORDER	Cost Object	MOV		0COSTOBJ

Characteristics/ Time variant	Identification	Update rule	Type	Source fields
0CURTYPE	Currency Type			0CURTYPE
0ID_DOCNUM	Document Number			0ID_DOCNUM

Characteristics/ Time variant	Identification	Update rule	Type	Source fields
OID_ITMNUM	Document Item Number			OID_ITMNUM
OREC_TYPE	Record Type			OREC_TYPE
OSOURSYSTEM	Source System ID			OSOURSYSTEM
OVERSION	Version			OVERSION
OVTYPE	Value Type			OVTYPE
OFISCVARNT	Fiscal Year Variant			OFISCVARNT
OFISCPER	Fiscal Year/Period			OFISCPER

Key Figure	Identification	Update rule	Type	Source fields
OCO_AREA	Controlling area	MOV		OCO_AREA

Characteristics/ Time variant	Identification	Update rule	Type	Source fields
OCURTYPE	Currency Type			OCURTYPE
OID_DOCNUM	Document Number			OID_DOCNUM
OID_ITMNUM	Document Item Number			OID_ITMNUM
OREC_TYPE	Record Type			OREC_TYPE
OSOURSYSTEM	Source System ID			OSOURSYSTEM
OVERSION	Version			OVERSION
OVTYPE	Value Type			OVTYPE
OFISCVARNT	Fiscal Year Variant			OFISCVARNT
OFISCPER	Fiscal Year/Period			OFISCPER

Key Figure	Identification	Update rule	Type	Source fields
0CUST_GROUP	Customer Group	MOV		0CUST_GROUP

Characteristics/ Time variant	Identification	Update rule	Type	Source fields
0CURTYPE	Currency Type			0CURTYPE
0ID_DOCNUM	Document Number			0ID_DOCNUM
0ID_ITMNUM	Document Item Number			0ID_ITMNUM
0REC_TYPE	Record Type			0REC_TYPE
0SOURSYSTEM	Source System ID			0SOURSYSTEM
0VERSION	Version			0VERSION
0VTYPE	Value Type			0VTYPE
0FISCVARNT	Fiscal Year Variant			0FISCVARNT
0FISCPER	Fiscal Year/Period			0FISCPER

Key Figure	Identification	Update rule	Type	Source fields
0DISTR_CHAN	Distribution Channel	MOV		0DISTR_CHAN

Characteristics/ Time variant	Identification	Update rule	Type	Source fields
0CURTYPE	Currency Type			0CURTYPE
0ID_DOCNUM	Document Number			0ID_DOCNUM
0ID_ITMNUM	Document Item Number			0ID_ITMNUM
0REC_TYPE	Record Type			0REC_TYPE
0SOURSYSTEM	Source System ID			0SOURSYSTEM

Characteristics/ Time variant	Identification	Update rule	Type	Source fields
0VERSION	Version			0VERSION
0VTYPE	Value Type			0VTYPE
0FISCVARNT	Fiscal Year Variant			0FISCVARNT
0FISCPER	Fiscal Year/Period			0FISCPER

Key Figure	Identification	Update rule	Type	Source fields
0DIVISION	Division	MOV		0DIVISION

Characteristics/ Time variant	Identification	Update rule	Type	Source fields
0CURTYPE	Currency Type			0CURTYPE
0ID_DOCNUM	Document Number			0ID_DOCNUM
0ID_ITMNUM	Document Item Number			0ID_ITMNUM
0REC_TYPE	Record Type			0REC_TYPE
0SOURSYSTEM	Source System ID			0SOURSYSTEM
0VERSION	Version			0VERSION
0VTYPE	Value Type			0VTYPE
0FISCVARNT	Fiscal Year Variant			0FISCVARNT
0FISCPER	Fiscal Year/Period			0FISCPER

Key Figure	Identification	Update rule	Type	Source fields
0DOC_NUMBER	Sales Document	MOV		0DOC_NUMBER

Characteristics/ Time variant	Identification	Update rule	Type	Source fields
0CURTYPE	Currency Type			0CURTYPE
0ID_DOCNUM	Document Number			0ID_DOCNUM
0ID_ITMNUM	Document Item Number			0ID_ITMNUM
0REC_TYPE	Record Type			0REC_TYPE
0SOURSYSTEM	Source System ID			0SOURSYSTEM
0VERSION	Version			0VERSION
0VTYPE	Value Type			0VTYPE
0FISCVARNT	Fiscal Year Variant			0FISCVARNT
0FISCPER	Fiscal Year/Period			0FISCPER

Key Figure	Identification	Update rule	Type	Source fields
0S_ORD_ITEM	Item	MOV		0S_ORD_ITEM

Characteristics/ Time variant	Identification	Update rule	Type	Source fields
0CURTYPE	Currency Type			0CURTYPE
0ID_DOCNUM	Document Number			0ID_DOCNUM
0ID_ITMNUM	Document Item Number			0ID_ITMNUM
0REC_TYPE	Record Type			0REC_TYPE
0SOURSYSTEM	Source System ID			0SOURSYSTEM
0VERSION	Version			0VERSION
0VTYPE	Value Type			0VTYPE

Characteristics/Time variant	Identification	Update rule	Type	Source fields
OFISCVARNT	Fiscal Year Variant			OFISCVARNT
OFISCPER	Fiscal Year/Period			OFISCPER

Key Figure	Identification	Update rule	Type	Source fields
OGI_DATE	Goods Issue	MOV		OGI_DATE

Characteristics/Time variant	Identification	Update rule	Type	Source fields
OCURTYPE	Currency Type			OCURTYPE
OID_DOCNUM	Document Number			OID_DOCNUM
OID_ITMNUM	Document Item Number			OID_ITMNUM
OREC_TYPE	Record Type			OREC_TYPE
OSOURSYSTEM	Source System ID			OSOURSYSTEM
OVERSION	Version			OVERSION
OVTYPE	Value Type			OVTYPE
OFISCVARNT	Fiscal Year Variant			OFISCVARNT
OFISCPER	Fiscal Year/Period			OFISCPER

Key Figure	Identification	Update rule	Type	Source fields
OINDUSTRY	Industry	MOV		OINDUSTRY

Characteristics/Time variant	Identification	Update rule	Type	Source fields
OCURTYPE	Currency Type			OCURTYPE
OID_DOCNUM	Document Number			OID_DOCNUM

Characteristics/ Time variant	Identification	Update rule	Type	Source fields
0ID_ITMNUM	Document Item Number			0ID_ITMNUM
0REC_TYPE	Record Type			0REC_TYPE
0SOURSYSTEM	Source System ID			0SOURSYSTEM
0VERSION	Version			0VERSION
0VTYPE	Value Type			0VTYPE
0FISCVARNT	Fiscal Year Variant			0FISCVARNT
0FISCPER	Fiscal Year/Period			0FISCPER

Key Figure	Identification	Update rule	Type	Source fields
0MAINMATGRP	Main Material Group	MOV		0MAINMATGRP

Characteristics/ Time variant	Identification	Update rule	Type	Source fields
0CURTYPE	Currency Type			0CURTYPE
0ID_DOCNUM	Document Number			0ID_DOCNUM
0ID_ITMNUM	Document Item Number			0ID_ITMNUM
0REC_TYPE	Record Type			0REC_TYPE
0SOURSYSTEM	Source System ID			0SOURSYSTEM
0VERSION	Version			0VERSION
0VTYPE	Value Type			0VTYPE
0FISCVARNT	Fiscal Year Variant			0FISCVARNT
0FISCPER	Fiscal Year/Period			0FISCPER

Key Figure	Identification	Update rule	Type	Source fields
0MATL_GROUP	Material Group	MOV		0MATL_GROUP

Characteristics/ Time variant	Identification	Update rule	Type	Source fields
0CURTYPE	Currency Type			0CURTYPE
0ID_DOCNUM	Document Number			0ID_DOCNUM
0ID_ITMNUM	Document Item Number			0ID_ITMNUM
0REC_TYPE	Record Type			0REC_TYPE
0SOURSYSTEM	Source System ID			0SOURSYSTEM
0VERSION	Version			0VERSION
0VTYPE	Value Type			0VTYPE
0FISCVARNT	Fiscal Year Variant			0FISCVARNT
0FISCPER	Fiscal Year/Period			0FISCPER

Key Figure	Identification	Update rule	Type	Source fields
0ME_REFDOC	CO-PA Ref. Doc. No.	MOV		0ME_REFDOC

Characteristics/ Time variant	Identification	Update rule	Type	Source fields
0CURTYPE	Currency Type			0CURTYPE
0ID_DOCNUM	Document Number			0ID_DOCNUM
0ID_ITMNUM	Document Item Number			0ID_ITMNUM
0REC_TYPE	Record Type			0REC_TYPE
0SOURSYSTEM	Source System ID			0SOURSYSTEM

Characteristics/ Time variant	Identification	Update rule	Type	Source fields
0VERSION	Version			0VERSION
0VTYPE	Value Type			0VTYPE
0FISCVARNT	Fiscal Year Variant			0FISCVARNT
0FISCPER	Fiscal Year/Period			0FISCPER

Key Figure	Identification	Update rule	Type	Source fields
0ME_REFITEM	CO-PA Ref. item	MOV		0ME_REFITEM

Characteristics/ Time variant	Identification	Update rule	Type	Source fields
0CURTYPE	Currency Type			0CURTYPE
0ID_DOCNUM	Document Number			0ID_DOCNUM
0ID_ITMNUM	Document Item Number			0ID_ITMNUM
0REC_TYPE	Record Type			0REC_TYPE
0SOURSYSTEM	Source System ID			0SOURSYSTEM
0VERSION	Version			0VERSION
0VTYPE	Value Type			0VTYPE
0FISCVARNT	Fiscal Year Variant			0FISCVARNT
0FISCPER	Fiscal Year/Period			0FISCPER

Key Figure	Identification	Update rule	Type	Source fields
0PSTNG_DATE	Posting Date	MOV		0PSTNG_DATE

Characteristics/ Time variant	Identification	Update rule	Type	Source fields
0CURTYPE	Currency Type			0CURTYPE
0ID_DOCNUM	Document Number			0ID_DOCNUM
0ID_ITMNUM	Document Item Number			0ID_ITMNUM
0REC_TYPE	Record Type			0REC_TYPE
0SOURSYSTEM	Source System ID			0SOURSYSTEM
0VERSION	Version			0VERSION
0VTYPE	Value Type			0VTYPE
0FISCVARNT	Fiscal Year Variant			0FISCVARNT
0FISCPER	Fiscal Year/Period			0FISCPER

Key Figure	Identification	Update rule	Type	Source fields
0SALESEMPLY	Sales Employee	MOV		0SALESEMPLY

Characteristics/ Time variant	Identification	Update rule	Type	Source fields
0CURTYPE	Currency Type			0CURTYPE
0ID_DOCNUM	Document Number			0ID_DOCNUM
0ID_ITMNUM	Document Item Number			0ID_ITMNUM
0REC_TYPE	Record Type			0REC_TYPE
0SOURSYSTEM	Source System ID			0SOURSYSTEM
0VERSION	Version			0VERSION
0VTYPE	Value Type			0VTYPE

Characteristics/Time variant	Identification	Update rule	Type	Source fields
0FISCVARNT	Fiscal Year Variant			0FISCVARNT
0FISCPER	Fiscal Year/Period			0FISCPER

Key Figure	Identification	Update rule	Type	Source fields
0SALES_DIST	Sales District	MOV		0SALES_DIST

Characteristics/Time variant	Identification	Update rule	Type	Source fields
0CURTYPE	Currency Type			0CURTYPE
0ID_DOCNUM	Document Number			0ID_DOCNUM
0ID_ITMNUM	Document Item Number			0ID_ITMNUM
0REC_TYPE	Record Type			0REC_TYPE
0SOURSYSTEM	Source System ID			0SOURSYSTEM
0VERSION	Version			0VERSION
0VTYPE	Value Type			0VTYPE
0FISCVARNT	Fiscal Year Variant			0FISCVARNT
0FISCPER	Fiscal Year/Period			0FISCPER

Key Figure	Identification	Update rule	Type	Source fields
0SALES_GRP	Sales Group	MOV		0SALES_GRP

Characteristics/Time variant	Identification	Update rule	Type	Source fields
0CURTYPE	Currency Type			0CURTYPE
0ID_DOCNUM	Document Number			0ID_DOCNUM

Characteristics/Time variant	Identification	Update rule	Type	Source fields
0ID_ITMNUM	Document Item Number			0ID_ITMNUM
0REC_TYPE	Record Type			0REC_TYPE
0SOURSYSTEM	Source System ID			0SOURSYSTEM
0VERSION	Version			0VERSION
0VTYPE	Value Type			0VTYPE
0FISCVARNT	Fiscal Year Variant			0FISCVARNT
0FISCPER	Fiscal Year/Period			0FISCPER

Key Figure	Identification	Update rule	Type	Source fields
0SALES_OFF	Sales Office	MOV		0SALES_OFF

Characteristics/Time variant	Identification	Update rule	Type	Source fields
0CURTYPE	Currency Type			0CURTYPE
0ID_DOCNUM	Document Number			0ID_DOCNUM
0ID_ITMNUM	Document Item Number			0ID_ITMNUM
0REC_TYPE	Record Type			0REC_TYPE
0SOURSYSTEM	Source System ID			0SOURSYSTEM
0VERSION	Version			0VERSION
0VTYPE	Value Type			0VTYPE
0FISCVARNT	Fiscal Year Variant			0FISCVARNT
0FISCPER	Fiscal Year/Period			0FISCPER

Key Figure	Identification	Update rule	Type	Source fields
0VALUATION	Valuation View	MOV	▲▦	0VALUATION

Charateristics/ Time variant	Identification	Update rule	Type	Source fields
0CURTYPE	Currency Type		▲▦	0CURTYPE
0ID_DOCNUM	Document Number		▲▦	0ID_DOCNUM
0ID_ITMNUM	Document Item Number		▲▦	0ID_ITMNUM
0REC_TYPE	Record Type		▲▦	0REC_TYPE
0SOURSYSTEM	Source System ID		▲▦	0SOURSYSTEM
0VERSION	Version		▲▦	0VERSION
0VTYPE	Value Type		▲▦	0VTYPE
0FISCVARNT	Fiscal Year Variant		▲▦	0FISCVARNT
0FISCPER	Fiscal Year/Period		▲▦	0FISCPER

Key Figure	Identification	Update rule	Type	Source fields
ZEVERSION	Version	MOV	▲▦	ZEVERSION

Characteristics/ Tima base	Identification	Update rule	Type	Source fields
0CURTYPE	Currency Type		▲▦	0CURTYPE
0ID_DOCNUM	Document Number		▲▦	0ID_DOCNUM
0ID_ITMNUM	Document Item Number		▲▦	0ID_ITMNUM
0REC_TYPE	Record Type		▲▦	0REC_TYPE
0SOURSYSTEM	Source System ID		▲▦	0SOURSYSTEM

Characteristics/ Time base	Identification	Update rule	Type	Source fields
0VERSION	Version			0VERSION
0VTYPE	Value Type			0VTYPE
0FISCVARNT	Fiscal Year Variant			0FISCVARNT
0FISCPER	Fiscal Year/Period			0FISCPER

Key Figure	Identification	Update rule	Type	Source fields
0FISCYEAR	Fiscal Year	MOV		0FISCPER

Characteristics/ Time variant	Identification	Update rule	Type	Source fields
0CURTYPE	Currency Type			0CURTYPE
0ID_DOCNUM	Document Number			0ID_DOCNUM
0ID_ITMNUM	Document Item Number			0ID_ITMNUM
0REC_TYPE	Record Type			0REC_TYPE
0SOURSYSTEM	Source System ID			0SOURSYSTEM
0VERSION	Version			0VERSION
0VTYPE	Value Type			0VTYPE
0FISCVARNT	Fiscal Year Variant			0FISCVARNT
0FISCPER	Fiscal Year/Period			0FISCPER

Key Figure	Identification	Update rule	Type	Source fields
0FISCPER3	Posting Period	MOV		0FISCPER

Characteristics/ Time variant	Identification	Update rule	Type	Source fields
0CURTYPE	Currency Type			0CURTYPE
0ID_DOCNUM	Document Number			0ID_DOCNUM
0ID_ITMNUM	Document Item Number			0ID_ITMNUM
0REC_TYPE	Record Type			0REC_TYPE
0SOURSYSTEM	Source System ID			0SOURSYSTEM
0VERSION	Version			0VERSION
0VTYPE	Value Type			0VTYPE
0FISCVARNT	Fiscal Year Variant			0FISCVARNT
0FISCPER	Fiscal Year/Period			0FISCPER

Key Figure	Identification	Update rule	Type	Source fields
0ACCRDFR_CS	Accrued Freight Costs	MOV		0ACCRDFR_CS

Characteristics/ Time variant	Identification	Update rule	Type	Source fields
0CURTYPE	Currency Type			0CURTYPE
0ID_DOCNUM	Document Number			0ID_DOCNUM
0ID_ITMNUM	Document Item Number			0ID_ITMNUM
0REC_TYPE	Record Type			0REC_TYPE
0SOURSYSTEM	Source System ID			0SOURSYSTEM
0VERSION	Version			0VERSION
0VTYPE	Value Type			0VTYPE
0FISCVARNT	Fiscal Year Variant			0FISCVARNT
0FISCPER	Fiscal Year/Period			0FISCPER

Key Figure	Identification	Update rule	Type	Source fields
0ADMNSTRTN	Administration	MOV		0ADMNSTRTN

Characteristics/ Time variant	Identification	Update rule	Type	Source fields
0CURTYPE	Currency Type			0CURTYPE
0ID_DOCNUM	Document Number			0ID_DOCNUM
0ID_ITMNUM	Document Item Number			0ID_ITMNUM
0REC_TYPE	Record Type			0REC_TYPE
0SOURSYSTEM	Source System ID			0SOURSYSTEM
0VERSION	Version			0VERSION
0VTYPE	Value Type			0VTYPE
0FISCVARNT	Fiscal Year Variant			0FISCVARNT
0FISCPER	Fiscal Year/Period			0FISCPER

Key Figure	Identification	Update rule	Type	Source fields
0CASH_DSCNT	Cash Discount	MOV		0CASH_DSCNT

Characteristics/ Time variant	Identification	Update rule	Type	Source fields
0CURTYPE	Currency Type			0CURTYPE
0ID_DOCNUM	Document Number			0ID_DOCNUM
0ID_ITMNUM	Document Item Number			0ID_ITMNUM
0REC_TYPE	Record Type			0REC_TYPE
0SOURSYSTEM	Source System ID			0SOURSYSTEM
0VERSION	Version			0VERSION
0VTYPE	Value Type			0VTYPE
0FISCVARNT	Fiscal Year Variant			0FISCVARNT
0FISCPER	Fiscal Year/Period			0FISCPER

Key Figure	Identification	Update rule	Type	Source fields
0COPAREVEN	Revenue	MOV		0COPAREVEN

Characteristics/Time variant	Identification	Update rule	Type	Source fields
0CURTYPE	Currency Type			0CURTYPE
0ID_DOCNUM	Document Number			0ID_DOCNUM
0ID_ITMNUM	Document Item Number			0ID_ITMNUM
0REC_TYPE	Record Type			0REC_TYPE
0SOURSYSTEM	Source System ID			0SOURSYSTEM
0VERSION	Version			0VERSION
0VTYPE	Value Type			0VTYPE
0FISCVARNT	Fiscal Year Variant			0FISCVARNT
0FISCPER	Fiscal Year/Period			0FISCPER

Key Figure	Identification	Update rule	Type	Source fields
0COPASLQTY	Sales Quantity	MOV		0COPASLQTY

Characteristics/Time variant	Identification	Update rule	Type	Source fields
0CURTYPE	Currency Type			0CURTYPE
0ID_DOCNUM	Document Number			0ID_DOCNUM
0ID_ITMNUM	Document Item Number			0ID_ITMNUM
0REC_TYPE	Record Type			0REC_TYPE
0SOURSYSTEM	Source System ID			0SOURSYSTEM
0VERSION	Version			0VERSION
0VTYPE	Value Type			0VTYPE

Characteristics/ Time variant	Identification	Update rule	Type	Source fields
OFISCVARNT	Fiscal Year Variant			OFISCVARNT
OFISCPER	Fiscal Year/Period			OFISCPER

Key Figure	Identification	Update rule	Type	Source fields
OCUST_DSCNT	Customer Discount	MOV		OCUST_DSCNT

Characteristics/ Time variant	Identification	Update rule	Type	Source fields
OCURTYPE	Currency Type			OCURTYPE
OID_DOCNUM	Document Number			OID_DOCNUM
OID_ITMNUM	Document Item Number			OID_ITMNUM
OREC_TYPE	Record Type			OREC_TYPE
OSOURSYSTEM	Source System ID			OSOURSYSTEM
OVERSION	Version			OVERSION
OVTYPE	Value Type			OVTYPE
OFISCVARNT	Fiscal Year Variant			OFISCVARNT
OFISCPER	Fiscal Year/Period			OFISCPER

Key Figure	Identification	Update rule	Type	Source fields
ODIRMAT_CS	Direct Material Costs	MOV		ODIRMAT_CS

Characteristics/ Time variant	Identification	Update rule	Type	Source fields
OCURTYPE	Currency Type			OCURTYPE
OID_DOCNUM	Document Number			OID_DOCNUM

Characteristics/ Time variant	Identification	Update rule	Type	Source fields
OID_ITMNUM	Document Item Number			OID_ITMNUM
OREC_TYPE	Record Type			OREC_TYPE
OSOURSYSTEM	Source System ID			OSOURSYSTEM
OVERSION	Version			OVERSION
OVTYPE	Value Type			OVTYPE
OFISCVARNT	Fiscal Year Variant			OFISCVARNT
OFISCPER	Fiscal Year/Period			OFISCPER

Key Figure	Identification	Update rule	Type	Source fields
OFIXPROD_CS	Fixed Prod. Costs	MOV		OFIXPROD_CS

Characteristics/ Time variant	Identification	Update rule	Type	Source fields
OCURTYPE	Currency Type			OCURTYPE
OID_DOCNUM	Document Number			OID_DOCNUM
OID_ITMNUM	Document Item Number			OID_ITMNUM
OREC_TYPE	Record Type			OREC_TYPE
OSOURSYSTEM	Source System ID			OSOURSYSTEM
OVERSION	Version			OVERSION
OVTYPE	Value Type			OVTYPE
OFISCVARNT	Fiscal Year Variant			OFISCVARNT
OFISCPER	Fiscal Year/Period			OFISCPER

Key Figure	Identification	Update rule	Type	Source fields
0MARKETING	Marketing	MOV		0MARKETING

Characteristics/ Time variant	Identification	Update rule	Type	Source fields
0CURTYPE	Currency Type			0CURTYPE
0ID_DOCNUM	Document Number			0ID_DOCNUM
0ID_ITMNUM	Document Item Number			0ID_ITMNUM
0REC_TYPE	Record Type			0REC_TYPE
0SOURSYSTEM	Source System ID			0SOURSYSTEM
0VERSION	Version			0VERSION
0VTYPE	Value Type			0VTYPE
0FISCVARNT	Fiscal Year Variant			0FISCVARNT
0FISCPER	Fiscal Year/Period			0FISCPER

Key Figure	Identification	Update rule	Type	Source fields
0MATOVHD	Material Overhead Costs	MOV		0MATOVHD

Characteristics/ Time variant	Identification	Update rule	Type	Source fields
0CURTYPE	Currency Type			0CURTYPE
0ID_DOCNUM	Document Number			0ID_DOCNUM
0ID_ITMNUM	Document Item Number			0ID_ITMNUM
0REC_TYPE	Record Type			0REC_TYPE
0SOURSYSTEM	Source System ID			0SOURSYSTEM

Characteristics/Time variant	Identification	Update rule	Type	Source fields
0VERSION	Version			0VERSION
0VTYPE	Value Type			0VTYPE
0FISCVARNT	Fiscal Year Variant			0FISCVARNT
0FISCPER	Fiscal Year/Period			0FISCPER

Key Figure	Identification	Update rule	Type	Source fields
0OTHER_OVHD	Other Overhead Costs	MOV		0OTHER_OVHD

Characteristics/Time variant	Identification	Update rule	Type	Source fields
0CURTYPE	Currency Type			0CURTYPE
0ID_DOCNUM	Document Number			0ID_DOCNUM
0ID_ITMNUM	Document Item Number			0ID_ITMNUM
0REC_TYPE	Record Type			0REC_TYPE
0SOURSYSTEM	Source System ID			0SOURSYSTEM
0VERSION	Version			0VERSION
0VTYPE	Value Type			0VTYPE
0FISCVARNT	Fiscal Year Variant			0FISCVARNT
0FISCPER	Fiscal Year/Period			0FISCPER

Key Figure	Identification	Update rule	Type	Source fields
0OTHER_VRNC	Other Variances	MOV		0OTHER_VRNC

Characteristics/ Time variant	Identification	Update rule	Type	Source fields
0CURTYPE	Currency Type			0CURTYPE
0ID_DOCNUM	Document Number			0ID_DOCNUM
0ID_ITMNUM	Document Item Number			0ID_ITMNUM
0REC_TYPE	Record Type			0REC_TYPE
0SOURSYSTEM	Source System ID			0SOURSYSTEM
0VERSION	Version			0VERSION
0VTYPE	Value Type			0VTYPE
0FISCVARNT	Fiscal Year Variant			0FISCVARNT
0FISCPER	Fiscal Year/Period			0FISCPER

Key Figure	Identification	Update rule	Type	Source fields
0PRICE_VRNC	Price Variance	MOV		0PRICE_VRNC

Characteristics/ Time variant	Identification	Update rule	Type	Source fields
0CURTYPE	Currency Type			0CURTYPE
0ID_DOCNUM	Document Number			0ID_DOCNUM
0ID_ITMNUM	Document Item Number			0ID_ITMNUM
0REC_TYPE	Record Type			0REC_TYPE
0SOURSYSTEM	Source System ID			0SOURSYSTEM
0VERSION	Version			0VERSION
0VTYPE	Value Type			0VTYPE

Characteristics/ Time variant	Identification	Update rule	Type	Source fields
0FISCVARNT	Fiscal Year Variant			0FISCVARNT
0FISCPER	Fiscal Year/Period			0FISCPER

Key Figure	Identification	Update rule	Type	Source fields
0PROD_DSCNT	Product Discount	MOV		0PROD_DSCNT

Characteristics/ Time variant	Identification	Update rule	Type	Source fields
0CURTYPE	Currency Type			0CURTYPE
0ID_DOCNUM	Document Number			0ID_DOCNUM
0ID_ITMNUM	Document Item Number			0ID_ITMNUM
0REC_TYPE	Record Type			0REC_TYPE
0SOURSYSTEM	Source System ID			0SOURSYSTEM
0VERSION	Version			0VERSION
0VTYPE	Value Type			0VTYPE
0FISCVARNT	Fiscal Year Variant			0FISCVARNT
0FISCPER	Fiscal Year/Period			0FISCPER

Key Figure	Identification	Update rule	Type	Source fields
0QTY_DSCNT	Quantity Discount	MOV		0QTY_DSCNT

Characteristics/ Time variant	Identification	Update rule	Type	Source fields
0CURTYPE	Currency Type			0CURTYPE
0ID_DOCNUM	Document Number			0ID_DOCNUM

Characteristics/ Time variant	Identification	Update rule	Type	Source fields
0ID_ITMNUM	Document Item Number			0ID_ITMNUM
0REC_TYPE	Record Type			0REC_TYPE
0SOURSYSTEM	Source System ID			0SOURSYSTEM
0VERSION	Version			0VERSION
0VTYPE	Value Type			0VTYPE
0FISCVARNT	Fiscal Year Variant			0FISCVARNT
0FISCPER	Fiscal Year/Period			0FISCPER

Key Figure	Identification	Update rule	Type	Source fields
0QUANT_VRNC	Quantity Variances	MOV		0QUANT_VRNC

Characteristics/ Time variant	Identification	Update rule	Type	Source fields
0CURTYPE	Currency Type			0CURTYPE
0ID_DOCNUM	Document Number			0ID_DOCNUM
0ID_ITMNUM	Document Item Number			0ID_ITMNUM
0REC_TYPE	Record Type			0REC_TYPE
0SOURSYSTEM	Source System ID			0SOURSYSTEM
0VERSION	Version			0VERSION
0VTYPE	Value Type			0VTYPE
0FISCVARNT	Fiscal Year Variant			0FISCVARNT
0FISCPER	Fiscal Year/Period			0FISCPER

Key Figure	Identification	Update rule	Type	Source fields
0RSRCH_DEV	R&D	MOV		0RSRCH_DEV

Characteristics/ Time variant	Identification	Update rule	Type	Source fields
0CURTYPE	Currency Type			0CURTYPE
0ID_DOCNUM	Document Number			0ID_DOCNUM
0ID_ITMNUM	Document Item Number			0ID_ITMNUM
0REC_TYPE	Record Type			0REC_TYPE
0SOURSYSTEM	Source System ID			0SOURSYSTEM
0VERSION	Version			0VERSION
0VTYPE	Value Type			0VTYPE
0FISCVARNT	Fiscal Year Variant			0FISCVARNT
0FISCPER	Fiscal Year/Period			0FISCPER

Key Figure	Identification	Update rule	Type	Source fields
0SALES_CMSN	Sales Commission	MOV		0SALES_CMSN

Characteristics/ Time variant	Identification	Update rule	Type	Source fields
0CURTYPE	Currency Type			0CURTYPE
0ID_DOCNUM	Document Number			0ID_DOCNUM
0ID_ITMNUM	Document Item Number			0ID_ITMNUM
0REC_TYPE	Record Type			0REC_TYPE
0SOURSYSTEM	Source System ID			0SOURSYSTEM

Characteristics/ Time variant	Identification	Update rule	Type	Source fields
0VERSION	Version			0VERSION
0VTYPE	Value Type			0VTYPE
0FISCVARNT	Fiscal Year Variant			0FISCVARNT
0FISCPER	Fiscal Year/Period			0FISCPER

Key Figure	Identification	Update rule	Type	Source fields
0SALES_CS	Sales Costs	MOV		0SALES_CS

Characteristics/ Time variant	Identification	Update rule	Type	Source fields
0CURTYPE	Currency Type			0CURTYPE
0ID_DOCNUM	Document Number			0ID_DOCNUM
0ID_ITMNUM	Document Item Number			0ID_ITMNUM
0REC_TYPE	Record Type			0REC_TYPE
0SOURSYSTEM	Source System ID			0SOURSYSTEM
0VERSION	Version			0VERSION
0VTYPE	Value Type			0VTYPE
0FISCVARNT	Fiscal Year Variant			0FISCVARNT
0FISCPER	Fiscal Year/Period			0FISCPER

Key Figure	Identification	Update rule	Type	Source fields
0SPCDSLS_CS	Special Direct Costs of Sales	MOV		0SPCDSLS_CS

Characteristics/ Time variant	Identification	Update rule	Type	Source fields
0CURTYPE	Currency Type			0CURTYPE
0ID_DOCNUM	Document Number			0ID_DOCNUM
0ID_ITMNUM	Document Item Number			0ID_ITMNUM
0REC_TYPE	Record Type			0REC_TYPE
0SOURSYSTEM	Source System ID			0SOURSYSTEM
0VERSION	Version			0VERSION
0VTYPE	Value Type			0VTYPE
0FISCVARNT	Fiscal Year Variant			0FISCVARNT
0FISCPER	Fiscal Year/Period			0FISCPER

Key Figure	Identification	Update rule	Type	Source fields
0VARPROD_CS	Var. Prod. Costs	MOV		0VARPROD_CS

Characteristics/ Time variant	Identification	Update rule	Type	Source fields
0CURTYPE	Currency Type			0CURTYPE
0ID_DOCNUM	Document Number			0ID_DOCNUM
0ID_ITMNUM	Document Item Number			0ID_ITMNUM
0REC_TYPE	Record Type			0REC_TYPE
0SOURSYSTEM	Source System ID			0SOURSYSTEM
0VERSION	Version			0VERSION
0VTYPE	Value Type			0VTYPE

Characteristics/ Time variant	Identification	Update rule	Type	Source fields
OFISCVARNT	Fiscal Year Variant			OFISCVARNT
OFISCPER	Fiscal Year/Period			OFISCPER

Key Figure	Identification	Update rule	Type	Source fields
OVOL_REBATE	Volume Rebate	MOV		OVOL_REBATE

Characteristics/ Time variant	Identification	Update rule	Type	Source fields
OCURTYPE	Currency Type			OCURTYPE
OID_DOCNUM	Document Number			OID_DOCNUM
OID_ITMNUM	Document Item Number			OID_ITMNUM
OREC_TYPE	Record Type			OREC_TYPE
OSOURSYSTEM	Source System ID			OSOURSYSTEM
OVERSION	Version			OVERSION
OVTYPE	Value Type			OVTYPE
OFISCVARNT	Fiscal Year Variant			OFISCVARNT
OFISCPER	Fiscal Year/Period			OFISCPER

Key Figure	Identification	Update rule	Type	Source fields
OCURRENCY	Currency	MOV		OCURRENCY

Characteristics/ Time variant	Identification	Update rule	Type	Source fields
OCURTYPE	Currency Type			OCURTYPE
OID_DOCNUM	Document Number			OID_DOCNUM

0ID_ITMNUM	Document Item Number			0ID_ITMNUM
0REC_TYPE	Record Type			0REC_TYPE
0SOURSYSTEM	Source System ID			0SOURSYSTEM
0VERSION	Version			0VERSION
0VTYPE	Value Type			0VTYPE
0FISCVARNT	Fiscal Year Variant			0FISCVARNT
0FISCPER	Fiscal Year/Period			0FISCPER

Key Figure	Identification	Update rule	Type	Source fields
0COPASLQTU	Sales QU	MOV		0COPASLQTU

Characteristics/ Time variant	Identification	Update rule	Type	Source fields
0CURTYPE	Currency Type			0CURTYPE
0ID_DOCNUM	Document Number			0ID_DOCNUM
0ID_ITMNUM	Document Item Number			0ID_ITMNUM
0REC_TYPE	Record Type			0REC_TYPE
0SOURSYSTEM	Source System ID			0SOURSYSTEM
0VERSION	Version			0VERSION
0VTYPE	Value Type			0VTYPE
0FISCVARNT	Fiscal Year Variant			0FISCVARNT
0FISCPER	Fiscal Year/Period			0FISCPER

E.2 Update Rules 8ZECOPAO1 in InfoCube ZEKDABC1

E.2.1 InfoSource 8ZECOPAO1

Key Figure	Identification	Update rule	Type	Source fields
ZEBETRAG	Amount	ADD		Routine ZEBE-TRAG

Characteristics/ Time variant	Identification	Update rule	Type	Source fields
0SOURSYSTEM	Source System ID			0SOURSYSTEM
0CURTYPE	Currency Type			0CURTYPE
0VERSION	Version			0VERSION
0VTYPE	Value Type			0VTYPE
0COMP_CODE	Company Code			0COMP_CODE
0PLANT	Plant			0PLANT
0SALESORG	Sales Organization			0SALESORG
0MATERIAL	Material			0MATERIAL
0CUSTOMER	Customer			0CUSTOMER
0BILL_TYPE	Billing Type			0BILL_TYPE
0CUST_GROUP	Customer Group			0CUST_GROUP
0DISTR_CHAN	Distribution Channel			0DISTR_CHAN
0DIVISION	Division			0DIVISION
0SALESEMPLY	Sales Employee			0SALESEMPLY
0SALES_DIST	Sales District			0SALES_DIST
0SALES_GRP	Sales Group			0SALES_GRP

0SALES_OFF	Sales Office		0SALES_OFF
0VALUATION	Valuation View		0VALUATION
ZEVERSION	Version		ZEVERSION
0FISCVARNT	Fiscal Year Variant		0FISCVARNT
0FISCPER	Fiscal Year/Period		0FISCPER
0FISCYEAR	Fiscal Year		0FISCPER
0FISCPER3	Posting Period		0FISCPER
0CURRENCY	Currency		0CURRENCY

Update Rules: Routines

InfoSource	8ZECOPAO1	InfoObject	

1   * TABLES: ...

2   * DATA: ...

InfoSource	8ZECOPAO1	InfoObject	ZEBETRAG

1   * fill the internal table "MONITOR" to make monitor entries

2

3   if COMM_STRUCTURE-REC_TYPE = 'A' or COMM_STRUCTURE-REC_TYPE = 'F'.

4

5   RESULT = COMM_STRUCTURE-COPAREVEN

6   - (COMM_STRUCTURE-CUST_DSCNT + COMM_STRUCTURE-PROD_DSCNT

7   + COMM_STRUCTURE-QTY_DSCNT) .

8

9   if COMM_STRUCTURE-REC_TYPE = 'F'.

10   RESULT = - RESULT.

11   endif.

12

```
13    RETURNCODE = 0.

14

15    else.

16

17    RETURNCODE = 0.

18

19    endif.

20

21    * if abort is not equal to zero, the update process will be canceled

22    ABORT = 0.

23
```

F   Transaction Codes

F.1   Transactions in the SAP BW System

Transaction	Description
BAPI	BAPI Explorer
CMOD	Project administration of SAP enhancements
FILE	Maintenance of logical file paths
LISTCUBE	List viewer for data targets (→ BasisCubes, ODS objects, Characteristic InfoObjects)
LISTSCHEMA	Schema viewer for BasicCubes (including aggregates)
PFCG	Role maintenance
RRC1, RRC2, RRC3	Creating/changing/viewing currency exchange rate definitions
RRMX	Starting BEx Analyzer
RS12	Displaying and deleting lock entries (in tables)
RSA1	Administrator Workbench (→ Modeling)
RSA11	Administrator Workbench (→ InfoProvider)
RSA12	Administrator Workbench (→ InfoSources)
RSA13	Administrator Workbench (→ Source systems)
RSA14	Administrator Workbench (→ InfoObjects)
RSA3	Extractor checker SAPI 3.0
RSA5	Transferring DataSources from Business Content
RSA6	Postprocessing DataSources and component hierarchy
RSA7	Maintaining the delta queue
RSA9	Transferring application component from Business Content
RSBBS	Maintaining jumps for the RRI (Report-to-Report Interface)
RSCUSTV1	Modifying the settings of flat files (→ Thousand, decimal, and field separators as well as field delimitators)
RSCUSTV6	Modifying the threshold values for data loading processes (→ Package size, PSA partition size, frequency status IDoc)
RSCUSTV8	Changing the aggregate change run settings (→ Threshold value for rebuild, block size)
RSD1, RSD2, RSD3	Maintaining InfoObjects of characteristics/key figures/units type

Transaction	Description
RSD4, RSD5	Processing technical and time characteristics
RSDBC	DB Connect: Selecting tables and views
RSDDV	Maintaining aggregates
RSDIOBC	Editing InfoObjectCatalogs
RSDMD	Maintaining master data for a characteristic
RSDMPROM	Editing MultiProviders
RSDODS	Editing ODS objects
RSDV	Maintaining the validity slice (→ BasicCubes containing key figures of the "non-cumulative value" type)
RSFH	Testing tool for transaction-data extractors
RSIMG	BW Customizing Guidelines
RSISET	Maintenance of InfoSets
RSKC	Maintenance of additional characters allowed in BW
RSMD	Testing tool for master-data extractors
RSMO	Monitor
RSMON	Administrator Workbench (→ Monitoring)
RSMONCOLOR	Valuation of requests
RSO2	Maintenance of generic DataSources
RSO3	Setting up of delta extraction for attributes and texts
RSOR	Administrator Workbench (→ Metadata Repository)
RSORBCT	Administrator Workbench (→ Business Content)
RSPC	Maintenance of Process Chains
RSRT	Query Monitor
RSRTRACE	Query Trace
RSRV	Analysis and repair of BW objects
RSSM	Maintenance of reporting authorization objects
RSU1/RSU2/RSU3	Creating/changing/viewing update rules (→ BasicCubes and ODS objects)
SARA	Archive administration
SBIW	Viewing the Guidelines (→ Customizing extractors)
SE03	Transport Organizer Tools

Transaction	Description
SE09	Transport Organizer
SE11	ABAP Dictionary
SE16	ABAP Data Browser
SE37	Function Builder ($\rightarrow$ Maintenance of function modules)
SE38	ABAP Editor ($\rightarrow$ Maintenance of ABAP programs)
SE80	Object Navigator
SICF	System Internet Communication Framework Maintenance
SM04	User list
SM12	Selecting lock entries
SM21	Online evaluation system log
SM37	Job overview
SM38	Queue (Job) — Definition
SM50	Process overview
SM59	Maintenance of RFC connections
SM62	Maintenance of events
SM66	Global work process overview
SMX	System $\rightarrow$ own jobs
SPRO	Customizing guidelines
SQ02	SAP Query/InfoSets Maintenance
SQ10	Assigning Query/InfoSets to user and role
ST03	BW statistics
ST05	Performance analysis ($\rightarrow$ SQL Trace)
ST22	ABAP dump analysis
SU01	User maintenance
SU24	Maintenance of role templates
SU53	Resolving error codes at the authorization level
TRSA	Testing tool for service API

F.2   Transactions Relevant to BW in the SAP R/3 System

Transaction	Description
LBWE	Logistics extract structures customizing cockpit
KEB0	Creating/viewing/deleting CO-PA DataSource
RSA3	Extractor checker SAPI 3.0
RSA5	Transferring DataSources from Business Content
RSA6	Postprocessing DataSources and component hierarchy
RSA7	Maintaining the delta queue
RSA9	Transferring application component from Business Content
RSO2	Maintenance of generic DataSources
RSO3	Setting-up of delta extraction for attributes and texts
SBIW	Viewing the Guidelines (→ Customizing extractors)
SMQ1	qRFC Monitor (outbound queue)
TRSA	Testing tool for service API

G   Metadata Tables

G.1   InfoObject

Table	Description
RSDIOBJ	List of all InfoObjects
RSDIOBJT	Texts of InfoObjects
RSDATRNAV	Navigation attributes
RSDATRNAVT	Navigation attributes
RSDBCHATR	Master data attributes
RSDCHABAS	Basic characteristics (for characteristics, time characteristics, and units)
RSDCHA	Characteristics catalog
RSDDPA	Data package characteristics
RSDIOBJCMP	Compounding (dependencies) of InfoObjects
RSKYF	Key figures
RSDTIM	Time characteristics
RSDUNI	Units

G.2   InfoCube

Table	Description
RSDCUBE	List of the InfoCubes
RSDCUBET	Texts for the InfoCubes
RSDCUBEIOBJ	Navigation attributes
RSDDIME	List of dimensions
RSDDIMET	Texts for dimensions
RSDDIMEIOBJ	InfoObjects per dimension (where-used list)
RSDCUBEMULTI	InfoCubes that are part of MultiCube
RSDICMULTIIOBJ	MultiProviders: selection/identification of InfoObjects
RSDICHAPRO	InfoCube-specific characteristic properties

Table	Description
RSDIKYFPRO	InfoCube-specific key-figure properties
RSDICVALIOBJ	InfoObjects from the inventory validity table of the InfoCube

G.3 Aggregate

Table	Description
RSDDAGGRDIR	List of aggregates
RSDDAGGRCOMP	Description of aggregates
RSDDAGGRT	Texts for the aggregates

G.4 ODS Objects

Table	Description
RSDODSO	List of all ODS objects
RSDODSOT	Texts of ODS objects
RSDODSOIOBJ	InfoObjects of the ODS object
RSDODSOATRNAV	Navigation attributes for the ODS object
RSDODSOTABL	List of all ODS object tables

G.5 PSA

Table	Description
RSTSODS	List of all PSA tables

G.6 DataSource (= OLTP Source)

Table	Description
ROOSOURCE	Header table for SAP BW DataSources (SAP source system/ BW system)
RODELTAM	BW delta procedure (SAP source system)
RSOLTPSOURCE	Replica table for DataSources in SAP BW

G.7　InfoSource

Table	Description
RSIS	List of InfoSources with flexible updating
RSIST	Texts for InfoSources with flexible updating
RSISFIELD	InfoObjects of an InfoSource

G.8　Communication Structure

Table	Description
RSKS	▶ Communication structure for InfoSources with flexible updating ▶ Communication structure (view) for attributes of InfoSource with direct updating
RSKSFIELD	Texts for InfoSources with flexible updating
RSISFIELD	InfoObjects of an InfoSource with flexible updating

G.9　Transfer Structure

Table	Description
RSTS	Transfer structure in BW
ROOSGEN	Generated DataSource objects (for example, transfer structure) in SAP source system

G.10　Mapping

Table	Description
RSISOSMAP	Mapping between InfoSources and DataSources (= OLTP sources)
RSOSFIELDMAP	Mapping between DataSource fields and InfoObjects

G.11 BW Statistics

Table	Description
RSDDSTAT	Basic table InfoCubes/Queries
RSDDSTATAGGR	Detailed table for aggregate building
RSDDSTATAGGRDEF	Detailed table: navigations per InfoCube/Query

H   Glossary

Ad-hoc Query Designer
Web item that enables you to create and change ad-hoc queries in a Web application. You can use the Ad-hoc Query Designer in the Web Application Designer to design Web applications in which you can create or change queries.

ADK
see: Archiving Development Kit

Administrator Workbench (AWB)
Central tool for controlling, monitoring, and maintaining all processes involved in data retrieval and processing in SAP BW. The tasks are executed in the following functional areas:

▶ **Modeling** (Transaction RSA1)
This functional area handles the creation and maintenance of (meta) objects in SAP BW relevant to the process of retrieving or loading data.

▶ **Monitoring** (Transaction RSMON)
Monitoring enables you to observe and control the data loading process and other data processing activities in SAP BW.

▶ **Reporting Agent** (Transaction RSA1 • Pushbutton **Reporting Agent**)
Tool for scheduling and executing reporting functions in the background (batch). The functions include evaluating exceptions and printing queries.

▶ **Transport connection** (Transaction RSA1 • Pushbutton **Transport connection**)
With the transport connection, you can collect newly created and modified BW objects and use the Change and Transport Organizer (CTO) to transport them into other BW systems.

▶ **Documents** (Transaction RSA1 • Pushbutton **Documents**)
This functional area enables you to link and search one or more documents in various formats, versions, and languages.

▶ **Business Content** (Transaction RSORBCT)
Business Content offers preconfigured roles and task-related information models based on consistent metadata (*see:* Business Content).

▶ **Translation** (Transaction RSA1 • Pushbutton **Translation**)
You can translate short and long texts of BW objects in this functional area.

▶ **Metadata Repository** (Transaction RSOR)
The HTML-based BW Metadata Repository centrally administers all BW metaobjects and their links to each other, which enables a consistent and homogeneous data model across all source systems (*see:* Metadata Repository).

Aggregate
Stores the dataset of a BasicCube redundantly and persistently in a summarized form in the database. Because aggregates use the same form of storage (fact and

dimension tables) as BasicCubes, they are often called aggregate cubes. Aggregates enable you to access BasicCubes quickly for reporting. Therefore, aggregates help to improve performance. Because a BasicCube can have several aggregates, the Optimizer of the OLAP processor automatically accesses the most appropriate aggregate during execution of a query. In other words, the decision to use a Basic-Cube or an aggregate for reporting is not transparent to the end user. Information on aggregates, such as technical, content, and status properties, are stored in table RSDDAGGRDIR. Maintenance of aggregates in SAP BW:

▶ Transaction RSDDV

▶ Initial access: **AWB** · **Modeling** · **InfoProvider** · **Select InfoArea** · Select **maintain aggregate** in the context menu of the selected BasicCube.

When building an aggregate from the characteristics and navigation attributes of a BasicCube, you can group the data according to different aggregation levels:

▶ **All characteristic values (*)**
Data is grouped according to all values of the combined characteristics or navigation attributes that define the aggregate.

▶ **Hierarchy level (H)**
The data is grouped according to the nodes of a hierarchy level.

▶ **Fixed value (F)**
The data is filtered and grouped according to an individual value of a characteristic or navigation attribute.

Logical data packages are used to load new data (requests) into an aggregate. When loading data, note the distinction between filling and rolling up. Aggregates enable you to access InfoCube data quickly for reporting. Thus, aggregates help to improve performance.

▶ **Activate and fill**
This function builds the aggregate and fills it for the first time. An active and filled aggregate is used for reporting and can be populated with additional data by rolling up data packages.

▶ **Roll-up**
Loads data packages (requests) that are not yet contained in the aggregates of a BasicCube into all aggregates of the BasicCube. A roll-up is required as soon as the data of the BasicCube has changed to ensure the consistency of data between the aggregate and the BasicCube. After the roll-up, the new data is used in queries.

▶ **Roll-up hierarchy (aggregate hierarchy)**
The roll-up hierarchy displays the dependency of aggregates to a BasicCube and among aggregates in terms of the roll-up. In other words, it displays whether an aggregate is filled by a superior aggregate or directly by the Basic-Cube during a roll-up. You can use the roll-up hierarchy to identify similar aggregates and then use this information as the basis for manual and targeted optimization of the aggregates.

Additional functionalities:

▶ **On/Off Switch**
If an aggregate is temporarily switched off, it is not used in the execution of a query. When the aggregate is switched back on, it does not have to be reactivated and refilled. This feature allows you to compare the runtime of the query with and without the aggregate to determine whether using the aggregate is advisable.

▶ **Deactivate**
Deactivation of an aggregate means that all the data of the aggregate is deleted, although the structure of the aggregate remains in place.

▶ **Delete**
Deletion deactivates the aggregate and its structure.

▶ **Compress**
Compression of aggregates corresponds to the compression of BasicCubes. In other words, compressed requests can no longer be deleted from the aggregate. However, you can switch compression off after the roll-up so that the aggregate request remains in place.

▶ **Hierarchy/Attribute Change Run**
If the hierarchy and navigation attributes of characteristics used in aggregates change, structural modifications are needed in the aggregates to adjust the data accordingly. A structure modification affects the aggregates of all BasicCubes affected by modifications of hierarchies and navigation attributes:

▶ Initial access: **AWB · Tools · Execute Hierarchy/Attribute Modifications for Reporting**

▶ You can use the ABAP program "RSDDS_CHANGE" "RUN_MONITOR" to determine the attributes, hierarchies, and aggregates to be adjusted during the change run. Modifications of master data become effective only if a change run is executed for the master data. At a certain size of the change run, modification of the aggregates involves more work than rebuilding it. You can set this threshold value yourself:

> ▶ Transaction RSCUSTV8

> ▶ Initial access: **BW Customizing Guidelines · Business Information Warehouse · General BW Settings · Parameters for Aggregates**

Aggregation Level
Choice of characteristics and navigation attributes of an InfoCube from which aggregates are constructed. You have the following aggregation options:

▶ **All characteristic values (*)**
Data is grouped by all values of the characteristic or the navigation attribute.

▶ **Hierarchy level (H)**
The data is grouped according to the nodes of a hierarchy level.

▶ **Fixed value (F)**
Data is filtered according to a single value.

ALE
see: Application Link Enabling

Alert Monitor
A monitoring tool for displaying exceptions whose threshold values have been exceeded or have not been reached. The exceptions that occur are found in background processing with the help of the reporting agent. They are then displayed in the alert monitor as a follow-up action. Exceptions are displayed in the BEx Analyzer as well as in the reporting agent scheduler of the Administrator Workbench. Exceptions can be displayed as an alert monitor in a Web application.

And Process
Collective process of process chain maintenance. The use of an And process in process chain maintenance starts the application process only after successful triggers of all events of the preceding processes, including the last of the events for which it waited.

API Service
see: SAPI

Application Component Hierarchy

▶ **In the SAP source system**
The component hierarchy is an element of the SAP source system Business Content that is imported with the plug-in. You can also maintain the hierarchy manually. The hierarchy helps organize DataSources. Modify component hierarchy:

  ▶ Transaction RSA8

  ▶ Initial access: **Transaction SBIW · Postprocessing of DataSources · Modify Component Hierarchy**

▶ **In the SAP BW system**
The component hierarchy is also an element of SAP BW—Business Content; you can maintain it manually here. It helps to organize the InfoSource tree and PSA tables in the PSA tree.

Application Link Enabling (ALE)
ALE supports the configuration and operation of distributed application systems between SAP systems themselves and between SAP systems and external systems. For communication (data exchange) among distributed application systems, ALE provides tolls and services, such as consistency checks, monitoring of data transfer, error handling, and synchronous and asynchronous connections. It guarantees controlled data exchange among the distributed application systems and consistent data storage.

Application Process
A process that is automated in process chain maintenance. Example: a data loading process or an attribute change run.

Archiving

Data archiving enables you to archive data from BasicCubes and ODS objects (tables with active data). In other words, you can store the data as a flat structure in a file system and delete it from the BasicCube or ODS object. You archive data for the following purposes:

▶ To lessen the volume or data and thus save storage space

▶ To improve performance because of the smaller volume of data—during analyses, updates, roll-ups, and change runs, for example

▶ To meet legal requirements for the storage of data

see also: Archiving Development Kit, Archiving Process, and Archiving Objects

Archiving Development Kit (ADK)

The ADK of mySAP Technology—Basis is used for archiving. The ADK provides the runtime environment for archiving. It primarily helps to read and write data to and from archive files. The ADK guarantees platform and release independence for archived data.

Archiving Objects

All archiving requires archiving objects that describe related business data with a data structure and that are used to define and execute reading, writing, and deleting in the context of the archiving process. They are the link between the ADK and SAP BW objects. C3reating an archiving object:

Initial access: **AWB · Modeling · InfoProvider ·** select **InfoArea**. In the context menu of the selected BasicCube or ODS object, select **Modify · Extras · Archiving**

Archiving Process

The archiving process in SAP BW consists of the following subprocesses:

▶ **Writing data to the archive (Transaction SARA)**

▶ **Deleting the archived data from the BasicCube/ODS Object (Transaction SARA)**
If you delete archived data from a BasicCube, it is also deleted from the aggregate that belongs to the BasicCube. If you delete data from an ODS object, archiving does not affect the data targets populated with data from the ODS object.

▶ **Restoring archived data in the BW system**
You can restore archived data with the export DataSource of the BasicCube or ODS object from which the data was archived. The ADK provides functions for reading archived data. Later updates occur with the familiar data loading processes in the BW system.

Attributes

Attributes are InfoObjects (characteristics or key figures) used to describe characteristics in more detail. Example: For the "cost center" characteristic, you can assign the following attributes:

▶ "Cost center manger" (characteristic as attribute)

▶ "Size of the cost center in square meters" (key figure as attribute)

When you maintain an InfoObject for a characteristic, you can also assign attributes with attribute properties to the characteristic:

▶ **Display**
Attributes with this property can be used in reporting only as supplemental information in combination with the characteristic. That means that you cannot navigate in queries. Note the special case that occurs when you define InfoObjects. You can define InfoObjects (characteristics or key figures) as exclusive attributes. You cannot use these attributes as navigation attributes; you can use them only as display attributes.

▶ **Navigation Attribute**
You can define attributes of InfoObject type "characteristic" as navigation attributes. These types of attributes can be used for navigation much like (dimension) characteristics in queries: all navigation functions of (dimension) characteristics in queries also apply to navigation attributes. Unlike (dimension) characteristics, navigation attributes enable current and key-date data views at the query layer (→ Tracking History). To make these attributes available in reporting as navigation attributes, you must also switch them on at the data-target layer. A characteristic used as a navigation attribute can also have its own navigation attributes called transitive attributes (= two-level navigation attribute). You can also switch on the transitive attributes and make them available for navigation in queries.

▶ **Time Dependency**
You can flag both display and navigation attributes as time-dependent attributes if a validity area is required for each attribute value.

AWB
see: Administrator Workbench

Balanced Scorecard (BSC)
Robert S. Kaplan, professor of management at Harvard Business School, and Dr. David Norton introduced this management instrument in 1992 and triggered lasting change in performance management at leading companies. The *Harvard Business Review* calls the concept the most important management idea in the last 75 years.

The core of the theory is that the economic success of a company rests on influencing factors behind the target financial values that determine the ability to reach the financial objective. The BSC usually considers meeting objects from the perspective of finances, processes, customers, and innovation. The evidence of historical key figures is supplemented by a knowledge of future developments.

BAPI (Business Application Programming Interface)

BAPIs are open, standard interfaces defined at the application layer (Transaction: BAPI). These interfaces provided by SAP enable communication between SAP systems and applications developed by third parties. Technically, calling a BAPI calls a function module with RFC or tRFC. *See also:* Staging BAPI

BasicCube

▶ Creating BasicCubes:

▶ Initial access: **AWB** · **Modeling** · **InfoProvider** · select **InfoArea**. In the context menu of the selected InfoArea, select **Create InfoCube** and select the type of BasicCube

▶ Maintenance of BasicCubes: Transaction RSDCUBE

A BasicCube is a data container; reports and analyses in SAP BW are based on BasicCubes. It is an InfoCube that represents a closed, topically related dataset on which queries can be defined. A BasicCube contains two types of data: key figures and characteristics. It is supplied with transaction data relevant to analysis by one or more InfoSources with update rules. A BasicCube is the InfoCube relevant for multidimensional modeling because only objects that contain data are considered for the BW data model.

Technically, a BasicCube is a set of relational tables placed together according to the star schema: a large fact table in the center, surrounded by several dimension tables. The fact table is used to store all key figures at the lowest level of detail. The dimension tables help store the characteristics required in reporting and during analysis of the key figures. Dimension tables are considered independently of each other. Only the fact table links the dimensions to the key figures. Consequently, all data is stored multidimensionally in the BasicCubes:

▶ **Fact Tables**
A BasicCube consists of two fact tables, each of which stores the key figures.

  ▶ F table: Normal fact table (→ partitioned with respect to the request ID)

  ▶ E table: Compressed fact table (→ F table without request ID)

  ▶ A maximum of 233 key figures can be stored. Use of the E table is optional (*see also:* Compression).

▶ **Dimension Tables**
A BasicCube consists of a maximum of 16 dimension tables. Of these, the system automatically generates the time dimension and data package dimension tables. The system generates a unit dimension table only when at least one key figure is of the "amount" or "quantity" type. In this case, you must also supply a fixed or variable currency/unit along with the key figure (*see also:* Key Figures).

▶ **SID Tables/Master Data Tables**
The relationship between the master data tables for a characteristic InfoObject and the dimension tables is created by system-generated INT4 keys, or SIDs (surrogate identifications) of each characteristic InfoObject. Dimension tables store only SIDs of each characteristic InfoObject; they never store characteristic values. A dimension table can contain a maximum of 248 SIDs of each charac-

teristic InfoObject. The relationship between a fact table and the related dimension tables is created with artificially generated INT4 keys, or DIM IDs (dimension identifications).

Administering BasicCubes:

▶ **Selective Deletion (Content tab)**
With this function and a previous selection, you can delete targeted data records that correspond to the selection criteria from a BasicCube. If you use selective deletion to delete erroneous data records from the BasicCube, you can replace the records with correct(ed) data records by using a repair request in the scheduler (**Scheduler · Maintain InfoPackage**).

▶ **Check, Delete, or Repair Indices (Performance tab)**
An index of BasicCubes is created on the fact table for each DIM ID. The indices are required to guarantee optimal finding and selection of data. However, the database system must adjust the indices during write access, which can lead to considerable degradations of performance. The Delete Indices function enables you to accelerate write access during the updating of the BasicCubes. After the update ends, you must rebuild the indices with the Repair Indices function. You can use the Check Indices function to determine whether indices are deleted (red light), rebuilt (yellow light), or active (green light).

▶ **Delete Requests (Requests tab)**
You can use this function to delete selected requests loaded into the BasicCubes (if they have not been rolled up into aggregates).

▶ **Rebuild Requests (Rebuild tab)**
You can use this function to recreate deleted requests for a BasicCube. You can also use these requests for other BasicCubes. This function works only if the PSA tables store the requests.

▶ **Roll-Up Requests (Roll-Up tab)**
see: **Aggregate · Roll-Up**

▶ **Compress (Compress tab)**
Every BasicCube has a data package dimension table (set by the system) that stores the SID for the 0REQUID (request ID) technical characteristic. Every load process fills this dimension table. Consequently, the fact table stores data with a higher level of detail than required from a business viewpoint. Depending on the modeling of the BasicCube, the frequency of load processes, and the composition of loaded data, the level of detail can significantly affect the volume of data in the BasicCubes. After the disappearance of the request ID, the data volume can be reduced considerably without having to accept any disadvantages from the perspective of the business. To enable this reduction, each BasicCube consists of two fact tables:

▶ F table: Normal fact table

▶ E table: Compressed fact table (= F table without request ID)

The **Compress** function fills the E table with data from the F table. The entire F table can be compressed or only an older portion of the requests can be compressed. New requests are written to the F table and can then be compressed.

The compression of aggregates behaves similarly. The disadvantage of compression is that it cannot be reversed.

BCT
see: Business Content

BEx
see: Business Explorer

BI Cockpit
see: Business Intelligence Cockpit

BIS
see: Business Intelligence Systems

BSC
see: Balanced Scorecard

Business Application Programming Interface
see: BAPI

Business Content (BCT)
An important advantage of SAP BW over and against other data warehouse solutions is the Business Content (BCT) that SAP delivers with SAP BW. SAP continues ongoing development of BCT, which involves a comprehensive, predefined information model for the analysis of business processes. It contains the entire definition of all required SAP BW objects, including the following: InfoAreas, InfoObjectCatalogs, roles, workbooks, query elements, InfoCubes, InfoObjects, ODS objects, update rules, InfoSources, transfer rules, currency conversion types, extractors, and DataSources. Accordingly, two areas of BCT are distinguished:

▶ BCT for source systems (component hierarchy and DataSources, for example)

▶ BCT for the BW system

BCT for SAP source systems (SAP R/3 systems: = Release 3.1 I) is imported with plug-ins. If BW systems are connected to other BW systems as source systems, the importation of plug-ins is not required. Before you can use elements of BCT, you must adopt or activate them explicitly. You do so with transaction SBIW in the source system and with transaction RSORBCT in the BW system.

▶ **Object Versions**
All BW objects are first delivered in the D(elivered) version with BCT. The adoption of these objects from BCT creates an A(ctive) version; the D version remains in place. If the activated objects are modified, a new, M(odified) version is created. You can activate the M version and thus overwrite the older active version. Modifications of BW objects adopted from the BCT are not overwritten by adoption of a newer content version.

Business Explorer (BEx)
The BEx is the analysis and reporting tool of SAP BW. You can use it to evaluate centrally stored data that comes from various sources. The BEx optimizes the following areas:

▶ **Query Design and Application Design**
  BEx Query Designer and BEx Web Application Designer

▶ **Analysis and Reporting**
  BEx Analyzer, BEx Web Applications, and Mobile Intelligence

▶ **Formatted Reporting**
  Crystal Reports integration

▶ **Organization**
  BEx Browser

Business Explorer Analyzer (BEx Analyzer)

▶ Transaction RRMX

Analysis and reporting tool of Business Explorer. It is embedded as an add-in in Microsoft Excel and can thus access all Excel functionality. In the Business Explorer Analyzer, you can use navigation to analyze selected InfoProvider Data in queries created in the BEx Query Designer and generate various views of the data—query views. BEx Analyzer is used for the following:

▶ To create and modify reports

▶ To analyze reports and navigate within reports

▶ To call and to save reports in roles or as personal favorites

▶ To publish reports for Web reporting

Business Explorer Browser (BEx Browser)
A tool to organize and manage workbooks and documents. You can use it to access all documents in SAP BW that have been assigned to your role and that you have stored in your list of favorites. You can work with the following types of documents in the BEx Browser:

▶ SAP BW workbooks

▶ Documents stored in the Business Document Service (BDS)

▶ Links (references to the file system and shortcuts)

▶ Links to Internet sites (URLs)

▶ SAP transaction calls

▶ Web applications and Web templates

▶ Crystal Reports

Business Explorer Map (BEx Map)
Geographical Information System (GIS) of Business Explorer that enables you to display and evaluate data with geographical references (characteristics such as

customer, sales region, and country, for example) along with key figures relevant to the business on a map.

Business Explorer Mobile Intelligence (BEx Mobile Intelligence)
The use of Web applications for mobile devices with an online connection to the SAP BW system.

Business Explorer Query Designer (BEx Query Designer)
A tool used to define queries based on selected characteristics and key figures (InfoObjects) or reusable structures of an InfoProvider. In BEx Query Designer, you can parameterize queries by defining variables for characteristic values, hierarchies, hierarchy nodes, texts, or formulas. You can make the selection of Info-Objects more precise by the following:

▶ Limiting characteristics and key figures to characteristic values, characteristic value intervals, and hierarchy nodes

▶ Defining calculated and limited key figures for reuse

▶ Defining structures for reuse

▶ Defining exceptions

▶ Defining conditions

▶ Defining exception cells

All queries defined in BEx Query Designer can also be used for OLAP reporting and for flat reporting.

Business Explorer Web Application (BEx Web Application)
Web-based application in Business Explorer for data analysis, reporting, and analytical applications on the Web. You can format and display your data in various ways in BEx Web Application Designer with a series of Web items (tables, filters, charts, maps, documents, and so on). In this manner, you can create Web applications (such as BI cockpits) individually and access them over the Internet or via an enterprise portal.

Business Explorer Web Application Designer (BEx Web Application Designer)
Desktop application for creating websites with SAP BW content. With the BEx Web Application Designer, you can place queries and HTML documents on an intranet or on the Internet. With the BEx Web Application Designer, you create an HTML page that contains BW-specific content such as tables, charts, and maps. Such HTML pages serve as the basis for Web applications with complex interaction, such as BI cockpits. You can save Web applications as a URL and then access them over an intranet or from mobile end devices. You can also save Web applications as an iView and integrate them into an enterprise portal.

Business Explorer Web Application Wizard (BEx Web Application Wizard)
An assistant that supports you in the creation of Web pages with SAP BW-specific content. It enables a simplified design procedure with an automated, step-by-step sequence. The Web Application Wizard is integrated into the Web Application Designer.

Business Intelligence Cockpit (BI Cockpit)
Synonyms: Web cockpit and information cockpit

Web-based switchboard with business intelligence content. Much like a cockpit in an airplane, it displays an overview of all relevant business data to a company's management. With the BEx Web Application Designer, you can create individual BI cockpits that display the relevant data in tables, charts, or maps. You can recognize at a glance critical data that has exceeded a threshold with the alert monitor integrated into the BI cockpit. You can also insert additional data, such as documents, sketches, or hyperlinks, into the business data. BI cockpits offer the following options:

▶ Data can be collected from various data sources and visualized in various ways (tables, charts, maps, and so on).

▶ Structured (BI content) and unstructured (documents and so on) information supplement each other

▶ Personalized access: Parameters are automatically filled with user-specific values (references to the cost center, region, and so on)

▶ Role-specific variations: various BI cockpits for various roles

You can get a quick overview of various business information much like you would when reading the front page of a newspaper. You can then perform a detailed query with easy-to-use navigation elements like hyperlinks, dropdown boxes, buttons, and so on.

Business Intelligence Systems (BIS)
Business Intelligence Systems (BIS) refer to a family of IT systems tailored to the requirements of a specific user group: knowledge workers. Both observers of the IT industry and analysts differentiate between operating systems and business intelligence systems:

▶ Operative systems help to automate routine, predictable tasks.

▶ They are characterized by a multitude of small transactions whose effects are normally limited and that convert data into a format that can be processed by a computer.

▶ Business intelligence systems help research, analyze, and present information.

▶ They typically involve a relatively small number of queries that are often comprehensive, or that have a great deal of influence.

▶ The type of queries that might arise in the future cannot be predicted. Such systems always involve mining information from the system.

Characteristic

▶ Creating a characteristic InfoObject in the InfoObject tree:
  ▶ Initial access: **AWB · Modeling · InfoObjects · Select InfoArea ·** Select **InfoObjectCatalog** of type characteristic. Select **Create InfoObject** in the context menu of the InfoObjectCatalog

▶ Maintenance of characteristics: Transactions RSD1 through RSD5

Type of InfoObject. Organization term, like company code, product, customer group, fiscal year, period, or region. Characteristic InfoObjects (such as customer or item) are reference objects. They are used to describe, select, and evaluate key figures. In addition, characteristic can carry master data (attributes, texts, and hierarchies) as master data tables:

▶ Attributes

▶ Texts

▶ Hierarchies

Characteristics indicate the classification options of a data set. In general, an Info-Cube contains only a subset of the characteristic values from the master data table. The master data comprises the permitted values of a characteristic, the characteristic values. Characteristic values are discrete descriptions. For example, the "region" characteristic has the following properties:

▶ North

▶ Central

▶ South

Characteristics that carry master data can also be used as an InfoSource with direct update for loading master data. (Exception: Reference characteristics, unit Info-Objects, and characteristic 0SOURSYSTEM). Note the following special characteristics:

▶ Units (0CURRENCY (currency key) and 0UNIT (quantity unit), for example)

▶ Time characteristics (0CALYEAR (calendar year), for example)

▶ Technical characteristics (0REQUID (request ID), for example)

see also: Reference Characteristic

Chart
Web item that refers to the data of a query view to create a diagram for a Web application. You can select from a variety of display options for the diagram. You can also navigate in interactive charts and analyze the data displayed in them.

Cleansing
Cleaning data before posting, checking data for plausibility before posting, or suppressing records with errors. You can use transfer rules and update rules to homogenize and harmonize data from the source systems in terms of data structure and semantics before posting it to the data targets. You can filter out, cleanse, or correct erroneous information.

Collective Process
In process chain maintenance, a collective process enables you to combine several process strands into one, which makes multiple scheduling of the actual application process unnecessary. Process chain maintenance makes the following collective processes available:

▶ **And process (last)**
The application process starts only after successful triggers of all events of the preceding processes, including the last of the events for which it waited.

▶ **Or Process (every)**
The application process starts every time an event of the preceding process is triggered successfully.

▶ **Exor Process (first)**
The application process starts only when the first event of the preceding process has been triggered successfully.

Common Warehouse Metamodel (CWM)
A standard recognized by the Object Management Group (OMG): it describes the exchange of metadata in the following areas:

▶ Data warehousing

▶ Business intelligence

▶ Knowledge management

▶ Portal technologies

CWM uses:

▶ UML to model metadata

▶ MOF to access metadata

▶ XMI to exchange metadata

You can find the specifications for CWM Version 1.0 at *http://www.omg.org*.

Communication structure
The communication structure is independent of the source system and depicts the structure of an InfoSource. It contains all the InfoObjects that belong to an InfoSource. Data is updated into InfoCubes from this structure. The system always accesses the active, saved version of the communication structure.

An InfoSource with direct update always contains one communication structure for attributes and one for texts. Both are automatically generated by the system as an InfoSource during the creation of a characteristic. A communication structure for hierarchies is generated only if you select "PSA" as the transfer method.

The technical properties (length and type, for example) of the fields in the communication structure correspond to the InfoObjects of SAP BW.

Compounding
You will frequently need to compound characteristic values to enable the unambiguous assignment of characteristic values. Compounding is implemented during the maintenance of characteristic InfoObjects. You can use multiple characteristics as compounded characteristics. In general, you should use as few compounded characteristics as possible to avoid a negative affect on performance (→ compounded characteristics are elements of the primary key of the corresponding SID and

master data tables). Example: Cost center 100 in controlling area 1000 is purchasing, and in controlling area 2000, it is sales. Therefore, unambiguous evaluation is impossible. Compounding the cost center to the controlling area guarantees no ambiguity.

Condenser
A program that compresses the contents of an InfoCube fact table.

Control Query
An auxiliary query executed in the Web template before the queries whose results are used to parameterize the Web template.

CO-PA Updating
Transfer of account assignment data from Contract Accounts Receivable and Payable (FI-CA) into Profitability Analysis (CO-PA).

Crystal Enterprise
Server component for executing reports, scheduling reports, caching reports, and outputting reports to the Web. Content and user administration occur over the SAP BW server in the context of integration.

Crystal Reports Designer
Design component to create a Crystal Report; it contains the layout (report definition).

Crystal Report
BW object type. A report definition created with Crystal Reports Designer and stored in SAP BW. Several queries can be embedded in a Crystal Report (similar to an Excel workbook). A Crystal Report does not contain any current data.

CWM
see: Common Warehouse Metamodel

Data Dictionary (DDIC)

▶ Transaction SE11

The (ABAP) Data Dictionary enables central description and management of all the data definitions used in the system. The DDIC is completely integrated into the ABAP Workbench. The DDIC supports the definition of user-defined types (data elements, structures, and table types). You can also define the structure of database objects (tables, indices, and views) in the DDIC. You can use this definition for automatic creation of the objects in the database.

Data Granularity
Data granularity describes the level of detail of data. Very detailed data has a low granularity; increasing aggregation produces a higher granularity. Granularity affects disk space, the quantity of information, and read performance. In SAP BW,

detailed data for reporting is stored in ODS objects; aggregated data in stored in BasicCubes or aggregates.

Data Manager
Part of the OLAP processor: it executes the database accesses that result from the definition of a query. Part of warehouse management: it writes data to the database.

Data Marts
see: Data Mart Interface

Data Mart Interface
The data mart interface enables updating data from one data target into an additional data target. It allows updating within an SAP BW system (Myself Data Mart/Myself System) and among multiple BW systems. If you use several BW systems, the system that delivers the data is called the source BW; the receiving system is called the target BW. Individual BWs in such a landscape are called data marts.

A transfer of data from one data target into another requires an export DataSource derived from the structure of the source data target. If the source data target is an ODS object, the export DataSource is automatically generated when you activate a newly created ODS object (which differs from the case with a BasicCube).

Data Providers
An object that delivers data for one or more Web items. A data provider reflects the navigational status of a query at a specific point in time. The star view of a data provider corresponds to a query view. Navigation through the data or parameterization of the call can modify the state of a data provider.

Data Quality
Quality of data in terms of its usefulness for reporting and analysis.

Data Requirement
Describes the requirement set on the source system by the scheduler, the quantity of data and information generated in SAP BW, and the source system because of the requirement, and the loading procedure.

Data Staging
Formatting process for retrieving data in SAP BW.

Data Target
A data target is a BW object into which data can be loaded: it is a physical object. These objects include BasicCubes, ODS objects, and InfoObjects (characteristics with attributes, texts, or hierarchies). Note the distinction between pure data targets for which queries cannot be created or executed, and data targets for which queries can be defined. The latter are also called InfoProviders. A data target is a

physical object that is important during the modeling of the BW data model and when loading the data. Data targets can include the following:

▶ BasicCubes

▶ ODS objects

▶ Characteristic InfoObjects

Data Warehouse (DWH)

A DWH is a system that stores data relevant to decisions in terms of topics, persistently, and time. The functions of a data warehouse are to combine data from sources within a firm and outside of it, to cleanse the data, to consolidate the data, and to make it available consistently with analysis, reporting, and evaluation tools. The knowledge gained in this manner creates the foundation for decision-making that applies to the control of a company. A data warehouse is therefore a system primarily used to support enterprise control.

The integration of OLAP tools in a DWH system is not mandatory. Nevertheless, manufacturers currently offer increasingly more DWH systems with integrated OLAP tools. Such DWH systems are often called OLAP systems or DWH solutions. Accordingly, SAP BW is a DWH solution.

Database Shared Library

see: DB Connect

DataSource

Comprises a quantity of fields in SAP BW offered in a flat structure, the extract structure, to transfer data. It also describes the properties of the corresponding extractor in terms of transferring data into SAP BW.

A DataSource describes a business unit of master data (material master data, for example) and transaction data (sales data, for example). From the viewpoint of the source system, metainformation (fields and field descriptions of the master and transaction data and programs) belongs to each DataSource; the metainformation describes how the extraction is executed. This information is specific to each source system: a DataSource is dependent on the source system. In SAP source systems, the DataSource information (or properties) is stored in tables ROOSOURCE and RODELTAM; in SAP BW systems, it is stored in table RSOLT-PSOURCE. Technically, a DataSource distinguishes between two types of field structures:

▶ Extract structure

▶ Transfer structure

Note the following types of DataSources:

▶ DataSources for transaction data

▶ DataSources for master data attributes

▶ DataSources for master data attributes

▶ DataSources for master data hierarchies

The definition of generic DataSources allows you to extract data from any DDIC tables and view, SAP queries, and InfoSets, or function modules from SAP source systems. Therefore, you can extract data from SAP source systems that is not extracted by BCT DataSources (transaction RSO2). You cannot extract data for external hierarchies with generic DataSources.

DB Connect

Enables the connection to various (external) relational database systems and the transfer of data from tables or views from the database system into SAP BW.
SAP DB MultiConnect is used to create a connection to the database management system (DBMS) of the external database. Reading metadata and the original data makes it easy to generate the required structures in SAP BW and to load the data.

The precondition is that SAP supports the DBMS involved. You can then use Data-Sources to make the data known to SAP BW and to extract it. SAP supports the following DBMS:

▶ SAP DB

▶ Informix

▶ Microsoft SQL Server

▶ Oracle

▶ IBM DB2 390//400/UDB

In addition, you must also install the SAP-specific part of the Database Shared Library (DBSL) interface on the SAP BW application server for each source DBMS.

DBSL (Database Shared Library)
see: DB Connect

DDIC
see: Data Dictionary

Decision-Support System (DSS)

Development of decision-support systems began in the 1970s: Managers wanted query and analysis instruments that were based on flexible database systems and allowed them to perform what-if scenarios and ad-hoc analyses. Three main reasons contributed to the failure of this DSS design:

▶ The DSS offered at the time used complex languages and inflexible model structures; they required a great deal of effort to learn and had prohibitively high start-up costs.

▶ To justify the enormous investments in the DSS infrastructure and the high cost of IT specialists, increasingly more lists and reports were created. The sheer quantity and resulting unmanageability of the reports and lists made it impossible to make reasonable management decisions.

▶ It soon became apparent that endless lists of numbers for the controller did not determine the success of an enterprise. Success depended on the consistent implementation of strategic goals, coupled with quick decisions.

Delta Process
Extractor feature. It specifies how the data is to be transferred. As a DataSource attribute, it specifies how the DataSource data is to be transmitted to the data target. The user can determine, for example, with which data targets a DataSource is compatible, how the data is to be updated, and how serialization is to take place.

Delta Queue
Data storage in the source system of a BW system. Data records are automatically written to the delta queue in the source system with a posting procedure, or are written to a data request from BW via extraction with a function module. The data is transferred to SAP BW during a delta requirement of the BW scheduler.

Delta Update
A delta update requests only data that has been created since the last update. It fills the corresponding data targets with the (new) data. Before you can request a delta update, you must initialize the data process. A delta update is independent of the DataSource. In SAP source systems, the DataSource properties are stored in tables ROOSOURCE and RODELTAM; in SAP BW systems, the DataSource is stored in table RSOLTPSOURCE.

DIM ID
see: Dimension Identification

Dimension
A dimension is the grouping of logically related characteristics into one generic term. A total of 248 characteristics can be combined within one dimension. From a technical viewpoint, a dimension consists of a BasicCube from a dimension table (if it is not a line item dimension), SID tables, and master data tables. During the definition of an InfoCube, characteristics are summarized into dimensions to store them in a table of the star schema (dimension table). *See also*: Line Item Dimension

Dimension Identification (DIM ID)
The relationship between a fact table and its dimension tables to a BasicCube is created with a system-generated INT4 key, also called DIM IDs. During the loading of transaction data into the BasicCube, DIM ID values are assigned non-ambiguously: Each DIM ID value is assigned unambiguously to a combination of SID values of the various characteristics.

Dimension Table
see: BasicCube

Drill Down
Hierarchies can be defined for every dimension. The hierarchies can contain multiple levels. The higher the hierarchy level is, the higher the aggregation level of the displayed data. The deeper a user goes into the hierarchy, or drills down into it, the more detailed the information becomes. Drilldown can occur within a

dimension (by moving in the product hierarchy from main product groups, to product groups, and then to individual products), or by inserting characteristics from other dimensions. *See also:* Hierarchy

DSS
see: Decision Support System

DWH
see: Data Warehouse

DWH Systems
see: Data Warehouse

EIS
see: Executive Information System

Elementary Test
Component of a test that cannot be split up into subtests. An elementary test checks the consistency of logical objects that belong together.

Error Handling
You can use the error-handling function on the **Update Parameters** tab in the InfoPackage of the scheduler when loading data with the PSA table to control the behavior of SAP BW when data records with errors appear. You then have the following options:

▶ No posting and no reporting (default)

▶ Posting of valid records and no reporting (request is red)

▶ Posting of valid records and reporting is possible (request is green)

You can also determine after how many error records the loading process aborts. If you do not make any entries here, the loading process aborts when the first error occurs.

The request is considered an error if the number of received records does not agree with the number of posted records (key figure: "Aggregation not allowed").

E Table
see: BasicCube

ETL Process
An ETL process consists of the following subprocesses:

▶ Extraction of data from a source system

▶ Transformation of the data (including cleansing and data quality assurance)

▶ Loading the data into the BW system

Event

A signal to background control that a specific state in the SAP system has been reached. Background control then starts all the processes waiting for the event.

Event Collector

An event collector is a set of several, independent, and successfully completed events to which background processing is to react. The event collector corresponds to the "And" process of process chain maintenance. If an application process is scheduled with a event collector, it starts when all the events of the preceding processes have been triggered successfully.

Executive Information System (EIS)

After the era of controllers and the decision-support systems of the 1970s, evolution of planning systems took an entirely new path in the 1980s. Instead of automatic decision generators or decision-support systems operated by expensive specialists, developers decided to focus on what they could actually accomplish.

▶ Upper management was to be supported by executive information systems (EIS).

▶ If a decision-maker needed information, it was to be available almost at the push of a button.

▶ No one wanted to be limited to a company's own data, but wanted to try to integrate external data.

But the EIS approach failed technologically. It was too expensive and did not offer good enough performance. The continuing weaknesses of EIS tools, especially regarding the integration of external data, and a lack of acceptance among upper management also contributed to the failure of this approach. Instead, divisional solutions came into being, such as marketing, sales, financial, and product information systems.

Export DataSource

see: Data Mart Interface

eXtensible Markup Language

see: XML

External Hierarchies

In SAP BW, the term "external hierarchy" is understood as presentation hierarchies that store the properties of a characteristic for structuring in hierarchy tables. In other words, they are triggered by the attributes and texts of a characteristic InfoObject and can thus be maintained independently of the attributes and texts of the characteristic InfoObject. When the **With Hierarchy** flag is set in characteristic maintenance, you can also create hierarchies for a characteristic (not reference characteristics) within SAP BW and load them from the SAP source system or with flat files into SAP BW.

Maintenance of hierarchies for a characteristic:

▶ Transaction RSH1

▶ Initial access: **AWB · Modeling · InfoObjects · Select InfoArea · Select Create Hierarchy** in the context menu of the selected characteristic InfoObject

Existing hierarchies for a characteristic are displayed in the InfoObject tree beneath this characteristic and can be edited from the corresponding context menu.

Properties of external hierarchies:

▶ **Version-independence**
External hierarchies can be used in various versions. Version-dependent hierarchies can be used for planning and other reporting tasks similar to simulation. In other words, hierarchy versions can be compared with each other in a query.

▶ **Time-dependence**
Note the following distinctions related to time-dependence:

▷ **Time-dependent whole hierarchy**
The time-dependence refers to the hierarchy root and is therefore transferred to all nodes of the hierarchy. Depending on the key data chosen in the query, you can use various hierarchies.

▷ **Time-dependent hierarchy structure**
The time-dependence refers to the nodes of the hierarchy. Here you can determine the time period of the nodes for which the hierarchy should stand at the indicated location.

▶ **Hierarchy interval**
You can append characteristic properties as intervals beneath a hierarchy node. For example, instead of appending the cost element properties to material costs individually in a cost element hierarchy, you can specify cost element properties as cost elements 100 through 1000.

▶ **Plus/minus sign reversal for nodes**
You can use this function to reverse the plus or minus sign of values assigned in a hierarchy node.

External System
An external, non-SAP data source for a BW system used to transfer data and metadata with staging BAPIs. External systems are non-SAP systems (including SAP R/3 system and SAP R/3 systems with a release level lower than 3.1I) that make data available to SAP BW and thus act as a source system. The extraction, transformation, and loading of this data can occur with staging BAPIS and third-party tools.

Extractor
A program that fills the extract structure of a DataSource with data from the data stored in the SAP source system. Extractors are imported into the SAP source system with the DataSources as a plug-in. An extractor is a program for the following:

▶ To make metadata from an SAP source system available with the extract structure of a DataSource

- ▶ To process data requests
- ▶ To perform the extraction

Extract Structure

- ▶ Transaction in the source system: SBIW

In the extract structure, the data of a DataSource is made available in the source system. The extract structure contains all the fields of the SAP source system that the extractors make available in the source system for the data-loading process. You can define, edit, and extend the extract structures of DataSources in the source system. The extract structure contains the number of fields that are offered by the extractor in the source system for the data-loading process in SAP BW.

F Table
see: BasicCube

Fact Tables
A table in the middle of the star schema of an InfoCube. It contains the key fields of the dimension table and the key figures of the InfoCube. The key is built with reference to the entries of the dimensions of the InfoCube. Together with the dimension tables assigned to it, the fact table builds the InfoCube (for transaction data). *See also:* BasicCube and InfoCube

Filter (QD)
A Web item that displays the filter values for a query view generated by navigation in a Web application and enables selection of individual values.

The data container includes a column for a filter flag. You can use this flag to have a data contained use several graphic proxies but to access different data sets. This feature makes the creation of a specific data container for every graphic proxy superfluous.

Flat File
Data can be imported into SAP BW with a file interface. Two data formats are supported as source files for SAP BW:

- ▶ **ASCII (American Standard Code for Information Interchange)**
  Files with fixed field lengths
- ▶ **CSV (Comma Separated Value)**
  Files with variable length: users can define the separator (transaction RSCUSTV1)

You can use flat files to reduce the number of problems involved with interfaces, but you must maintain the metadata (the transfer structure, for example) manually in SAP BW.

Formatted Reporting
Design for reports with master data, ODS objects, and multidimensional InfoProviders. You can use formatted reporting to make data available for interactive ana-

lyses and in formatted print layouts. Formatted reporting is based on the queries defined in the BEx Analyzer. Formatted reporting uses Crystal Reports from Crystal Decision, which is integrated into SAP BW.

Formatted reporting contains all the elements of formatting reports: fonts, font sizes, colors, graphics, and styles. It enables pixel-exact assignment of reporting elements without being limited to a tabular display. It focuses on form-based reports and print output. No analytical functionality: Options for interaction are considered when the report is designed.

Full Update
A full update requests all the data that corresponds to the selection criteria set in **Scheduler · InfoPackage.** Contrary to a delta update, every DataSource supports a full update.

Generation Template
A template from which a program is generated. A generation template is used when the desired program cannot be written generically and therefore must be generated anew and appropriately for each new situation.

Granularity
Refinement or level of detail of data.

Hierarchy
A hierarchy usually means an array of objects related to each other. In this sense, SAP BW has hierarchies in the dimension, attribute, and hierarchy tables. In DWH terminology, the term hierarchy is closely related to the term drilldown (→ predefined drilldown path). *See also:* External Hierarchies

Hierarchy Attribute
Attribute that mirrors the properties of the entire hierarchy. (The level table type is an example: It indicates the form of the level table.)

IDoc (Intermediate Document)
A (data) IDoc is a data contained for the exchange of data among SAP systems, non-SAP systems, and external systems. It uses ALE technology. An IDoc consists of:

▶ **Header record**
The header contains information on the sender, recipient, and the type of message and IDoc.

▶ **Connected data segments**
Every data segment contains a standard header that consists of a sequential segment number and a description of the segment type, and a 1000 byte field list that describes the data of the segment.

▶ **Status records**
Status records describe the previous processing steps of the IDoc.

These IDocs are used to load data into the SAP BW system if transfer method PSA was selected in maintenance of the transfer method.

InfoAreas

InfoAreas help organize metaobjects in SAP BW. They are the highest organization criterion of InfoProviders and InfoObjects in SAP BW. You can use InfoObject-Catalogs to assign InfoObjects a data target property; you can also sign them to various InfoAreas.

Every data target is assigned to an InfoArea. The Administrator Workbench (AWB) then displays this hierarchy. The hierarchy organized the objects in appropriate trees:

▶ InfoProvider tree

▶ InfoObject tree

Every InfoProvider must be assigned to exactly one InfoArea in the InfoProvider. You can assign InfoObjects to various InfoAreas in the InfoObject tree with Info-ObjectCatalogs. As is the case with other SAP BW objects, you define InfoAreas with a technical name and a description and create them within the InfoProvider tree or InfoObject tree.

InfoCube

▶ Creating an InfoCube in an InfoProvider tree:

  ▷ Initial access: **AWB** · **Modeling** · **InfoProvider** · Select **InfoArea** · Select **Create InfoCube** in the context menu of the InfoArea.

▶ Editing InfoCubes: Transaction RSDCUBE

InfoCubes are the central objects in SAP BW; multidimensional analyses and reports are based on InfoCubes. From a reporting viewpoint (the viewpoint of the end user of reporting), an InfoCube describes a closed data set of a business report. Queries are defined and executed on an InfoCube. The data set can be evaluated with BEx Query. InfoCubes can function as both data targets and Info-Providers.

An InfoCube is a set of relational tables placed together according to the star schema: a large fact table in the center, surrounded by several dimension tables. SAP BW distinguishes among the following types of InfoCubes:

▶ BasicCube

▶ General RemoteCube

▶ SAP RemoteCube

▶ Virtual InfoCube with services

InfoObject

▶ Creating an InfoObject in the InfoObject tree:

  ▶ Initial access: **AWB** · **Modeling** · **InfoObjects** · Select **InfoArea** · Select **InfoObjectCatalog** · Select **Create InfoObject** in the context menu of the InfoObjectcatalog

▶ Maintenance of InfoObjects: Transactions RSD1 through RSD5

In SAP BW, business evaluation objects (customers, revenue, and so on) are called InfoObjects. They are therefore the smallest information module (field) that can be identified unambiguously with their technical name. InfoObjects are divided into characteristics, key figures, units, time characteristics, and technical characteristics, (such as a request number, for example).

As a component of the Metadata Repository, InfoObjects carry the technical and user information of the master and transaction data in SAP BW. They are used throughout the system to build tables and structures, which allows SAP BW to map the information in a structured form. InfoObjects are subdivided in the following classes, according to their function and task:

▶ **Key figure (revenue and quantity, for example)**
Key figure InfoObjects supply the values that are to be evaluated with characteristics and characteristic combinations.

▶ **Characteristic (material, customer, and source system ID, for example)**
Characteristic InfoObjects are business reference objects used to evaluate the key figures.

▶ **Time characteristic (calendar day or month, for example)**
Time characteristics build the reference framework for many data analyses and evaluations. These characteristics are delivered with BCT; you can also define your own time characteristics.

  ▶ **Unit (currency key or quantity unit, for example)**
  InfoObjects can be entered along with the key figures to enable linkage between the values of the key figures and the related units in the evaluations.

  ▶ **Technical characteristic**
  These characteristics have an organizational meaning in SAP BW. For example, technical characteristic "OREQUID" supplies the numbers assigned by the system during the loading of requests. Technical characteristic "OCHNGID" supplies the numbers assigned during aggregate change runs.

InfoObjectCatalog

▶ Creating an InfoObjectCatalog in the InfoObject tree:

  ▶ Initial access: **AWB** · **Modeling** · **InfoObject** · Select **InfoArea** · Select **Create InfoObjectCatalog** in the context menu of the InfoArea.

▶ Editing InfoObjectCatalogs: Transaction RSDIOBC

An InfoObjectCatalog is a grouping of InfoObjects according to application-specific viewpoints. It is a purely organizational aide and has no evaluative purpose. An InfoObjectCatalog is assigned to an InfoArea in the InfoObject tree. The type of InfoObjectCatalog is either "characteristic" or "key figure" and thus contains a characteristic or key figure, depending on its type.

InfoPackage

An InfoPackage describes which data is to be requested from a source system with a DataSource. The data can be selected with selection parameters, such as only from controlling area 001 in period 10.1997. An InfoPackage can request the following types of data:

▶ Transaction data

▶ Attributes of master data

▶ Hierarchies of master data

▶ Master data texts

You can define several InfoPackages for a DataSource. You can define several InfoPackages for a DataSource.

▶ Creating an InfoPackage in the InfoObject tree:

> Initial access: **AWB** · **Modeling** · **InfoSources** · Select **InfoSource** · Select **Source System** · Select **Create InfoPackage** (and schedule in the scheduler) in the context menu of the source system)

Existing InfoPackages are displayed in the InfoSource tree beneath the source system and can be edited with the context menu.

InfoPackage Group

Combines logically related InfoPackages.

InfoProvider

An InfoProvider is an SAP BW object that you can use to create and execute queries. InfoProviders include objects that physically contain data: data targets like InfoCubes, ODS objects, and InfoObjects (characteristics with attributes, texts, or hierarchies. They also include objects that do not represent physical data storage: RemoteCubes, SAP RemoteCubes, and MultiProviders. InfoProviders are objects or views integral to reporting. InfoProviders can be the following:

▶ InfoCubes (BasicCubes and virtual cubes)

▶ ODS objects

▶ Characteristic InfoObjects (with attributes or texts)

▶ InfoSets

▶ MultiProviders

Information Cockpit

see: Business Intelligence Cockpit

InfoSet

▶ Creating an InfoSet in an InfoProvider tree:

  ▶ Initial access: **AWB** · **Modeling** · **InfoProvider** · Select **InfoArea** · Select **Create InfoSet** in the context menu of the InfoArea.

▶ Maintenance of InfoSets: Transaction RSISET

An InfoSet is an InfoProvider that does not contain any data. It involves a query definition that can usually be read in the BW system with joins of ODS objects or characteristic InfoObjects (with attributes or texts) at the runtime of data analysis. Unlike a traditional InfoSet, this view of the data is specific to SAP BW.

Reporting on master data is a possible use of InfoSets. InfoSets are created and modified in the InfoSet Builder. Based on InfoSets, you can define reports with the Query Designer.

InfoSet Builder
A tool to create and modify InfoSets with SAP BW repository objects (InfoObjects with master data and ODS objects).

InfoSet Query (ISQ)
Corresponds to the InfoSet query (BC-SRV-QUE) familiar in SAP R/3 Basis. A tool to create lists. The data to be evaluated is combined in InfoSets. SAP List Viewer is the output medium for InfoSet query.

InfoSource

▶ Creating an InfoSource in the InfoSources tree:

  ▶ Initial access: **AWB** · **Modeling** · **InfoSources** · Select **Create InfoSource** in the context menu of an application component · Select **InfoSource type**

A set of all the data available on a business event or a type of business events (such as cost center accounting, for example). An InfoSource is a set of logically related InfoObjects that contain all the information available on a business process (such as cost center accounting, for example). InfoSources can include transaction data and master data (attributes, texts, and hierarchies).

The structure that stores InfoSources is called the communication structure. Unlike the transfer structure, the communication structure is independent of the source system. You can assign several DataSources to an InfoSource. However, you can assign a DataSource to only one InfoSource within a source system. Note the following two types of InfoSources:

▶ **InfoSource with direct update**
With this type of InfoSource, the master data (attributes and texts) of a characteristic InfoObject is updated directly (one to one with a communication structure) to the corresponding master data tables (exception: a transfer routine is created for a characteristic used as an InfoSource with direct update). The following applies to hierarchies: If you select transfer method "PSA," the system generates a communication structure used to load the data into the corresponding hierar-

chy tables. If you select transfer method "IDoc," the system does not generate a communication structure: The data is updated directly with the transfer structure. In this case, you cannot define any (local) transfer rules. (With hierarchies, transfer method "PSA" is independent of DataSources: see table ROOSOURCE.) InfoSources with direct update cannot be used for transaction data.

▶ **InfoSource with flexible update**
With this type of InfoSource, you can use update rules to load attribute, text, and transaction data into data targets (BasicCubes, ODS objects, and characteristic InfoObject) with a communication structure. You cannot update hierarchies flexibly.

InfoSpoke
Object for data export within Open Hub Services. The following are defined in the InfoSpoke:

▶ The open hub data source from which the data is extracted

▶ The extraction mode in which the data is delivered

▶ The open hub destination into which the data is delivered

Intermediate Document
see: IDoc

Key Figure

▶ Creating a key figure InfoObject in the InfoObject tree:

   ▷ Initial access: **AWB** · **Modeling** · **InfoObjects** · Select **InfoArea** · Select **InfoObjectCatalog of key figure type** · Select **Create InfoObject** in the context menu of the InfoObjectcatalog.

▶ Maintenance of key figures: Transactions RSD1 through RSD5

Values or quantities. In addition to the key figures stored in the database, you can also define calculated (derived) key figures during query definition in Business Explorer. You can calculate such key figures with a formula from the key figures of the InfoCube.

Examples for key figures:

▶ Revenue, Fixed costs, Sales quantity, Number of employees

Examples for derived key figures:

▶ Revenue per employee, Deviation in percent, Contribution margin

Key figure InfoObjects like revenue and quantity deliver the values to be evaluated with characteristics or combinations of characteristics. SAP BW differentiates among the following types of key figures:

▶ Amount

▶ Quantity

▶ Number

- Integer
- Date
- Time

If you select the amount of quantity type of key figure, you must also enter corresponding units: the key figured is linked to a unit InfoObject or to a fixed value for a unit.

- **Key figure as cumulative value** (= value that refers to a period of time)
  Values for this key figure must be posted in every time unit for which values are to be calculated for this key figure (revenue, for example).

- **Key figure as non-cumulative value** (= value that refers to a specific point in time)
  For non-cumulative values, values must be stored for only selected points in time. The values of the other points in time are calculated from the value in a specific point in time and the intermediary balance sheet changes (such as warehouse inventory). You have two options for defining non-cumulative values:

  - **Non-cumulative with balance sheet changes**
    Definition of the non-cumulative values also requires a cumulative value as a key figure InfoObject, a balance sheet change, which agrees with the non-cumulative value to be defined in the definition of the type.

  - **Non-cumulative with acquisitions and retirements**
    Definition of the non-cumulative value requires two cumulative values, "acquisition" and "retirement," which agree with the non-cumulative value to be defined in the definition of the type.

- **Aggregation of Key Figures**

  - **Standard Aggregation (SUM/Max/Min)**
    With standard aggregation, you set how the key is aggregated in the Basic-Cube in key figure maintenance. This setting plays a role with an ODS object only when you select "addition" (you do not choose "overwrite") as the update type in maintenance of the update rules.

  - **Exception aggregation (last value, first value, maximum, minimum, and so on)**
    With exception aggregation, which you set in key figure maintenance, you can perform more complex aggregations of key figures. Example: The "number of employees" key figure is total with the "cost center" characteristic ($\rightarrow$ Standard-Aggregation). In this case, you could also enter a time characteristic as a reference characteristic for exception aggregation "last value."

- **Reference key figure**
  You can create a key figure with a reference to another key figure (= reference key figure). You usually need a reference key figure for the elimination of intercompany sales.

Line Item
see: Line Item Dimension
see: Dimension

Line Item Dimension
Characteristics can be defined as line items, which means that no additional characteristics can be assigned to a dimension along with this characteristic. Such a dimension is called a line item dimension (= degenerate dimension). Unlike a typical dimension, a line item dimension does not receive a dimension table. The SID table of the line item is linked directly with the fact table here over a foreign–primary key relationship. This option is used if a characteristic, such as an order number, has a large quantity of values. Using this option can improve the performance of queries. *see also:* Dimension

List of Conditions
Web item that lists the existing conditions with their states (active/not active/not applicable/not used) for a query view in a Web application.

List of Exceptions
Web item that lists the existing conditions with their states (active/not active) for a query view in a Web application.

Master Data ID (SID)
Internal key (type INT4) used for characteristics carrying master data to master data, especially for hierarchy nodes and for characteristic names.

Master data IDs and characteristic values are stored in a master data table (SID table). Information on time-independent and time-dependent master data stored in a P or Q table is stored once again in an X or Y table by using SIDs in place of the characteristic values.

MDX
Multidimensional expressions. Query language for queries on data stored in multidimensional cubes.

Metadata Repository
The Metadata Repository contains the various classes of metadata. This type of data storage and presentation results in a consistent and homogenous data model across all source systems. The Metadata Repository comprises all metaobjects (InfoCubes, InfoObjects, queries, and so on) in SAP BW and their relationships to each other.

▶ Transaction: RSOR

▶ Initial access: **AWB** • **Metadata Repository**

Metadata
Metadata is data or information about data. Metadata describes the origin, history, and other aspects of the data. Metadata enables the effective use of the information stored in SAP BW for reporting and analysis. Note the following types of metadata:

- ▶ **Technical metadata**
  For example: the storage structure of the data, like the number format of a key figure

- ▶ **Business metadata and effective metadata**
  For example: the person responsible for data and the origin of the data

Mobile Application
A Web application on a mobile device with an online connection to the BW system. Superordinate term of: PDA application and WAP application

MOLAP (Multidimensional OLAP)
Multidimensional online analytical processing. Multidimensional data storage in special data structures based on arrays or cubes. MOLAP is mostly used in comparison with or as an alternative to ROLAP. *See also*: OLAP

MOLAP Storage
see: MOLAP

MOLAP Aggregate
Aggregate of a MOLAP cube. Like the MOLAP cube itself, the aggregate is stored in MOLAP storage.

MOLAP Cube
A BasicCube whose data is physically stored in MOLAP storage. Superordinate term: MOLAP Storage

Monitor
Monitoring tool of the Administrator Workbench (AWB). You can use the monitor to keep an eye on data requests and processing in SAP BW.

You can use the monitor to check data requests and processing within the AWB.

- ▶ Transactions: RSMON (monitoring) and RSMO (monitor)
- ▶ Initial access: **AWB · Monitoring**

Multidimensional Expressions
see: MDX

Multidimensional Online Analytical Processing
see: MOLAP

Multidimensional OLAP
see: MOLAP

MultiProviders
Initial access: **AWB · Modeling · InfoProvider ·** Select **InfoArea**. In the context menu of the selected InfoArea, select **Create MultiProvider** and select the Info-Provider.

A MultiProvider is a special InfoProvider that merges data from several InfoProviders and makes the data available for reporting. The MultiProvider itself does not contain any data. Its data comes exclusively from the InfoProviders upon which it is based. Like InfoProviders, MultiProviders are objects or views integral to reporting. A MultiProvider can merge various combinations of InfoProviders:

▶ InfoCube

▶ ODS object

▶ Characteristic InfoObject (with attributes or texts)

▶ InfoSet

Myself Data Mart
see: Myself System

Myself System
A system connected to itself for data extraction over the data mart interface. Such a connection means that data from data targets can be updated to additional data targets. *See also:* Data Mart Interface

Navigation
Analysis of InfoProvider data by displaying various views of a query's data or of a Web application. You can use navigation functions (such as Set Filter Value, Insert Outline After) to generate various views of the data (query views) that are then presented in the results area of the query or in a Web application. Changing views is referred to as navigation.

Navigation Attribute
Attribute in which the query can be selected.

Nodes
Objects that build a hierarchy. A node can have subnodes. Note the distinction between the following two types of 6nodes:

▶ Nodes that can be posted to

▶ Nodes that cannot be posted to

Node Attribute
An attribute at the node level: every node of the hierarchy has this attribute. (For example: date fields DATETO ad DATEFROM if the hierarchy structure is time-dependent.)

ODS Objects
An operational data store (ODS) object stores consolidated and cleansed data (transaction or master data) at the document level. An ODS object contains key fields (characteristics) and data fields that can also be key figures and characteristics, which differs from a BasicCube.

An ODS object describes a consolidated data set from one or more InfoSources. You can evaluate the data set with a BEx query. An ODS object contains a key (such as a document number or item) and data fields that can also contain character fields (such as customer) as key figures. The data of an ODS object can be updated with a delta update into InfoCubes or additional ODS objects in the same system or across systems. Contrary to multidimensional data storage with InfoCubes, the data of ODS objects is stored in flat database tables. Unlike BasicCubes, ODS objects consists of three (flat)tables:

▶ **Activation queue** (= initial table of ODS objects)
New data is stored in this table before it is activated. Its structure is similar to that of a PSA table: The key is built from the request, data package, and data record number. After all the requests in the activation queue have been successfully activated, they are deleted from the activation queue.

▶ **Table with the active data**
This table stores the current state of the data. This table has a semantic key (such as an order number or item) that the modeler can define. Reporting draws upon this table. If the connected data targets are supplied in the full update method of updating, the data targets are updated with the active data from this table.

▶ **Change log** (= output table for connect data targets)
During an activation run, the modifications are stored in the change log. The change log therefore contains all the complete (activation) history of the modifications because the contents of the change log are not automatically deleted. If the connected data targets are supplied from the ODS object in a delta process, the data targets are updated from the change log. The change log is a PSA table and can be maintained in the PSA tree of the AWB. Accordingly, the change log has a technical key derived from the request, data package, and data record number.

The new state of the data is written in parallel into the change log and into the table with the active data. Note the following types of ODS objects:

▶ **Standard ODS object**

  ▶ Creating a standard ODS object:
  Initial access: **AWB** · **Modeling** · **InfoProvider** · Select **InfoArea** · Select **Create ODS Object** in the context menu of the selected InfoArea

  ▶ Editing standard ODS objects: Transaction RSDODS

  ▶ Managing a standard ODS object:
  Initial access: **AWB** · **Modeling** · **InfoProvider** · Select **InfoArea** · Select **Manage** in the context menu of the selected ODS object
  This object involves the ODS object (→ three tables) described above. As is the case with BasicCubes, ODS objects are supplied with data from one or more InfoSources with update rules.
  The update rules include rules that apply to BasicCubes and an additional option to overwrite data fields.

  ▶ **Selective deletion (Contents tab):**
  Similar to the situation with a BasicCube, you can opt to delete targeted

data records that correspond to the selection criteria from the ODS object. Selective deletion affects only the table with the active data, that is, only entries in this table are deleted.

If you use selective deletion to delete erroneous data records from the ODS object, you can replace the records with correct(ed) data records by using a repair request in the scheduler (→ **Scheduler** · **Maintain InfoPackage**).

▶ **Delete requests (Requests tab)**
You can use this function to delete targeted requests that have been loaded into the ODS object, if they have not yet been updated into the connected data targets. Note the following two initial situations:

▶ **Non-activated requests**
In this case, the requests are deleted only from the activation queue.

▶ **Activated requests**
In this case, the requests are deleted from the table with the active data and from the **Change Log**.

▶ **Rebuild requests (Rebuild tab)**
You can use this function to recover previously deleted requests for an ODS object. The recovered requests are then stored once again in the activation queue. This function works only if the PSA table stored the requests.

▶ **Delete change log**
You can use this function to delete requests from the **Change Log**, requests that are no longer needed for updates or to rebuild the connected data targets. We recommend that you delete change log requests if you don't need the **Change Log**.

▶ Management: **Environment** · **Delete Change Log Data**

▶ **Transactional ODS Object**

▶ Creating a transactional ODS object:
Initial access: **AWB** · **Modeling** · **InfoProvider** · Select **InfoArea** · Select Create ODS Object in the context menu of the selected InfoArea Select ODS object under the Type settings · Select **Modify Type** in the context menu

▶ Editing standard ODS objects: Transaction RSDODS
This type of ODS object has only the table with active data. Accordingly, this ODS object cannot be linked to the staging process because neither the activation queue nor the Change Log are used. These ODS object types can be filled by APIs and read with a BAPI. They help store data for external applications, such as SAP Strategic Enterprise Management (SAP SEM). Transactional ODS objects are not automatically available for reporting. You must first define an InfoSet with these ODS objects; you can then use the InfoSet to define and execute queries.

OLAP (Online Analytical Processing)
The core of this software technology is multidimensional retrieval of data. Multi-

dimensionality allows for the creation of very flexible query and analysis tools that enable rapid, interactive, and flexible access to the relevant information.

▶ **ROLAP (Relational OLAP)**
The task of the ROLAP engine is to format relational data (with the star schema) in a multidimensional structure to enable efficient access. SAP BW is an example of a ROLAP system.

▶ **MOLAP (Multidimensional OLAP)**
Data is physically stored here in multidimensional structures (cell and array structures), so that further formatting of the analysis tools is no longer necessary. This approach requires rapid response times for queries and calculations. So far, MOLAP systems are less appropriate than ROLAP systems for large sets of data.

OLAP Reporting

Reporting based on multidimensional data sources. OLAP reporting enables simultaneous analysis of multiple dimensions (such as time, location, product, and so on). The goal of OLAP reporting is the analysis of key figures, such as a revenue analysis of a specific product over a specific period. The business question is formulated in a query that contains key figures and characteristics; the query is required for analysis and a response to the question. The data displayed in the form of a table serves as the starting point for detailed analysis that can address a multitude of questions.

Several interaction options—such as sorting, filtering, exchanging characteristics, recalculating values, and so on—enable the flexible navigation in the data at runtime. In SAP BW, the data in the Business Explorer can be analyzed in the following areas:

▶ In BEx analyzer in the form of queries

▶ In BEx Web Applications

Unlike table-based reporting, the number of columns is dynamic here. Data analysis is the primary concern. The layout, formatting, and printing of the reports are secondary.

Synonyms: analytical reporting and multidimensional reporting

OLAP Systems
see: Data Warehouse

OLAP Tools
see: Data Warehouse

OLAP (Online Transaction Processing)

The core of this software technology is the relational retrieval of data for processing and the documentation of business processes (billing and inventory management, for example). However, the required standardization (→ as a rule, the third standard form → guarantees data consistency and referential integrity) makes the queries more complex because many tables must be read. (The traditional SAP R/3 system in an example of an OLTP system.)

Online Analytical Processing
see: OLAP

Online Transaction Processing
see: OLTP

Open Hub Service
A service that enables sharing data from an SAP BW system with non-SAP data marts, analytical applications, and other applications. The open hub service guarantees the controlled distribution and consistency of data across several systems.

Operational Data Store Object
see: ODS Objects

Or Process
Collective process of process chain maintenance. When you use or process in process chain maintenance, the application process starts each time that an event of the preceding process was triggered successfully.

Original Source System
Source system from which newly created or modified objects are transported into another system, the target source system. In the context of a system landscape consisting of OLTP and BW systems, an original source system is an OLTP development system. The target source system is the OLTP system linked to the BW target system. To be able to transport objects specific to a source system (such as transfer structure), you must enter the logical system name for the source system into a mapping table in the BW target system before and after the transport.

P Table
Master data table for time-independent master data. This table includes the following fields:

▶ The characteristic that carries master data itself

▶ The characteristics associated with this characteristic ("superordinate characteristics")

▶ All time-independent attributes

CHANGED (D: record to delete; I: insert record; space: no modification; modifications are evaluated only with activation.)

OBJEVERS (A: active version; M: modified and thus not the active version)

These fields build the key.

PDA Application
Web application on a PDA device with Pocket IE.

Persistent staging area (PSA)
The persistent staging area (PSA) represents the initial view into SAP BW architecture. The PSA consists of transparent database tables (PSA tables) that can be used for (temporary) storage of unmodified data from the source system. One PSA is created for each DataSource and source system. The basic structure of PSA tables corresponds to the transfer structure. It consists of the following fields: key fields of the PSA + fields of the transfer structure. The key consists of the request, data package, and data record number. The system generates PSA tables (technical name: /BIC/B000*) for each DataSource at activation of the transfer rules only if you selected "PSA" as the transfer method in maintenance of the transfer rules.

You can select from the following posting types in the scheduler when loading data into data targets (characteristic InfoObject, BasicCube, and ODS object):

▶ **PSA followed by data target (by package)**
This type of posting first extracts a data package of a request from the source system and writes it to the PSA table. Posting of the data to the data targets begins as soon as the data package has been completely transferred into the PSA table. Extraction of the next data package begins at the same time as the posting, so that extraction and posting are executed in parallel.

▶ **PSA followed by data targets in parallel (by package)**
Parallel posting to the data targets begins at the same time as writing the data packages to the PSA table.

▶ **Only PSA followed by updating to the data targets**
This type of posting first posts all the data packages of a request to the PSA table and then to the data targets. Posting and extraction do not occur in parallel here.

▶ **Only PSA**
This posting type enables you to store all the extracted data packages of a request in a PSA table without updating them to the data targets. You can trigger follow-up posting at a later time.

▶ **Only data target**
The data packages of a request are posted directly to the data targets. The data packages are not stored temporarily in a PSA table.

Process
A procedure within or external to an SAP system. A process has a defined beginning and end.

Process Chain

▶ Maintenance of Process Chains: Transaction RSPC

A process chain is a series of processes that are scheduled in the background (= batch) and are waiting for an event. Some of the processes trigger their own event, which can then start other processes. You can use process chains for the following:

▶ To automate complex flows (like the loading process) in SAP BW with event-driven processing

▶ To visualize flows with the use of network graphics.

▶ To control and monitor processing of the processes centrally

Process Instance
A property of a process. The process instance contains the most important information that the process might want to communicate to subsequent processes. During a loading process, for example, this information would be the name of the request. The instance is determined by the process itself at runtime. The logs for the process are stored beneath the process instance.

Process Type
The type of process, such as the load process. The process type determines the tasks that a process has and what properties it has in maintenance.

Process Variant
Name of the process. A process can have various variants. For example, with the loading process, the name of the InfoPackage represents the variant of the process. Users define a variant at scheduling.

PSA
see: Persistent Staging Area

PSA Table
see: Persistent Staging Area

Q Table
Master data table for time-dependent master data. In terms of its fields, the Q table corresponds to the P table.

Query
A combination of characteristics and key figures (InfoObjects) to analyze the data of an InfoProvider. You can use a query to combine characteristics and key figure InfoObjects in the query designer to analyze the data of an InfoProvider. A query always refers to one InfoProvider, but any number of queries can be defined for an InfoProvider.

A query is defined in BEx query designed by selecting InfoObjects or reusable structures of an InfoProvider and setting a view of the data (query view) by distributing filters, rows, columns, and free characteristics. You can save the defined starting view of the query in the query designer among your favorites or roles. You use the saved query view as the basis for data analysis and reporting in BEx analyzer, BEx Web applications, BEx mobile intelligence, or formatted reporting.

Query Designer
see: Business Explorer Query Designer

Query View
Saved navigational view of a query.

Record
In a relational database table: a set of related values. A record is store in the relational database management system (DBMS) as a line.

Referential Integrity
A check of **referential integrity** can occur only for transaction and master data updated flexibly ($\rightarrow$ InfoSource with flexible update). The check determines the valid values of the InfoObject. The check occurs after filling the communication structure, but before application of the update rules. The check occurs against the SID table of a characteristic, or against an ODS object highlighted in maintenance of a characteristic InfoObject. In order to use the check for **referential integrity**, you must select the option to **post data always, even if no master data for the data exists**, in the **Update** table of the scheduler (**Maintain InfoPackage**). You must also flag the characteristic InfoObjects that are to be checked against SID tables and ODS objects in the **Referential Integrity** column in InfoSource maintenance.

Reference Characteristic
You can use reference characteristics to reuse defined characteristic InfoObjects. Reference characteristics deliver technical properties to another characteristic. You can maintain these properties only with a reference characteristic. Technical properties include master data tables (attributes, texts, and hierarchies), data type, length, number and type of compounded characteristics, lowercase letters, and conversion routines. *see also*: Characteristic

Relational OLAP
see: ROLAP

Relational Online Analytical Processing
see: ROLAP

Remote Function Call (RFC)
You can use RFC to transfer data reliably between SAP systems and programs that you have developed. RFC called a function module in another SAP system, BW system, a program you have developed, or within an SAP system. The data is transmitted with TCP/IP or X.400 as a byte stream. If the call is asynchronous, it is referred to as a transactional RFC (tRFC).

RemoteCube

An InfoCube whose transaction data is managed externally rather than in SAP BW. Only the structure of the RemoteCube is defined in SAP BW. The data is read with a BAPI from another system for reporting.

Reporting Agent

A tool you can use to schedule reporting functions in the background. You can execute the following functions:

► Evaluation of exceptions

► Printing of queries

► Precalculation of Web templates

Results Area

In Business Explorer Analyzer, the result area is the portion of the worksheet that shows the results of a query. The results area corresponds to the Web item table in Web applications.

Reusable Structure

A component of a query stored for reuse in an InfoCube. You define a query template when you want to use parts of a query definition in other queries. For example, you can save structures as query templates. Structures are freely defined evaluations that consist of combinations of characteristics and basic key figures (as calculated or limited key figures, for example) of the InfoCube. For example, a structure can be a plan–actual comparison or a contribution margin scheme.

RFC

see: Remote Function Call

ROLAP

Relational Online Analytical Processing. The storage of multidimensional data in a relational database: in tables organized in a star schema. Opposite model: MOLAP. *See also:* OLAP

Source SAP BW (Source SAP Business Information Warehouse

SAP BW that serves as the source system for additional BW servers. *See also:* Data Mart Interface

Source System

System available to SAP BW for data extraction. Source systems are instances that deliver data to SAP BW.

► External Systems (Non-SAP Systems, SAP R/2 Systems, and SAP R/3 Systems <3,1I)

► SAP systems

► BW systems (data marts)

► Databases (DB connect)

- Flat files (CSV and ASCII files)
- Flat files for external market data (from Dun & Bradstreet (D&B), for example)
- XML file

SAP Exit
A type of processing for variables delivered with SAP BW Business Content. The variables are processed by automatic substitution in a default substitution path (SAP Exit).

SAP RemoteCube
Access to transaction data in other SAP systems, based on an InfoSource with flexible update. The objects in SAP BW that do not store data include: InfoSets, RemoteCubes, SAP RemoteCubes, virtual InfoCubes with services, and MultiProviders. *See also:* InfoProvider

SAPI (Service API)
The (BW) SAPI is the interface imported with the plug-in. SAPI is used for communication and data exchange among SAP systems (SAP SEM, SAP CRM, SAP APO, and SAP R/3) and the SAP BW system, between XML files and the SAP BW system, and between SAP BW systems. The SAPI is based exclusively on SAP technology and is available for SAP systems as of Basis Release 3.1I. SAP BW service API technology is used in various places within the architecture of SAP BW, for example:

- To transfer data and metadata from SAP systems
- To transfer data between SAP BW data targets within an SAP BW system
- (data mart Myself interface) or into another SAP BW system (data mart interface)
- To transfer data from XML files

Scheduler
You use the scheduler to determine which data (transaction data, master data, texts, or hierarchies) is requested and updated from which InfoSource, DataSource, and source system at which point in time.

Scheduling Package
Logical combination of multiple reporting agent settings for background processing.

SID
see: Surrogate Identification

SID Table
see: Master Data Tables

Staging
The process of retrieving data in a data warehouse.

Staging BAPI
You can use staging BAPIs to transfer data (metadata, master data, and transaction data) from external systems in SAP BW. *See also:* BAPI

Standardization
see: Cleansing

Star Schema
The classic star schema is intended for the use of relational database systems at the physical design level. A drawing of the start schema resembles a star in which multidimensional data structures are mapped in two types of tables:

▶ **In a single fact table**
The table contains the key figures and a combined key with an element for each dimension.

▶ **In dimension tables (one per dimension)**
These tables are completely non-normalized and contain a composed primary key from all the attributes needed for nonambiguity, the hierarchical structure of the related dimension, and a level attribute that displays all the individual entries on affiliation for a hierarchy level.

see also: BasicCube

Start Process
Defines the start of a process chain.

Surrogate Identification (SID)
SIDs are system-generated INT4 keys. An SID key is generated for each characteristic. This assignment is implemented in an SID table for each characteristics: The characteristic is the primary key of the SID table. The SID table is linked to the related master data tables (if present) with the characteristic key. If a characteristic is assigned to a BasicCube when it is created, the SID table of the characteristic is linked to the corresponding dimension table after activations of the BasicCube. SID values are generated during loading of master data or transaction data and written to the appropriate SID tables. For transaction data, the values are also written to the dimension tables to set up the DIM ID. Use of INT4 keys (SID and DIM ID keys) enables faster access to the data than do long alphanumeric keys. The SID technique in the SAP BW star schema also enables the use of master data across BasicCubes.

Surrogate Index
A special SAP BW index of all key figures of a fact table. The surrogate index is created on a fact table in place of the primary index. Unlike the primary index, the surrogate index does not have a UNIQUE limitation.

Reporting is based on one-dimensional tables: Analysis is limited to one dimension with its attributes. Unlike OLAP reporting, you can assign columns in any way that you want during the design of a query in tabular editing mode of BEx query designer. For example, you can place a characteristics column between two key figure columns. The column presentation is fixed and set at the time of design.

Target BW
A BW system connected to another BW system as a source system and into which data can be loaded with export DataSources. *See also*: Data Mart Interface

TCT
see: Technical Content

Technical Content (TCT)
TCT makes the required SAP BW objects and tools available for the use of SAP BW Statistics. SAP BW Statistics is a tool for the analysis and optimization of processes, such as access time to data with queries and loading times. The data of SAP BW Statistics is stored in SAP BW and is based on a MultiProvider that comprises several SAP BW BasicCubes. TCT is transferred in the same manner as BCT.

To use SAP BW Statistics, you must activate it ahead of time for selected InfoProviders. (Initial access: **AWB · Tools · BW Statistics for InfoProviders**).

Temporal Join
A join that contains at least one time-dependent characteristic. The time dependencies are evaluated to determine the set of results. Each record of the set of results is assigned a time interval valid for that record (valid time interval).

Test
A check for the consistency of internal information with SAP BW objects. A repair is offered in some circumstances. A test consists of a series of elementary tests. To avoid performing unnecessary checks, you can select elementary tests individually. *Synonym:* Analysis

Test Package
A sequence of elementary tests as the result of a selection of specific tests or elementary tests. You can save a test package and schedule it for a later run.

Text
Texts (such as the description of a cost center) belong to master data in SAP BW, as do attributes and hierarchies. In the maintenance of a characteristic Info Object (→ Master Data/Texts tab), you can determine whether the characteristic should have texts. If it should, you must select at least one text: short, medium, and long text (20, 40, and 60 characters). You can also determine whether the texts are time- or language-dependent. Texts are stored in a master data table for texts related to the characteristic.

T-Logo Object
Logical transport object. A T-logo object consists of the total of several table entries that are transported together. Example: The T-logo object "InfoObject" con-

sists of table entries of the InfoObject table, the characteristics table, the text table, and the basic characteristics table.

Traditional InfoSet
Corresponds to the InfoSet familiar in SAP R/3 Basis: Element of an SAP query. An InfoSet determines the tables or table fields to which a query refers. InfoSets are primarily created with table joins or logical databases.

Transaction BasicCube
Transaction BasicCubes are typically used with SAP Strategic Enterprise Management (SEM). Data of such a BasicCube is accessed in a transactional manner: Data is written to the BasicCube (sometimes by several users simultaneously) and can be read immediately. Standard BasicCubes are not appropriate for such use. You should use standard BasicCubes for read-only access.

Transaction Data
The transaction data of a system has a dynamic character.

Transfer Routine
In maintenance of a characteristic InfoObject, you can create a (global) transfer routine (ABAP routine/no formula editor). Contrary to a local transfer rule, you can use a global transfer routine across all source systems. The transfer routine is used only if the characteristic is used as an InfoSource with direct update. If both a local and a global transfer routine are used, the local transfer routine runs first, followed by the global transfer routine.

Transfer Rule

▶ Editing transfer rules:

Initial access: **AWB** · **Modeling** · **InfoSources** · Select **Application Component** · Select **InfoSource** · Select **Source System** · Select **Modify/Delete Transfer Rules**

The transfer rules determine how source data is transferred to the communication structure over the SAP BW transfer structure, that is, transfer rules apply only to the data from one source system. Therefore, these rules are often referred to as local transfer rules. Note the differentiation of the following transfer rules:

▶ Data is updated 1:1.

▶ Supply with a constant: During the load process, the fields of the communication structure can be supplied with fixed values: the fields are not supplied via the transfer structure.

▶ You can use ABAP routines and the formula editor to design transfer rules.

see also: Cleansing

Transfer Structure

The structure in which data from the source system is transferred into SAP BW. The transfer structure helps BW retrieve all the metadata of an SAP source system on a business process or a business unit. The structure represents the selection of the fields of an extract structure of the SAP source system. In the maintenance of the transfer structure in SAP BW, you assign the DataSource and InfoSource to determine which fields should be used for the load process. When you activate the transfer rules, the transfer structure is generated in the SAP BW system and in the SAP source system. The transfer structure in the SAP BW system is stored in table RSTS; in the SAP source system in table ROOSGEN. The data is copied 1:1 from the transfer structure of the SAP source system into the transfer structure of SAP BW and then transmitted to the communication structure of SAP with the transfer rules. If the source system is a file system, the metadata is maintain in SAP BW, so that the transfer structure must also be defined manually in SAP BW. The structure of the transfer structure must describe the structure of the file. *See also*: InfoSource

UD Connect

Universal Data Connect. SAP BW component that enables you to access all relational multidimensional data sources via SAP Web AS J2EE connectivity. To connect to the data sources, UD Connect uses the Bi Java connectors as a resource adapter. The data can either be transferred to SAP BW or read directly via a RemoteCube.

UML

Unified Modeling Language. UML is the standard recognized by the Object Management Group (OMG) for semantic analysis of objects and for the design of object-oriented models with graphic tools. The UML standard is integrated in XMI. You can find the specifications for UML at *www.omg.org*.

Unified Modeling Language

see: UML

Update Rules

Via the communication structure of an InfoSource with flexible updating, the master data and transaction data are transferred into the data targets (BasicCubes, ODS objects, and characteristic InfoObjects with attributes or texts) based on the logic defined in the update rules.

Therefore, update rules are not specific to a source system, but to a data target, which is how they differ from transfer rules. However, you can copy the update rules of one data target for use with another data target. These rules help you to supply the data targets of one or more InfoSources. They help post data in the data targets and with modifications and enhancements of the data.

Definition of update rules: Initial access: **AWB · Modeling · InfoProvider** · Select **InfoArea** · Select **Create Update Rules** in the context menu of the selected data target.

Examples of update rules include the following:

▶ Reading master data attributes

▶ Filling fields in the data target with constants

▶ Using a routing (ABAP coding) or a formula (transformation library) to supply the fields of a data target

▶ Currency conversion

With an update, you must select one of the following update types:

▶ **Addition/Maximum/Minimum**
The standard aggregation behavior of a key figure is set in the maintenance of key figures and offered in the update rules for this key figure as addition, maximum, or minimum. In particular, addition is an option for data fields of ODS objects, as long as the ODS objects have a numeric data type. This update type is invalid for characteristic InfoObjects as a data target.

▶ **Overwrite**
This type of update is not available for BasicCubes; it is available only for ODS objects and characteristic InfoObjects.

▶ **No update**
If you select this type of update, no value is calculated for the affected key figure. In addition, no calculation is performed for the corresponding characteristics and key fields.

see also: Cleansing

Update Types
see: Update Rules

Variables
Parameters of a query created in BEx query designer. The parameters are filled with values only when the query is inserted into a workbook. Variables function as placeholders for characteristic values, hierarchies, hierarchy nodes, texts, and formula elements. They can be processed in various ways. Variables in SAP BW are global variables: They are defined unambiguously and are available for the definition of all queries.

Virtual Cube
Virtual cubes are special InfoCubes in SAP BW. A virtual cube represents a logical view. Unlike BasicCubes, however, virtual cubes do not physically store any data. The data is retrieved from the source systems during the execution of queries. In terms of data collection, note the following types of virtual cubes:

▶ **SAP remote cube**
An SAP RemoteCube allows definition of queries with direct access to the transaction data in other SAP systems. Requirements for the use of SAP RemoteCubes:

▶ The functionality of BW SAPI is installed (contained in the plug-in of the SAP source system).

▶ The release level of the source system is at least 4.0B.

▶ DataSources from the source system are assigned to the InfoSource of the RemoteCube. The DataSources are released for direct access, and no transfer rules are active for this combination. To determine whether a DataSource supports direct access, view table ROOSOURCE: Direct access is supported if field VITCUBE is populated with a 1 or a 2.

▶ **General RemoteCube**
A general RemoteCube enables reporting on data from non-SAP systems. The external system uses BAPIs to transfer the requested data to the OLAP processor. The data must be delivered in the source system because it is required for analysis: You cannot define any transfer rules in the SAP BW system.

▶ **Virtual InfoCube with services**
This type of virtual cube enables you to analyze the data with a self-developed function module. It is used for complex calculations that queries with formulas and exception aggregations cannot perform, such as those involved in strategic enterprise management.

Web Application
see: Business Explorer Web Application

Web Application Designer
see: Business Explorer Web Application Designer

Web Application Wizard
see: Business Explorer Web Application Wizard

Web Cockpit
see: Business Intelligence Cockpit

Web Item
An object that refers to the data of a Data Provider and makes it available as HTML in a Web application. Examples: generic navigation block, table, filter, text element, alert monitor, map, chart, and so on.

Web Item Paging
A mechanism to distribute the Web items of Web template to several pages that are linked to an overview page that is generated automatically.

Web Template
HTML document that helps set the structure of a Web application. It contains placeholders for Web items, Data Providers, and SAP BW URLs. Superordinate term of: Master Web template, standard Web template, and device-specific Web template

Wireless Application Protocol

A transmission protocol optimized for compression transfer of the Wireless Markup Language (WML) content in mobile networks.

Wireless Markup Language

see: WML

WML

Wireless Markup Language An Internet language standard to describe pages for mobile WAP devices.

Workbook

A file with several worksheets (an expression from Microsoft Excel terminology). You insert one or more queries in the workbook to display them in the Business Explorer Analyzer. You can save the workbook in your favorites or in your rolls.

XMI (XML Metadata Interchange)

A standard, XML-based format to exchange metadata between UML-based modeling tools and MOF-based metadata repositories in distributed, heterogeneous development environments. The exchange occurs with data flows or files.

Along with UML and MOF, XMI forms the core of the Metadata Repository architecture of the Object Management Group (OMG). You can find the specifications for XMI at *www.omg.org*.

XML (eXtensible Markup Language)

A descriptive markup language that can be enhanced. XML is a subset of the Standard Generalized Markup Language (SGML) developed for users on the World Wide Web. XML documents consist of entities that contain parsed or unparsed data. A parsed entity contains text: a sequence of characters. Note the following types of characters:

▶ Character data

▶ Markup (smart tags, end tags, tags for empty elements, entity references, character references, comments, limits for CDATA sections, document-type declarations, and processing instructions)

The XML 1.0 specification was designed by the Word Wide Web Consortium (W3C) and accepted by the W3C as a recommendation in 1998. You can view the specification at *www.w3.org*.
Several standards (XLink, Xpointer, XSL, XSLT, and DOM, for example) have been developed based on XML. More standards are still being developed.

XML for Analysis

A protocol specified by Microsoft to exchange analytical data between client applications and servers via HTTP and SOAP as a service on the Web. XML for Analysis is not limited to a specific platform, application, or development language.

You can view the specification for XML for Analysis at *http://www.msdn.micro-soft.com/library* **Web Development • XML and Web Services • XML (General) • XML for Analysis Spec**. The use of XML for Analysis in SAP BW enables direct communication between a third-party reporting tool connect to SAP BW and the online analytical processing (OLAP) processor.

XML Integration

Data exchange with XML is based on standards defined by the Object Management Group (OMG). The OMG attempts to developed industry standards for data exchange among various systems. In SAP BW, such transfer methods for the integration of data is implemented with XML. Transfer of XML data into SAP BW occurs with the Simple Object Access Protocol (SOAP) and the use of the Hypertext Transfer Protocol (HTTP). The data is described in XML format. The data is first written to the delta queue and then updated over a DataSource for the Myself source system into the desired data targets. Do not use this transfer method for mass data; use the flat file interface for large data sets.

XML Metadata Interchange

see: XMI

X Table

Attribute SID table for time-independent master data. This table includes the following fields:

▶ The SID of the characteristic

▶ OBJEVERS (object version); both fields build the key

▶ The values of the superordinate characteristics

▶ The value of the characteristic itself carries master data

▶ CHANGED

▶ SIDs of the time-independent attributes

For more information on OBJEVERS and CHANGED,
see: P Table

Y Table

Attribute SID table for time-dependent master data. In terms of its fields, the Y table corresponds to the X table.

I   Literature

Balanced Scorecard Institute: *http://www.balancedscorecard.org*.

Codd, Edgar Frank: A Relational Model of Data For Large Shared Data Banks, Communications of the ACM 26, No. 1, January 1983.

Codd, Edgar Frank et al.: Providing OLAP (Online Analytical Processing) to User-Analysts: An IT Mandate, 1993. See also: *http://www. fpm.com/refer/codd.html*.

Egger, Norbert: SAP BW Professional, SAP PRESS, 2004.

Egger, Norbert; Fiechter, Jean-Marie R.; Rohlf, Jens: SAP BW—Data Modeling, SAP PRESS, 2005.

Fischer, Roland: Business Planning with SAP SEM, SAP PRESS, 2004.

Imhoff, Claudia; Galemmo, Nicholas; Geiger, Jonathan G.: Mastering Data Warehouse Design: Relational and Dimensional Techniques, John Wiley, 2003.

Inmon, William H.: Building the Data Warehouse, John Wiley, 3. Edition 2002.

Inmon, William H.; Imhoff, Claudia, Sousa, Ryan: Corporate Information Factory, John Wiley, 2. Edition 2000.

Kaiser, Bernd-Ulrich: Corporate Information with SAP-EIS: Building a Data Warehouse and a MIS-Application with Insight. Academic Press, 1998.

Kaplan, Robert S.; Norton, David P.: The Balanced Scorecard. Translating Strategy Into Action, 1996.

Kimball, Ralph; Merz, Richard: The Data Warehouse Toolkit: Building the Web-Enabled Data Warehouse, John Wiley, 2000.

Kimball, Ralph; Reeves, Laura; Ross, Margy; Thornthwaite, W.: The Data Warehouse Lifecycle Toolkit: Expert Methods for Designing, Developing, and Deploying Data Warehouses, John Wiley, 1998.

Kimball, Ralph; Ross, Margy: The Data Warehouse Toolkit: The Complete Guide to Dimensional Modeling, John Wiley, 2. Edition 2002.

Pendse, Nigel: The OLAP Report. What is OLAP? An analysis of what the increasingly misused OLAP term is supposed to mean, *http://www.olapreport.com*.

Rafanelli, Maurizio: Multidimensional Databases: Problems and Solutions, Idea Group Publishing, 2003.

Thomsen, Erik: OLAP Solutions: Building Multidimensional Information Systems, John Wiley, 2. Edition 2002.

Totok, Andreas: Modellierung von OLAP- und Data-Warehouse-Systemen, Deutscher Universitäts-Verlag, 2000.

The SAP BW Library

With this special edition, SAP PRESS offers you valuable, expert knowledge on every aspect of SAP BW. All volumes share the same, practical approach. Step by step and with easily understood sample cases, you'll learn how to master all the important topical areas in SAP BW. All authors are SAP BW specialists of the Cube-Serv Group. This ensures profound, expert knowledge and a uniform, application-oriented conception of all the books.

Egger, Fiechter, Rohlf
SAP BW Data Modeling
This book delivers all the essential information needed for successful data modeling using SAP BW. In a practice-oriented approach, you'll learn how to prepare, store, and manage your data efficiently. Essential topics such as data warehousing concepts and the architecture of SAP BW are examined in detail. You'll learn, step-by-step, all there is to know about InfoObjects, InfoProviders, and SAP Business Content, all based on Release SAP BW 3.5.
ISBN 1-59229-043-4

Egger, Fiechter, Rohlf, Rose, Schrüffer
SAP BW Reporting and Analysis
Quick and targeted access to the information you want. This book offers a fundamental guide to setting up, executing, and optimizing (Web) reporting, Web applications, and the resulting analysis options in SAP BW for your specific needs. The book first familiarizes you with the basic concepts of BEx Query Designer, BEx Web Application Designer, BEx Web Applications, BEx Analyzer, and SAP Business Content. It then takes you through the creation of individual reports and analyses step by step. You'll learn how to create your own SAP BW Web Cockpit successfully. Based on Release SAP BW 3.5.
ISBN 1-59229-045-0

Egger, Fiechter, Rohlf, Rose, Weber
SAP BW Business Planning and Simulation
Active enterprise control with SAP BW-BPS: This is the only book available that introduces you to this current and supplemental topic in SAP BW. A walk-through introduces you step by step to the new functions in SAP BW 3.5. Whatever your interest—planning environment, manual planning, or Web interface builder—this book offers you the basic knowledge you need to execute successful planning with SAP BW. Learn about recent innovations and take advantage of all the SAP BW functionality.
ISBN 1-59229-046-9

J   Authors

CubeServ.

The authors of this book are all acknowledged BW specialists of the CubeServ Group (*www.cubeserv.com*). The CubeServ Group (CubeServ AG, CubeServ GmbH, and CubeServ Technologies AG) specializes in Business Intelligence (BI) solutions and has practical experience with SAP Business Information Warehouse (SAP BW) dating back to 1998, having worked on countless projects with SAP BW and SAP Strategic Enterprise Management (SAP SEM).

Norbert Egger is the Managing Director of the CubeServ Group, which specializes in business intelligence solutions. In 1996, he established the world's first data warehouse based on SAP. Since then, he has realized more than 200 projects with SAP BW and SAP SEM. He has many years of experience in the operation of SAP-based business intelligence solutions.

Norbert Egger (*n.egger@cubeserv.com*) is the author of Chapter 3, *Sample Scenario,* and Chapter 6, *ETL Process: Transaction Data.*

Jean-Marie R. Fiechter has worked as a data warehousing consultant at CubeServ AG (Jona, Switzerland) since 2003 and is a certified mySAP Business Intelligence consultant. He has international, practical experience in the areas of data warehousing, business intelligence, massively parallel processing, and management information systems (MIS). For several years, he has lectured on data warehousing at universities and technical colleges.

Jean-Marie R. Fiechter (*j-m.fiechter@cubeserv.com*) is the author of Chapter 1, *Data Warehousing and SAP BW,* and Chapter 2, *Data Acquisition: ETL Concepts and Their Implementation in SAP BW.*

Robert Salzmann works as a consultant at Cube-Serv AG (Jona, Switzerland), which specializes in business intelligence solutions. He has many years of experience with projects in the SAP BW area and is currently involved in several SAP BW projects in medium-size and large European companies.

Robert Salzmann (*r.salzmann@cubeserv.com*) is the author of Chapter 7, *SAP BW Business Content*.

Ralf Patrick Sawicki is an SAP BW consultant at CubeServ GmbH (Flörsheim am Main, Germany). In the SAP BW area, his main focus is on data modeling, extraction, and reporting. Ralf Patrick Sawicki graduated in business information systems technology at the technical college in Reutlingen, Germany. He has many years of experience with SAP Business Information Warehouse and SAP R/3 and has been involved in numerous national and international projects with well-known companies.

Ralf Patrick Sawicki (*rp.sawicki@cubeserv.com*) is the author of Chapter 4, *Extractors: Overview of the Techniques*.

Thomas Thielen is a senior consultant for business intelligence solutions at CubeServ AG (Jona, Switzerland). He holds a degree in Business Administration, Accounting, and Fiscal Law. In May 2002, SAP Europe certified Thomas Thielen as an Application Consultant for SAP Business Warehouse Systems. Since then he has managed and successfully implemented numerous projects with SAP BW and SAP SEM.

Thomas Thielen (*t.thielen@cubeserv.com*) is the author of Chapter 5, *ETL Process: Master Data*.

 **Wiebke Hübner** joined the CubeServ Group in 2004 as Project Manager for SAP publications. She has many years of experience in the preparation and communication of specialized topics. After graduating with a degree in Liberal Arts, she worked in project management for a cross-regional museum. In 2001, she became editor at Galileo Press (Bonn, Germany) for business-oriented SAP literature.

Index

Performance 391, 402
  considerations 83
  problems 391
Period values 132
Persistent staging area 58
Plan cost rates 72
Plan data 72
Plan prices 72
Planning and Simulation 67
Planning functions 72
Planning horizon 72
Planning interface 74
Plug-in 332
Posting period 280, 303
Post-processing DataSources 126
Post-processing transfer rules 366
PowerCenter 53
Preaggregations 27
Presentation tools 31
Presummarization 396
Process chain 57, 389
Process integration 53
Process steps 44
Processing 233
Product Cost Controlling 113
Product Lifecycle Management 396
Profit and loss accounting 332
Profit margin 71
Profitability analysis 70, 73, 75, 113, 124,
  259, 267, 287, 288, 289, 295, 303,
  308, 329, 396
  data 323
  extractors 321
  non-SAP 278, 282
Profitability segment number 115
Protocol 62
Provider 62
Proxy communication 60
PSA 58, 112, 166, 170, 182, 236, 237, 241
  and Data Targets in Parallel 236
  table 236
Pseudo delta 144
Pull mechanism 116
Pull mode 116
Pulled delta 390
Push mode 84
Push technique 148
Pushed delta 390

Q
qRFC monitor 110
Qualitative data 29
Quantitative data 29
Query 38, 62, 66, 116, 167, 331
  language 66
  optimization 27
Queued delta 91, 93, 100, 108

R
R/3 migration 84
R/3 System 92
Realignment 115
Real-time data 26
Reconciliation account 125
Reconstruction 103, 104
  protocol 104
  table 86, 398
Record type 278, 323
Recovery 45
Referential integrity 188, 189
Relational data source 53
Relational database 77, 163
Relational detail data layer 28
Relational query model 65
Reloading 45
Remote access 40
Remote function call 35
RemoteCube 37, 78, 528
RemoteCube technology 78
Replicated DataSource 124, 132
Replication 119, 172, 336
  method 397
Report 34
Reporting 31, 39, 61, 121
  agent 41
  tools 74
Reporting and Analysis 67
  tools 40
Repository 24, 34
Request 88, 112, 236
  processing 236
Resource adapter 62
Return 90
Revenue reduction 71, 72
Reverse image 90
RFC 35, 148, 153
  capability 161
  connection 62
  destinations 63

Interested in reading more?

Please visit our Web site for all
new book releases from SAP PRESS.

www.sap-press.com